## CSWE's Core Competencies and Practice Behavior Examples in this Text

| Competency | Chapter |
|---|---|
| **Professional Identity** | |
| *Practice Behavior Examples...* | |
| Serve as representatives of the profession, its mission, and its core values | 11 |
| Know the profession's history | 8 |
| Commit themselves to the profession's enhancement and to their own professional conduct and growth | 9 |
| Advocate for client access to the services of social work | |
| Practice personal reflection and self-correction to assure continual professional development | |
| Attend to professional roles and boundaries | |
| Demonstrate professional demeanor in behavior, appearance, and communication | |
| Engage in career-long learning | |
| Use supervision and consultation | |
| **Ethical Practice** | |
| *Practice Behavior Examples...* | |
| Obligation to conduct themselves ethically and engage in ethical decision-making | 1 |
| Know about the value base of the profession, its ethical standards, and relevant law | 1, 9, 10 |
| Recognize and manage personal values in a way that allows professional values to guide practice | |
| Make ethical decisions by applying standards of the National Association of Social Workers Code of Ethics and, as applicable, of the International Federation of Social Workers/International Association of Schools of Social Work Ethics in Social Work, Statement of Principles | |
| Tolerate ambiguity in resolving ethical conflicts | 3 |
| **Critical Thinking** | |
| *Practice Behavior Examples...* | |
| Know about the principles of logic, scientific inquiry, and reasoned discernment | 3, 5 |
| Use critical thinking augmented by creativity and curiosity | |
| Requires the synthesis and communication of relevant information | |
| Distinguish, appraise, and integrate multiple sources of knowledge, including research-based knowledge, and practice wisdom | |
| Analyze models of assessment, prevention, intervention, and evaluation | |
| Demonstrate effective oral and written communication in working with individuals, families, groups, organizations, communities, and colleagues | |
| **Diversity in Practice** | |
| *Practice Behavior Examples...* | |
| Understand how diversity characterizes and shapes the human experience and is critical to the formation of identity | 9 |
| Understand the dimensions of diversity as the intersectionality of multiple factors including age, class, color, culture, disability, ethnicity, gender, gender identity and expression, immigration status, political ideology, race, religion, sex, and sexual orientation | |

| Competency | Chapter |
|---|---|
| Appreciate that, as a consequence of difference, a person's life experiences may include oppression, poverty, marginalization, and alienation as well as privilege, power, and acclaim | |
| Recognize the extent to which a culture's structures and values may oppress, marginalize, alienate, or create or enhance privilege and power | 2 |
| Gain sufficient self-awareness to eliminate the influence of personal biases and values in working with diverse groups | 8, 11 |
| Recognize and communicate their understanding of the importance of difference in shaping life experiences | 2 |

| Competency | Chapter |
|---|---|
| **Human Rights & Justice** | |
| *Practice Behavior Examples...* | |
| Understand that each person, regardless of position in society, has basic human rights, such as freedom, safety, privacy, an adequate standard of living, health care, and education | 6 |
| Recognize the global interconnections of oppression and are knowledgeable about theories of justice and strategies to promote human and civil rights | 7, 11 |
| Understand the forms and mechanisms of oppression and discrimination | 1, 2 |
| Advocate for human rights and social and economic justice | 4 |
| Understand the forms and mechanisms of oppression and discrimination. Advocate for human rights and social and economic justice | 10 |
| Engage in practices that advance social and economic justice | 2 |
| **Research Based Practice** | |
| *Practice Behavior Examples...* | |
| Use practice experience to inform research, employ evidence-based interventions, evaluate their own practice, and use research findings to improve practice, policy, and social service delivery | 3 |
| Comprehend quantitative and qualitative research and understand scientific and ethical approaches to building knowledge | 2 |
| Use practice experience to inform scientific inquiry | |
| Use research evidence to inform practice | |
| **Human Behavior** | |
| *Practice Behavior Examples...* | |
| Know about human behavior across the life course; the range of social systems in which people live; and the ways social systems promote or deter people in maintaining or achieving health and well-being | 1, 7, 8, 9, 10. 11 |
| Apply theories and knowledge from the liberal arts to understand biological, social, cultural, psychological, and spiritual development | 1, 3 |
| Utilize conceptual frameworks to guide the processes of assessment, intervention, and evaluation | 1 |
| Critique and apply knowledge to understand person and environment. | 1, 4, 5, 6 |

# CSWE's Core Competencies and Practice Behavior Examples in this Text

| Competency | Chapter |
|---|---|
| **Policy Practice** | |
| *Practice Behavior Examples...* | |
| Understand that policy affects service delivery and social workers actively engage in policy practice | 4, 7 |
| Analyze, formulate, and advocate for policies that advance social well-being | 10 |
| Collaborate with colleagues and clients for effective policy action | |
| **Practice Contexts** | |
| *Practice Behavior Examples...* | |
| Keep informed, resourceful, and proactive in responding to evolving organizational, community, and societal contexts at all levels of practice | |
| Recognize that the context of practice is dynamic, and use knowledge and skill to respond proactively | |
| Continuously discover, appraise, and attend to changing locales, populations, scientific and technological developments, and emerging societal trends to provide relevant services | 6 |
| Provide leadership in promoting sustainable changes in service delivery and practice to improve the quality of social services | 8 |
| **Engage, Assess Intervene, Evaluate** | |
| *Practice Behavior Examples...* | |
| Identify, analyze, and implement evidence-based interventions designed to achieve client goals | |
| Use research and technological advances | |
| Evaluate program outcomes and practice effectiveness | |
| Develop, analyze, advocate, and provide leadership for policies and services | |
| Promote social and economic justice | 3 |
| A) Engagement | |
| Substantively and effectively prepare for action with individuals, families, groups, organizations, and communities | |
| Use empathy and other interpersonal skills | |
| Develop a mutually agreed- n focus of work and desired outcomes | |
| B) Assessment | |
| Collect, organize, and interpret client data | |
| Assess client strengths and limitations | 5 |
| Develop mutually agreed-on intervention goals and objectives | |
| Select appropriate intervention strategies | |
| C) Intervention | |
| Initiate actions to achieve organizational goals | |
| Implement prevention interventions that enhance client capacities | |
| Help clients resolve problems | |
| Negotiate, mediate, and advocate for clients | |
| Facilitate transitions and endings | |
| D) Evaluation | |
| Critically analyze, monitor, and evaluate interventions | |

SIXTH EDITION

# Human Behavior and the Social Environment

## Shifting Paradigms in Essential Knowledge for Social Work Practice

Joe M. Schriver

*University of Arkansas*

**PEARSON**

Boston  Columbus  Indianapolis  New York  San Francisco  Upper Saddle River
Amsterdam  Cape Town  Dubai  London  Madrid  Milan  Munich  Paris  Montréal  Toronto
Delhi  Mexico City  São Paulo  Sydney  Hong Kong  Seoul  Singapore  Taipei  Tokyo

VP and Editorial Director: Jeffery W. Johnston
Editorial Assistant: Andrea Hall
Senior Product Manager: Julie Peters
Program Manager: Alicia Ritchey
Executive Marketing Manager: Krista Clark
Marketing Coordinator: Elizabeth Mackenzie Lamb
Operations Specialist: Maura Zaldivar-Garcia
Senior Art Director: Diane Lorenzo
Manager, Rights and Permissions: Ben Ferrini

Image Permission Coordinator: Martha Shethar
Cover Art: Fotolia © Olga Lyubkin
Media Producer: Allison Longley
Full-Service Project Management:
   PreMediaGlobal, Inc./Sudip Sinha
Composition: PreMediaGlobal, Inc.
Printer/Binder: LSC Communications
Cover Printer: LSC Communications
Text Font: Dante MT Std

Credits and acknowledgments borrowed from other sources and reproduced, with permission, in this textbook appear on appropriate page within text.

**Library of Congress Cataloging-in-Publication Data**

Schriver, Joe M.
   Human behavior and the social environment : shifting paradigms in
essential knowledge for social work practice / Joe M. Schriver, University of Arkansas.—Sixth edition.
      pages cm
   Includes bibliographical references and index.
   ISBN 978-0-205-92436-3—ISBN 0-205-92436-0
   1. Social psychology. 2. Behavioral assessment. 3. Social interaction. 4. Social systems.
5. Paradigms (Social sciences) 6. Social service. I. Title.
   HM1033.S373 2014
   302—dc23

                                                                            2014004851

4  17

PEARSON

Student Edition
ISBN 10: 0-205-92436-0
ISBN 13: 978-0-205-92436-3

# Contents

*To Cathy and Andrew*

# Preface

This text begins with a presentation of the basic purposes and foundations of social work and social work education. Principles and fundamental concepts necessary for acquiring and organizing knowledge about human behavior and the social environment (HBSE) are also presented. Next, a conceptual framework for thinking about both traditional and alternative ways in which knowledge about human behavior and the social environment is created and valued is outlined. This conceptual framework is accompanied by discussion of some widely used approaches and fundamental themes guiding social workers in the creation, selection, organization, and use of knowledge about human behavior and the social environment. The book then uses the notions of traditional and alternative paradigms to organize and present a variety of models, theories, and concepts concerning HBSE. At least one full chapter (two chapters are included on individual behavior and development) is devoted to content about each of the social system levels required of professional social work education by the Educational Policy and Accreditation Standards (EPAS) of the Council on Social Work Education. Knowledge for practice with individuals, families, groups, organizations, communities, and global contexts as well as content on the interaction among these systems is presented.

In this, the sixth edition, significant changes in both organization and content have been made. The overall intention here is to add new content, streamline by removing redundancies, and improve the logic and flow of content throughout the book. The reader, of course, will determine if my intention has been achieved.

The most significant changes in this edition include:

- The most exciting change has been the transition to the book's availability as an e-book with many more engaging and interactive opportunities for learning the content.
- New sections on environmental social work, mindfulness, new urbanism, neoliberalism, food insecurity, the Millennial generation (Gen Y), and the Multi-System Life Course perspective.
- The addition of a chapter expanding the current Chapter 3 and including more tools for social work practice (new Chapter 4).
- Removal of Illustrative Readings. Given the knowledge explosion and the availability of full-text databases, readings related to chapter content become quickly outdated and are more current and readily available through electronic access. This has also improved the flow of content from one chapter to the next.
- New mechanisms for connecting the CSWE required core competencies and practice behaviors to the content throughout the book.

*To read about the full chapter-by-chapter changes, please visit* www.pcarsonhighered.com.

## Features

There are many features of this text to enhance your experience; however, they are only as useful as you make them. By engaging with this text and its resources, you'll learn about human behavior through:

- **An applied focus** – bridging knowledge about influences on human behavior and decision-making in varied social work practice settings.
- **A topical approach** – providing a focus on issues while noting the influence of developmental considerations, allowing for easy identification of information.
- **A multidimensional framework** – providing in-depth examination of biological, psychological, social, cultural, spiritual, environmental, and systemic influences.
- **Well-tested theories and current evidence** – including helpful diagrams, figures, graphs, and tables to promote students ability to grasp concepts.
- **Current topics** – such as immigration, trauma and abuse, and discrimination, sexual orientation, gender identity, sustainability, the environment, war, globalization, poverty, and health care.
- **Multimedia resources** – including videos, case examples, and narratives.

## Learning Outcomes

Students will be able to achieve a variety of learning outcomes by using this text and its resources including:

- **Critical Thinking skills** – students can develop their critical thinking skills by reviewing the competency boxes (indicated by the Core Competencies series icon) and engaging with the multimedia resources highlighted in blue boxes throughout the chapter.
- **Oral Communication skills** – students can develop their oral communication skills by engaging with others in and out of class to discuss their comprehension of the chapter based on the chapter's learning objectives.
- **Assessment and Writing skills** – students can develop their assessment and writing skills in preparation for future licensing exams by completing topic-based and chapter review assessments for each chapter.
- **CSWE Core Competencies** – students can develop their comprehension and application of CSWE's core competencies and practice behaviors by discussing the competency box critical thinking questions.

## A Note about Bias and the Author

I should make it explicit that I am biased. I recognize the contributions of traditional perspectives and approaches to creating and valuing knowledge, but I believe that we as humans will not realize our collective (and individual) potential for well-being as long as we do not embrace alternative perspective and worldviews such as those described in this book. Therefore, while traditional perspectives and paradigms are presented in this book, the reader should keep in mind that the author generally finds these perspectives lacking. This author believes that the perspectives used to define and describe "normal" or "optimal" human behavior and experiences too often represent the beliefs and realities of only a privileged few. This privileged few too often includes only those who have the power, the good fortune, the gender, the color, the wealth, or the sexual orientation consistent with and reflected in traditional perspectives and worldviews.

The reader should also be aware that, though in many respects this book is a critique of traditional paradigm thinking, this author is a product of the traditional institutions that create and enforce those traditional perspectives and worldviews. This author also shares many of the characteristics of the "privileged few." Therefore, writing this book has been an effort to question, to examine, and to expand my own worldview.

## Acknowledgments

Those friends and colleagues from around the country and internationally whom I listed in prior editions remain a most supportive community for me. That community is ever expanding and for that I am most grateful.

Special thanks to reviewers for all editions: Yvonne Barry, John Tyler Community College; Brian Flynn, Binghampton University; and Valandra, St. Catharine University.

I noted in the first edition that my son, Andrew, then almost two years old, had taught me more about human behavior and the social environment than anyone else. Andrew, now at an amazing twenty-two years old, you continue to be the best of teachers as you share your curiosity, knowledge, and wonder about humans and our worlds. Cathy Owens Schriver, as with the other editions—you have been the most important and patient supporter of my work I could wish for.

This text is available in a variety of formats—digital and print. To learn more about our programs, pricing options, and customization, visit www.pearsonhighered.com.

**1**

JEFF GREENBERG/PHOTOEDIT

# Human Behavior and the Social Environment (HBSE) and Paradigms

## INTRODUCTION

**Who should use this book and how should it be used?** Instructors in both undergraduate and graduate social work education programs can use this book to help their students gain HBSE content. The book is designed to meet the requirements of the Council on Social Work Education for HBSE foundation content at either the undergraduate or graduate level. At the undergraduate level, the book may work best in programs with a two-course HBSE sequence designed to provide content on HBSE from a multi-systems perspective (individual, family, group, organization, community, and global systems). At the foundation graduate level, the book can be effectively used as the text in a single HBSE course or a two-course sequence designed to provide basic content across system levels and, in the case of graduate programs, prior to delivering advanced HBSE content. In addition, this book integrates content from the other CSWE required competencies into the HBSE area.

The purpose of human behavior and the social environment content in social work education is to provide us with knowledge for practice. We need to continually look at this content for how to apply what we are learning about human behavior and the social environment to social work practice and to our lives. As we move through the material in this book, we will struggle to integrate what we are learning here with what we have learned and are learning from our own and others' life experiences, from our other social work courses, and from our courses in the liberal arts and sciences. We will try to weave together all these important sources of knowing and understanding into an organic whole that can help us become life-long learners and guide us in our social work practice.

## PURPOSE AND ASSUMPTIONS

Moving through the content of this book can be compared to a journey. Before we begin our journey, we will place the content and purposes of this human behavior and the social environment (HBSE) book within the context of the purpose of social work as the Council on Social Work Education (CSWE) has defined it. The Council on Social Work Education is the organization responsible for determining and monitoring the accreditation standards for undergraduate and graduate (MSW) social work education programs in the United States.

### Purpose

According to the Council on Social Work Education:

> The purpose of the social work profession is to promote human and community well-being. Guided by a person and environment construct, a global perspective, respect for human diversity, and knowledge based on scientific inquiry, social work's purpose is actualized through its quest for social and economic justice, the prevention of conditions that limit human rights, the elimination of poverty, and the enhancement of the quality of life for all persons. (CSWE, 2008: 1)

The purpose of social work will guide us throughout our journey to understand HBSE content. The purpose emerges from the history of the social work profession and its continuing concern for improving quality of life, especially for vulnerable populations.

### Assumptions

In addition to the purpose of social work, our journey through this book will be guided by several very basic assumptions:

1. How we view the world and its people directly affects the way we will practice social work.
2. The way we view the world and its people already affects the way we behave in our daily lives.
3. Our work as social workers and our lives are not separate from each other.
4. Our lives are not separate from the lives of the people with whom we work and interact.

5. While our lives are interconnected with the lives of the people with whom we work and interact, we differ from each other in many ways.

6. The assumptions we make about ourselves and others are strongly influenced by our individual and collective histories and cultures.

7. Change is a constant part of our lives and the lives of the people with whom we work.

Such assumptions as these are reflected in what we will come to conceptualize as an alternative paradigm for thinking about social work.

## CORE COMPETENCIES

Social work education programs (BSW and MSW) are required to prepare all students to demonstrate mastery of 10 core competencies

It is difficult to imagine that competence in HBSE can be achieved without including content related to the other core competencies:

- The development of your professional identity as a social worker
- Ethical behaviors and dilemmas
- Critical thinking skills
- Diversity in Practice
- Human rights and social and economic justice
- Research-informed practice and practice-informed research
- Human behavior and the social environment
- Social policy practice
- Practice contexts
- Engage, assess, intervene, evaluate: The processes involved in doing social work

It is difficult as well to imagine that achieving competence in the ten areas, in addition to the HBSE competency, listed above could be accomplished without HBSE content. In essence, this book is intended to be an integral and interdependent part of your overall social work education.

## CORE VALUES

In addition, the content of this book is grounded in the basic and fundamental or core values of the social work profession as identified by the CSWE:

- Service
- Social justice
- The dignity and worth of the person
- The importance of human relationships
- Competence
- Human rights
- Scientific inquiry (CSWE, 2008)

These values are and have historically been the underpinning for all of social work education and practice.

---

**Ethical Practice**

**Practice Behavior Example:** Know about the value base of the profession, its ethical standards, and relevant law

**Critical Thinking Question:** How might the fundamental values of the social work profession be reflected in and guide our efforts to gain knowledge about human behavior and the social environment?

# HUMAN BEHAVIOR AND THE SOCIAL ENVIRONMENT

So, specifically what does the CSWE expect of us in order to attain the required competence in HBSE? In order to become competent in applying "knowledge of human behavior and the social environment," we are expected to be knowledgeable about:

- Human behavior across the life course
- The range of social systems
- The ways social systems promote or deter people in maintaining or achieving health and well-being

In addition, we are expected to be able to:

- Apply theories and knowledge from the liberal arts to understand biological, social, cultural, psychological, and spiritual development

We will know we have achieved these expectations when we can:

- Utilize conceptual frameworks to guide the processes of assessment, intervention, and evaluation
- Critique and apply knowledge to understand person and environment. (CSWE, 2008:6)

In addition to being guided by the requirements of CSWE regarding HBSE, our journey through this book will be guided by several very basic concepts and perspectives. The most basic concept that will guide us is that of paradigm.

## PARADIGMS AND SOCIAL WORK

A **paradigm** "is a world view, a general perspective, a way of breaking down the complexity of the real world" (Lincoln and Guba, 1985:15). Paradigms constitute "cultural patterns of group life" (Schutz, 1944). More specifically, Kuhn (1970 [1962]:175) defines a paradigm as "the entire constellation of beliefs, values, techniques, and so on shared by the members of a given community." Paradigms shape and are shaped by values, knowledge, and beliefs about the nature of our worlds and are often so "taken for granted" that we are virtually unaware of their existence or of the assumptions we make because of them. For social workers the notion of paradigm is particularly important, because if we can become conscious of the elements that result in different worldviews, this awareness can provide us with tools to use to think about and to understand ourselves, others, and the environments we all inhabit. The notion of paradigm can help us understand more completely the past perspectives, current realities, and future possibilities about what it means to be human. Furthermore, the notion of paradigm can help us understand our own and others' roles in creating and re-creating the very meaning of humanness.

Specifically, thinking in terms of paradigms can provide us with new ways of understanding humans' behaviors in individual, family, group, organizational, community, and global contexts. The concept of paradigm can serve us very well to organize our thinking about and increase our understanding of multiple theories and perspectives about human behavior and the social environment. Using the concept of paradigm can help us understand the way things are and, equally important for social workers, it can help us understand the way things might be. Throughout this book, we will explore paradigms from two different types of paradigms: traditional or dominant and alternative or possible.

## TWO TYPES OF PARADIGMS: TRADITIONAL AND ALTERNATIVE

Traditional (dominant) and alternative (possible) paradigms are quite different from each other but are not mutually exclusive kinds of paradigms. We explore in some detail the characteristics of both of these types of paradigms in Chapter 2. For now, when we refer to traditional or dominant paradigms, we simply mean the paradigms or worldviews that have most influenced the environments that make up our worlds. When we refer to alternative or possible paradigms, we mean worldviews that have had less influence and have been less prominent in shaping our own and others' views about humans and their environments. However, alternative or possible paradigms reflect worldviews that are of significant importance to social workers and many of the people we serve. They are called alternative paradigms only in the sense that they have for too long been overlooked and undervalued in a world that disproportionately reflects traditional or dominant worldviews.

## PARADIGMS: BOTH/AND NOT EITHER/OR

Much of the emphasis in this book is on shifting to alternative paradigms and transcending the limits of traditional and dominant paradigm thinking. It is important to realize, though, that our journey to understanding Human Behavior and the Social Environment will not take us to either one or the other worldview. Our journey will take us to both traditional and alternative destinations along the way. After all, traditional scientific worldviews have revealed much valuable knowledge about ourselves and our worlds.

We will try in this book to learn about alternative paradigms and to challenge us to think beyond traditional paradigms in which science is the single source of understanding. However, in order to understand alternative paradigms, we need to be cognizant of traditional theories about human behavior and development. We will challenge traditional paradigms as incomplete, as excluding many people, and as reflecting biases due to the value assumptions and historical periods out of which they emerged. These inadequacies, however, render traditional theories nonetheless powerful in the influences they have had in the past, that they currently have, and that they will continue to have on the construction and application of knowledge about human behavior and the social environment. Traditional approaches provide important departure points from which we may embark on our journey toward more complete, more inclusive, and less-biased visions (or at least visions in which bias is recognized and used to facilitate inclusiveness) of HBSE. Many of the alternative paradigms we will visit began as extensions or adaptations of existing traditional worldviews.

There is another very practical reason for learning about theories that emerge from and reflect traditional paradigms. The practice world social workers inhabit and that you will soon enter (and we hope transform) is a world constructed largely on traditional views of human behavior and the social environment. To survive in that world long enough to change it, we must be conversant in the discourse of that world. We must have sufficient knowledge of traditional and dominant paradigms of human behavior and development to make decisions about what in those worldviews we wish to retain because of its usefulness in attaining the goal of maximizing human potential. Knowledge of traditional and dominant paradigms is also necessary in deciding what to discard or alter to better serve that same core concern of social work. To help us understand paradigms in the context of social work, we need to be able to conduct a paradigm analysis.

## PARADIGM ANALYSIS

Put simply, **paradigm analysis** is learning to "think paradigm." It is a process of continually asking questions about what the information, both spoken and unspoken, we send and receive reflects about our own and others' views of the world and its people, especially people different from ourselves. It is a process of continually "thinking about thinking." Paradigm analysis requires us to continuously critically evaluate the many perspectives we will explore for their consistency with the core values of social work.

Paradigm analysis involves asking a set of very basic questions about each of the perspectives we explore in order to determine its compatibility with the core values of social work. These questions are:

1.  Does this perspective contribute to preserving and restoring human dignity?
2.  Does this perspective recognize the benefits of, and does it celebrate, human diversity?
3.  Does this perspective assist us in transforming our society and ourselves so that we welcome the voices, the strengths, the ways of knowing, and the energies of us all?
4.  Does this perspective help us all (ourselves and the people with whom we work) to reach our fullest human potential?
5.  Does the perspective or theory reflect the participation and experiences of males and females; economically well off and poor; white people and people of color; gay men, lesbians, bisexuals, transgendered, and heterosexuals; old and young; temporarily able-bodied and people with disabilities?

**Test your understanding of Paradigms by taking this short** Quiz.

The answers we find to these questions will tell us generally if the perspective we are exploring is consistent with the core values of social work. The answer to the final question will tell us about how the paradigm came to be and who participated in its development or construction. The questions above can also help us decide whether the paradigm or perspective being examined should change or "shift" in order to help fulfill the purposes of social work.

# PARADIGM SHIFT

A **paradigm shift** is "a profound change in the thoughts, perceptions, and values that form a particular vision of reality" (Capra, 1983:30). To express the fundamental changes required of a paradigm shift, Thomas Kuhn (1970) uses the analogy of travel to another planet. Kuhn tells us that a paradigm shift "is rather as if the professional community had been suddenly transported to another planet where familiar objects are seen in a different light and are joined by unfamiliar ones as well" (1970, p. 111). The elements of this analogy—travel, another planet or world, viewing both familiar and new objects in a different light—are consistent with our efforts in this book to travel on a journey toward a more complete understanding of HBSE. Our journey will take us to other people's worlds and it will call upon us to view new things in those worlds and familiar things in our own worlds in new ways and through others' eyes. As we continue on our journey we should try to appreciate that the process of taking the trip is as important and enlightening as any final destination we might reach.

Paradigms are not mysterious, determined for all time, immovable objects. Paradigms are social constructs created by humans. They can be and, in fact, have been changed and reconstructed by humans throughout our history (Capra, 1983:30). Kuhn ([1962] 1970:92), for example, discusses scientific and political revolutions that result in paradigm shifts and changes. Such changes, Kuhn suggests, come about when a segment of a community, often a small segment, has a growing sense that existing institutions are unable to adequately address or solve the problems in the environment—an environment those same institutions helped create. The actions taken by the dissatisfied segment of the community can result in the replacement of all or parts of the older paradigm with a newer one. However, since not all humans have the same amount of influence or power and control over what a paradigm looks like and whose values and beliefs give it form, efforts to change paradigms involve conflict and struggles (Kuhn, [1962] 1970:93).

Use of the notion of paradigm shift will enable us to expand our knowledge of human behavior and the social environment and to use this additional knowledge in our practice of social work. It can free us from an overdependence on traditional ways of viewing the world as the only ways of viewing the world. It can allow us to move beyond these views to alternative possibilities for viewing the world, its people, and their behaviors.

The concept of paradigm shift allows us to make the transitions necessary to continue our journey to explore alternative paradigms and paradigmatic elements that represent the many human interests, needs, and perspectives not addressed by or reflected in the traditional and dominant paradigm. The concept of paradigm shift is also helpful in recognizing relationships between traditional and alternative paradigms and for tracing how alternative paradigms often emerge from traditional or dominant ones. Traditional or dominant paradigms and alternative or possible paradigms for human behavior are not necessarily mutually exclusive.

As we will see in the discussion of paradigms and history, different paradigms can be described as different points in a progression of transformations in the way we perceive human behavior and the social environment. The progression from traditional and dominant to alternative and possible that we envision here is one that reflects a continuous movement (we hope) toward views of human behavior more consistent with the core values of social work and away from narrow perspectives that include only a privileged few and exclude the majority of humans. In some cases, this progression will mean returning to previously neglected paradigms. Such a progression, then, does not imply a linear, forward-only movement. It might more readily be conceived as a spiral or winding kind of movement. The worldviews illustrated in our discussion of history, for example, represented the perspectives almost exclusively of Europeans. Very different worldviews emerged in other parts of the world. Myers (1985:34), for example, describes an Afrocentric worldview that emerged over 5,000 years ago among Egyptians that posited the real world to be both spiritual and material at once. This holistic perspective found God manifest in everything. The self included "ancestors, the yet unborn, all of nature, and the entire community" (Myers, 1985:35).Many scholars suggest that this paradigm continues to influence the worldviews of many people of African descent today. This Afrocentric paradigm clearly offers an alternative to European humanist or scientific paradigms that emerged during the Renaissance. Such an alternative emphasizing the interrelatedness of individuals and community and their mutual responsibility for one another encompasses much that is valuable and consistent with the core values of social work. The notion of a continuum helps us to understand the importance and usefulness of knowing about dominant paradigms at the same time that we attempt to transcend or shift away from the limits of traditional paradigms and move toward ones that are more inclusive and that more fully reflect the core values of social work.

## Paradigm Shift, Social Work, and Social Change

The concept of paradigm change has significant implications for us as social workers. If you recall from earlier discussion, the basic purposes of social work include social change or social transformation and call upon us to be involved in social and political action to promote social and economic justice. Social change is also required in our call to enhance human well-being and to work on behalf of oppressed persons denied access to opportunities and resources or power. When we as social workers become a part of the processes of changing paradigms and the institutions that emerge from them, we are, in essence, engaging in fundamental processes of social change and transformation.

We can use the information we now have about paradigms and paradigm analysis to change or replace paradigms that create obstacles to people meeting their needs and reaching their potential. Since paradigms are reflected throughout the beliefs, values, institutions, and processes that make up our daily lives, we need not limit our thinking about paradigms only to our immediate concerns here about human behavior and the social environment. We can apply what we know about paradigms and paradigm change throughout our education and practice. For us as students of social work, that means we must become aware of the nature of the paradigms reflected throughout all areas of our studies in social work necessary to achieve the 10 core competencies required of professional social workers. We certainly also must begin to analyze the nature and assumptions of the paradigms we encounter through our course work in the arts and humanities (music, theater, visual arts, philosophy, literature, English, languages, religious studies), social sciences (economics, political science, psychology, sociology, anthropology, history), and natural sciences (biology, physics, chemistry, geology, geography), as well as through our own personal histories and life experiences.

**Socialization** is the process of teaching new members the rules by which the larger group or society operates. Socialization involves imparting to new members the knowledge, values, and skills according to which they are expected to operate. For example, the social work education process in which you are currently involved is a process for socializing you to the knowledge, values, and skills expected of professional social workers.

In a more general sense, we are socialized to and interact with others in the social environment from paradigmatic perspectives. These perspectives are not only imparted to us through formal education in the schools but also through what we are taught and what we learn from our families, religious institutions, and other groups and organizations as well. We are influenced by worldviews and we reflect the worldviews to which we have been socialized. The worldview likely to have influenced us most if we were socialized through the educational system in the United States is the traditional or dominant paradigm. The influence of this paradigm is pervasive, even if the worldviews of our families or cultures are in conflict with parts or all of the traditional or dominant paradigm. Because of the power accorded thinking consistent with the traditional paradigm, it is extremely difficult for alternative paradigms to be accorded legitimacy. It is not, however, impossible. As we shall see, it is quite possible through understanding traditional and alternative paradigms and the dynamics of paradigm change that we can exercise choice in the paradigms or worldviews through which we lead our lives. We suggest here that social changes resulting from shifts in worldviews inherently and inextricably flow from changes in the way we as individuals view our worlds. This position is consistent with the suggestion of much alternative paradigm thinking, in particular that of feminism, that *the personal is political*.

In order to use our understanding of paradigms to support processes of social change/transformation, we must first engage in the process of paradigm analysis we described earlier. Paradigm analysis, you might recall, requires us to ask a set of questions that can guide us, in our education and practice, toward adopting and adapting approaches to understanding human behavior and the social environment that incorporate perspectives consistent with the core values of social work.

As suggested earlier, a significant responsibility for us as social workers is assisting people whose needs are not met and whose problems are not solved by the institutions and processes in the social environment that emerge from and reflect the dominant/ traditional paradigms. Much of what social work is about involves recognizing, analyzing, challenging, and changing existing paradigms. An essential step in fulfilling this important responsibility is learning to listen to, respect, and effectively respond to the voices and visions that the people with whom we work have to contribute to their own well-being and to the common good. In this way, paradigms that too often have been considered permanent and unchangeable can be questioned, challenged, altered, and replaced. More important, they can be changed to more completely include the worldviews of persons previously denied participation in paradigm-building processes.

Such a perspective on knowledge for practice allows us to operate in partnership with the people with whom we work. It allows us to incorporate their strengths, and it provides us an opportunity to use social work knowledge, skills, and values in concert with those strengths in our practice interactions.

The possible or alternative paradigms are those that enrich, alter, or replace existing paradigms by including the voices and visions—values, beliefs, ways of doing and knowing—of persons who have usually been left out of the paradigm building that has previously taken place. It is interesting, but not coincidental, that the persons who have usually been left out of paradigm-building processes are often the same persons with whom social workers have traditionally worked and toward whom the concerns of social workers have historically been directed.

**Human Rights & Justice**

**Practice Behavior Example:** Understand the forms and mechanisms of oppression and discrimination

**Critical Thinking Question:** How can the concept of power and its inequitable distribution help us understand oppression and discrimination?

# POWER: SOCIAL AND ECONOMIC JUSTICE

Of major concern to social workers are power and resource differences (social and economic justice) that result from one's gender, color, sexual orientation, gender identity, religion, age, ability, culture, income, and class (membership in populations-at-risk). These differences have resulted in the exclusion of many persons from having a place or a voice in dominant or traditional paradigms that guide decision-making in this society. Differences such as those listed above have resulted in the worldviews of some individuals and groups having much more influence than others on the institutions and processes through which human needs must be met and human potential reached. It is the contention in this book that when some of us are denied opportunities to influence decision-making processes that affect our lives we are all hurt. We all lose when the voices and visions of some of us are excluded from paradigms and paradigm-building processes. By listening to the voices and seeing the world through the eyes of those who differ from us in gender, color, sexual orientation, religion, age, ability, culture, income, and class we can learn much about new paradigms or worldviews that can enrich all our lives. Close attention to and inclusion of the voices and visions of persons different from us can greatly expand, with exciting new possibilities, our understanding of human behavior and the social environment—and our understanding of what it means to be human.

Much of our work as we proceed through the remaining chapters of this book will involve understanding, critiquing, and analyzing traditional or dominant paradigms as well as alternative, more inclusive paradigms. We will engage in these processes as we explore theories and information about individual human behavior in the contexts of families, groups, organizations, communities, and globally.

# PARADIGMS AND HISTORY

To help us apply a critical thinking approach to explore either traditional or alternative paradigms, we need to acquire a historical perspective about the contexts out of which these worldviews emerged. Neither the traditional nor their alternative counterparts came about in a historical vacuum. They instead emerged as points along a historical continuum marked by humans' attempts to understand their own behaviors, the behaviors of others, and the environments in which they lived.

## Pre-modern/Pre-positivism

A historical perspective can help us appreciate that the paradigms we will explore as traditional and currently dominant were considered quite alternative and even radical at the times of their emergence. For example, the emergence of humanism—a belief in the power of humans to control their own behaviors and the environments in which they lived—in Europe at the opening of the Renaissance (mid-1400s) and at the ending of the Middle Ages (the early 1400s) was an alternative, and for many a radical, paradigm at that time. Humanism was considered by many, especially those in power, to be not only alternative but also dangerous, wrong, and heretical. Humanism was considered an affront to scholasticism, the traditional paradigm or worldview that had been dominant throughout much of Europe in the Middle Ages (approximately a.d. 476–mid-1400s). Scholasticism (approximately a.d. 800–mid-1400s) was a worldview that saw a Christian god, represented by the Roman Catholic Church, as the sole determiner and judge of human behavior. This Christian god was the controller of the entire natural world or environment in which humans existed. Similarly, Protestantism was a worldview placed in motion by Martin Luther during the early 1500s. It questioned the absolute authority of the Roman Catholic Church and the Pope as the sole representative of God, and was seen as another radical alternative affronting the existing worldview. The emergence of both humanism and Protestantism were alternative ways of viewing humans and their environments that called into question, and were seen as significant threats to, the then existing dominant and traditional ways of viewing the world (Manchester, 1992; Sahakian, 1968).

## Modernism/Positivism

Another important perspective from which to get a sense of the historical continuum out of which paradigms emerge is that of the birth of worldviews explaining human behavior and the environments we inhabit through science. The emergence of worldviews that explained the world through science was in some ways an extension of the humanistic paradigm. Science was a powerful tool through which humans could gain control of their behaviors and of the universe they inhabited. Science allowed humans to understand the world by directly observing it through the senses and by carefully measuring, experimenting, and analyzing what was observed. The emergence of scientific thinking or positivism during the period called the Enlightenment or the "Age of Reason" in the 17th and 18th centuries, however, was also a significant challenge to humanism and represented an alternative paradigm itself. Scientific thinking questioned humanism's central concern for gaining understanding through such expressions as art, literature, and poetry. A scientific worldview saw humanism and its reflection in the humanities as a traditional and insufficient way of viewing the world.

Science sought to extend, if not replace, humanism's ways of knowing and understanding the world with a more reliable and comprehensive perspective that was cosmos centered rather than [hu]man centered (Sahakian, 1968:119). The humanities raised questions and sought answers by looking to and rediscovering the great ideas and expressions of humans from the past, such as the classic works of the Romans and Greeks. Science offered keys to unlocking the secrets of the universe and the future through new ways of asking and answering questions. Science promised not only new questions and new ways of posing them but also answers to questions both new and old (Boulding, 1964).

The empirical observations of Galileo Galilei in the first half of the 1600s confirming the earlier findings of Copernicus in the early 1500s, for example, literally provided a new view of the world ( Manchester, 1992:116–117). This new and alternative view moved the earth from the stable and unmoving center of the universe to one in which the earth was but one of many bodies revolving around the sun. The threat posed by such a dramatically different view of the world as that of Copernicus to the traditional Roman Catholic theology-based paradigm is captured eloquently by Manchester in his book *A World Lit Only by Fire:*

> The Scriptures assumed that everything had been created for the use of man. If the earth were shrunken to a mere speck in the universe, mankind would also be diminished. Heaven was lost when "up" and "down" lost all meaning—when each became the other every twenty-four hours. (1992:229)

According to Manchester, it was written in 1575 that "No attack on Christianity is more dangerous . . . than the infinite size and depth of the universe" (1992:229). Much about the traditional paradigms that we explore in the next chapters has its roots in science and scientific ways of thinking that we virtually take for granted today. These approaches to understanding our worlds are centered in empirical observation and rational methods of gaining knowledge. So, science offers us a current example of what was, in a historical sense, an alternative paradigm becoming a traditional paradigm today. As has historically been the case, changes in paradigms currently taking place—what we will call alternative paradigms—call into question, challenge, and seek to extend our worldviews beyond those that have science and a scientific approach as the central tool for understanding human behavior and the social environment.

## Postmodernism/Post-positivism

Berman (1996), for example, notes that the basic methods and assumptions of the traditional scientific paradigm that emerged during the 17th-century Enlightenment have not solely resulted in progress for people and the earth. Berman (1996:33) argues that the scientific, also referred to as "the mechanical paradigm sees the earth as inert, as dead, or at best as part of the solar system, which is viewed as a kind of clockwork mechanism . . . and one consequence of [this view] was the opening of the door to the unchecked exploitation of the earth." In addition Berman suggests that science leaves little room for the spiritual and subjective elements of the world and its mechanistic tendencies leave little motivation for seeing the world as a living system. He makes an important observation that: "As a tool, there is nothing wrong with the mechanistic paradigm. But for some reason, we couldn't stop there; we had to equate it with all of reality and so have arrived at a dysfunctional science and society at the end of the twentieth century" (Berman, 1996:35). We will explore in more detail both the elements of scientific method and alternatives to the scientific paradigm in the next two chapters.

For now we simply need to recognize that today there is considerable discussion and considerable disagreement as well, about whether we have moved or are moving in history to the point that we live in a post-positivist or postmodern world in which science and scientific reasoning are less likely to be considered the only, the best, or even the most accurate means for understanding the world around us. Lather (1991) provides a helpful summary of the three historical periods focused on knowledge production, views of history itself, and the nature of the economy.

Following are three historical eras profiled by Lather (1991:160–161):

1. Pre-modern: Centrality of church/sacred basis of determining truth and knowledge; feudal economy; history as divinely ordered.

2. Modern: Centrality of secular humanism, individual reason, and science in determining truth; the industrial age, capitalism, and bureaucracy as bases of economic life; history as linear in the direction of constant progress driven by human rationality and science.

3. Postmodern: Existing/traditional knowledge and knowledge creation processes intensely questioned. Emphasis on multiple ways of knowing through processes that are nonhierarchical, feminist influenced, and participatory; economy more and more based on information, technology, and global capitalism; view of history as nonlinear, cyclical, continually rewritten.

## Post-Postmodernism

Currently, there is growing discussion and disagreement about whether we are moving toward a *post-postmodern* worldview. This emerging discussion and the theories being generated as a result involves the revolutionary impact of technology, connectivity, and globalization.

One example of post-postmodern theory is referred to as *digimodernism*. **Digimodernism** suggests the most critical event in current culture is the clash between computerization or a digitally driven world and the written word or "text" and is reflected in such contemporary manifestations as Web 2.0 and video games. (Kirby, 2010).

Web 2.0 involved a paradigm shift from the relatively static ways we used the internet early on such as "surfing the web" to much more fluid and interactive options such as Facebook. The list below contains many of the features now available via what is termed *Web 2.0.*

- Users as first class entities in the system, with prominent profile pages, including such features as: age, sex, location, testimonials, or comments about the user by other users.
- The ability to form connections between users, via links to other users who are "friends," membership in "groups" of various kinds, and subscriptions or RSS feeds of "updates" from others.
- The ability to post content in many forms: photos, videos, blogs, comments, and ratings on other users' content, tagging of own or others' content, and some ability to control privacy and sharing.
- Other more technical features, including a public API to allow third-party enhancements and "mash-ups," and embedding of various rich content types (e.g., Flash videos), and communication with other users through internal e-mail or IM systems (Cormode & Krishnamurthy, 2008).

Another theory is called *altermodern*. **Altermodern** is defined as culture shaped by the forces of economic globalization (Bourriaud cited in Kirby, 2010). Still another theory,

*For each of these photos choose one of the historical periods: Pre-modern/Pre-positivism; Modernism/ Positivism; or Postmodernism/Post-positivism you would associate with the photo? Why did you choose as you did?*

*automodernity*, "sees a new world formed by the encounter between digital automation and personal autonomy" (Samuels cited in Kirby, 2010).

Understanding the historical flow or continuum out of which differing worldviews emerged or are emerging over time is an important means of recognizing the changes in perspectives on the world that at any given moment are likely to seem stable, permanent, and unchangeable. Even the changes occurring over time in the Western worldviews illustrated in the examples above give us a sense that permanency in approaches to understanding our worlds is less reality than perspective at any particular point in time.

**Test your understanding of Paradigms and History by taking this short** Quiz.

## SOCIAL WORK HISTORY: SCIENCE AND ART

A scientific approach to doing social work has been a major avenue used by social workers to attempt to understand and intervene in the world during the short history of social work as a field of study and practice. Although we have claimed allegiances to both art and science, many of us have preferred that science guide our work. This is not surprising given the power and faith in the scientific approach that has pervaded the modern world of the 19th and 20th centuries. The period of the late 19th and 20th centuries coincides with the birth and development of social work as an organized field of knowledge and practice.

Many of the historical arguments and issues concerning traditional and alternative paradigms—humanism, science, religion—for understanding our worlds and ourselves have parallels in the history of social work. The mission, values, and purposes of social work all reflect beliefs about the nature of the world and people. The concern of social work with individuals, families, and communities in interaction and interdependence, as well as its concern for social reform to bring about improvements in individual and collective well-being, reflects important beliefs about the nature of the world and its inhabitants.

In 1990, the late social work scholar Howard Goldstein (1990:33–34) suggested social work has followed two quite distinct tracks to put its mission into practice. These two distinct tracks parallel in a number of ways the two quite different worldviews or paradigms represented by humanistic (social work as an art) and scientific perspectives. Goldstein reminded us that, while social work adopted a scientific approach to pursuing its mission, it did not discard completely its humanistic inclinations. These divergent paths have led us to multiple approaches to understanding humans' behaviors and the environments they inhabit and within which they interact. These paths have at times led social work to emphasize "Freudian psychology, the empiricism of behavioral psychology, and the objectivity of the scientific methods of the social sciences" (1990:33). At other times, we have followed much different paths in "existential, artistic, and value-based" alternatives (1990:35). Goldstein found social workers in 1990 (as he found the social sciences generally) turning again toward the humanistic, subjective, or interpretive paths. This is a direction quite consistent with the alternative paradigms for understanding human behavior and the social environment that we will explore in the chapters to come. This alternative path allows social workers "to give more serious attention to and have more regard for the subjective domain of our clients' moral, theological, and cultural beliefs, which . . . give meaning to the experiences of individuals and families" (England 1986 in Goldstein, 1990:38). However, in 2012, with social work's emphasis on evidence-based practice (EBP), a shift toward a scientific approach seems to be occurring again. Goldstein might be shocked at the recent focus in colleges and universities on the so-called "STEM" (Science, Technology, Engineering, and Mathematics) disciplines and the accompanying shift away from disciplines in the social sciences and humanities.

## Social Work and the Liberal Arts

In order to prepare us for effective 21st century social work practice, we contend that a balance between science and art in social work education remains essential. Both areas are necessary to provide the tools to become critical thinkers and understand the wide and complex range of worldviews held by the people with whom we work in an increasingly diverse U.S. society and interconnected global worlds. We will search for ways to become aware of the many paradigmatic elements that influence our day-to-day lives and those of the people with whom we work. One way this is accomplished is through requirements that social work education be based on a foundation of studies in a wide range of multidisciplinary liberal arts and sciences courses. Our studies in these courses can provide us new avenues to understand our own cultures and the cultures of others.

Social workers have recognized these valuable avenues to understanding human behavior and the social environment for a long time. They are considered so important in the overall education of social workers that content in the liberal arts and sciences disciplines is part of the knowledge required to achieve competence in applying knowledge of human behavior and the social environment in your social work practice (CSWE, 2008). As we proceed, we will try, through this book, to connect what we are thinking and learning about human behavior and the social environment with the experiences and knowledge we have (we all have a great deal!) and are continually gaining through the liberal arts and sciences.

Lather suggests a helpful way of thinking about the liberal arts and sciences as "human sciences" which encompass social, psychological, and biological sciences as they relate to humans. The definition of "human science" she puts forth suggests a broader, more inclusive approach to understanding human behavior through the liberal arts and sciences. Human science "is more inclusive, using multiple systems of inquiry, a science which approaches questions about the human realm with an openness to its special characteristics and a willingness to let the questions inform which methods are appropriate" (Polkinghome quoted in Lather 1991:166). This more inclusive and open approach to achieving understanding is consistent with the perspective we take in this book toward alternative paradigms for understanding HBSE.

Howard Goldstein (1990) contends that broad knowledge from the liberal arts (the humanities) helps us do better social work. He suggests that much understanding about the continuously unfolding and complex nature of the lives of the people with whom we work (and of our own lives) can be achieved through study in the liberal arts. According to Goldstein, this broad range of knowledge includes art, literature, drama, philosophy, religion, and history.

Because paradigmatic elements are so interwoven with the many expressions of cultures and societies, it is essential for social workers to have as wide a range of opportunities as possible to learn and to think about these important elements and expressions. Creative thinking that helps us ask questions that lead us toward understanding the experiences and the worlds of the people with whom we work, as well as our own, is central to what social work practice is all about.

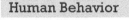

**Human Behavior**

**Practice Behavior Example:** Apply theories and knowledge from the liberal arts to understand biological, social, cultural, psychological, and spiritual development

**Critical Thinking Question:** Can you think of an example from one of your liberal arts courses where you attained understanding of processes of spiritual development?

# PARADIGMS, CULTURE, AND SOCIETY

A paradigm, as the concept is used here, encompasses a number of different but interrelated elements. Among the elements that can help us understand the complexities and variations of worldviews or paradigms held by different people are culture and society. Each of these terms has a variety of meanings and is used in different ways depending on the context of their use and the worldview held by their users. For example, each of these concepts, in the hands of their users, can either be a very strong and positive force for unity and cooperation or an equally strong and negative force for divisiveness and domination. We will examine some of the interrelated meanings of these concepts next.

Paradigms or worldviews simultaneously shape and reflect the institutions and processes shared by people in a society. However, there is a great deal of variation in the specific paradigmatic elements—the parts that constitute a paradigm—and the degree to which different persons in the same society share these parts. This is especially true in the United States, although it is often unrecognized. Paradigmatic elements include the processes, beliefs, values, and products that make up cultures and give multiple meanings to such concepts as ethnicity and race. They include and are reflected in such varied expressions of cultures as art, music, science, philosophy, religion, politics, economics, leisure, work, and education. As Logan (1990:25) suggests, "culture must be viewed in the sense of the spiritual life of a people as well as material and behavioral aspects." As in the case of the concept of society, there is tremendous variation in the nature of the paradigmatic elements that constitute different cultures and the degree to which these elements are shared by the peoples of the United States and the world. It is contended here that this variation, this diversity, is a rich and essential, although underutilized, resource for understanding human behavior and the social environment.

## Culture and Society: Multiple Meanings

A very basic and traditional definition of culture is that it is the "shared values, traditions, norms, customs, arts, history, folklore, and institutions of a group of people" (NCCC, 2004). Even more basic is the definition offered by Herskovits that culture is "the human-made part of the environment" (Lonner, 1994:231). Society can be defined as a "group of people who share a heritage or history" (Persell, 1987:47–48). The concepts of culture and society are linked. Lonner (1994:231) suggests that culture is "the mass of behavior that human beings in any society learn from their elders and pass on to the younger generation." In other words, culture can be learned from and passed on by others in the society. The transmission of culture can happen in two ways. It can occur through socialization, which is teaching the culture by an elder generation to a younger one very explicitly through formal instruction and rules. This transmission process can also occur through enculturation by "implicitly or subtly" teaching the culture to the younger generation "in the course of everyday life" (Lonner, 1994:234). These definitions and concepts reflect the sense that culture is constructed by groups of people (societies), is made up of beliefs, practices, and products (artifacts), and is passed from one generation to another.

The definitions above all emphasize similarities and commonalties among the people who make up cultures and societies. It is very important for us as social workers to be careful not to overgeneralize about these similarities. We need to recognize that "culture does not simply make people uniform or homogenize them: It rather sets trends from which in some cases it allows, and in other case even encourages, deviation: be it by attributing differentiating roles, or simply by encouraging individual differences in fashion, imagination, or style. In other words, a culture seems to need both uniformity and individuality" (Boesch 1991 in Lonner, 1994:233).

## SOCIAL WORK AND CULTURAL COMPETENCE

It is not enough for social workers to simply understand the abstract complexities that make up definitions of culture and society. Because respect for diversity is so central to social work values and practice and because culture is such an important tool for understanding human diversity, social workers make considerations about culture and cultural differences central to what we consider to be competent social work practice. The notion of culturally competent social work practice and what it involves has been described for multiple levels and areas of practice, including individual practitioners and clients, families and agencies.

Cultural Competence is a set of cultural behaviors and attitudes integrated into the practice methods of a system, agency, or its professionals, that enables them to work effectively in cross cultural situations (National Center for Cultural Competence, 2004). According to the National Center for Cultural Competence (NCCC), cultural competence comprises two dimensions:

- Surface Structure: Use people, places, language, music, food, and clothing familiar to and preferred by the target audience.
- Deep Structure: Involves sociodemographic and racial/ethnic population differences and the influence of ethnic, cultural, social, environmental, and historical factors on behaviors (National Center for Cultural Competence, 2004).

The NCCC also suggest three major characteristics of culturally competent service delivery (see box below).

Culturally competent social work practice—its meaning and its application—is emerging as one of the most critical aspects of social work practice. It is especially important as the diversity of the U.S. population continues to increase. Culturally competent practice is also increasingly important as we become more and more interrelated with other people in the world as a result of the rapid shifts toward ever more global economics, communication, and transportation. Cultural competence is addressed in more detail in Chapter 3.

**Test your understanding of Paradigms, Culture, and Society by taking this short Quiz.**

---

### Characteristics of Culturally Competent Service Delivery

**Available:** Availability of services refers to the existence of health services and bicultural/ bilingual personnel

**Accessible:** Accessibility is contingent on factors such as cost of services, the hours of service provision, and the geographic location of a program.

**Acceptable:** Acceptability is the degree to which services are compatible with the cultural values and traditions of the clientele. (National Center for Cultural Competence, 2004)

## SUMMARY/TRANSITION

This chapter presented you with information and perspectives in a number of areas. It has introduced you to the place and importance of human behavior and the social environment content in the social work curriculum. It has described HBSE content as required content for all accredited social work education programs that, in concert with a wide range of content from the liberal arts and sciences, builds a foundation of knowledge upon which to base social work practice. This chapter has presented a number of guiding assumptions about the interrelationships among us, others, and social work practice.

Definitions of the concept of paradigm or worldview have been presented, along with discussions of the related notions of paradigm analysis and paradigm shift and their significance for social workers and social change. This chapter has introduced the notions of traditional or dominant paradigms and alternative or possible paradigms. These concepts have been placed in context through discussion of their emergence and change over time along a historical continuum. Attention has been given in this chapter to the purposes and foundations of social work that form its historic mission to enhance human and community well-being and alleviate poverty and oppression. The exclusion of many diverse persons from traditional and dominant paradigms has been introduced. In addition, the concepts of culture, society, and cultural competence were introduced. The concepts and issues in this chapter present the basic themes that will guide us through-

**Recall what you learned in this chapter by completing the Chapter Review.**

out our journey to understanding human behavior and the social environment in the chapters that comprise this book. The concepts and issues presented in this chapter are intended to provide a base from which to explore in more detail dimensions of traditional and alternative paradigms in the next chapter.

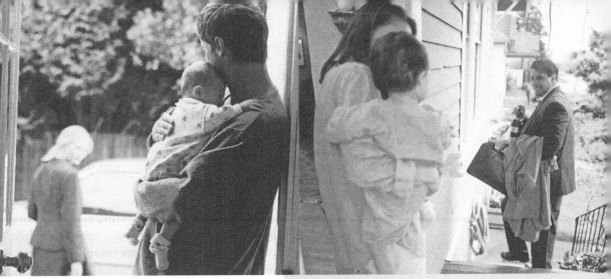

RANALD MACKECHNIE/GETTY IMAGES,
RYAN MCVAY/PHOTODISC/GETTY IMAGES

# 2

# Traditional and Alternative Paradigms

## INTRODUCTION

**This chapter outlines the conceptual framework we will use** throughout this book. Traditional and alternative paradigms for gathering and organizing knowledge for social work practice are described, compared, and contrasted in this chapter. Five dimensions of traditional and alternative paradigms are outlined. These five dimensions offer some basic perspectives social workers can use to organize a wide range of information about human behavior and the social environment (HBSE) from a number of different disciplines. This framework provides the basic vehicles we will use on our journey to more comprehensive and critical understanding of human behavior and the social environment.

## DIMENSIONS OF TRADITIONAL AND DOMINANT PARADIGM

Like paradigms or worldviews in general, the traditional and dominant paradigm is viewed here as a set of interrelated and interlocking dimensions through which what and how we know about the world around us is created, communicated, and controlled.

These dimensions include methods (processes), attributes, perspectives, standards, and ways of relating. When these dimensions come together to form the traditional and dominant paradigm, they represent in large part what we are taught to believe in the United States to be right and true.

The traditional and dominant paradigm gains its specific identity in the following ways. It gives primacy to the use of **positivistic, scientific, objective, and quantitative methods (processes)** for creating knowledge upon which to base actions and beliefs. The dominant paradigm places primary value on and reflects **masculine attributes and patriarchal perspectives.** The dominant paradigm evaluates persons' worth and importance according to standards of **whiteness.** Relations with others are constructed with concern for maintaining high degrees of **separateness and impersonality.** Within the dominant paradigm, concepts and people tend to be placed in **oppositional or competitive positions** in relation to each other. **Privileged status** is awarded according to the degree to which one displays and adheres to the methods (processes), attributes, perspectives, standards, and ways of relating to others that characterize the traditional and dominant paradigm. We will explore in more depth these dimensions of the traditional and dominant paradigm in the sections that follow.

## Positivistic/Scientific/Objective/Quantitative: Ways of Knowing

An important means of understanding the traditional and dominant paradigm is the examination of methods or processes through which knowledge or information is gained and evaluated. These methods or processes are in themselves important components of the traditional and dominant paradigm at the same time that they are mechanisms for creating that worldview. They represent both "ways of knowing" and what is considered "worth knowing." They are central "processes" and essential qualities of "products" in the traditional paradigm. In other words, they are in many respects both *how* and *what* we need to know according to the traditional and dominant paradigm.

Elements of this dimension of the traditional and dominant paradigm are: **positivistic, scientific, objective, and quantitative.** These dual-purpose characteristics are presented here as an interrelated group. These characteristics are considered together because they are so often applied almost interchangeably in references to the "ways of knowing" and to what is accorded "worth knowing" (or valid knowledge) according to the traditional paradigm. However, separate descriptions and discussions of these process/product characteristics are presented below for clarity. While we discuss each of these interrelated characteristics separately, we must keep in mind that these characteristics combine to form a single perspective or standpoint from which the world is viewed and evaluated.

### Research Based Practice

**Practice Behavior Example:** Comprehend quantitative and qualitative research and understand scientific and ethical approaches to building knowledge

**Critical Thinking Question:** Does the dimension of the traditional paradigm discussed in this section assist us in comprehending quantitative or qualitative approaches to knowledge building? Why?

### Positivistic

The first of these characteristics is a positivistic approach or positivism. Positivism is also often referred to as **empiricism** (Bottomore, 1984:22–23; Imre, 1984:41). The words **positivism** and **empiricism** refer to *the belief that knowledge is gained through objective observations of the world around us.* Conclusions drawn about that world must be based only on those objective observations (Dawson et al., 1991:247–248, 432; Manheim, 1977:12–14). The positivist or empiricist standpoint suggests that *we can know* *the world with certainty only if we can observe it through our senses.* This perspective carries the assumption that any capable person observing the same event, experience, or object will see, feel, taste, smell, or hear that event, experience, or object in exactly the same way. This is also referred to as replication. "Truth" or "knowledge" is in fact verified or strengthened in this way and only in this way (Dawson et al., 1991:19–20; Manheim, 1977:12). While many researchers consider positivism and empiricism synonymous, other scholars differentiate the terms. They suggest that *positivism* is a more narrow concept, always based on use of the scientific method (see below) to determine what is knowledge. *Empiricism* is sometimes considered a broader or more inclusive concept that may be applied to ways of gaining knowledge other than through scientific method, such as through qualitative approaches (Heineman Pieper, 1995:xxiii; Tyson, 1995:9).

## Scientific

The second characteristic necessary for knowing and evaluating the world according to the traditional and dominant paradigm is science or the scientific approach. Like the positivistic or empiricist standpoint, a scientific approach requires observation of experiences, events, or objects through our senses. In addition, the **scientific approach** requires *"systematic, controlled, empirical, and critical investigation of hypothetical propositions about the presumed relations among natural phenomena"* (Kerlinger, 1973:11). A scientific approach also assumes that it is through this kind of investigation of the relationship among observable phenomena that we come to know the world and its occupants according to the scientific approach. It is difficult to understate the power accorded the scientific approach to determining what we know and what is worth knowing in dominant U.S. society. In the box below is a summary of the scientific method.

## Objective

Central to the scientific approach is the third characteristic necessary for knowing and evaluating the world according to the traditional and dominant paradigm—objectivity. An **objective approach** *places a premium on being "unbiased, unprejudiced, detached, impersonal."* **Objectivity** is *"the characteristic of viewing things as they 'really' are"* (Manheim, 1977:10). Objectivity requires that the values of the studier be kept completely separate from any event, experience, or object being studied. The person with a scientific perspective "believes . . . that there is some ultimate link between logical thinking and empirical facts . . . that objective reality not only exists, but is essentially in one piece, so that there should be no disparity between what is logical and what is empirical" (Dawson et al., 1991:20).

## Quantitative

It is not surprising that a paradigm such as the traditional and dominant paradigm—with so much emphasis on gathering and validating knowledge through systematic,

## Steps in Scientific Method

1. Choosing research topics
2. Constructing hypotheses
3. Selecting methods
4. Collecting data
5. Analyzing data
6. Interpreting findings and drawing conclusions (Alix 1995:41)

objective observations, using our human senses and the senses of others for verifying that knowledge—places great importance on keeping a record of the nature and number of the events, experiences, or objects observed. Thus, the fourth ingredient necessary for knowing and evaluating the world according to the traditional and dominant paradigm is quantitative. A **quantitative approach** *assumes that "all materials are potentially quantifiable"* (Kerlinger, 1973:529). *This approach seeks answers to questions by making generalizations about people and things "based on precisely measured quantities"* (Dawson et al. 1991:436). Value, veracity, importance, and power are determined by how often and how much or how many of a given commodity has been observed or accumulated.

As we continue our exploration of other dimensions of the traditional and dominant paradigms, we need to keep in mind their interrelatedness with this powerful and fundamental traditional paradigm dimension. It is through struggling with the complexities of the interwoven nature of the dimensions of the traditional and dominant paradigm that we can come to appreciate the power of this paradigm in our own and others' lives. Just as these four characteristics—positivistic, scientific, objective, and quantitative—depend upon and reinforce each other throughout this "way of knowing" and this means of judging what is "worth knowing," we must recognize the interdependence of this group of processes/products with other dimensions of the traditional and dominant worldview.

## Masculinity/Patriarchy

The traditional and dominant paradigm places great value on, and reflects attributes that have come to be associated with, maleness or masculinity. This emphasis on valuing masculine attributes has resulted in a system or set of perspectives and institutions referred to as a patriarchy. Interestingly, we will see in our exploration of the masculinity/patriarchy dimension of the traditional and dominant paradigm that a number of the processes/products discussed above—positivistic, scientific, objective, quantitative—have come to be associated closely with maleness or masculinity. These processes/products are also important elements of patriarchal perspectives and institutions.

### Patriarchy

Literally, **patriarchy** means *"the rule of the fathers."* In the social sciences, the meaning of patriarchy is very close to this literal definition. "A **patriarchy** *is a society in which formal power over public decision and policy making is held by adult men"* (Ruth 1990:45). This is a helpful definition for us to use in our exploration of the traditional and dominant paradigm. It implies that the nature of the society and institutions in which we live, their values and priorities, are determined almost exclusively through patriarchy, which is the "embodiment of masculine ideals and practices" (Ruth, 1990: 45).

We can find evidence and examples of patriarchy and its influence in areas of our lives other than politics. Belenky et al. (1986:5–6), for example, remind us "that conceptions of knowledge and truth that are accepted and articulated today have been shaped throughout history by the male-dominated culture." They assert that men have drawn on their own perspectives and visions to construct prevailing theories, to write history, and to set values "that have become the guiding principles for men and women alike."

### Human Rights & Justice

**Practice Behavior Example:** Engage in practices that advance social and economic justice

**Critical Thinking Question:** How does the Masculinity/Patriarchy dimension of the traditional paradigm help us understand the importance of advancing human rights and social and economic justice, especially regarding women?

**Masculinity**

If patriarchy is the embodiment of control over decision and policy making by men, what are some of the attributes of maleness or masculinity that are reflected in patriarchal decisions and policies? Different observers differ somewhat about the specific attributes of masculinity. Ruth provides one useful list of attributes that are representative of what she calls the **"patriarchal ideal of masculinity."** These attributes include: *"aggressiveness, courage, physical strength and health, self-control and emotional reserve, perseverance and endurance, competence and rationality, independence, self-reliance, autonomy, individuality, sexual potency"* (Ruth, 1990:47).

## Whiteness

The traditional and dominant paradigm is inordinately influenced by, and its content controlled by, white persons of European descent. What this has come to mean is that all persons, both white and nonwhite, have come to be judged or evaluated in virtually all areas of life according to standards that reflect the values, attitudes, experiences, and historical perspectives of white persons, specifically white persons of European descent. This perspective is so influential that the traditional and dominant worldview is often referred to as Eurocentric.

**Whiteness, power, and social institutions**

The dimension of whiteness, as in the cases of the masculinity/patriarchy and positivistic/scientific/objective/quantitative dimensions, permeates processes and products that make up our worlds and that shape and are shaped by the traditional and dominant worldview. For examples of the predominance of whites in positions of power in this society, one need only look to the public decision- and policy-making arenas. According to Lyubansky (2011), there are several different approaches to defining whiteness. These include: 1) racial identity or whiteness as a group identity distinct from non-white people and groups; 2) racial bias or discrimination directed by white people toward non-white people; and 3) racial privilege or the unearned and often unconscious benefits accrued simply as a result of being white.

Pharr (1988) suggests that we also examine through a lens of color the leadership of other social institutions, such as finance and banking, churches and synagogues, and the military. Such an examination will reveal that not only does whiteness predominate in the leadership of social institutions, but it permeates the very nature of what is communicated through those social institutions as well. Pharr reminds us that "in our schools, the primary literature and history taught are about the exploits of white men, shown through the white man's eyes. Black history, for instance, is still relegated to one month, whereas 'American history' is taught all year round" (Pharr, 1988:54).

Collins (1989:752) reminds us that when one group, white males, for example, controls fundamental social processes such as the "knowledge-validation" or education/research processes, other voices and ways of knowing are suppressed. She notes that "since the general culture shaping the taken-for-granted knowledge of the community of experts is one permeated by widespread notions of Black and female inferiority, new knowledge claims that seem to violate these fundamental assumptions are likely to be viewed as anomalies." In fact, questions about such notions are unlikely even to be raised "from within a white-male-controlled academic community" (Collins, 1989:752).

## Separate/Impersonal/Competitive

The traditional and dominant paradigm places primacy in relations and relationships on separation, impersonality, and on viewing the world in oppositional or competitive ways. Often this has meant the world has been viewed in what has been referred to as binary or competing and oppositional terms such as "either/or" and "we/they" rather than in cooperative and inclusive terms such as "both/and" and "us" (Derrida in (Scott, 1988:7).

### Separateness and impersonality

In Western philosophy this focus on separateness is seen in the traditional concern for separation of mind (thought) from body (physical). In the natural and the social sciences, emphasis is placed, as we saw earlier in our discussions of the scientific approach, on separating personal values from the empirical process of knowledge building. In carrying out the scientific process, any integration of subjective and objective elements has long been seen as contaminating the process of knowledge building. Science, in order to be scientific, must be conducted impersonally. The education of natural scientists continually stresses the importance of being value-free, of being objective, of separating studier from studied (subject from object). The social sciences and many in social work have modeled their approaches to knowledge building on the impersonal and value-free tenets of the natural sciences.

Impersonality and separateness are also associated closely with such valued masculine attributes as independence, autonomy, and individuality. These, you will recall, are elements of the "patriarchal ideal of masculinity." The value placed on these attributes in combination with the importance placed on separateness and impersonal approaches has heavily influenced the nature and focus of research on human development and behavior. Belenky et al., for example, remind us that "the Western tradition of dividing human nature into dual . . . streams" has resulted in our learning "a great deal about the development of autonomy and independence . . . while we have not learned as much about the development of interdependence, intimacy, nurturance, and contextual thought" (Belenky et al. 1986:6–7).

We will look in some detail at issues of autonomy and interdependence in Chapters 4 and 5 when we explore traditional and alternative approaches to understanding individual behavior and development. Belenky et al. also point out that "the mental processes that are involved in considering the abstract and the impersonal have been labeled 'thinking' and are attributed primarily to men, while those that deal with the personal and interpersonal fall under the rubric of 'emotions' and are largely relegated to women" (1986:7). Again, the interweaving of the dimensions of the traditional and dominant paradigm is obvious.

### Competitiveness: binaries and hierarchies

When ideas or characteristics are divided into **dichotomies or binary oppositions**—as French philosopher/linguist Jacques Derrida refers to this tendency to separate into opposite and competing forces—the opposing sides tend to be hierarchical, with one dominant or primary, the opposite subordinate and secondary (Scott, 1988:7). Collins also stresses the tendency of such dichotomous thinking to carry strong implications of systemic inequality. She stresses that "dichotomous oppositional differences invariably imply relationships of superiority and inferiority, hierarchical relationships that mesh with political economies of domination and subordination" (Collins, 1986:20).

The Western philosophical tradition, Derrida argues, rests on these binary oppositions or dichotomies in many other areas such as unity/diversity, identity/difference, presence/absence (Scott, 1988). Collins addresses the meaning of dichotomous thinking from an African American feminist perspective in the context of human oppression. In doing so she demonstrates the interlocking and interdependent nature of the several dimensions of the traditional/dominant paradigm. "Either/or dualistic thinking, or . . . the construct of dichotomous oppositional difference, may be a philosophical linchpin in systems of race, class, and gender oppression," she believes. "One fundamental characteristic of this construct is the categorization of people, things, and ideas in terms of their difference [separateness] from one another." The examples of dichotomies she provides—black/white, male/female, reason/emotion, fact/opinion, and subject/object (Collins, 1986:20)—speak loudly of the dichotomies implicit in the traditional and dominant paradigm.

Social work also has a history of struggling with dichotomies or dualities. Berlin points out that social work "is built on a foundation of dualities." She notes, for example, our contrasting commitments to "individual adaptation and social change" and "to humanistic values and scientific knowledge development." Social work continues to struggle over which of these dualities to align itself with or how to provide a more balanced alignment. Over our history we have moved from side to side at different points—sometimes moving toward a focus on individual change, sometimes toward social change; sometimes emphasizing our humanistic values as primary, sometimes emphasizing scientific aspects of social work. Many would argue that our alignments have more often gone with individual adaptation and science than with social change and humanistic values. That the struggle and tension continue to involve both sides of these dichotomies rather than shifting entirely to one side and remaining there can be considered a strength of the field (Berlin, 1990:55).

## Privilege

The impact of the traditional and dominant paradigm in all its varied manifestations is hardly neutral or value-free. The paradigmatic elements that we have explored so far all carry with them differential meanings and very different results for different people. Those who benefit are those who define, fit, and enforce the processes, attributes, perspectives, standards, and ways of relating that characterize the traditional and dominant paradigm. The set or system of benefits that accrue to these persons is referred to as **privilege.** We end our examination of the elements of the traditional and dominant paradigm with a brief exploration of privilege. The concept of privilege will be a continuing concern for us as we move on in our journey toward greater understanding of human behavior and the social environment.

**Privilege** is that powerful but often unspoken and taken-for-granted sense that one fits, that one is an active and powerful participant and partner in defining and making decisions about one's world. It is that sense that one's worldview is in fact dominant. Privilege is the total of the benefits one accrues as a result of that dominance. Unfortunately, such a definition of privilege is accompanied by the reality that this privilege is gained and maintained at the expense of others: It is exclusive.

### Human Rights & Justice

**Practice Behavior Example:** Understand the forms and mechanisms of oppression and discrimination

**Critical Thinking Question:** How do the concepts of privilege and white privilege assist us in gaining this understanding?

### Norm of rightness

Privilege is used synonymously here with what Pharr (1988:53) refers to in discussing the common elements of oppressions as a **"defined norm, a standard of rightness and often righteousness."** This norm is used to judge all other persons. It is backed up by institutional and economic power; by institutional and individual violence. In the United States, Pharr characterizes the determiner and enforcer of this norm as "male, white, heterosexual, Christian, temporarily able-bodied, youthful with access to wealth and resources." She makes an important observation about this "defined norm" that is essential to our understanding of privilege. She urges us to remember "that an established norm does not necessarily represent a majority in terms of numbers; it represents those who have the ability to exert power and control over others" (Pharr, 1988:53).

### White privilege

In U.S. society, the ability to exert power and control over others is often associated with whiteness, what one might refer to as *white privilege*. However, white people are often unaware or unwilling to recognize how closely whiteness is associated with privilege in the United States. Helms (1994:305) suggests that the reality, existence, and persistence of white privilege is often denied by white people. This denial may even take the form of denying that an identifiable privileged white racial group exists. She argues that "disavowal of the existence of White privilege takes the form of denying that a White *racial* group exists that benefits from White privilege."

Peggy McIntosh, a feminist scholar, offers dramatic, real-life examples of the benefits that accrue to those of us who reflect characteristics of the "norm of rightness" and who "fit" the dimensions of the traditional and dominant paradigm. McIntosh specifically addresses what she refers to as "skin-color privilege," or what we have referred to here as "whiteness." However, implications for the meaning of privilege flowing from other attributes of the "norm of rightness" can be drawn from her examples as well. The following are some particularly illuminating and concrete examples of what it means on a day-to-day basis to have white privilege. These examples can help bring to a conscious level many of the "taken-for-granted" aspects of both whiteness and other elements of privilege.

As a white person, McIntosh, points out:

- I can turn on the television or open to the front page of the paper and see people of my race widely and positively represented.
- I can be sure that my children will be given curricular materials that testify to the existence of their race.
- I can be reasonably sure that if I ask to talk to "the person in charge," I will be facing a person of my race.
- I can easily buy posters, postcards, picture books, greeting cards, dolls, toys, and children's magazines featuring people of my race.
- I can be late to a meeting without having the lateness reflect on my race.
- I can choose blemish cover or bandages in "flesh" color and have them more or less match my skin. (McIntosh, 1992:73–75)

Tim Wise, a current proponent of recognizing and addressing white privilege, provides an example of the economic privilege accrued as a result of white privilege:

> How is it not an issue that the typical white family in America, thanks to this history, this legacy of institutionalized oppression for some and advantage and privilege for others, how is it not news that the average white family in America, not the average rich white family, the average white family has 12 times the accumulated net worth of the average African American family, 8 times the accumulated net worth of the average Latino family. (Wise in (Ryan, 2011)

**Test your understanding of the Dimensions of Dominant/Traditional Paradigm by taking this short Quiz.**

Next we will explore the dimensions and characteristics of alternative or possible paradigms.

# DIMENSIONS OF ALTERNATIVE/POSSIBLE PARADIGMS

As is the case with paradigms in general, alternative paradigms are sets of interrelated and interlocking dimensions through which what and how we know about the world around us is created, communicated, and controlled. Like all paradigms, alternative paradigms include methods (processes), attributes, perspectives, standards, and ways of relating.

Alternative paradigms incorporate **interpretive, intuitive, subjective, and qualitative** products and processes for creating knowledge upon which to base actions and beliefs. Alternative paradigms do not necessarily exclude the processes and products (positivistic, scientific, objective, and quantitative) of the traditional/dominant paradigm. They do not, however, recognize those processes and products as the only or necessarily the most appropriate avenues to understanding and action. The alternative paradigms we consider, value, and reflect **feminine attributes and feminist perspectives.** They do not give primacy to masculine attributes or patriarchal perspectives. The alternative paradigms we explore evaluate persons' worth and importance according to standards of the inherent worth and dignity of all humans, and they especially recognize the benefits of **human diversity.** Persons are not evaluated according to standards of whiteness. The alternative paradigms we will explore structure relations with others around recognition of the **interconnected and personal** nature of our relationships with other persons and with the elements of the worlds around us. Separateness and impersonality are seen as obstacles to constructing effective relationships. The alternative paradigms with which we are concerned do not assume a competitive stance in which people or ideas are in opposition to one another. They instead focus on the **integrative and complementary** nature of differences among people and ideas. The alternative paradigms through which we will attempt to view our worlds seek recognition of **oppressions** and the elimination of conditions and relations that allow some persons and groups privilege at the expense of others. These are the critical dimensions of alternative paradigms through which we will attempt to find and create new ways to view our worlds. These interrelated dimensions are explored in more detail in the following sections.

## Interpretive/Intuitive/Subjective/Qualitative: Ways of Knowing

In our discussion of the traditional and dominant paradigm, we noted that examination of the methods and processes through which knowledge or information is gained and evaluated is essential for understanding that paradigm. The methods and processes for gaining and evaluating information and knowledge are essential components of and avenues for creating alternative worldviews as well. Our alternative paradigms are characterized by an emphasis on "ways of knowing" that are more interpretive, intuitive, subjective, and qualitative than those of the dominant paradigm we explored earlier in this chapter. These characteristics also represent alternative types of knowledge "worth knowing." Although these alternative ways of knowing and of evaluating what is worth knowing often have not been valued within the purview of the traditional and dominant paradigm, they offer essential avenues for social workers to gain a more complete understanding of humans, our behaviors, and the social environments we construct and inhabit.

**Practice Behavior Example:** Comprehend quantitative and qualitative research and understand scientific and ethical approaches to building knowledge

**Critical Thinking Question:** How does the alternative paradigm dimension of "Interpretive/ Intuitive/Subjective/Qualitative: Ways of Knowing" addressed in this section reinforce the importance of comprehending qualitative research?

The interpretive, intuitive, subjective, and qualitative dimension of alternative paradigms for understanding human behavior is discussed in some detail next. Although we discuss the characteristics—interpretive, intuitive, subjective, and qualitative—of this dimension separately, it is important to keep in mind that all these characteristics are interrelated and combine to form the process/products of the alternative worldviews we are seeking to understand.

### Interpretive knowledge

The first characteristic of alternative paradigm knowledge building and validating processes we will consider is the interpretive aspect. While they are often controversial, shifts toward more interpretive approaches to understanding humans and their behaviors have been under way for some time. (In Chapter 1, you might recall, we explored in some detail the concept and consequences of "shifts" in paradigms.) Edmund Sherman (1991:69) discusses shifts occurring in the ways we think about and gather information in the social sciences. He notes that many people in these fields "are questioning just how scientific the social sciences can and should be." Rather than using the "science" dimension of the traditional/dominant paradigm as the sole methodology for understanding our worlds, some social scientists are shifting to methods more characteristic of those used in the liberal arts, specifically, the humanities.

Sherman suggests that representative of this shift are changes in the language used to describe knowledge-gathering methods or processes in the social sciences. He notes that many social scientists are using words such as " 'interpretation' and 'hermeneutics,' in describing an alternative mode of inquiry that draws as much from the humanities as from the natural sciences, if not more" (Winkler, 1985 in Sherman, 1991:69). These descriptors—interpretation and hermeneutics—are much more consistent with knowledge-gathering processes in the liberal arts and humanities than those in the natural sciences. It should come as no surprise that those of us who depend on knowledge of human behavior to do our work would look to the "humanities"—"the branches of learning having primarily a cultural character" (Webster, 1983)—for help in understanding the human condition.

A term often used as a synonym for these **interpretive approaches** to gaining understanding is **hermeneutics.** According to Webster, "Hermeneutics can be most simply defined as 'the science of interpretation'" (1983:851). Perhaps a good way to expand our understanding of interpretive or hermeneutic approaches to knowledge building is to visit some of the humanities from which the concept is taken—philosophy and history. Philosopher and historian Wilhelm Dilthey used the term **hermeneutics** to denote "the discipline concerned with the investigation and interpretation of human behavior, speech, institutions, etc., as essentially intentional" (Dilthey in Sherman, 1991:71). Lorenz points out that in the natural sciences "hermeneutics has been recognized even by theoretical physicists like Niels Bohr as a necessary and complementary epistemology that frees inquiry from the "tyranny" of positivism" (2012, p. 497).

This interpretive, hermeneutic approach is quite similar to what social workers mean when we talk about such basic concepts as "**empathy**" and "**beginning where the client is.**" These interpretive approaches to knowing are concerned in large part with understanding the meaning of human experiences. These attempts to understand the meaning of human experiences take us well beyond the realm of traditional scientific approaches to knowledge building. They take us out of the laboratory and into the everyday worlds we and the people with whom we work actually live.

This search involves going from the detached observation characteristic of science to the kind of expressive involvement more often associated with the arts. Reason and Hawkins (in Reason, 1988:80) suggest that understanding the meaning of experience is accomplished "when we tell stories, write and act in plays, write poems, meditate, create pictures, enter psychotherapy, etc. When we partake of life we create meaning; the purpose of life is making meaning." These diverse methods/processes for expanding our understanding of human behavior and experience hold rich and varied potential (some already in use, such as art therapy, others virtually unexplored) for use by social workers. These approaches or "ways of knowing" are unavailable through the knowledge-building processes of the traditional/dominant paradigm.

### Intuitive knowledge

A second characteristic of alternative routes to knowing and understanding is **intuition** or **intuitive knowledge.** Fritjof Capra (1983), a physicist, explains that "**intuitive knowledge** . . . is based on a direct, nonintellectual experience of reality arising in an expanded state of awareness. It tends to be synthesizing, holistic, and nonlinear." Reason (1981) offers a similar description in the profile proposed by Jung to describe persons who use intuition as a way of knowing. These persons "take in information through their imagination, and are interested in the whole, in the gestalt; they are idealists, interested in hypothetical possibilities, in what might be, in the creation of novel, innovative viewpoints" (Reason, 1981:44). This kind of holistic thinking, the ability to see the "big picture," is essential to social work knowledge and practice. The intuitive element of our alternative paradigm is often difficult to grasp, especially for those of us (and that is virtually all of us) who have been educated almost exclusively to think according to the dominant paradigm.

### Subjective understanding/knowing

A third element valued in alternative approaches to gaining knowledge and closely related to intuitive ways of knowing is **subjective understanding.** Subjective understanding, like intuitive ways of knowing, respects personal experience as an important/valuable/valued influence on what is known and how we view the world. Belenky et al. describe **subjective knowledge** as "a perspective from which truth and knowledge are conceived of as personal, private, and subjectively known or intuited" (1986:15).

### Experiencing Intuition by Zukav 1980:40

The next time you are awed by something, let the feeling flow freely through you and do not try to 'understand' it. You will find that you *do* understand, but in a way that you will not be able to put into words. You are perceiving intuitively.

### Subjective Understanding by James Hillman 1975 in Reason 1988:80

My soul is not the result of objective facts that require explanation; rather it reflects subjective experiences that require understanding.

Subjective knowledge calls into question the exclusive focus on objectivity as *the* most valuable path to knowing that is characteristic of the dominant paradigm. Belenky et al. remind us of the Eurocentric bias at work in thinking of objectively derived knowledge as the only real or legitimate knowledge. Such a perspective is not universal: "In many non-Western and non-technological societies, subjective knowledge and intuitive processes hold a more esteemed place in the culture" (Belenky et al., 1986:55). To accept as valuable knowledge that which comes about through personal, subjective experience is an example of respecting and learning through diverse non-Western alternative paradigms.

In a study of the ways women derive and validate knowledge, Belenky et al. identified "subjective knowers." Their description of subjective knowers suggests how neglected and unrecognized intuitive or subjective sources of understanding remain. One of the women in their study eloquently described the intuitive/subjective dimensions of these avenues to knowing about and understanding the world around her: "There's a part of me that I didn't even realize I had until recently—instinct, intuition, whatever. It helps me and protects me. It's perceptive and astute. I just listen to the inside of me and I know what to do" (Belenky et al., 1986:69). This woman articulates not only the personal and powerful nature of this way of knowing, but she also reminds us that we are often unaware of this important and personally affirming dimension of knowing. Social workers who recognize, respect, and trust this way of knowing open up important pathways to insight into human behavior at the same time that we facilitate the active, personal involvement in the knowledge-building process of those persons with whom we work.

## Qualitative approaches

A fourth approach to gaining knowledge valued in alternative paradigms is **qualitative data** and **research methods.** Capra suggests that "a true science of consciousness will deal with qualities rather than quantities, and will be based on shared experience rather than verifiable measurements" (Capra, 1983:376). Our alternative paradigm for gathering and creating social work knowledge respects and values qualitative ways of knowing. This area of knowledge seeking and understanding is especially fitting for studying HBSE because of its consistency with social work values, practices, and goals. The qualitative characteristic is interwoven with the other characteristics—interpretive, subjective, intuitive—of this dimension of alternative paradigm thinking we have discussed here.

Cobb and Forbes (2002:M197) explain what qualitative social work researchers might actually do in relation to practice settings. Such researchers "go into a particular setting such as a nursing home, clinic, or community, and, over time, they watch, listen, ask questions, take notes, and try to understand as fully as possible how persons in that setting see and experience their world. Qualitative research requires the researcher to be engaged in the lives of the people studied—to hear their stories, grasp their point of view, and understand their meanings." Cobb and Forbes (2002:M198) note there are three commonly used qualitative approaches:

- Ethnography has as its purpose the description of a culture and the meaning of human behaviors within the cultural context.
- The goal of a grounded theory study is to inductively develop a theory "grounded" in data obtained through direct observation, interviewing, and field work.
- Phenomenological studies rely primarily on in-depth interviews with a small number of people who share a common experience, often one that is difficult to measure, such as an emotion like suffering or courage. The goal is to identify and describe the essence of the experience as it is lived by those who have the experience.

## Multiple Definitions of Feminism*

[Feminism] is an entire worldview or gestalt, not just a laundry list of "women's issues." Feminist theory provides a basis for understanding every area of our lives, and a feminist perspective can affect the world politically, culturally, economically, and spiritually. (Charlotte Bunch, *Learning Our Way*, 1983)

Feminism means finally that we renounce our obedience to the fathers and recognize that the world they have described is not the whole world. . . . Feminism implies that we recognize fully the inadequacy for us, the distortion, of male-created ideologies, and that we proceed to think, and act, out of that recognition. (Adrienne Rich, *Of Woman Born*, 1976)

Feminism is the political theory and practice to free all women; women of color, working-class women, poor women, physically challenged women, lesbians, old women, as well as white economically privileged heterosexual women. Anything less than this is not feminism . . . (Barbara Smith in Cherríe Moraga and Gloria Anzaldúa, *This Bridge Called My Back*, 1981)

It is a commitment to eradicating the ideology of domination that permeates Western Culture on various levels—sex, race, and class, to name a few—and a commitment to reorganizing U.S. society, so that the self-development of people can take precedence over imperialism, economic expansion, and material desires. (bell hooks, *Ain't I a Woman*, 1981)

*From Kramarae and Treichler's *Feminist Dictionary* in Ruth 1990:30.

---

Qualitative ways of knowing respect the importance of "subjective meanings of events to individuals and groups" (Epstein in Dawson et al., 1991:244). This approach also "allows the acceptance of multiple rationales, conflicting value systems, and separate realities" (Rodwell in Dawson et al., 1991:244). In this way it shares with social work an appreciation of diversity and of the importance of participation and partnership by all persons involved.

## Feminisms

Feminism offers a significant and far-reaching approach to developing alternative paradigms for understanding human behavior and the social environment. Feminism or feminist thinking is both an essential dimension of the alternative paradigm we wish to develop and explore and an alternative paradigm or worldview in itself. Feminism is multidimensional and has many meanings to different people. It is perhaps really more accurate to think in terms of feminisms than in terms of feminism. Ruth (1990:3) suggests the comprehensive, multidimensional nature of feminism. She presents feminism as "a perspective, a worldview, a political theory, a spiritual focus, or a kind of activism."

Van Den Bergh and Cooper, social workers, offer a definition of feminism that reflects the consistency between this worldview and the purposes and values of social work: "*Feminism* is a conceptual framework and mode of analysis that has analyzed the status of women (and other disempowered groups), cross-culturally and historically to explain dynamics and conditions undergirding disparities in sociocultural status and power between majority and minority populations" (1995, p. xii).

### Feminisms: Three Waves

The history of feminism in the United States can be summarized by thinking in terms of "waves."

1. **First Wave Feminism** focused primarily on attaining basic rights for women. Among the most important of these rights was "suffrage" or the right to vote. Though the battle for this basic right had begun much earlier, the 1848 first

National Women's Rights Convention at Seneca Falls, New York is considered by many to mark the beginning of the movement to gain equal voting rights for women in the United States. However, it was not until 1920, with the ratification of the 19th Amendment to the Constitution, that women finally won the right to vote.

2. The **Second Wave** is considered to be the "Women's Liberation Movement" of the 1970s. This wave was marked by a heavy focus on activism to enact laws against sexual discrimination, for abortion rights, and the unsuccessful attempt to ratify the proposed Equal Rights Amendment to the Constitution.

3. **Third Wave Feminism** is considered by many to be the current wave and is more focused on personal fulfillment. Many third wave feminists are young, having been born approximately between 1976 and 1997. Third wave feminism celebrates women's multiple identities in the world today. It is more focused on individual fulfillment than on the social change philosophy embodied in the two earlier waves (Rampton, 2008).

## African American Feminism, Standpoint Theory, and Global Feminism

Within the context of standpoint determined by hierarchical power relations, Patricia Hill Collins, a leading African American feminist scholar, suggests that standpoint theory and feminism have different interpretations and implications for understanding the lives and experiences of African American women and other women. In addition, she suggests these different interpretations can also assist in defining and understanding a more global approach to feminist analyzes. She notes significant developments in these analyzes from the perspectives of women of color over the past 20 years:

> African American women . . . developed a "voice," a self-defined, collective black women's standpoint about black womanhood (Collins, 1990). Moreover, black women used this standpoint to "talk back" concerning black women's representation in dominant discourses (hooks, 1989). As a result of this struggle, African American women's ideas and experiences have achieved a visibility unthinkable in the past (Collins, 1996:9).

These developments, according to Collins, have allowed deeper understanding among African American women of the interplay of multiple standpoints within what had been considered a monolithic group. In other words, it has allowed a fuller recognition of the diversity within diversity (see the following section, "Diversities," for a detailed discussion of "diversity within diversity"). She points out that, specifically, "the new public safe space provided by black women's success allowed longstanding differences

## Shared Characteristics Between Social Work and Feminist Worldviews

- The development of all human beings through service
- The intrinsic worth and dignity of all human beings
- The intrinsic importance of active participation in society
- The necessity for removing obstacles to self-realization

- The prevention and elimination of discrimination in services, work, employment, and common human needs.

_Source:_ Wetzel in Swigonski 1994:389

among black women structured along axes of sexuality, social class, nationality, religion, and region to emerge." As a result of this heterogeneity, "ensuring group unity while recognizing the tremendous heterogeneity that operates within the boundaries of the term 'black women' comprises one fundamental challenge now confronting African American women." Given this heterogeneity, she suggests that commitments to social justice and participatory democracy provide key ground rules for individuals within the larger group to relate to each other across differences (Collins, 1996).

Collins uses this expanded and more diverse perspective to outline some of the elements of a global feminist agenda. She suggests that this agenda includes four major areas for attention. First is the *economic status* of women, that of global poverty reflected in the areas of "educational opportunities, industrial development, environmental racism, employment policies, prostitution, and inheritance laws concerning property." Second is *political rights* for women. Specific areas of concern are "gaining the vote, rights of assembly, traveling in public, officeholding, the rights of political prisoners, and basic human rights violations against women such as rape and torture." Third is *marital and family issues* "such as marriage and divorce laws, child custody policies, and domestic labor." Fourth is *women's health and survival issues.* These issues include "reproductive rights, pregnancy, sexuality, and AIDS" (Collins, 1996).

**Test your understanding of Feminisms by taking this short Quiz.**

## Diversities

A key to conceptualizing an alternative paradigm for understanding human behavior and the social environment is recognition of the centrality of **diversity and difference.** The importance of human diversity is interwoven with all the other dimensions of our alternative paradigm. Diversity is central to alternative routes to knowledge building, to feminism, to interrelatedness, and to understanding and eliminating oppressions. Our alternative paradigm recognizes human diversity as a source of strength, creativity, wonder, and health. This alternative paradigm is one in which processes of discovery are central. It is one in which there is not one answer but many answers; not one question but many questions. Only by recognizing both our differences and our similarities as humans can we proceed toward reaching our full potential. The search for an alternative paradigm is at its core a search for diversity. It is a search for new ways to answer age-old questions. It is a process of attempting to allow voices, long silenced, to be heard. Our alternative paradigm is one in which the complex questions of human behavior welcome and respect multiple answers suited to the multiple needs and views of the humans with whom social workers interact.

The human diversities with which we are concerned include those resulting from gender, color, sexual orientation, religion, age, disabling condition, culture, income, and class. Acquainting ourselves with the voices and visions of these different individuals and groups will provide us with important, useful, and creative alternative ways of thinking about such basic concerns of social work and HBSE as individuals, families, groups, organizations, communities, and nations. Next, we will explore some examples of how the worldviews of diverse people and groups can provide social workers with new ways to think about HBSE.

### Diversity in Practice

**Practice Behavior Examples:** Recognize and communicate their understanding of the importance of difference in shaping life experiences

**Critical Thinking Question:** How does the alternative paradigm dimension of "Diversities" discussed in the section help us understand the complex nature of meeting this expectation?

**Diversities and worldviews: what can we learn from others?**

One example of diverse avenues to understanding human experience more completely can be found in elements of a worldview based on the experiences and history of many persons of African descent. These experiences and shared history translate into values and perspectives that shape a worldview quite different from that reflected in the dominant paradigms. According to Graham (1999) in (Bent-Goodley, 2005):

> The African-centered worldview goes beyond the issues of historical oppression and draws on historical sources to revise a *collective text—the best of Africa*—to develop social work approaches and patterns which support the philosophical, cultural, and historical heritage of African people throughout the world. (emphasis added)

Bent-Goodley (2005:199–200) summarizes a number of interrelated principles that reflect an "African-centered paradigm" and that can inform social work practice with African Americans. These include the principles of *fundamental goodness, self-knowledge, communalism, spirituality, self-reliance, language and oral tradition,* and *thought and practice* (emphasizes combining knowledge with social action). These principles will be explored further in Chapter 6. Respect for and understanding of this complex set of values is essential to expanding our understanding of HBSE.

The experiences and perspectives of lesbians and gay men also have rich potential for providing new insight into questions of human behavior. These experiences and perspectives have much to offer, not only in terms of understanding the complexities of sexual orientation—lesbian, gay, bisexual, transgendered, and heterosexual—but also in providing new perspectives on such wide-ranging but essential concerns as human diversity itself, innovative alternative structures for family, and strengths-based perspectives on help seeking.

We can learn about what it means to be bicultural through the experiences of lesbians and gay men who must function simultaneously in both the heterosexual and gay/lesbian worlds. We will discuss **biculturality** or the ability to function in two cultures simultaneously in more detail in later chapters. At this point we simply need to be aware that members of diverse groups such as lesbians and gay men and people of color are expected to be able to function effectively according to the expectations of both the dominant paradigm and their own alternative worldviews. This ability to be bicultural, however, is usually not expected of members of the dominant group. Models for becoming bicultural are important for us as social workers, since we will frequently be called upon to work with persons from many different cultural backgrounds.

Alternative perspectives of some American Indian cultures offer helpful models for seeing strength in diversity. These cultures offer models not of merely accepting such differences as those between gay and nongay persons, but of finding respected roles and responsibilities for these special members of the community. Evans-Campbell and colleagues note, "many indigenous societies in North America have historically acknowledged and incorporated the existence of diverse gender and sexual identities among community members. . . . Although there were exceptions, these community member tended to be well integrated within Native communities and often occupied highly respected social and ceremonial roles." For example, they point out, "Native LGBTQT-S (lesbian, gay, bisexual, transgender, queer or two-spirit)" people often have cultural roles and responsibilities focused on caregiving (Evans-Campbell et al., 2007:78). These cultures perceive of their gay and lesbian members as transcending limits imposed by roles traditionally assigned to people based on gender.

Many other similarly significant alternatives to traditional paradigm thinking can be found by exploring diversity. Belief systems about the appropriate relationship of humans to the natural environment of many American Indian, Asian American, Muslim American, and African American people also offer much that might well be essential to our very survival on this planet. These diverse groups have shared a historic sense that humans must exist in harmony with all the elements of the natural world—human, animal, or inanimate. Such belief systems result in a deep respect and concern for preserving the natural world. This sense of interconnectedness and mutual responsibility is quite consistent with core concerns of social work as well as alternative paradigm dimensions. This perspective is quite different from dominant perspectives based on the belief that the natural world is to be controlled and harnessed in service to humans. The dominant perspective has resulted too often in the abuse and destruction of the natural environment in order to control and exploit it for the immediate benefit of some humans.

Learning about diversity can expand our understanding of still another area of concern to social workers. We can find helpful alternative perspectives on the roles of elders and their contributions to the common good. Many American Indian, African American, Asian American, and Hispanic families and communities reserve positions of great respect and importance for their elder members. Many families and communities of African heritage, for example, see elders as holding the wisdom of the culture, and they entrust them to impart their wisdom and the history of the people to younger members through oral tradition. Other meaningful roles for elders, especially for grandparents, are found in actively participating in child rearing and in assuming foster and adoptive parent roles for the family's children when necessary. In many African American families and communities, responsibilities for child rearing may be shared among parents and grandparents as well as other adult and elderly members of the community who function as grandparents and care givers outside the traditional blood-related or legally sanctioned family network. Such inclusiveness not only creates more opportunities for meaningful roles for elders, it also affords a larger system of caregivers for the community's children. Through such extended systems as these there is the opportunity for mutual benefits and obligations across generations and traditional family boundaries Beaver, 1990:224; Turner in Everett et al., 1991: 50–51.

## Diversity within diversity: beyond binaries

The traditional paradigm tendency to view the world in binary terms of either/or greatly oversimplifies the richness and multiple realities of many persons. The historic tendency of the dominant group (whites) literally to see the world in "black and white" reflects this binary tendency.

The Census This binary tendency to deny multiple racial realities was perhaps most clearly reflected in traditional U.S. Census Bureau policy. However, this is changing. According to the AmeriStat Population Reference Bureau and Social Science Data Analysis Network, "the shifting labels and definitions used in the U.S. census reflect the growing diversity of the population and changing political and social climate." According to AmeriStat:

> The first population census in 1790 asked enumerators to classify free residents as white or "other." Slaves were counted separately. By 1860, the census requested that residents be classified as white, black, or mulatto (mixed race), American Indian and Chinese were added as separate categories in 1870. In the 1890 census, census-takers were instructed to distinguish the color of household members as white, black, octoroon (one-eighth black), quadroon (one-quarter black), mulatto (one-half black), or as Chinese, Japanese, or American Indian. (AmeriStat, 2000)

For the first time, the year 2000 census, and continued in the 2010 census, allowed respondents to mark multiple categories. With this change as many as 63 racial combinations were possible. The year 2000 census was also more responsive to persons of Hispanic heritage. The Census Bureau coding (including the option of writing in specific group of origin, such as Salvadoran, Nicaraguan, Argentinean, etc.) allowed over 30 Hispanic or Latino(a) groups to be specified. This is a significant change, allowing multiracial people to more accurately report their multiracial identities (Armas, 2000; Bureau of the Census, 2000). The issues of racial and ethnic identity are particularly pertinent to members of the Hispanic population because Hispanic persons can be any race. Currently, the Census Bureau is attempting to more effectively address this issue by proposing and testing a question that combines "race or origin" to make self-identification simpler and increase the number of respondents of Hispanic heritage. Thus far, the experiment with the option to select "some other race or origin" shows an increase in response rates without a reduction in the size of this population (Population Reference Bureau, 2013). Clearly, the meanings of race and racial identity will continue to change. For example, as intermarriage continues to increase, the boundaries between racial groups increasingly blur as well (Population Reference Bureau, 2010).

**Multiple diversities**

In addition to multiple diversities in terms of race, culture, and ethnicity, there is growing recognition that individuals may identify with other multiple diversities. It is extremely important to recognize that diversity is not a unitary status, though it is often considered to be so. There is considerable variability among the members of any one diverse group. In addition, individuals may simultaneously have membership in multiple diverse groups. For example, an individual may identify as a gay male, person of color, with a physical disability. All of these identifications have significance for how people see themselves and how others view them. These multiple identities interact in complex ways as a person grows and develops and interacts in different social environments.

The above examples demonstrate that, like feminism, diversity is much more than a single dimension of an alternative paradigm for thinking about HBSE. The notion of diversity opens doors to a multitude of alternative paradigms. Through the door of diversity we can enter worlds offering vastly differing and rich ways of thinking about the world and the individuals, families, groups, organizations, communities and nations that make it up. Diversity, then, is not a single dimension of a single alternative paradigm; it offers both a cornerstone and an organizing framework for our attempts to think more broadly, more progressively, more creatively, more humanely about HBSE in every chapter at every point throughout this book.

## Interrelatedness

The alternative paradigms with which we are concerned are characterized by a recognition of the **interrelatedness and interconnectedness** of all humans. Many Afrocentric, American Indian, and Asian influenced worldviews share this sense of the interrelatedness of humans with all elements of the environment in which we exist. Such a holistic and integrative perspective is useful and appropriate for social work with its concern for human behavior in the context of the larger environment. Alternative paradigm thinking challenges us to take the broadest most inclusive approach possible to what constitutes context or environment including both the built and natural environments.

Capra suggests that from new perspectives in physics emerges a picture of the physical world characterized by an extremely high degree of interrelatedness. He suggests that the new perspectives in physics have significant implications for and connections with the "human sciences." The new perspectives in physics are based on "the harmonious interrelatedness" of all components of the natural world. Capra finds this view of the world inconsistent with dominant paradigm perspectives that see society made up of unconnected and competing forces (1983:17–18). Such a statement from the perspective of a physicist about social change has striking and interesting links to core social work values and philosophy.

Ann Weick, a social worker, also suggests that we look to emerging alternatives to the traditional paradigm in the natural sciences to inform our thinking about society. She, like Capra, suggests that new perspectives in physics (quantum theory) illustrate the centrality of interrelatedness. Using the findings in physics as a metaphor, she believes, we can recognize "that human behavior is set within a web of relationships where dynamic interaction is a key feature. It is not possible to isolate one element in the web without disrupting the pattern or patterns in which it exists" (Weick, 1991:21).

An important aspect of interrelatedness especially significant to social workers is that of mutuality or partnership between the actors involved in human interactions. This mutuality is central to the approaches we take to understanding HBSE in this book. We learn about ourselves through our attempts to understand the behaviors of others and we learn about others through our attempts to understand our own behaviors. Such a perspective emphasizes that as social workers we are not separate from the persons with whom we interact and work. We are, instead, partners in a mutual process of seeking meaning and understanding. Out of this mutual meaning and understanding can come action to help us and the people with whom we work reach our fullest potential.

Alternative paradigms of concern to us also recognize the importance and power of personal experience and action to understand and transform the elements of our worlds. This standpoint emphasizes that our personal day-to-day experiences, challenges, accomplishments, and struggles have meaning and importance. For it is through our personal day-to-day experiences that we come to know our worlds. It is through sharing our personal experiences with those around us that we recognize similarities and differences between our experiences of the world and those of others.

The process of sharing personal experiences and analyzes of those experiences results not only in more fully understanding the world around us, but it can result in joining with others around us to transform that world to allow ourselves and others more opportunity to reach our human potential.

The personal characteristic of an alternative paradigm requires a rethinking of traditional approaches in many areas. Alternative approaches, unlike traditional approaches to the study of history, for example, see history not simply as a story of "great" people and "great" events, it is the stories of all of us and of *all* of the events that shape *all* our lives. Respecting and valuing our personal experiences and perspectives can be an important source of empowerment, especially for persons whose experiences and lives are not reflected in histories and institutions that emerge from the dominant/traditional paradigm. Collins (1986:16) suggests that recognizing and valuing the importance of our own personal experiences in the face of oppressive forces that seek to devalue those personal experiences are important in overcoming oppression.

## Oppressions

Collins (1990) finds oppositional or binary thinking that places differences (among people, beliefs, etc.) in direct opposition to or competition with one another to be an important part of dominant paradigm approaches for ordering and valuing people and information. In this respect, she finds binary thinking a major component linking oppressions. If this is the case, then more integrative and cooperative processes are likely to offer means for reducing interlocking oppressions. Integrative approaches call for us to think in terms of both/and rather than in dichotomous either/or terms. Such an integrative perspective also allows us to take seriously such diverse approaches as Eastern philosophical notions of balance, and quantum notions of interrelatedness of observer and observed.

### Oppressions and oppressors

Paulo Freire (1992) looked at the mutual impact of oppression on both the oppressed and the oppressor: "Once a situation of violence and oppression has been established, it engenders an entire way of life and behavior for those caught up in it—oppressors and oppressed alike. Both are submerged in this situation, and both bear the marks of oppression" (Freire in Myers and Speight 1994:108). According to (Freire, 1993, p. 47), "the situation of oppression is a dehumanized and dehumanizing totality affecting both the oppressors and those whom they oppress." Freire argues "as the oppressors dehumanize others and violate their rights, the themselves also become dehumanized" (1993, p. 56). In addition, "the oppressed cannot perceive clearly the" system of oppression, "having internalized the image of the oppressor" (Freire, 1993, p. 62). In other words, the oppressed experience what has become known as "internalized oppression."

### Interlocking oppressions

In our explorations we will seek recognition and awareness of what Collins (1990: 222ff.) refers to as "**interlocking systems of oppression.**" We will focus our concern on oppressions as they manifest themselves throughout the institutions and systems that constitute U.S. society and increasingly in global society. This alternative approach recognizes the interrelatedness of oppressions and the interconnections between oppressions and the other dimensions of both traditional/dominant and alternate paradigms. We will recognize that oppression in any institution directed toward any individual or group is connected with and results in oppression in other institutions and of many other individuals and groups. This interrelated or interlocking quality gives oppression its systemic nature.

Such a multifaceted and interconnected conceptualization of oppression requires a significant change in thinking for many of us. Collins suggests that we must move away from simple additive approaches that may recognize oppression in multiple institutions or directed toward multiple persons or groups, but do not recognize the interplay of these oppressions among different systems. Collins illustrates the interlocking nature of oppressions from the perspective of African American women. She suggests that Black feminist thought offers an alternative paradigm for understanding oppressions by calling for "a fundamental paradigmatic shift that rejects additive approaches to oppression. Instead of starting with gender and then adding in other variables such as age, sexual orientation, race, social class, and religion, Black feminist thought sees these distinctive systems of oppression as being part of one overarching structure of domination" (Collins, 1990:222). This perspective assumes "that each system needs the others in order to function" (Collins, 1990:222).

"Attention to the interlocking nature of race, gender, and class oppression is a . . . recurring theme in the works of Black feminists" (Collins, 1986:19) and recognition of these complex and mutually reinforcing dynamics is essential for social workers. The implications of this alternative perspective on oppression are multiple for social workers. As Collins points out, "this viewpoint shifts the entire focus of investigation from one aimed at explicating elements of race or gender or class oppression to one whose goal is to determine what the links are among these systems" rather than prioritizing one form of oppression as being primary (Collins, 1986:20). As students of social work and of HBSE, we must critically examine each theory, perspective, or paradigm that we explore, whether traditional or alternative, for its implications for recognizing and challenging existing systems of oppression.

**Test your understanding of Dimensions of Alternative/ Possible Paradigms by taking this short** Quiz.

## SUMMARY/TRANSITION

In this chapter we have outlined a conceptual framework for approaching human behavior and the social environment content. The conceptual framework is built around the notions of traditional and alternative paradigms. A traditional paradigm was explored through five interrelated dimensions: 1) positivistic/scientific/objective/quantitative; 2) masculinity/patriarchy; 3) whiteness; 4) separate/impersonal/competitive; and 5) privilege. An alternative paradigm was explored also through five interrelated dimensions: 1) interpretive/intuitive/subjective/qualitative; 2) feminism; 3) diversity; 4) interrelatedness/personal/integrative; and 5) oppressions.

In Chapters 3 and 4, we will explore ways of using our new understandings of dominant and alternative paradigms for gathering knowledge for use in social work practice. We will also explore some of the tools available to social workers to do our work.

**Recall what you learned in this chapter by completing the** Chapter Review.

# Social Work Knowledge for Practice: Tools for Social Workers

## INTRODUCTION

This chapter presents content about tools we can use to understand traditional and alternative views of human behavior and the social environment (HBSE). These tools include frameworks, concepts, models, and theories. We will use these tools as we would use maps or directions when trying to find our way to a destination we have not visited before. These maps and directions can help guide us on our journey through traditional and alternative paradigms in our search for more complete understandings of human behavior and the social environment.

In addition to frameworks, concepts, models, and theories, we will use a number of other tools to help us "think about thinking" including: metaphor, appreciation for ambiguity, the intersection of personal and political issues (or individual and social change), the importance of language and words, and social work assessment.

We will use all these different forms of guidance to help us make connections between traditional and alternative paradigms and issues important to us as social workers. The tools, directions, and maps we explore in this chapter are intended to be of assistance to us on the journey we shall take in this book. They can help us gain a more complete understanding of humans' individual, family, group, organizational, community, and international behaviors and of the social environments that influence and form the contexts in which human behavior takes place. Equally important, these tools can help us do our work as social workers.

## TOOLS FOR THINKING ABOUT THINKING

Before we explore some specific tools for practice, we will explore some tools for thinking about thinking. These tools are intended to help us understand the processes involved in creating and organizing knowledge.

We previously defined paradigm as the "entire constellation of beliefs, values, techniques, and so on shared by the members of a given community" (Kuhn, [1962] 1970). Others (Dawson et al., 1991:16; Brown, 1981:36) add that research paradigms incorporate theories, models, concepts, categories, assumptions, and approaches to help clarify and formulate research. All these notions are central to the approach taken in this book, but what do we really mean when we use such terms? There is a good deal of overlap among and ambiguity about the meanings of these terms. However, they also have some commonly accepted meanings that we might agree upon for use in this book. Perhaps our most important tool for thinking is the process of learning to think critically.

## CRITICAL THINKING

Critical thinking has been defined in many ways and has a long history in many disciplines. Critical thinking is rooted in the "concept of scepticism - the questioning of the source of truthfulness and the reliability of knowledge." According to Facione "Critical thinking is thinking with a purpose" (Fancione, 2000 and Brechin, Brown, and Eby, 2000 in Tilbury, Osmond, & Scott, 2009, p. 33). Rudd provides a definition developed through a synthesis of a number of existing definitions: "Critical thinking is reasoned, purposive and reflective thinking used to make decisions, solve problems and master concepts" (in Rudd, 2007, p. 46). Today it is seen as a combination of several processes and characteristics that include both skills, and attitudes or values that resonate with those required of social workers. Table 3.1 illustrates the kinds of cognitive (thinking) skills and attitudes (values) of an effective critical thinker (Tilbury, et al., 2009, p. 34).

More specific tools for thinking about thinking in addition to the broader notion of critical thinking are described next.

### Ontology and Epistemology

Two important terms for helping understand the creation and organization of knowledge are *ontology* and *epistemology*. Stanley and Wise (in Van Den Berg, 1995) suggest that *ontology* is a "theory about what is real." (The meaning of "theory" is addressed later in this section.) Van Den Bergh suggests on a larger scale that social work's *ontological* perspective about clients and their problems (we might add their strengths as well)

| Critical Thinking |
| --- |

**Practice Behavior Example:**

Know about the principles of logic, scientific inquiry, and reasoned discernment.

**Critical Thinking Question:** How do the skills and attitudes included in Table 3.1. reflect the use of principles of logic and reasoned discernment in critical thinking?

---

**Table 3.1** Critical thinking skills and attitudes for social workers (a summary from the literature)

Skills

---

**Analyse**

- Examine information in detail
- Prioritise important information
- Identify underpinning political ideologies, assumptions, values, and biases (eg., role of state, position of client, professional authority, gender roles, cultural, and racial stereotypes, tropes of deserving and undeserving)

**Think Creatively**

- Problematize "taken for granted" issues
- Consider different, "non-standard" possibilities and approaches

**Problem Solve**

- Dismantle problems and goals into constituent parts
- Formulate plausible hypotheses and predictions
- Articulate rationale for decisions (make defensible decisions)

**Reason**

- Reduce errors in thinking or logical flaws
- Make decisions precise, clear, balanced (not vague)
- Integrate information to identify necessary conclusions
- Make judgments deliberate and purposeful

**Evaluate**

- Recognize micro and macro contextual factors that impact upon issues—will it work in this situation? Will it work for this individual, family, or community?
- Assess whether or not information is relevant to purpose.

Source: Brechin, Brown and Eby 2000; Ennis 1996; Facione 2006; Gambrill 2006in Tilbury, et al., 2009, pp. 37–38.

---

"is that they are contextually based in the client's history or 'life space'" [environment]. *Epistemology* can be defined as "the study of knowledge and knowledge-generating processes" (1995:xii). An *epistemology* is a "theory about how to know" what is reality (Tyson, 1995:10). It is the study of how knowledge is created. The discussions in Chapter 2 about how knowledge is created according to traditional and alternative paradigms, then, can be referred to as discussions and comparisons of two very different approaches to the study of knowledge and knowledge-creation processes (epistemologies) and two approaches to determining the nature of reality (ontology).

*Concepts* are "general words, terms, or phrases that represent a class of events or phenomena in the observable world. . . . and help us make sense of experience" (Martin and O'Connor, 1989:39). Examples of concepts relevant to our work here include "social class," "gender," or "racism." We will consider many other concepts as we proceed on our journey. "A *conceptual framework* ... is defined as a set of interrelated concepts that attempt to account for some topic or process. Conceptual frameworks are less developed than theories but are called theory anyway" (Martin and O'Connor, 1989:39). The meaning we give to *conceptual framework* in this book is that of a conceptual scheme consisting of a set of interrelated concepts that can help explain human behavior in the context of environment. The "conceptual framework" used in this book consists of the two kinds of paradigms—traditional and alternative—that we outlined in the previous chapter. Each of these paradigms was divided into five dimensions. The dimensions include theories, feminist theory, for example, and concepts such as diversity or oppression.

Mullen (in Grinnell, 1981:606) uses Siporin's definition of a *model* as "a symbolic, pictorial structure of concepts, in terms of metaphors and propositions concerning a specific problem, or a piece of reality, and of how it works . . . a problem-solving device." A related notion is that of construct. A construct is a way of defining or describing something that is abstract rather than concrete. For example, a smart phone is easy to visualize because it is a concrete object we can see and touch. One the other hand, the notion of "well-being" is much more abstract. But by determining, defining, and measuring specific aspects of well-being, such as the degree of ability to obtain decent housing or health care, a construct of well-being can be created.

Dawson et al. (1991:438) describe *theory* as "a reasoned set of propositions, derived from and supported by established evidence, which serves to explain a group of phenomena." Shafritz and Ott (1987:1) suggest "by *theory* we mean a proposition or set of propositions that seeks to explain or predict something." These definitions of theory are helpful because they suggest that theories function to give us directions or they act as guides that suggest some explanation about why something happens as it does. It is important to recognize that theories are only guesses based on observations about how and why things happen as they do. Theories do not offer absolute answers.

The theories with which we are concerned in this book are those that seek to explain a variety of aspects of human behavior. We are concerned with the traditional theories we have relied most heavily on for explaining our behaviors, their environmental contexts, and the possible interplay of person and environment. We are also interested in alternative theories that offer other possible explanations in addition to traditional and dominant theories of human behaviors, their environmental contexts, and the interaction of person and environment. Examples of theories we will explore include "Freudian theory," "conflict theory," and "feminist theory." Many other theories are also discussed throughout this book.

What do we mean when we refer to environment? When we refer to *environment* we mean the social and physical context of the surroundings in which human behavior occurs. In addition to the social and physical context, we concur with Germain (1986:623) that environment also includes such elements as time and space. These unseen but influential aspects of environment are especially important to social workers when working across cultures. Different cultures emphasize very different perspectives on such unseen elements as time and space. For example, members of one culture may arrange their activities and environments according to very precise time schedules (as is the case with most members of urban, dominant, white society in the United States). Members of other cultures may arrange their activities in an environment organized by much more natural and less specific divisions of time such as morning, afternoon, and evening or according to seasonal changes (as is the case with many American Indian cultures and with many traditional rural and agrarian people). If we are not aware of alternative perspectives on these unseen but critical environmental characteristics, we risk insult and misunderstanding in our interactions with others.

## The Meaning of Metaphor

Another tool for helping us understand HBSE is metaphor. Much thinking in social work directed toward understanding HBSE is done with the assistance of metaphors. Social work is not alone in this respect, for much social science thinking is carried out with the assistance of metaphors. Certainly metaphors are used often to communicate ideas about ourselves and the world around us. An example of a metaphor is "education is the key to success." The word "key" might suggest the importance of education to your future well-being. The word "key" might also suggest education's potential to "open doors" that can lead to your future success. Aristotle defined *metaphor* as "giving a thing a name that belongs to something else" (Aristotle quoted in Szasz, 1987:137). Metaphor and analogy are often used interchangeably, but they do not mean the same thing. The word "is" indicates a metaphor, while "as if" indicates an analogy. For example, "my boss is a beast" is a metaphor and "he ran as if his house was on fire" is an analogy. Much of our ability to understand the world and the behaviors of humans comes from our ability to use metaphors. We attempt to explain something we do not yet understand by comparing it to or describing it in terms of something we do understand.

In the introduction to this chapter, we employed metaphors to describe the things we are going to try to achieve in this chapter. We used the concepts of tools, maps, and the process of receiving directions to a new destination as metaphors for what we are attempting to do in this chapter. The comparison of our efforts in this book to develop understanding of HBSE to the processes and tasks involved in traveling on a journey is also a metaphor. We must recognize the limits of metaphors at the same time that we appreciate their helpfulness. When we say something is comparable or similar to something else, we are not saying the two things are exactly the same. Social systems thinking is similar to a map, for example, but it is not in fact a map as maps are traditionally defined. As with all tools for improving our understanding of HBSE, we must use metaphors critically. We must appreciate what they are as well as what they are not. These cautions about the use of metaphors to help us understand and explain phenomena suggest a need to be conscious of ambiguity.

## The Necessity of Appreciating Ambiguity

To be ambiguous or to exhibit ambiguity is often considered a negative attribute. This is especially true when our thinking is confined to traditional "either/or" approaches to understanding the world around us. Such approaches leave no room for the vagaries or subtleties that alternative approaches incorporate as essential elements for understanding the complexity and richness of human experience and behavior.

**Watch the video** "Tolerating Ambiguity in Resolving Conflicts" **to see how ambiguity is reflected in a practice situation.**

Critical Thinking Question: Can you describe the three sources of ambiguity faced by the client in the video?

In our travels we will try to make room for and appreciate the usefulness of ambiguity. We will try to suspend our dependence on the need for certainty. We will attempt to recognize that appreciating ambiguity can lead to more complete understanding. *Ambiguity* is a healthy sense of "maybe" or "could sometimes be" rather than a need to always be able to answer a question "definitely" or "must always be." Let's explore the implications for social workers of the concept of ambiguity.

If we think for a moment about human behavior from the perspective of quantum theorists, Weick suggests, we will find ourselves including ambiguity as a necessary element for achieving understanding. This alternative way of thinking, however, requires us to shift from the traditional natural science paradigm that suggests that certainty and predictability are the keys to understanding to alternative paradigms flexible enough to allow room for ambiguity. Such alternative perspectives recognize that humans are at least as likely to behave unpredictably as they are to behave in completely predictable ways.

Using this comparison can help us recognize that "the nature of [human] relationships is not governed by determinism. Human behavior is acausal, in the sense that human action, except in the most narrow sense, cannot be predicted from prior behavior" (Weick, 1991:21). Prediction is really only possible when based on the aggregate behavior of large groups. One cannot accurately or consistently predict the behavior of any single individual within the group. As social workers we need to recognize this as an important limitation of statistics that present aggregate data. Such data are helpful in pointing out patterns or trends, but they are much less useful as tools for predicting the behavior of any one individual. For example, aggregate data may help us recognize a dramatic increase in the number of teenage pregnancies over time. However, these data do not tell us with any certainty about the specific factors leading to the pregnancy of the teenage client sitting at our desk.

**Ethical Practice**

**Practice Behavior Example:**

Tolerate ambiguity in resolving ethical conflicts.

**Critical Thinking Question:** Why do you think understanding ambiguity is an important part of the process of resolving ethical conflicts?

## The Substantive Nature of Language and Words

It is vitally important that social workers recognize and continually reflect on the content and messages conveyed by the language and words we and others use. Language and words are primary means through which we communicate the nature of the paradigms we use to understand human behavior and the social environment. Language and words also play an important part in shaping our own and others' views of the world. The implications of language and words for us as social workers include but go well beyond the narrow and traditional meanings of these words. They are themselves important vehicles for assisting us in our journey toward fuller understanding of HBSE.

### Language, texts, and discourse

Joan Scott (1988:34) describes an expanded view of language that reflects its substantive nature as a vehicle for increasing our understanding of our worlds. Scott's description offers us a means to better appreciate the central place of language and words in understanding HBSE. She describes *language* as "not simply words or even a vocabulary and set of grammatical rules but, rather, a meaning-constituting system: that is, any system—strictly verbal or other—through which meaning is constructed and cultural practices organized and by which, accordingly, people represent and understand their world, including who they are and how they relate to others."

Scott (1988) suggests "texts" are not only books and documents (like this book, for example) but also a wide range of expressions through which we communicate at many levels including rituals such as those surrounding marriage, birth, and death in many cultures. Michel Foucault uses the term discourse rather than text to describe the process through which meaning is constructed, conveyed, and enforced. This notion of discourse certainly includes the languages and texts we create and use to describe and define our worlds, but it goes beyond this to include organizations and institutions that make up our worlds. This notion of discourse also incorporates the important concepts of conflict and power through which meanings are contested, controlled, or changed. This expanded vision of language and texts offers a helpful way for social workers to build and practice our analytical skills as we seek to examine alternative and traditional paradigms for their consistency with the core concerns of social work. In fact such a vision allows us to incorporate in our analyzes such core concerns as power, empowerment, and conflict.

As social workers, we need to continually "read" or "deconstruct" the world around us for the meanings it conveys about the core concerns of social work. This is especially important for us as we examine theories and models for understanding HBSE, for it is through these theories and models that we construct our social work practice. This perspective on language and words also underscores the importance of such basic social work skills as listening, clarifying, and restating. (If you have not already explored and/or practiced these skills, you will in all likelihood get the opportunity to do so before you complete your social work education.)

This notion of our worlds as made up of fields of discourse through which meanings are created and conveyed suggests that the meanings created can and do change over time according to the historical, political, and social contexts of the times. These meanings, created by humans, can therefore be changed by human efforts. The process of changing meanings and the organizations and institutions through which those meanings are constructed and communicated reflects the essence of the process of social change or social transformation.

## Language: Exclusiveness versus Inclusiveness

Several of the perspectives we have discussed come together around issues of inclusiveness versus exclusiveness in our efforts to understand HBSE and to practice social work. Concern for the emergent and process nature of knowledge and knowledge building, concern for the unity of personal and political dimensions, and concerns about the power of words and language all can be thought of in relation to the issue of inclusiveness or exclusiveness.

An important example of the complex interplay of the personal and political implications of language and words as we construct knowledge about others is reflected in the words used to name the diverse peoples of the United States. The process of naming or labeling has important implications for social work and for thinking about issues of inclusiveness and exclusiveness.

## Language: labels and people of color

Asamoah et al. point out that the *labels* applied to racial/ethnic groups are of major significance. They are "structural perceptions with implications for access to power, distribution of resources, and for social policy and practice." In addition, labels "can be inclusive or exclusive, can promote unity or divisiveness, can blur or highlight the distinctions between cultural, political and national identity, and can positively or negatively affect daily social interaction among and between groups" (1991:9).

Central to both the personal identity implications and the political meanings of labels of diverse peoples is the issue of who controls the naming or labeling. In reference to African Americans, Harding (in Asamoah et al., 1991:10) "suggested that self-identification is the foundation on which a sense of peoplehood develops." So, in accordance with this suggestion and with social workers' concern for self-determination, we should find out from and respect the names preferred by the persons with whom we work rather than assume that the name with which we may be most familiar and comfortable is appropriate. This is especially the case with persons who have historically been oppressed and denied access to power. It is also important to recognize that even self-determined labels can change over time in accordance with the changing perspectives and experiences of individuals and groups. For example, the terms Negro, Black, and African American have all been self-identification preferences for African Americans at different points in history. Today the term "Negro" is no longer an accepted term by most African Americans; "African American" is now preferred. It is the responsibility of the social worker to remain current with the descriptive labels preferred by the range of diverse persons with whom we work.

## The meanings of "minority"

Another issue related to specific labels for diverse peoples is the more general word *minority*. Minority is used to describe a person or a group who is not part of dominant white society and can refer to race or ethnicity, persons with disabilities, people who are low-income, GLBTQ persons, members of a particular religion, as well as other people and groups. As a result, the term leads to gross overgeneralizations about people. A more accurate and respectful term for a non-white individual is "person of color" and for non-white groups is "people of color." The term *minority* is also inaccurate in reference to persons and groups, such as women, who are a numerical majority.

As indicated above, key to the personal and political implications of labeling is the issue of whether the label is determined by members inside the group or by persons external to the group. Whenever the label is imposed externally by persons other than members of the group being named, the members of the group end up being evaluated "in terms of how or whether they measure up to some external standard, the parameters of which may not even be totally known to them" (Asamoah et al., 1991:20). A large body of sociological theory referred to as labeling theory focuses on this aspect of labeling.

*How many different ways might the people in the photograph describe their identity? How might others (you, for example) identify the people? Would there be differences, depending on who is describing the identities?*

AP IMAGES

*Labeling theory* "describes the ability of some groups to impose a label of 'deviant' on certain other members of society" (Persell, 1987:163).

A consequence, then, for members of oppressed groups of naming themselves is empowerment. As Asamoah et al. (1991:20) remind us, "Once we define ourselves, it no longer matters what 'they' call us. What matters is what 'we' answer." Clearly, again, the interplay of the various vehicles for achieving understanding of HBSE is apparent when we think about the importance of words and naming for their ability to determine who is included and who is excluded in the worldviews we create.

### Language: Inclusiveness and persons with disabilities

Patterson et al. stress that it is important to remember that a "disability represents only one facet of any person" (1995:76). According to the U.S. Census Bureau "approximately 56.7 million people (18.7 percent) of the 303.9 million in the civilian noninstitutionalized population had a disability in 2010" (Brault, 2012:4). Language is a significant element of both defining and reflecting a paradigm that is inclusive and respectful of persons with disabilities. Patterson et al. suggest that **inappropriate language is language that:**

1. reinforces myths [and] stereotypes about people with disabilities:

   - "wheelchair bound," "confined to a wheelchair," "afflicted," "suffers from" vs. "uses a wheelchair"

   - "you do that just like a normal person" implies the person with a disability is abnormal versus "able-bodied"

   - disability, sickness, and disease are not synonyms

2. equates the person with the disability by using the disability as a noun

   - "the disabled," "the handicapped," "the blind": "they equate people with their disability . . . the disability is . . . only one characteristic of a unique and complex person."

3. uses demeaning and outdated words and phrases when referring to people with disabilities.

   - terms that no longer have scientific meaning: "crippled," "idiot," "handi-capped." (1995:77–78)

Patterson et al. stress that *disability* is the preferred term, and refers to "a physical, mental, emotional or sensory condition that limits a person in any major life area, such as self-care, transportation, communication, mobility, activities of daily living, and work" (1995:78).

## Technology

As we noted in Chapter 1 new technologies are increasingly providing new tools for social work education and practice. Online learning technologies such as Web-based Blackboard, for example, supplement traditional courses and allow complete courses to be offered online. In addition, such technologies as real-time video conferencing (Skype, Facetime) are expanding the tools available for social work education.

However, new technological tools are also sometimes criticized for their lack of personal face-to-face exchanges among students and teachers. It is important

**Test your understanding of Tools for Thinking About Thinking by taking this short** Quiz.

to recognize these new technologies as tools for enhancing opportunities for education, rather than as mechanisms for replacing traditional approaches to education. It is also important to recognize the lack of equal access to these new tools for many individuals and agencies.

New skills are necessary to teach and learn using these technologies. *Digital literacy* requires the use of critical thinking skills. Gilster emphasizes that "you can't understand information you find on the Internet without evaluating its sources and placing it in context" (in Pool, 1997).

Technology is also providing a range of new tools for assisting social workers in practice with individuals, groups, organizations, and communities. In addition to e-mail, listservs, social networking sites (for example, Facebook, Twitter), and conferencing technologies that allow professionals new ways of communicating with each other and with consumers of their services, there are also technologies for use at the community, international, and policy levels. Among these are geographic information systems (GIS). GIS are "computer systems for capturing, storing, manipulating, analyzing, displaying, and integrating spatial (that is, geographical or locational) and non-spatial (that is, statistical or attribution) information" (Queralt and Witte, 1998). GIS technology combines global positioning (GPS) and mapping systems with data such as census data and agency data on client demographics to generate reports and maps that can show both patterns and trends of service use and service needs. According to Queralt and Witte, some of the uses of GIS technology include:

- To assess the sociodemographic characteristics of the neighborhoods served by the agency
- To assess whether the supply of services in a given community is adequate and appropriate for the target population in order to determine which areas may be in special need of outreach initiatives, such as activities to encourage the development of services in neighborhoods where the supply appears deficient
- To help determine the locations of new branch offices, client groups to be targeted, and services to be offered
- To delineate catchment areas for various facilities (for example, special schools, transitional aid offices, specialized health services, outpatient psychiatric services), taking into consideration maximum distances and travel times appropriate to the life situations of potential clients
- To map the flow of clients to and from various community services; for example, to compute travel times and distance from areas with large concentrations of elderly people to the closest geriatric hospital or from home to work for those transitioning from welfare to work
- To plan routes; for example, in community policing, to develop daily police patrol routes that cover the areas where crimes are most frequently reported (1998).

## Social Work and Assessment

Much of HBSE is about gaining information and perspectives to effectively assess the social contexts and the people with whom you are working to determine how to appropriately interact with people for effective practice. Norman and Wheeler suggest a three-dimensional model of social work assessment. They assert "practitioners must keep in mind that each individual is unique, with unique experiences, perceptions, feelings,

**Engage, Assess Intervene, Evaluate**

**Practice Behavior Example:** Promote social and economic justice.

**Critical Thinking Question:** How does the approach to assessment described here support the promotion of social and economic justice when doing assessments?

and behaviors, and yet has much in common with other human beings." They offer a model that recognizes that any individual is:

1. like no other human being: "The fact that a client is a woman does not mean that she shares the views and experiences of other women."

2. like some others (other females or other males): "all humans are identified as belonging to subgroups or categories. Gender is one of those categories and should be considered in assessments or interventions."

3. like all others in the human community (female and male): "humans share common needs." Jung (1964 in Norman and Wheeler 1996) "proposed a 'collective unconscious,' a storehouse of latent memory traces inherited from humanity's ancestral past." "To fully understand a single human being, we must first comprehend all human beings, that is, the commonalties that connect us all." (1996:208–210)

While references in this model are to individuals, the authors suggest such a schema can assist in assessment with client systems of varying sizes. Try substituting family, group, organization, community, or an entire culture in each of the three dimensions above. At each system level we must recognize uniqueness, similarities with others in similar categories, and universal human commonalties.

Next we will explore two tools of particular interest and importance in assessment as well as most other social work processes necessary for effective practice. *Cultural competence* (discussed briefly in Chapter 1) and *evidence-based practice* are overarching tools and are reflected in or components of many other tools and skills.

## CULTURAL COMPETENCE

A cultural competence approach to thinking about and doing social work is emerging as one of the most essential perspectives for social work as it struggles to maintain its effectiveness and relevance in a 21st century marked by an increasingly diverse U.S. population. In addition, global economic, political, and technological realities make interacting with persons different from ourselves on an almost daily occurrence. This trend toward more diversity and globalization can be expected to increasingly influence not only our personal life experiences but our professional work as social workers as well. A number of scholars have worked to define what we mean by culturally competent social work practice (Green, 1999; Leigh, 1998; Lum, 1999; Weaver, 1999; Williams, 2006). Although a good deal of progress has been made toward a definition, we will likely continue to see the concept evolve in the future. Cultural competence is often described as a continual process of striving and learning rather than a clear end product. Diller, for example, describes cultural competence as "a developmental process that depends on the continual acquisition of knowledge, the development of new and more advanced skills, and an ongoing self-evaluation of progress" (Diller, 1999:10). Lum defines cultural competency as "the experiential awareness of the worker about culture, ethnicity, and racism; knowledge about historical oppression and related multicultural concepts; development of skills to deal effectively with the needs of the culturally diverse clients;" and the process of continuous learning to incorporate new multicultural knowledge (1999:174).

Williams (2006:110) suggests that, though social work has given considerable attention to defining and operationalizing what we mean by cultural competence, we continue to lack the necessary theoretical foundation upon which to base our understanding of cultural competence and to evaluate our effectiveness as practitioners in this arena. In response to this need she provides a helpful presentation of central issues related to cultural competence and organizes these issues around several traditional and alternative paradigms. She addresses cultural competence through the multiple epistemological lenses (approaches to studying the nature of knowledge, see Chapter 2) of postpositivism, constructivism, critical theory, and postmodernism. Briefly, these paradigms can be summarized as follows: postpositivism is somewhat similar to our earlier discussions of the traditional paradigm dimension of positivism and of the modernist historical period in its assumption that "reality is something that we can understand and capture probabilistically using the right tools." Postpositivism is differentiated from positivism and modernism by its acknowledgement that "research is influenced by the theories and biases of researchers." However, similar to positivism, researchers using this lens assume we "can pursue knowledge that is uncontaminated and reasonably stable" (2006:211). A constructivist paradigm suggests "reality is constructed through social interaction and dialogue. What we come to understand as knowledge is based on the shared experiences of groups and is inextricably connected to the participants who are involved in knowledge production" (2006:212). "The critical theory paradigm suggests that reality is produced through historically based social and political processes" that serve "the purposes of the powerful" (2006:213). Postmodernism, as we learned in Chapter 1, "suggests that reality is a moving target that cannot be reduced to reassuring regularities" (2006:214). Table 3.2 is helpful in organizing concepts and practices related to cultural competence.

**Table 3.2  Paradigms for culturally competent social work**

| Variable | Postpositivism | Constructivism | Critical Theory | Postmodernism |
|---|---|---|---|---|
| Nature of culture | Relatively stable, verifiable | Constructed in local and specific relationships | Historically derived from social, political, economic arrangements | Unfixed, constantly evolving |
| Practitioner role | Expert, anthropologist | Insider, cultural promoter | Advocate, mentor | Explorer, facilitator |
| Methods of practice | Learning cultural knowledge, including it in formulations | Immersion in cultural experience, using insider frame of reference | Consciousness raising, activism, collective participatory action | Not knowing, eliciting, reframing, reauthoring |
| Limitations | Stereotyping, overgeneralization | Cultural chauvinism, mainstream appropriation | Ideological barriers to implementation, neglecting individual problems | Not knowing is not feasible for practice |
| Goals, outcomes | Technically proficient practice across populations | Group affirmation and well-being | Empowerment and social change | Self-definition, multiple identities |
| Compatible social work models | Generic, etic | Culture-specific service provision | Anti-oppressive, feminist, anti-racist | Narrative, intersubjective |

Source: Adapted from Williams, C. (2006). The Epistemology of Cultural Competence. *Families in Society, 87*(2).

XXX
XX

**Research-Based Practice**

**Practice Behavior Example:** Use practice experience to inform research, employ evidence-based interventions, evaluate their own practice, and use research findings to improve practice, policy, and social service delivery.

**Critical Thinking Example:** Can you give one example from social work practice of the potential misuse of evidence-based practice?

Weaver summarizes three major principles of cultural competence:

- The human services provider must be knowledgeable about the group in question;
- The human services provider must be able to be self-reflective and to recognize biases in himself or herself and within the profession;
- The human services provider must be able to integrate this knowledge and reflection with practice skills. (Weaver, 1998:204)

## EVIDENCE-BASED PRACTICE (EBP)

More recently the profession has focused on evidence-based practice of which critical thinking is an essential component. *Evidence-based practice* (EBP) is "the conscientious, explicit, and judicious use of current best evidence in making decisions about the care of individuals" (Sackett, Richardson, Rosenberg, and Haynes, 1997 in Gambrill, 2007, p. 449). According to Gambrill EBP involves the following steps:

1. an individualized assessment;

2. a search for the best available external evidence related to the client's concerns and an estimate of the extent to which this applies to a particular client; and

3. a consideration of the values and expectations of clients (Sackett et al., 1977 in Gambrill 2007, p. 449).

Scheyett notes that while evidence-based practice, used appropriately, is an important development in social work, she also cautions against its misuse.

- Using it for reasons other than the best interests of clients, such as managed care organizations limiting reimbursement only to certain pre-approved interventions in order to save on costs.
- Equating evidence-based practice with quality practice by using it uncritically and without concern for contextual factors.
- Forgetting that the process of developing evidence-based practices is not infallible and one practice may be evidence-based initially, but further testing may dispute its effectiveness. (Scheyett, 2006, pp. 22–24)

**Test your understanding of Social Work and Assessment by taking this short** Quiz.

## TOOLS FOR SOCIAL WORKERS: TRADITIONAL THEORIES FOR PRACTICE

There are a number of traditional theories about humans' behavior and their interactions in the social environment that originate in the social and behavioral sciences. For example, if you have completed introductory level psychology, sociology, anthropology, or political sciences courses prior to taking this HBSE course, a number of the theories described in the following sections may be familiar to you. As we proceed through the other chapters in this book it may be helpful to refer back to the theories described here to help you connect the social work emphases on individuals, families, groups, organizations, communities, and global issues to these traditional approaches to understanding human behavior in a variety of contexts.

It is important to note that there are differing opinions in the profession about whether or not these traditional theories are supported by sufficient empirical evidence to warrant them as direct underpinnings of practice (Thyer, 2001).

## Functional Theory

According to Alix, "The functionalist perspective favors a consensus view of social order. It sees human beings as naturally caring and cooperative but also as rather undisciplined. They need some regulation to keep them from pursuing goals that are beyond their means. This control is exercised through consensus—agreement among most of a society's members" (1995:27). Henslin describes the central idea of *functional theory* as the belief "that society is a whole unit, made of interrelated parts that work together" (1996:11). Alix notes, however, that "critics . . . claim that the perspective's view that everything in society (including such negative arrangements as racial/ethnic and gender discrimination) somehow contributes to the functioning of society as a whole renders the perspective inherently conservative" (1995:29).

## Conflict Theory

Conflict theory offers a dramatic contrast to functional theory. "Unlike the functionalist who views society as a harmonious whole, with its parts working together, *conflict theorists* see society as composed of groups fiercely competing for scarce resources. Although alliances or cooperation may prevail on the surface, beneath that surface is a struggle for power" (Henslin, 1996:13). Karl Marx, the founder of conflict theory, believed "the key to all human history is class struggle. In each society, some small group controls the means of production and exploits those who do not" (Henslin, 1996:13). Basically, "*the conflict perspective* favors a coercion view of the social order." In this view, "human beings are self-interested and competitive, but not necessarily as the result of human nature. . . . We are forced into conflict with one another over such scarce resources as wealth and power. The *conflict perspective* sees as the basis of social order the coercion of less powerful groups and classes by more powerful groups and classes" (Alix, 1995:29).

## Interactionist Theory

This area of theory differs from either conflict or functional theory and focuses on the nature and meaning of the interactions between and among humans. There are several theoretical variations of interactionist theory. Interactionist theory takes a more micro (individuals or small groups) than macro (societal) approach to attempting to explain human behavior. It is also a bit less traditional in that it focuses on subjective meanings of behavior. From the *interactionist perspective* behavior is "much less scripted. Instead, it appears more fluid, more tentative, even negotiable. In other words, although people may have been given parts to play in society, they have a good deal of freedom in how they are going to play the parts—for example, with or without enthusiasm" (Alix, 1995:31). Alix describes the following 3 paragraphs:

> *Symbolic Interaction Theory* proposes that, in addition to any objective assessment of the costs and benefits of interacting with other people, you also are involved in a subjective, symbolic process . . . symbolic interaction theory proposes that, before

interacting, human beings size up one another in terms of these symbolic meanings. Ex. woman, instructor, student. . . . (1995:33–34)

*Exchange Theory* proposes that human interaction involves rational calculations. People calculate how much pleasure and pain they are likely to experience in current social situations based on their experience in past situations. . . . They seek to repeat pleasurable situations and to avoid painful ones. (1995:33)

*Dramaturgical Theory*. Goffman's (1922–1882 [sic]) more theatrical (and more cynical) view of human society . . . portrays people as actors in the literal sense. We act out our everyday lives on a succession of stages (social situations). We script scenes (interaction episodes) to serve our interests. We dress ourselves in the costumes of the characters we play. (1995:35)

## Role Theory

*Role theory* is another influential theory about human behavior. Role theory seeks to explain behavior as action taken in accordance with agreed-upon rules of behavior for persons occupying given positions. For example, we might behave in accordance with our roles as parent, sibling, worker, student, teacher, and so forth. We will explore roles people play as members of groups, in Chapter 8, and we will explore gender roles in the context of family in Chapter 7.

## Psychoanalytic Theory

*Psychoanalytic theory* is one of the most influential theories for explaining human behavior. We will explore psychoanalytic theory, in Chapter 4, as a traditional theory of individual development focusing on internal and often unconscious origins of human behavior.

## Behavioral/Learning Theory

*Behavioral theory or learning theory*, in contrast to psychoanalytic theory, sees human behavior as almost entirely determined through learning that takes place as a result of reinforcement of our behaviors by others or as a result of our observation of behaviors modeled by others. The reinforcement or modeling necessary for learning behaviors comes almost exclusively from the environment. In Chapter 6 we will explore alternative theories of individual development, such as theories of women's development, the development of ethnic identity, and gay and lesbian identity development. Many of these alternative theories see human development as a result of the interactions of multiple factors, some of which come from within us and some of which come from the social environment.

## Solution-Focused Brief Therapy (SFBT)

Another tool now commonly used in social work practice in a variety of settings is solution-focused brief therapy (SFBT). This approach has been used in medical settings, group settings, prisons, cross-cultural settings, and many others. The approach has also been evaluated in a number of studies to determine if

---

### Human Behavior

**Practice Behavior Example:** Apply theories and knowledge from the liberal arts to understand biological, social, cultural, psychological, and spiritual development.

**Critical Thinking Question:** Can you give an example of how you might use one of the traditional theories described in this section to understand social, cultural, psychological, or spiritual development of person you might be assisting?

there is empirical evidence to support its continued use (Gingerich, 2000). According to Lee (2003:387), the basis of SFBT is found in its efforts to find "what works in therapy."

According to Gingerich (2000:478), "SFBT evolved out of the clinical practice of Steve de Shazer, Insoo Kim Berg, and colleagues at the Brief Family Therapy Center in Milwaukee, Wisconsin, in the early 1980s. . . . As the name suggests, SFBT is defined by its emphasis on constructing solutions rather than resolving problems." Gingerich also provides a summary of the main elements of SFBT:

> The main therapeutic task is helping the client to imagine how he or she would like things to be different and what it will take to make that happen. Little attention is paid to diagnosis, history taking, or exploration of the problem. Solution-focused therapists assume clients want to change, have the capacity to envision change, and are doing their best to make change happen. Further, solution-focused therapists assume that the solution, or at least part of it, is probably already happening. . . . Treatment is brief, usually lasting less than six sessions. (2000:478)

In addition, Lee notes the connection to and consistency with SFBT and other tools and concepts we have addressed in earlier sections, including social constructivism, empowerment, strengths perspective, and cultural competence (2003:389).

Lee suggests, "the purpose of solution-focused intervention is to engage the client in a therapeutic conversation that is conducive to a solution-building process" (2003:390) focused on pragmatic goal setting with the client. Since its beginning in the 1980s a number of specific techniques have been developed to operationalize and implement SFBT. For example, emphasis is placed on several questions used by the practitioner with the client to create a dialog or conversation "to fully utilize the resources and potential of clients" in finding solutions (2003:390). These questions include:

- Exception questions ask clients to recall times when the problem is either absent, less intense, or dealt with in a manner that was acceptable to the client. . . . Examples: When don't you have this problem? When is the problem less bad? What is different about these times? (Lee, 2003: 390)
- Outcome questions help clients to envision life without the presenting complaint or with acceptable improvements in the problem. A widely used format is the miracle question. (Lee, 2003: 390)
- Miracle question: "Suppose that tonight, while you were asleep, there is a miracle and the problem that brought you here today has been solved. However, because you were asleep you were unaware that this miracle happened. Could you tell me, what would be different in the morning that would tell you a miracle has taken place?" (Newsome and Kelly, 2004:70)
- Coping questions help clients to notice times when they are coping with their problems and what they are doing when they are successfully coping. . . . Examples: How have you been able to keep going despite all the difficulties you've encountered? How are you able to get around despite language barriers? (Lee, 2003)
- Scaling questions ask clients to rank their situation and/or goal on a scale of 1 to 10. . . . Usually, one represents the worst possible scenario and 10 is the most desirable outcome. . . . A scaling question may be phrased as "On a one to 10 scale, with one being the worst possible outcome and ten the most desirable outcome, how would you rank your situation?" (Lee, 2003: 390)

- Relationship questions ask clients to imagine how significant others in their environment might react to their problem / situation and to the changes that the clients might make. . . . Examples: What would your mother (or spouse, sister, etc.) notice that is different about you if you are more comfortable with the new environment? On a scale of 1 to 10, how would your wife (or other significant others) rank your motivation to change? (Lee, 2003:390–391)

In addition, SFBT also includes the assignment of tasks or "homework" to help clients notice solutions in their day-to-day environment. "If clients are able to identify exception behaviors to the problem, clients are asked to 'do more of what works'" (Lee, 2003:391).

SFBT in a ranges of settings has been subjected to empirical study and analysis to determine its effectiveness. After completing a systematic review of literature and studies related to SFBT effectiveness, Gingerich concluded:

> Although the current studies [reviewed] fall short of what is needed to establish the efficacy of SFBT, they do provide preliminary support for the idea that SFBT may be beneficial to clients. The wide variety of settings and populations studied and the multiplicity of modalities used suggest that SFBT may be useful in a broad range of applications; however, this tentative conclusion awaits more careful study. All five of the well-controlled studies [analyzed] reported significant benefit from SFBT—four . . . found SFBT to be significantly better than no treatment or standard institutional services. (2000:496)

**Test your understanding of Traditional Tools for Social Workers by taking this short Quiz.**

## SUMMARY/TRANSITION

In this chapter we have explored some additional tools that can help organize and guide our thinking as we proceed to examine alternative and traditional perspectives on human behavior at a variety of levels—individual, family, group, organization, and community. We have explored meanings of epistemology and ontology, the use of metaphors, the need to appreciate ambiguity, the unity of personal or individual and political or social change, the power of language and words, and the need to consider inclusiveness and exclusiveness as we continue our journey. We summarized a number of traditional theories used by social workers to think about HBSE and in their practice of social work. We will next explore mid-range and alternative theories and perspectives available to social workers to think about and organize their approaches to practice both generally and in specific case situations.

**Recall what you learned in this chapter by completing the Chapter Review.**

# 4

## More Tools for Social Workers: Mid-Range and Alternative Theories for Practice

BUILDPIX/CONSTRUCTION PHOTOGRAPHY/ALAMY

## INTRODUCTION

In this chapter we will learn about additional tools we can use as guides for increasing our understanding of human behavior and the social environment (HBSE). While in chapter 3 we explored traditional theories and approaches, in this chapter we will extend our collection of tools to include mid-range theories and perspectives as well as alternative theories and perspectives to continue to fill our toolbox, so we will be better equipped not only to better understand human behavior and the social environment, but also use these new tools in our social work practice. Mid-range theories and perspectives are those that reflect dimensions of both traditional and alternative approaches. Alternative theories and perspectives are more contemporary or currently emerging tools for understanding HBSE. As has been the case thus far in this book, the alternative theories and perspectives we explore in this chapter attempt to provide more inclusive approaches to understanding the experiences and behaviors of persons who have often been rendered invisible or deficient when viewed through more traditional lenses and can be used to help us understand HBSE more comprehensively and holistically.

# MID-RANGE THEORETICAL APPROACHES

There are several theoretical approaches that we can consider mid-range theories to help us understand HBSE. These are theories that go beyond traditional theories and emphasize the importance of the social environment as a critical factor in human behavior. These middle-range theories also incorporate notions of change over time more than the traditional theories we explored earlier. However, these theories nevertheless flow from traditional paradigm thinking and tend not to emphasize dimensions of alternative paradigm thinking such as interpretive and intuitive ways of knowing, feminist approaches, diverse worldviews, and issues of power and oppression. The middle-range theories or perspectives we will consider here are human development, life span, life course, and social systems or ecological frameworks.

## Human Development

Theories of human development have been extremely important in social work approaches to understanding and assessing human behavior and the social environment. Bergen defines **human development** as

1. Changes in the structure, function, or behavior of the human organism

2. that occur over some period of time (which may be of long or brief duration)

3. and are due to an interactive combination of maturation and learning (heredity / environment interaction). (1994:13)

## Life Span Perspective

Another common framework used by social workers for organizing knowledge about human behavior is referred to as the life span perspective. This perspective is most often used in discussing human behavior at the individual level. However, life span perspectives can be applied also to families, groups, organizations, and even communities.

A life span perspective is sometimes used almost interchangeably with life cycle or stage theories about human behavior. The perspective on life span taken here is one that is broader and less linear than traditional life-cycle or stage-based theories. Newman and Newman (1991) outline a set of underlying assumptions about a life span perspective on individual development that is compatible with the broader, less-linear approach taken here.

The Newmans' approach to life span development of the individual is organized around four major assumptions:

1. Growth occurs at every period of life, from conception through old age.

2. Individual lives show continuity and change as they progress through time. An awareness of processes that contribute to both continuity and change is central to an understanding of human development.

3. We need to understand the whole person, because we function in an integrated manner on a day-to-day basis. To achieve such an understanding we

need to study the major internal developments that involve physical, social, emotional, and thinking capacities and their interrelationships.

4. Every person's behavior must be analyzed in the context of relevant settings and personal relationships. Human beings are highly skilled at adapting to their environment. The meaning of a given behavior pattern or change must be interpreted in light of the significant physical and social environments in which it occurs. (Newman and Newman, 1991:4)

These assumptions allow somewhat more emergent, holistic, and contextual alternatives to traditional ways of thinking about how individuals (and other social system levels) develop and change over time.

## Social Systems/Ecological Perspectives

Social systems perspectives (Anderson and Carter, 1990; Martin and O'Connor, 1989) and ecological perspectives (Germain, 1991) have for some time been important frameworks for organizing social work knowledge and for conceptualizing approaches to using that knowledge in practice. There is some disagreement about the similarities and differences between social systems and ecological approaches. It is clear that general systems theory, because its application includes the entire physical world as well as the human world, differs from both social systems and ecological perspectives that concern themselves primarily with humans and their interactions with each other and the world around them. The ecological perspective, however, explicitly defines the environment as including physical (nonhuman) elements. Social systems perspectives are less explicit about the place and role of nonhuman elements in the environment. Some would also argue that social systems and ecological approaches differ in their conceptualizations of boundaries and exchange across boundaries that occur in human interactions. Recognizing these areas of disagreement, we will consider these two perspectives similar enough to be treated together here.

Social systems or ecological perspectives can help us bridge the gap between traditional and alternative paradigms. Central to these approaches, for example, are notions of the interrelatedness or interconnectedness of the various components constituting individual behavior and the parts of the social environments in which individuals interact with each other. These approaches also tend to recognize that we must grasp both process and change if we are to understand HBSE. These notions are consistent with some of the dimensions of alternative paradigms we have explored.

While they recognize their importance for social workers, social systems and ecological perspectives, however, tend to be less focused on and offer less direction regarding fundamental social transformation or social change and the unity of personal and political issues than is the emphasis in much alternative paradigm thinking, such as that found in feminist or empowerment perspectives. Social systems perspectives recognize that systems are constantly changing or "in process," but they tend to emphasize these change processes as functional and self-righting much more than they emphasize the possibility of these processes to reinforce existing exclusion and oppression within systems.

Both social systems and ecological perspectives do recognize that adaptation sometimes involves altering the environment. Anderson and Carter (1990:39), for example, "reject the view that the adjustment must be made only by the system and not by the suprasystem or environment." Germain (1979:8), in her discussion of the ecological perspective, stresses that "living organisms adapt to their environments by actively changing their environment so that it meets their needs." She uses the examples of nest building by birds and tilling the land by humans. It is important to recognize that the level and intensity of alteration of the environment suggested by both social systems and eco- logical theorists is more incremental (adaptive) than the more fundamental structural or institutional changes called for by some alternative paradigm theorists. For example, feminists call for fundamental changes in the distribution of personal and political power and in the ways people relate to each other in the environment in order to bring an end to oppression of women and other groups denied equal power by the dominant group. Social systems and ecological perspectives nevertheless are helpful vehicles to use in our journey.

Systems models have been applied at many levels of human behavior. As we con- tinue our journey in this book, we will find systems perspectives among vehicles often used in social work to organize and guide thinking about human behavior of individuals, families, groups, organizations, communities, and globally. Sometimes systems models reflect traditional paradigms and sometimes they represent alternative paradigms.

### Social systems terms

The themes or assumptions of the various systems perspectives are often quite similar. However, there is considerable variation in the specific terms used to describe social sys- tems' structures and dynamics. Anderson and Carter's (1990) and, more recently, Anderson, Carter, and Lowe's (1999) treatment of social systems, perhaps the most widely used set of terminology for discussing social systems in HBSE courses in the United States, is summarized here to provide us a social systems map for HBSE. There are others, such as the "open systems applications" model of Martin and O'Connor (1989), that offer rather comprehensive social systems frameworks as well. The approach taken by Anderson and Carter is for the most part compatible with the systems perspectives you will find in the chapters that follow, although the specific terms used may vary.

Anderson and Carter (1990:266–267) define a *system* as "an organized whole made up of components that interact in a way distinct from their interaction with other enti- ties and which endures over some period of time." They offer a number of basic systems concepts that communicate the ideas essential to a social systems perspective. They sug- gest that all social systems, large or small, are simultaneously part of other systems and a whole in themselves. This they refer to as *holon.* They suggest it is essential, in order to use social systems thinking, that we set a perspective that allows us to focus by declar- ing a *focal system,* the system of primary concern. Only after a focal system has been declared can we begin to distinguish the parts or *subsystems* of which the focal system is composed from the parts and other entire social systems constituting the environment or *suprasystem* surrounding and influencing the focal system.

In addition to these basic perspective-setting concepts, Anderson and Carter suggest other fundamental aspects of social systems. Among these are the concept of *energy,* or the "capacity for action," "action," or the "power to effect change" (1990:11). Energy is a rather inclusive aspect of systems and suggests their dynamic or "process" nature. Energy is what allows systems to move, regardless of the direction in which they move. Energy is necessary for a social system to remain alive; it is the "stuff" that makes a sys- tem go. A healthy system can be characterized by *synergy* or the ability to use energy to create new energy. A system that is losing energy faster than it is creating or importing it is characterized by *entropy.* It is "running down"; it is in a state of decline (1990:13). Another fundamental aspect of social systems, according to Anderson and Carter, is organization. *Organization* is the "grouping and arranging of parts to form a whole, to put a system into working order" (1990:20). Organization provides structure for a system, just as energy provides movement and the ability to change. These concepts suggest that the system must be able to sufficiently organize or arrange its components to accomplish its goals or get its work done. Important concepts related to structure or organization of social systems include *boundary,* the means by which the parts of a system can be differentiated from the environment in which the system exists. Anderson and Carter offer an interactional definition of boundary as the location "where the intensity of energy interchange is greater on one side of a certain point than it is on the other, or greater among certain units than among others." They stress that boundary does not mean barrier, because systems must exchange energy with other systems across their boundaries in order to survive and thrive. This process of energy exchange is accomplished through *linkage.* A social system can be relatively *open* or relatively *closed* to energy exchange across its boundaries (Anderson and Carter, 1990:29–31).

Additional systems characteristics discussed by Anderson and Carter (and others) include *hierarchy,* the particular order in which system parts are arranged; *differentiation,* a division of labor among system parts, and *specialization,* a division of labor in which only certain parts can perform certain functions; *socialization,* imparting to system parts the rules for behavior, and *social control,* the pressure (persuasive or coercive) put on deviant system parts to return to behavior in accord with the rules of the system; *communication,* the transfer of energy to accomplish system goals, and *feedback,* the information received by systems about the progress toward goals and the system's response to that information (1990:31–38).

Together these basic concepts create a "language" of social systems that we will find useful at various points along our journey to understand HBSE. These concepts are often used in discussions of both traditional and alternative perspectives on HBSE. In this respect they tend to seem fairly neutral. Their real power flows from the context in which they are used and the purposes for which they are used. These basic concepts can be used to defend and maintain the status quo or they can be used to indicate the need for change. The perspective of the user of these concepts is essential to their meaning in any particular context.

## Social systems critiques

Given the potential for social systems thinking to be both a mechanism for maintaining the status quo and for indicating the need for change, we will explore some recent critiques of social systems thinking. As you think about these criticisms, consider whether you find the criticisms justified, whether some are justified and some are not, and what you might do as a social worker to minimize the weaknesses suggested by this criticism.

A number of criticisms have been raised about social systems thinking. Some critics suggest systems thinking is helpful in organizing information about human behavior and the social environment, but it does not actually explain anything. In addition, if all parts (subsystems) are of equal importance, power differences among the parts are not recognized. For example, one could hardly say equal power exists among the members in a family system characterized by intimate partner violence. This can result in "blaming the victim" for co-creating the violence against her. Other critics suggest social systems thinking is very conservative and supports the status quo because of its tenet that the natural state of a system is harmony. Feminist scholars, in particular, have criticized

**Test your understanding of Social Systems/Ecological Approaches by taking this short** Quiz.

social systems thinking for its neglect of biases against women built into systems. This has been especially true of criticisms directed to social systems approaches in family therapy. For example, feminist scholars point out that resources and power in society are "so unequally distributed to favor men over women and children" that it is impossible to be unbiased or rational in application of systems theories (Whitechurch and Constantine, 1993; Berman, 1996).

## Life Course Theory

Life Course theory is a contextual, process-oriented, and dynamic approach. It also addresses multiple system levels along the continuum of micro or small systems to macro or large systems by attending to individual, family, and community intersections during the life course (Bengston and Allen, 1993:469–499). George notes, "for more than two decades, the work of Glen Elder and his colleagues . . . has consistently demonstrated that life-course experiences, such as living through the Great Depression and military participation during World War II, have demonstrable effects on subjective outcomes (e.g., sense of self, levels of psychological distress, attitudes toward work and family life)" (George 1996:248). She describes some of the basic elements of Life Course theory, "first, at the broadest level, life-course research focuses on the intersection of social and historical factors with personal biography" (George, 1996:248ff). In addition:

> the concepts of transitions and trajectories have become key themes in life-course research. . . . Transitions refer to changes in status (most often role transitions) that are discrete and relatively bounded in duration, although their consequences may be observed over long time periods. Trajectories refer to long-term patterns of stability and change that can be reliably differentiated from alternate patterns. (emphasis added).

George points out the interrelatedness and overlapping of trajectories and transitions. For example, "trajectories often include multiple transitions . . . [and] transitions are always embedded in trajectories that give them distinctive form and meaning" (George, 1996:248ff). We will address Life Course Theory in more detail in Chapter 7 as it relates to families.

## Strengths-Based Perspective

### Human Behavior

**Practice Behavior Example:** Critique and apply knowledge to understand person and environment.

**Critical Thinking Question:** What are some examples from social systems perspectives, strengths-based approaches, and life course theory of knowledge that can help us understand person and environment in individual, family, group, organizational, community, or global contexts?

De Jong and Miller (1995) and Saleebey (1992, 1996) remind us that adopting a strengths perspective as individuals and as a profession requires a significant paradigm shift away from traditional approaches to practice. De Jong and Miller find that strengths "assumptions are grounded in the [postmodern] notion that social workers must increasingly respect and engage clients' ways of viewing themselves and their worlds in the helping process" (1995:729).

### Strengths: Related concepts and sources

There are a number of important concepts related to a strengths-based approach including resilience, membership, dialogue, collaboration, and suspension of disbelief.

An important concept related to a strengths perspective is resilience. Resilience "means the skills, abilities, knowledge, and insight that accumulate over time as people struggle to surmount adversity and meet challenges" (Saleebey, 1996:298). Scannapieco and Jackson expand the concept of resilience to go well beyond traditional notions of individual resilience. They suggest that while resilience "has been most often defined as an individual's ability to overcome adversities and adapt successfully to varying situations. . . . Recently, the concept of resilience has been used to describe families and schools and communities" (1996:190). Another key concept for understanding the strengths perspective is membership. According to Saleebey membership "means that people need to be citizens —responsible and valued members in a viable group or community. To be without membership is to be alienated, and to be at risk of marginalization and oppression" (1996:298–299). Membership suggests that "as people begin to realize and use their assets and abilities, collectively and individually, as they begin to discover the pride in having survived and overcome their difficulties, more and more of their capacities come into the work and play of daily life" (Saleebey, 1996:299). Saleebey illustrates that a "strengths based approach is an alternative to traditional pathology based approaches which underly much of social work knowledge and practice theory" (1996:298).

## Strengths-based assessment

Earlier in this chapter we explored the importance of assessment as an essential part of understanding HBSE and applying that understanding in practice. Assessment is central to the strengths perspective. Cowger reminds us that "If assessment focuses on deficits, it is likely that deficits will remain the focus of both the worker and the client during remaining contacts [and that]. . . . Assessment is a process as well as a product" (1994:264–265).

A strengths-based approach requires dialogue and collaboration with the people with whom we work. This requires the formation of a genuine relationship based on empathy, inclusiveness, and equality between the social worker and the person with whom she or he is working. Perhaps most important, it requires the social worker to listen, really listen, to what the other person has to say and to value the client's voice as essential to understanding and action. Collaboration requires the social worker to exchange the expert role for a role as partner with the client in completing a "mutually crafted" product. Finally, Saleebey calls for the strengths-based worker to suspend disbelief—in other words, we must not only listen to and really hear what the client has to say; the worker must believe the client and not assume the client has "faulty recall, distorted perceptions, and limited self-awareness" that render what the client says as somehow suspect or only partially true (Saleebey, 1997:10–11).

## Criticisms of strengths perspective

Many social workers are finding the strengths perspective to be a useful alternative to more traditional approaches to practice. However, the perspective has been questioned by some social workers in terms of whether it is a helpful alternative perspective.

For example, Gray criticizes the strengths perspective for being "too close to contemporary neoliberal [Neoliberalism is addressed in Chapter 11] notions of self-help and self-responsibility and glossing over the structural inequalities that hamper personal and social development" (Gray, 2011, p. 9).

Saleebey outlines some of the criticisms of the strengths perspective and offers a response from his position as an advocate for the strengths approach:

1. It's just "positive thinking" in disguise: Response: Strengths is more than uplifting words and sayings about everything being ok.

2. Reframing misery: The strengths approach simply reframes reality . . . clients are taught to "reconceptualize their difficulties so that they are sanitized and less threatening to self and others."

3. Pollyannaism: The strengths perspective "ignores how manipulative and dangerous or destructive clients and client groups can be. The argument is, apparently, that some people are simply beyond redemption." Response: There may be genuinely evil people, beyond grace or hope, but it is best not to make that assumption first."

4. Ignoring reality: Downplays real problems. Response: All social workers should assess and evaluate the sources of client problems. However, they must also "calculate how clients have managed to survive thus far and what they have drawn on in the face of misfortune" (Saleebey, 1996:302–303).

**Test your understanding of the Strengths-based perspective by taking this short** Quiz.

## Empowerment

Empowerment is a concept helpful to us as we think about the importance of power for understanding paradigms and its role in achieving the basic purposes of social work. Empowerment involves redistributing resources so that the voices and visions of persons previously excluded from paradigms and paradigm-building processes are included. Specifically, empowerment is the process through which people gain the power and resources necessary to shape their worlds and reach their full human potential. Empowerment suggests an alternative definition of power itself. African American feminists have suggested a very useful alternative definition of power. This definition rejects the traditional notion of power as a commodity used by one person or group to dominate another. It instead embraces "an alternative vision of power based on a humanist vision of self-actualization, self-definition, and self-determination" (Lorde, 1984; Steady, 1987; Davis, 1989; Hooks, 1989, cited in Collins, 1990:224). This alternate vision seems much more consistent with the purposes and foundations of social work than traditional conceptualizations of power that define power as "power over" someone else.

### Human Rights & Justice

**Practice Behavior Example:** Advocate for human rights and social and economic justice.

**Critical Thinking Question:** After reading this section on empowerment, give one example of how you might use an empowerment approach in practice to advocate for human rights and social and economic justice in practice with an individual.

As social workers we are especially concerned, in our explorations of alternative visions of power, with the empowerment of those persons who differ from the people whose voices and visions are represented disproportionately in the traditional and dominant paradigms. The persons most disproportionately represented in traditional paradigms are "male, white, heterosexual, Christian, temporarily able-bodied, youthful with access to wealth and resources" (Pharr, 1988:53). Our alternative vision seeks the empowerment of women, people of color, gay men and lesbians, non-Christians, non-young, persons with disabilities, non-European descended, low-income, and non-middle- or non-upper-socioeconomic-class persons.

The purpose of empowerment is in essence the purpose of social work: to preserve and restore human dignity, to benefit from and celebrate the diversities of humans, and to transform ourselves and our society into one that welcomes and supports the voices, the potential, the ways of knowing, the energies of us all. As we proceed we will continually weigh what we discover about any of the paradigms and perspectives we explore against the historic mission and core values of social work—"[the] quest for social and economic justice, the prevention of conditions that limit human rights, the elimination of poverty, and the enhancement of the quality of life for all persons" (CSWE, 2008:1). The tasks we set for ourselves as we continue our journey toward more complete understanding of HBSE are certainly challenging ones.

## Standpoint Theory

Swigonski defines a standpoint as "a social position from which certain features of reality come into prominence and other aspects of reality are obscured."

Standpoint theory emphasizes the strengths and potential contributions of marginalized groups because of their lived experiences. Swigonski calls upon researchers to identify areas of study out of the life experiences of marginalized groups and "to take these groups . . . out of the margins and place their day-to-day reality in the center of research" (1993:173). According to Swigonski, "Standpoint theory builds on the assertion that the less powerful members of society experience a different reality as a consequence of their oppression." As a result of this different reality, "to survive, they must have knowledge, awareness, and sensitivity of both the dominant group's view of society and their own—the potential for 'double vision' or consciousness—and thus the potential for a more complete view of social reality" (Swigonski, 1993:173).

# ALTERNATIVE THEORETICAL APPROACHES

Some emerging alternative theoretical approaches for understanding human behavior and the social environment call into question many of the taken-for-granted assumptions of traditional paradigm thinking. These theories provide social workers with alternative tools to use for understanding HBSE and for using that understanding in practice. These alternative approaches emphasize such dimensions of the alternative paradigm as subjective, interpretive, intuitive, qualitative thinking, interrelatedness, positive elements of human diversity, feminist thinking, and commitment to action to end oppression. We will also explore alternative extensions of social systems thinking including chaos, complexity, and Gaia theories. First, we will explore a new and more holistic conceptualization of social work education and practice called the Multi-System Life Course (MSLC) perspective.

## Multi-System Life Course Perspective (MSLC)

The MSLC perspective is an emerging approach to social work education and practice centered on "the multi-dimensional nature of the human experience" (Murphy et al., 2010, p. 673). Its proponents argue that it is more reflective of what 21st-century social workers actually do in contemporary practice. Rather than a discrete theory it is a perspective incorporating several traditional and alternative theories and perspectives including Life Course theory, social/ecological perspectives, intersectionality, symbolic interactionism, theories of social change (social and economic justice, human rights, oppression, power imbalances), and the traditional/alternative paradigm conceptual framework used in this book. These key theories and their components are described in detail in various sections of this chapter and chapter 3.

Key concepts and processes underlying MSLC are holistic, non-linear, and the inter-relatedness of biological, psychological, social, political, cultural, spiritual, global, and historical influences that converge to reflect the complexity and multi-layered nature of social work practice in today's world (Murphy et al., 2010).

MSLC uses a critical approach to examine the established theories listed above. The critical approach results in recognizing and maximizing the strengths of these theories while recognizing "one size does not fit all" in terms of their effectiveness in addressing the complex issues that characterize contemporary social work practice. Using intersectionality as a foundational element and the concept of integration as a driving force, MSLC offers a new perspective on social work practice and education. The architects of this approach provide a description of the dynamic, critical, and integrative nature of MSLC:

> While a good deal of attention has been paid to life course theory and its emphasis on social change with regard to changing social structures, life course theory alone, offers little direction with regard to social justice and social action. Similarly, while social work literature reveals much discussion of ecological social systems and its contributions regarding the importance of context, such discussions do not incorporate the depth, clarity, and specificity about place and time offered by life course theory. Nor do such discussions emphasize the significance of the meanings associated with social interactions that occur within and between various systems as emphasized in symbolic interactionism. Additionally, while theories of social change assist in understanding how issues such as privilege, oppression and power relate to social change, social justice and social action, as a stand-alone theory, the general conceptualizations of change as dialectical or dichotomous can minimize the significance of human agency and its relation to empowerment. Lastly, while symbolic interactionism offers much value at the micro level, it is less helpful when exploring macrostructures. (Murphy et al., 2010, p. 67)

MSLC is an approach that integrates all levels of practice—individuals through community and global practice concepts. It is an attempt to overcome the false divisions among micro (clinical), mezzo (families, groups) and macro (organizational, community, global) as well as administrative, policy, and research modalities of social work practice levels. Figure 4.1 provides an infographic outlining the MSLC perspective.

## Policy Practice

**Practice Behavior Example:** Understand that policy affects service delivery and social workers actively engage in policy practice.

**Critical Thinking Question:** How might you use the MSLC approach to actively engage in policy practice to improve services to individuals and families you realize are being disadvantaged by a state-level policy?

## Intersectionality

One recent approach to understanding the complexity and interwoven nature of human behavior and the social environment is intersectionality. This approach prevents us from taking an either/or approach to such issues as race, class, gender, and sexuality and, instead, suggests that any one of these dimensions can be more fully understood by appreciating the simultaneous interplay of each of these dimensions at any point in time. It, in effect, calls for a paradigm shift in social work at many levels. As Murphy et al. (2009:2) point out, "a paradigm shift that embraces

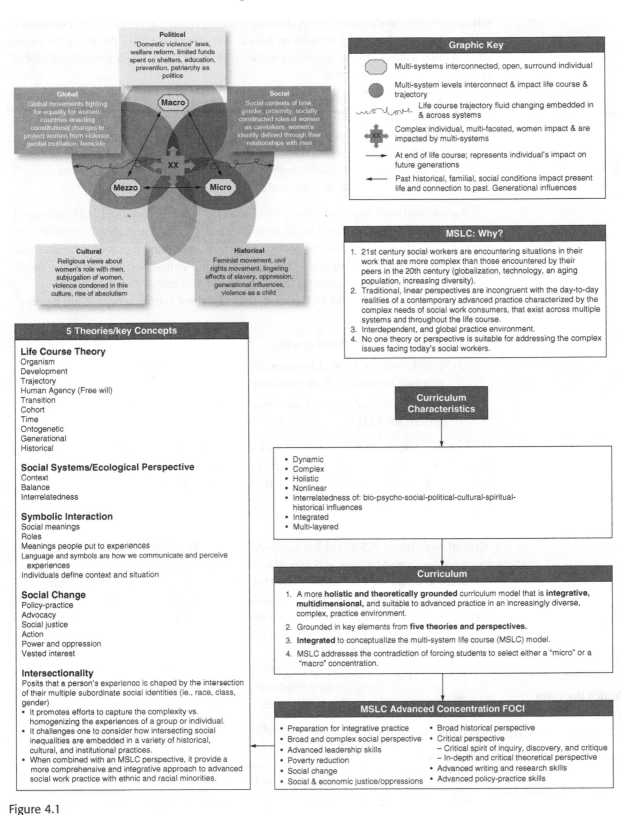

**Figure 4.1**
Multi-System Life Course (MSLC) Advanced Concentration

Source: Used with permission from Joe M. Schriver, PhD, Yvette Murphy-Erby, PhD, and Kameri Christy, PhD.

intersectionality in the most comprehensive manner is both appropriate and necessary to capturing the depth and breadth of human experiences within the complex social contexts that social workers encounter while working in increasingly diverse and global communities." They also stress:

> the intersectional perspective acknowledges the breadth of human experiences, instead of conceptualizing social relations and identities separately in terms of either race or class or gender or age or sexual orientation. An intersectional approach builds on theoretical contributions made by women of color to address their interactive effects. Additionally, an intersectional approach recognizes the power and complexity of socially constructed divisions. (2009:2)

An intersectional approach allows a more holistic understanding of both individual and group experiences by considering multiple characteristics and identities while also accounting for their social and political locations within dominant power structures and hierarchies. Cole and Omari note, "because every individual occupies multiple social locations, all identities are fundamentally intersectional" (2003:786).

According to Stewart and McDermott, there are three central tenets of intersectionality (2004:531-2):

1. no social group is homogenous,
2. people must be located in terms of social structures that capture the power relations implied by those structures, and
3. there are unique, nonadditive effects of identifying with more than one social group (2004:531-2).

Pastrana points out that consistent with the premises of intersectionality, "the notion of simultaneity, of being multiple things at the same time has also been quite visible in non-White feminist . . . and bisexual . . . investigations" (2004:81).

## Critical Race Theory

"Critical race theory (CRT) has been defined by a number of scholars as a legal counter-discourse generated by legal scholars of color concerned about issues of racial oppression in the law and society" (Lynn, 2004:155). Since its emergence in the late 1980s in the context of law and racial inequities within the legal system, CRT has been applied in critiques of the U.S. education system to examine its deficit-based treatment of people of color. It has received little attention within social work and social work scholarship (Abrams and Moio, 2009:252).

Within the arena of education and the preparation of teachers, Yosso outlines five basic tenets of CRT that are important in its understanding and are relevant to social work as well:

**Watch the video** *"Are Intelligence Tests Valid? (Drapetomania: Robert Guthrie)"* **to see how psychiatry was used to diagnose runaway slaves as having a mental illness.**

**Critical Thinking Question:** How do you think CRT would explain the creation of this diagnosis?

1. *The intercentricity of race and racism with other forms of subordination.* CRT starts from the premise that race and racism are central, endemic, permanent, and a fundamental part of defining and explaining how U.S. society functions.
2. *The challenge to dominant ideology.* CRT challenges White privilege. . . . CRT challenges notions of "neutral" research or "objective" researchers.

3. *The commitment to social justice.* CRT is committed to social justice and offers a liberatory or transformative response to racial, gender, and class oppression.

4. *The centrality of experiential knowledge.* CRT recognizes that the experiential knowledge of People of Color is legitimate, appropriate, and critical to understanding. . . . CRT draws explicitly on the lived experiences of People of Color by including such methods as storytelling, family histories, biographies, scenarios, parables, cuentos [stories], testimonios, chronicles and narratives.

5. *The transdisciplinary perspective.* CRT goes beyond disciplinary boundaries to analyze race and racism within both historical and contemporary contexts, drawing on scholarship from ethnic studies, women's studies, sociology, history, law, psychology, film, theatre, and other fields. (Yosso, 2005:74–75)

Abrams and Moio (2009:251–252) note, "CRT acknowledges the intersectionality of various oppressions and suggests that a primary focus on race can eclipse other forms of exclusion." They further note that reconciling the dilemma presented by placing a central focus on race, while also recognizing the importance of a "multidimensional framework" when addressing issues of oppression, is a subject of continuing ambivalence and discussion among CRT scholars (2009:251–252).

## Differential Vulnerability Versus "Equality-of-Oppressions" Theory

Here we address two theoretical positions that raise questions about the appropriateness and efficacy of the current "cultural competence" approach in social work education and practice. The following discussion demonstrates the complexity and multifaceted nature of approaches to effectively address oppression and social injustice within the social work community.

Schiele (2007:83–84) argues that because the accreditation standards of the Council on Social Work Education (CSWE) make no distinction "about the frequency, intensity, or pervasiveness of the various forms of oppression" among the categories of persons and groups that face oppression, social work has adopted what he calls an "equality-of-oppressions" paradigm. It should be kept in mind that the CSWE accreditation standards must be met by any social work education program in the United States wishing to receive or retain accredited status. In other words, all accredited social work programs are required to address all categories of diverse persons and groups through their classroom and field curricula as well as the broader learning context (implicit curriculum) in which the programs are located. These categories are age, class, color, culture, disability, ethnicity, gender, gender identity and expression, immigration status, political ideology, race, religion, sex, and sexual orientation (CSWE, 2008:5).

According to Schiele, the equality-of-oppressions paradigm "assumes that every source of oppression is equal to others in its severity, frequency, and production of human degradation." He contends that this paradigm "has weakened social work education's capacity to enhance content on people of color" (2007:84).

Schiele offers a different diversity / oppression model that is founded on "concept of differential vulnerability." Differential vulnerability would provide "a model to prioritize the various forms of oppression important to social work education" (2007:84). The concept of differential vulnerability originated within the public health discipline in which it is defined as "the recognition that 'at risk' populations vary in their level of susceptibility to stressful life events." Schiele contends, "if oppression is viewed as a stressful life event, the disadvantage generated by it may produce substantial variance" (2007:93). While recognizing that oppressed populations have similarities with each other, some oppressed groups may be at more risk than others for the damaging effects of oppressions.

Young outlines five different attributes or "faces" of oppression. These different elements of oppression may help clarify the concept of differential vulnerability. They are summarized below:

1. Exploitation is "a steady process of the transfer of the results of the labor of one social group to benefit another."

2. Marginalization can be defined by thinking in terms of a "group of people referred to as 'marginals.' Marginals are persons who lack, or who are blocked from obtaining, the training and skills necessary to locate and sustain gainful employment." Examples include the nonworking poor, persons who are severely disabled, or persons who are intensely stigmatized.

3. Powerlessness can be defined "as the extra liabilities endured by nonprofessionals, who are those with little or no advanced training or education." These persons "have less power in the workplace" and "often work for or are supervised by professionals."

4. Cultural imperialism speaks to the inequality in human values, experiences, and interpretations . . . that some groups have more power over determining which human values, experiences, and interpretations are valid. . . . [C]ultural imperialism is "the universalization of a dominant group's experience and culture, and its establishment as the norm." . . . Those whose culture and experience are most different from the dominant group are assumed to be the most marginalized in society.

5. "Violence implies physical abuse and harm." Examples of oppressed groups who are more vulnerable to violence include hate crimes, rape, and domestic abuse. Violence also includes "lesser forms of aggression, such as harassment, intimidation, and ridicule." (cited in Schiele, 2007:93–94)

Schiele points out limitations of the differential variability model. He suggests, "the most obvious limitation" of the model "is that it might lead some to engage in ruthless competition to underscore their group's subjugation." Such competition could lead to both intergroup and intragroup conflict that could have the effect of causing "some to deny the oppression of others" and lead some to the conclusion that the "lesser" types of oppression need not be addressed.

Schiele argues that the "five faces of oppression" model may help reach a balance between "recognizing the importance of all forms of oppression" and "prioritizing specific forms of oppression." At the same time it is necessary to recognize that "any one of the five faces is enough to consider a group oppressed." However, we also need to acknowledge "not all the faces are applicable to all groups." On the other hand, because of the history and power of racism in the United States, "Blacks and Latinos . . . often suffer all five forms of oppression" (Young, 1990 in Schiele, 2007:95). Schiele concludes as a result that people of color, especially African Americans and Hispanic Americans, "may need to receive additional attention in social work education" (Schiele, 2007:95).

Certainly, issues surrounding either an "equality-of-oppression" paradigm or the "differential vulnerability" model are controversial and unresolved in social work. It is necessary, though, to continue to think critically about how we address all oppressions and the related differing "faces of oppression."

These definitions and principles reflect the critical need for a culturally competent social worker to have knowledge about the members of the different cultures with which we work; self-awareness of our own culture, biases, and racism; a willingness to continually learn both about others and ourselves as cultural beings; and a willingness to incorporate our knowledge into practice skills. It is important to recognize that culturally competent practice is essential, whether working with individuals, families, groups, organizations, communities, and especially globally. Next we consider the emerging theory and practice arena of environmental social work.

## Environmental Social Work

The current conceptualization of the "environment" in social work education, focused almost entirely on the "social environment," is increasingly coming under fire by social work scholars who view it as too narrow to accommodate the more and more prominent influence of the larger environment (natural and built) on human well-being or even survival. A number of scholars are addressing this gap by suggesting new and more holistic approaches of incorporating the environment in social work education through a new social work practice focus referred to as "environmental social work" (Besthorn & McMillen, 2002; Gray, Coates, & Hetherington, 2012.

Gray, Coates, and Hetherington as well as other environmental social work scholars call for a "new paradigm" that would provide a "transition to a sustainable society." This new paradigm thinking about sustainable development is concerned with:

1. A dematerialization of the economy (substantial reduction in the overuse of natural resources including energy).
2. The fair distribution of wealth.
3. A new vision of human and planetary well-being. (Gray et al., 2012)

The United Nations Educational Scientific and Cultural Organization [UNESCO] (2004) in its Earth Charter suggests a more holistic perspective on the environment consisting of "Four Pillars." The pillars include:

1. Respect and care of the community of life.
2. Ecological integrity
3. Social and economic justice
4. Nonviolence and peace

Clearly, this perspective is consistent with several of the fundamental elements of the mission of the social work profession. Gray et al. suggest adding a new level of practice to our traditional conceptualization of the focus areas of social work:

- Mega—global
- Macro—community or policy
- Meso—organizational
- Micro—family and neighborhood (Gray et al., 2012, p. 270)

These scholars also see the need for "ecoliteracy" as part of the professional "toolbox" of all social workers. By this they mean a new and deeper understanding of the important role of nature's systems in fulfilling social work's mission. They suggest that, "to become ecologically literate is to relearn the processes of nature and our place in them."

Referring to the somewhat arrogant approach of traditional paradigm thinking that the earth, its systems, and resources exist solely for the benefit of humans, they counter that instead "Humans are not above or beyond the fundamentals of natural systems, but are rather entirely dependent upon them" (Gray et al., 2012, p. 221).

Gray et al. offer an outline of the essential elements of a new "Environmental Social Work Curriculum." This new foundational area of social work education would include three basic elements:

1. A body of knowledge, about natural systems and humans' place within these systems.

2. A critique of the existing situation that seeks to develop an understanding of what has gone wrong in the human-nature relationship.

3. A set of values that provide guidance for a way of living that reflects a deep ecological understanding and has the potential to take the profession forward to a sustainable future. (2012:220)

Besthorn and McMillen (2002) suggest that another aspect of a more holistic approach to understanding the importance of natural systems and their relationship to humans is a combination of an expanded notion of ecological or systems thinking and feminist theory. Ecofeminism seeks to reweave "the inherent interconnectedness in all of the universe through a revitalization of each person's direct, lived, and sensual experience with the complex whole of nature." Ecofeminism posits that "nature is one with and beneficial for humanity (Besthorn and McMillen 2002:226–227). They suggest, in summary:

[an] expanded ecological social work model . . . emphasizes interactions and actions based on caring and compassion rather than the dominance, competition, and exploitation inherent in our current competition-based social systems. (2002:229)

Environmental social work focuses on the importance of the environment beyond its social aspects to include the physical environments and conditions that endanger our potential for well-being. Next we shift from the "big picture approach" of environmental social work to the much more internally focused theory and practice of mindfulness.

## Mindfulness

Mindfulness training and practice is relatively new intervention for social work and is showing promise in addressing both physical and emotional challenges. Basically mindfulness "means 'paying attention in a particular way: on purpose, in the present moment and non-judgmentally' in a way which 'nurtures greater awareness, clarity, and acceptance of present moment reality'" (Hyland, 2012:187). More specifically, mindfulness is a contemplative practice that promotes "thinking, questioning, discussing, reflecting, and concentrating on self." The goal of this practice is to deepen our level of awareness about ourselves internally and of the world around us. Mindfulness practices include meditation, "silence, prayer, chanting, yoga, tai chi" and self-inquiry or deep reflection (McGarrigle & Walsh, 2011: 213–214). Basic to all forms of meditation is "cultivating mental focus" (Lang et al., 2012: 761).

Results of recent research on the effectiveness of meditation to reduce a variety of stress-related symptoms and to increase psychological well-being seem promising. (Bränström, Kvillemo, & Moskowitz, 2012: 540). One study used control and intervention groups, with the intervention group receiving mindfulness training and practice. The researchers found that continued use of meditation over time by the intervention group was "associated with a significant reduction in post-traumatic stress symptoms of avoidance" (Bränström et al., 2012: 535). Short-term reduction of stress symptoms for cancer patients as a result of mindfulness practice also has been demonstrated. Several studies using mindfulness training and practice with persons with developmental disabilities have shown promise in treating a number of problematic issues and behaviors.

In several studies using mindfulness training and practice to reduce aggression in people with autism spectrum disorders (ASD), aggressive behavior was reduced to zero. Similarly, continued mindfulness practice has shown positive and sustained results in weight reduction for obesity and reduction of smoking. For example, a smoker using the practice was able to reduce the number of cigarettes smoked from twelve to zero a day. Even more impressive was that with continued mindfulness practice the person remained smoke-free at three-year follow-up. In another review of 12 studies of the use of mindfulness practice with persons with developmental disabilities, all of the studies showed positive and consistent results in reducing some behavioral and psychological problems (Hwang & Kearney, 2013: 314–326).

## Transpersonal/Spirituality

It is helpful to begin to explore spirituality by understanding the major schools of thought about the basic nature of spirituality. Miovic (2004:106) defines three basic perspectives that define the nature of one's spiritual beliefs:

1. Theism is the belief in the existence of God (a Supreme Being or spiritual reality), an immortal soul, or any other type of deity or deities.

2. Atheism is the belief in the nonexistence of God (or any type of soul or deity), which in the modern world is often expressed as the materialist hypothesis that matter is the only reality.

3. Agnosticism is the belief that the question of whether or not God (or any type of soul or deity) exists either has not been or cannot be answered.

Cowley and Derezotes (1994) note that spirituality is considered by many to be a "universal aspect of human culture." However, they are also careful to point out (and as we differentiate below) "spirituality is not considered as equivalent with religion, religiosity, or theology. . . . The use of the word 'spiritual,' then is neither a statement of belief per se nor a measure of church attendance; indeed an atheist can have a profound spiritual life."

Sermabeikian uses Siporin's description of the transcendent and multi-system nature of spirituality. Siporin suggests that "It is in terms of a spiritual dimension that a person strives for transcendental values, meaning, experience and development; for knowledge of an ultimate reality; for belonging and relatedness with the moral universe and community; and for union with the immanent, supernatural powers that guide people and the universe for good and evil" (1994:180).

### Religion and spirituality

While spirituality is not the equivalent of religion or religiosity, as we noted above, the two concepts are often related in many ways. Canda (1989:39) differentiates between religion and spirituality. Spirituality is "the general human experience of developing a sense of meaning, purpose, and morality." Religion, on the other hand is the "formal institutional contexts of spiritual beliefs and practices" (Canda 1989:39).

Canda recommends a comparative approach to incorporating religious content into social work and offers a set of guidelines for approaching issues related to religion and spirituality in practice. The guidelines suggest the social worker:

1. Examines religion and spirituality as general aspects of human culture and experience
2. Compares and contrasts diverse religious behaviors and beliefs
3. Avoids both sectarian and anti-religious biases
4. Encourages dialogue that is explicit about value issues and respects value differences
5. Examines the potential benefit or harm of religious beliefs and practices
6. Emphasizes the relevance of the social worker's understanding of religion to providing effective service to clients. (1989:38–39)

It is important to develop an open and critical approach to understanding spirituality and religion and the roles they play in our personal, community, and social lives. For example, Sermabeikian notes the potential of spirituality and religion to be both helpful and harmful depending on the nature of their expression. As a human need, spirituality is multidimensional, and as such it can be manifested in healthy and unhealthy ways. Bergin (1991: 401) noted "spiritual phenomena have equal potential for destructiveness, as in the fundamentalist hate groups." Sermabeikian suggests further, that "Religious pathology, rigid ideologies, religious fervor associated with mental illness, cult involvement, and the non-constructive consequences of certain beliefs and practices present additional challenges to professionals" (1994:181-182).

As we noted in the discussion of spirituality in Chapter 2, this is an area many social work educators and practitioners believe has been neglected in both the contexts of social work education and of practice. We explore some current thinking here about transpersonal and humanistic psychology and their potential adaptability to social work education and practice. Clearly the areas of transpersonal and humanistic psychology and their applications to social work are currently considered alternative approaches.

Cowley and Derezotes suggest that "transpersonal means going beyond the personal level . . . to include the spiritual or higher states of consciousness" (1994:33). They place transpersonal psychology among the basic theoretical paradigms of the discipline. They note that Maslow referred to transpersonal psychology as the Fourth Force in psychology:

- First Force: Dynamic (psychoanalytic)
- Second Force: Behavioral
- Third Force: Experiential, humanistic, existential
- Fourth Force: Transpersonal (1994:34)

Transpersonal psychology was an alternative theory challenging the notion of such psychologists as Maslow that self-actualization was the highest level of human development. Transpersonal psychology is a synthesis of Eastern and Western psychologies that "offers an expanded notion of human possibilities that goes beyond self-actualization and beyond ego . . . and beyond the limitations of time and/or space" (Cowley and Derezotes, 1994:33).

Wilber argues that we need to use multiple paradigm approaches to help us understand the complexity of human behavior and the social environment. He suggests that there are three epistemological modes or ways of knowing:

1. *The sensory:* scientific approaches to knowing.
2. *The intellectual or symbolic:* hermeneutic or interpretive approaches.
3. *The contemplative:* intersubjective testing by masters/teachers in this realm. (Walsh and Vaughn, 1994:11–14).

While perhaps controversial, these notions of transpersonal realities that transcend those we experience through our senses every day may be valuable to us as we attempt to more fully understand the behaviors and worldviews of ourselves and those with whom we work.

## Alternative Extensions of Systems Approaches

Since social systems thinking has been and continues to be such an important force in conceptualizing and organizing the way social workers think about humans and their interactions with the social environment, we will now return to systems approaches and explore some more recent extensions of this approach. Recently systems thinking has been extended beyond using it to understand the basic order of systems to include disorder or chaos and other types of complexity within both human and other physical systems. Another interesting extension of systems thinking is the Gaia hypothesis which has called into question some of our basic thinking about human evolution and about the relationship of humans to the inanimate world.

## Chaos/Complexity

Krippner provides a definition of chaos theory that comes from the dynamical systems theory of mathematics. He explains that "chaos theory is the branch of mathematics for the study of processes that seem so complex that at first they do not appear to be governed by any known laws or principles, but which actually have an underlying order. . . . Examples of chaotic processes include a stream of rising smoke that breaks down and becomes turbulent, water flowing in a stream or crashing at the bottom of a waterfall, electroencephalographic activity of the brain, changes in animal populations, fluctuation on the stock exchange, and the weather. All of these phenomena involve the interaction of several elements and the pattern of their changes over time as they interact . . ." (emphasis added). Krippner explains that "Chaos theorists . . . look for patterns in nature that, while very complex, nonetheless contain a great degree of eloquent and beautiful order, and chaos theory attempts to direct investigators to a cosmic principle that can both simplify and deepen their understanding of nature" (1994:49).

James Gleick, in one of the first books about chaos theory published for readers outside of mathematics and the natural sciences, described the intense paradigm shift within the natural sciences that this theory was causing:

> Where chaos begins, classical science stops. For as long as the world has had physicists inquiring into the laws of nature, it has suffered a special ignorance about disorder in the atmosphere, in the turbulent sea, in the fluctuations of wildlife populations, in the oscillations of the heart and the brain. The irregular side of nature, the discontinuous and erratic side—these have been puzzles to science, or worse, monstrosities. (1987:3)

**Chaos and Order by Gleick 1987:6–8**

Physicists are beginning to return to serious consideration of phenomena on a human scale as opposed to either the cosmos or the tiniest of particles. And in this turn they are finding equal wonder at the complexity and unpredictability of these everyday phenomena. . . . They study not just galaxies but clouds. . . . The simplest systems are now seen to create extraordinarily difficult problems of predictability. Yet order arises spontaneously in those systems—chaos and order together.

Gleick believes that chaos cuts across the many different scientific disciplines and "poses problems that defy accepted ways of working in science. It makes strong claims about the universal behavior of complexity" (1987:5). Gleick believes this shift will help return the natural sciences to considering questions of more direct and immediate meaning to humans.

Gleick stresses that chaos and complexity theorists believe they have discovered that contrary to traditional scientific thinking "tiny differences in input could quickly become overwhelming differences in output—a phenomenon given the name 'sensitive dependence on initial conditions.' In weather, for example, this translates into what is only half-jokingly known as the Butterfly Effect—the notion that a butterfly stirring the air today in Peking [sic] can transform storm systems next month in New York" (1987:18).

### Order in disorder

According to Gleick: "Those studying chaotic dynamics discovered that the disorderly behavior of simple systems acted as a creative process. It generated complexity: richly organized patterns, sometimes stable and sometimes unstable, sometimes finite and sometimes infinite, but always with the fascination of living things" (1987:43). A related concept for describing this notion of order within disorder is that of fractal. Fractals are "geometric patterns with repetitive self-similar features have been called 'fractal' . . . because of their fractional dimensions." Mandelbrot, a scientist who studied "irregular patterns in natural processes" found "a quality of self-similarity. . . . Self-similarity is symmetry across scale. It implies recursion, pattern inside of pattern. . . . Self-similarity is an easily recognizable quality. Its images are everywhere in the culture: in the infinitely deep reflection of a person standing between two mirrors, or in the cartoon notion of a fish eating a smaller fish eating a smaller fish eating a smaller fish" (Gleick, 1987:103).

Gleick and others suggest that chaos and complexity theory reflect a paradigm shift of major proportions within science. Think about our discussion in Chapter 1 of history and how what were once alternative paradigms became traditional and dominant worldviews held universally by large groups of people. If traditional approaches to science are replaced by or even begin to substantively include notions of chaos and complexity, how might our definitions of both physical and social realities change? To many people today, this is not a question to consider in the future, it is a part of present discourse about the nature and behavior of reality.

## The Gaia Hypothesis

Perhaps the most controversial alternative extension of systems thinking flowing from chaos and complexity theory is known as the Gaia hypothesis. This is a perspective on systems thinking that goes well beyond the traditional notions of thinking in terms of specific systems, for example, social systems or human systems, to viewing the entire earth as a whole system. James Lovelock and Lynn Margulis are usually credited with formulating and putting forward the Gaia hypothesis. Lovelock and Margulis' Gaia hypothesis includes two fundamental components:

1. The planet is . . . a "super organismic system."
2. Evolution is the result of cooperative not competitive processes. (Lovelock, 2000)

Lovelock describes the "Earth as living organism" component of the Gaia hypothesis in the following excerpts:

> The entire range of living matter on Earth from whales to viruses and from oaks to algae could be regarded as constituting a single living entity capable of maintaining the Earth's atmosphere to suit its overall needs and endowed with faculties and powers far beyond those of its constituent parts.. [Gaia can be defined] as a complex entity involving the Earth's biosphere, atmosphere, oceans, and soil; the totality constituting a feedback of cybernetic systems which seeks an optimal physical and chemical environment for life on this planet. (Lovelock, 2000)

The Gaia hypothesis calls into question some of the basic Darwinian notions about survival of the fittest as the central component of evolution. Margulis has said Darwin's theory was not incorrect, but merely incomplete. She contended that her research on the evolution of certain organisms (referred to as endosymbiosis) revealed that a symbiotic, or mutually beneficial, relationship was central to their ongoing evolution. She contended that "symbiosis, not chance mutation (as Darwin had theorized), was the driving force behind evolution and that the cooperation between organisms and the environment are the chief agents of natural selection—not competition among individuals" (The Gaia Hypothesis, 1996, see http://www.mountainman.com.au/gaia.html).

Lovelock argued for this extended notion of symbiotic and system-like functioning as an enlargement of ecological theory:

> By taking the species and their physical environment together as a single system, we can, for the first time, build ecological models that are mathematically stable and yet include large numbers of competing species. In these models increased diversity among the species leads to better regulation.

## Gaia: Was Darwin Wrong?

In classical science nature was seen as a mechanical system composed of basic building blocks. In accordance with this view, Darwin proposed a theory of evolution in which the unit of survival was the species, the subspecies, or some other building block of the biological world. But a century later it has become quite clear that the unit of survival is not any of these entities. What survives is the organism-in-its-environment.

An organism that thinks only in terms of its own survival will invariably destroy its environment and, as we are learning from bitter experience, will thus destroy itself.

From the system point of view the unit of survival is not [an] entity at all, but rather a pattern of organization adopted by an organism in its interactions with its environment. (The Gaia Hypothesis, 1996, see http://www.mountainman.com.au/gaia.html)

**Test your understanding of Alternative Theories for Practice by taking this short** Quiz.

When the activity of an organism favors the environment as well as the organism itself, then its spread will be assisted; eventually the organism and the environmental change associated with it will become global in extent. The reverse is also true, and any species that adversely affects the environment is doomed; but life goes on. (The Gaia Hypothesis, 1996, see http://www.mountainman.com.au/gaia.html)

## SUMMARY/TRANSITION

In this chapter we have explored mid-range and alternative tools that can help organize and guide our thinking as we proceed to examine alternative and traditional perspectives on human behavior at a variety of levels—individual, family, group, organization, community, and global. We summarized a number of middle-range and alternative theories used by social workers to think about HBSE. Along with our knowledge of the dimensions of traditional and alternative paradigm thinking and traditional theories and perspectives, we will now use this collection of tools to continue our journey toward more complete understanding of human behavior and the social environment.

**Recall what you learned in this chapter by completing the** Chapter Review.

# 5

# Traditional/Dominant Perspectives on Individuals

## INTRODUCTION

As we proceed we need to continually weigh what we discover about any of the paradigms and perspectives we explore against the purpose of the social work profession—"to promote human and community well-being" and be guided by its principles and constructs, including:

> a person and environment construct, a global perspective, respect for human diversity, knowledge based on scientific inquiry. [a] quest for social and economic justice, the prevention of conditions that limit human rights, the elimination of poverty, and the enhancement of the quality of life for all persons (CSWE, 2008:1).

As we consider different perspectives (traditional in this chapter and alternative in the following chapter) on individuals, we need to keep in mind their potential roles in facilitating or hindering social change/transformation.

The tasks we set for ourselves as we continue our journey toward more complete understanding of HBSE are certainly challenging ones. However, like the assumptions of interconnectedness and interdependence we made in Chapter 1 about social work, ourselves, and the people with whom we work, all the chapters of this book are interconnected and interdependent. For example, in this chapter and the next one we focus on individuals, but we will not leave the things we learn and the questions we raise about individual development and behavior when we reach the end of the next two chapters. After we complete our exploration of traditional and alternative perspectives on the individual, in this chapter and the next one, the chapters that follow these—on familiness, groups, organizations, community(ies), and the global context—will continue to be heavily concerned with individual development. Families, groups, organizations, communities, and international issues are, in fact, fundamental contexts within which our own and others' individual development takes place. These contexts affect our development as, simultaneously, we affect the nature of these contexts.

# A CRITICAL PERSPECTIVE ON DEVELOPMENTAL JOURNEYS: LADDERS TO CLIMB?

Perhaps the most traditional and widely used models of individual behavior and development are linear approaches focusing on a chronological series of age-related developmental stages and tasks. These models or frameworks present the tasks and expectations of human development as though we each must "climb a developmental ladder." We step onto the first rung at conception or birth (depending on the particular model or theorist) and we step off the last rung at death.

These linear approaches are attractive because they offer an optimistic view of development as continuous growth and progress. They also lend simplicity, predictability, and order to the apparent chaos of human change (Steenbarger, 1991:288). However, these approaches tend to leave us with the impression that the "developmental ladder" is virtually the same for everyone and that the ladder is equally accessible to everyone. They oversimplify the complexities, diversities, and ambiguities that characterize human development.

## Critiques of Traditional Stage-Based Theories of Individual Development

A number of scholars have described a variety of criticisms of traditional theories of human development, especially strict adherence to linear stage theories of development. In order to maintain a critical approach to using traditional theories of development in our work as social workers, we should be aware of these critiques. The critiques later center around overemphasis on individual or internal influences and minimizing the impact of environmental influences on development; the inadequacy of chronological age to determine transitions from one stage to the next; overemphasis on development as achievement rather than simply change; and inadequacy for explaining or incorporating human diversity.

### Environmental, internal, chronological issues

Criticisms of stage-based theories include **failure to consider environmental influences sufficiently.** Miller notes that "Bronfenbrenner (1977) describes the greatest limitation of the study of human development as the failure to go beyond the focus on the individual;

he suggests that a full understanding of individual development requires an examination of the larger social ecology" (1992:34). Another criticism of stage theories is their *overemphasis on internal processes*. D'Augelli "suggests that many current models of lesbian and gay male identity formation suffer from an excessive emphasis on the internal processes of personal development, usually conceived of in stage-model terms" (in Trickett et al, 1994:324–328). A third criticism of stage theories stresses the *limits of chronological age*. Jendrek and other critics of age-stage-based approaches suggest that connections between chronological age and life periods (traditional role sets such as grandparenthood) have become blurred. They suggest instead the notion of "fluid-cycle" patterns. "This model also contains patterns and expectations, but they are *less* likely to be geared to age" (1994:207).

These increasing variations lead "proponents of the fluid-cycle model [to] argue, therefore, that it becomes difficult to distinguish major life events in terms of age. Despite the theme of orderliness in the life-course literature, research suggests "that 'disorder' may be more 'normal' than 'order'" (Jendrek, 1994:207).

### Developmental change as achievement

Bergen reminds us that the achievement orientation prevalent in dominant U.S. society has resulted in seeing "'development as achievement.' Thus, American parents and teachers see young children's developmental changes as the attainment of milestones or stages that mark progress." Bergen (quoting Feinman and Bruner) "questions our view that development is progress rather than just change" and urges us to remember that "human beings, whatever their age, are completed forms of what they are" (1994:13). This definition of "development as achievement" leads to such concepts as "'developmental delay,' which implies that, for some young children, developmental achievements have not occurred in a timely, sequential fashion." Bergen reminds us that "the sequences, milestones, and stages outlined by numerous researchers and theorists describe normative developmental features, usually called *universals* of development. However, these professionals, like most parents, have also found that wide *individual variations* occur within the universal developmental patterns. The individual variations form a range within typical development that has been called the 'range of normality.' Extreme variations that go beyond the borders of these ranges have traditionally been categorized as atypical developmental patterns or disabilities" (1994:13).

### Summary of critiques

Steenbarger (1991:288–289) summarizes "three particularly troublesome shortcomings" for which these models have been criticized.

1. "In their emphasis on linearity, stage-based models cannot account for the complexity of human development."

2. "In their emphasis on invariant sequences of structural unfolding, stage-based models cannot account for important situational influences in the developmental process."

3. "In an attempt to reduce development to uniform sequences, stage-based theories embody troublesome value premises."

---

### Critical Thinking

**Practice Behavior Example:** Know about the principles of logic, scientific inquiry, and reasoned discernment.

**Critical Thinking Question:** Using your critical thinking skills as you read this section, what conclusions do you reach regarding the value of traditional stage-based theories of individual development? You need not agree with the content of this section in reaching your conclusions. However, you do need to use your knowledge of principles of logic, scientific inquiry, and reasoned discernment.

**Test your understanding of a Critical Perspective on Developmental Journeys by taking this short Quiz.**

By emphasizing uniformity these theories "implicitly negate the values of pluralism and diversity."

### Stage theories and diversity

To explore these criticisms further, let us return to our "developmental ladder" analogy. Not only do traditional linear developmental approaches assume that for everyone the ladder is the same type or design, but they also assume that everyone's ladder has the same number of rungs (steps), the same distance between rungs (steps), the same total height, and the same width between the sides. Traditional developmental theories also too often assume that the context or environment in which the developmental ladder exists is virtually identical or at least equally benign for everyone. This assumption leads us to believe that for everyone the ladder is leaning at the same incline, against the same surface, and that each person climbing the ladder steps onto the first rung from the same surface at the bottom and steps off the last rung onto the same surface at the ladder's top.

We know, though, that the characteristics of ladders and the conditions or contexts in which they are used vary tremendously. (See Figure 5.1.) If all ladders were the same regardless of environmental conditions, they would be of extremely limited use. How can one use a five-foot stepladder to change the light bulb in a twenty-foot-high street light? A ladder's effectiveness depends a great deal on the task to be accomplished, the type of ladder available, the conditions in which it is used, and, perhaps most important, its effectiveness is determined by the skill and ability of the person using it. Effective approaches to human development must incorporate similarly diverse characteristics and conditions as well. Effective approaches to understanding human development must recognize that developmental ladders vary tremendously according to the needs, resources, and environments of individuals.

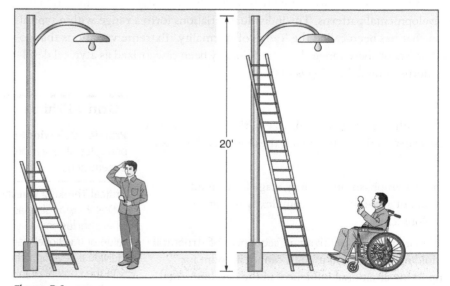

**Figure 5.1**
In the first illustration the person is unable to change the bulb in the streetlight because the ladder is not tall enough. In the second illustration the ladder is tall enough to reach the bulb but is inaccessible to the person in the wheelchair.

In addition to the tremendous variation in the characteristics of ladders and the conditions in which they are used, we also recognize that sometimes a ladder of any type is not the most appropriate or useful tool to get from one place to another. (And even if it is, we may not have a ladder available to us.) A ladder is of limited use, for example, if we need to get from Arkansas to Washington.

Sometimes a level sidewalk, a bridge, an inclined plane, a circular stair, an elevator, an automobile, a jet, a space shuttle, or even a "transporter" from the fictional *USS Enterprise* of *Star Trek* might be more appropriate and useful in moving us along. Lacking any of these alternatives, sometimes we might be forced simply to try to jump from one point to the next. Sometimes, depending on needs, conditions, final destinations, or available resources, a combination of or even *all* these tools for getting from one place to another might be useful. Ladders are but one tool for getting us from one place to another. Linear developmental ladder or stage models of human development are but one tool for understanding our developmental journeys.

## Developmental Perspectives: Commonality and Diversity

Recognizing, incorporating, and respecting developmental diversity does not require that we deny the many developmental tasks and needs shared by all humans. Certainly we have many developmental tasks and needs in common. These commonalities are a vital source of the bonds that serve to unify all people. These commonalities remind us that we are all linked in basic ways that define our common humanity and reflect common rights and responsibilities. However, it is the contention here that these commonalities should not overshadow or be valued any more than our rich diversities.

There are many common developmental tasks and needs, but all people do not develop at the same pace, in the same environments/conditions, or with the same resources or hindrances (obstacles). Unidimensional or linear approaches to individual behavior and development might result in ineffective social work practice and may be contrary to social work values. Such approaches deny the uniqueness of individuals and deprive many persons of the opportunity to celebrate their developmental uniqueness.

For example, a traditional developmental perspective is to assume that the task of walking unaided is a universal developmental task. However, development of the ability to walk unaided by other persons or devices is not a developmental task shared by all persons (or even by most persons). Consider, for a moment, realities such as developmental differences at birth, accidents, and physical changes as a result of aging or disease. Expanding the task of walking unaided to that of achieving sufficient mobility to negotiate one's environment and to allow one to maximize her/his human potential is inclusive of many more of us, at many more points in the life course.

To illustrate both commonality and diversity in development we will examine next the developmental universal, play, and then we will explore developmental risks and conditions that result in very different developmental experiences and results for different persons. We will also explore some common assessment tools used to assess developmental commonality and diversity.

### Play: A universal of human development

Play is an example of a developmental universal, shared by all developing humans, but unique to each developing human in the specific activities and contexts in which it takes place. Play is also a significant assessment context for social workers to understand individual and group human behavior and development. What follows is an examination of this developmental universal in terms of definition, learning, characteristics, and functions of play.

### Definition of Play

1. Play is the way children learn what no one can teach them. It is the way they explore and orient themselves to the actual world of space and time, of things, animals, structures, and people.
2. To move and function freely within prescribed limits.
3. Play is children's work.

### What Children Learn through Play

1. They are helped to develop social relationships and skills.
2. They learn to use play materials and equipment with others.
3. They learn to take turns.
4. They learn how to ask for what they want or need.
5. They understand the role of others (mother, baby, father, doctor, etc.).
6. They master skills.

### Characteristics of Play

1. Play is pleasurable (even when there are no signs of enjoyment, it is still gratifying to the players).
2. Play serves no particular purpose (it does not mean that play is unproductive).
3. Play is spontaneous and voluntary rather than obligatory.
4. Play actively involves the player.

### Functions of Play

1. Play may serve as a means of helping the child solve a problem.
2. Play serves as a means of self-assertion through which a child can declare his or her needs.
3. In play, contact with other children and the need to communicate with them help stimulate language growth.

Learning is a continuous process. In play, young children are learning to manage impulsive behavior, to gain skill in living, and to work with others (adapted from University of Arkansas Nursery School, 1996).

### Developmental risk assessment

Bergen (1994) provides a helpful approach to thinking about several types of vulnerabilities or developmental risks that may challenge the developmental processes of humans and result in diverse developmental experiences and outcomes. These vulnerabilities are often considered in assessment approaches and tools used by a variety of disciplines.

1. *Established Risk:* These "conditions include neurological, genetic, orthopedic, cognitive, or sensory impairments or other physical or medical syndromes that have been strongly linked to developmental problems. . . . Established risks are often called disabilities. They include diagnoses such as Down's syndrome, spina bifida, cerebral palsy, blindness, limb loss or deformity, and other such genetic, motor, sensory, and cognitive impairments."

2. *Biological Risk:* These "conditions are physical or medical trauma experiences that occur in the prenatal period, during the birth process, or in the neonatal period that have a high probability of resulting in developmental delay but that do not always cause delay. . . . For example, extremely low birth weight is often related to developmental delay; however, some children who are of low birth weight are able to overcome this condition and do not experience permanent delays in development."

3. *Environmental Risk:* These "conditions are those factors in the physical setting (e.g., substandard housing, exposure to lead paint) or in the family or other social institutions (e.g., parent caregiving capabilities, low socioeconomic level, cultural values that preclude medical care) that have the potential to influence negatively young children's developmental progress. Negative environmental conditions internal to the family (e.g., family violence, parental drug abuse) and external to the family (e.g., unemployment, lack of access to health care) have an impact both on the development of all family members and on the capacity of these families to provide appropriate environments for their young at-risk children" (Bergen, 1994:4–5).

## Normal and abnormal: Traditional and alternative perspectives

If we are concerned with traditional and alternative perspectives on individual behavior and development, we must question the very concepts of normal and abnormal as they are traditionally presented to us. To discuss human behavior in narrow terms of aggregates or so-called norms or average behaviors is consistent with dominant/traditional paradigm thinking. Others have gone even further to suggest "that a statistical concept of 'normal' can be pathological since it reflects only false consciousness. . . . [A] false consciousness of ideologies and norms imposed from outside the individual and resulting in social and organizational behaviors that are characteristically pathological and neurotic" (Fromm in Gemmill and Oakley, 1992:116).

When we recognize that social workers work with persons, groups, families, organizations, and communities with endless combinations of individual needs, histories, cultures, experiences, and orientations, the concept of "normal" must be questioned. We must seek some more holistic alternative for achieving understanding. Normal for whom?; in whose eyes?; according to whose values?; during what time period?; in what context?; under what conditions? we must ask.

We will try here to learn to think about multiple ranges and ways of ordering and understanding what is "normal" human behavior and development. In the next chapter, we will explore more holistic approaches in recognition of the diverse characteristics, needs, histories, and environments of the persons with whom

**Engage, Assess Intervene, Evaluate**

**Practice Behavior Examples:** Assess client strengths and limitations.

**Critical Thinking Question:** Assume you are working with an elementary school-age child and you determine the **child** has been exposed to all three types of developmental risks. Given the multiple limitations resulting from exposure to these risks, give one example for each risk condition of a potential strength the child might possess to mitigate the risk.

we interact. We can best accomplish this by seeking out developmental approaches/ perspectives/models that emerge from the persons who live and represent those experiences, conditions, and histories.

Traditional perspectives on what is "normal" human behavior leave much unanswered and much to be desired if we are searching for ways to make maximum use of the strengths of people and if we are attempting to respect people's differences as sources of strengths. Weick (1991:22) reminds us that traditional notions of "normal" flow from efforts to view human behavior only from a scientific or positivistic perspective. Such a perspective "searches for law-like occurrences in the natural world" or "norms." Weick argues for different approaches that help us build less rigid or limiting theories of human growth and development; that are "unhinged from the lockstep view of what is considered 'normal' development" (Weick, 1991:23). These alternative approaches should be "fluid models built on assumptions that recognize the creative and powerful energy underlying all human growth" (Weick, 1991:23).

"Normal" is assumed here to be extremely relative—to individual, environment, culture, gender, history, race, class, age, ability, and sexual orientation—and to the complex interplay of these diversities. To be "abnormal" is, in fact, "normal" for most of us, if we focus on our rich diversity. This contradictory-sounding assertion requires us to recognize that by "abnormal" we mean a wide range of differences, some of which fit traditional definitions of pathology such as schizophrenia or criminality, but most of which simply mean different from or alternative to the norms established according to traditional/dominant paradigms, theories, and assumptions about human behavior and development.

Our wide-ranging differences result in wide ranges of what can be considered normal. However, all of us as humans also share developmental "milestones" or expectations in the sense that if the milestone is not reached, or is not reached within some appropriate range of time, some adjustment will be required by the person or by others in the environment to allow the individual to continue on his/her developmental journey toward reaching her/his fullest human potential. For example, Table 5.1 provides an overview of traditional developmental principles, typical examples of developmental principles, and relation to risk conditions for each developmental principle.

To accommodate both the realities of diversity and the commonalities in human behavior, development approaches to gathering knowledge for practice that equally respect common developmental milestones and differences are required. Understanding both traditional and alternative approaches to individual development will help us achieve this balance.

Richards points out the costs of confusing diversity with abnormality and notes "How tragic if we mindlessly equate the abnormal with the pathological and demean the very diversity that can be enhancing and life-giving. To function fully as human beings, we need to broaden and redefine our acceptable 'limits of normality'" (1996:50).

## Traditional Notions of Intelligence: IQ

An example of one of the most influential traditional mechanisms for determining what is normal is that of traditional *Intelligence Quotient* or **IQ.** Traditional views of intelligence refer to a general level of intelligence that is most often referred to as "g" or general intelligence. *General intelligence* is defined "operationally as the ability to answer items on tests of intelligence." The test scores then infer underlying intelligence, called

**Table 5.1  Developmental Principles, Typical Examples, and Relation to Risk Conditions**

| Principles | Typical Examples | Risk Conditions |
|---|---|---|
| 1. Human beings are active in the process of their own development. | Infants actively seek stimulation by visual search and by grasping or moving toward novel phenomena. | Children who are at risk actively select and attend to environmental stimuli and attempt to act on these stimuli; if disabilities hamper self-efficacy, adaptive devices and social stimulation must be enablers of action. |
| 2. Development change can occur at any point in the life span. | Adolescent parents and middle adult parents experience developmental change when they have a child. | Those at risk may not reach some developmental milestones until they are older, but they will continue to make progress; education continues to make a difference throughout the life span. |
| 3. The process is not a smooth, additive one; it involves transitions and cycles, which include chaotic and disorganized as well as integrated and coordinated periods. | In the "terrible twos" the child strives for autonomy while still being dependent and so behavior fluctuates between seeking nurturing and gaining control of self and others. | Those at risk also experience setbacks, plateaux, disorganized periods, and new beginnings; these cycles may not be evidence of pathology but of developmental transition periods similar to those of typical children. |
| 4. Biological maturation and hereditary factors provide the parameters within which development occurs. | A child's physique (e.g., wiry or solidly built) may affect timing of walking. | Biological and hereditary factors affect the levels of progress and the end points of development in areas of risk. |
| 5. Environments can limit or expand developmental possibilities. | A child with poor nutrition or who is confined to a crib may walk later than is typical. | Certain types of delay (e.g., language, social) are very much influenced by home, school, and community environments. |
| 6. There are both continuity and discontinuity (i.e., gradual, stable growth, and abrupt changes) in development. | The temperament of a child (e.g., slow-to-warm-up) may be evident throughout life; thinking patterns will differ qualitatively from infancy to adolescence. | Continuity of development may be less easily recognized and discontinuities may be more noticeable or attributed to nondevelopmental causes in those at risk. |
| 7. Many developmental patterns and processes are universal (i.e., they follow similar time intervals, durations, and sequences of change in most individuals, no matter what their cultural group). | Children in all cultures use a type of "baby" grammar when they first learn to talk. | Children at risk will also show these patterns, although they may be distorted or delayed due to disabilities. |
| 8. There are unique individual biological characteristics as well as culturally and environmentally contingent qualities that influence timing, duration, sequence, and specificity of developmental change. | Most girls talk earlier than boys, but in cultures where mothers talk more to boys, they talk early; girls in some cultures are permitted to be active and in those cultures they show higher activity levels. | Children at risk are more likely to have unique characteristics and experiences that influence how universals of development are manifested. |
| 9. Developmental changes may be positive or negative, as they are affected by health and other factors. | A chronic illness may affect a child's progress and cause some regression to "baby" behavior. | Children with severe or progressive syndromes may show deteriorating development; a balance between maintenance of positive developmental signs and control of negative indicators may be required. |
| 10. Developmental change intervals tend to be of shorter time spans for younger than older individuals. | Infants' motor skills are very different at 6 months and at 1 year, but there is not much change in motor skills between ages 15 and 17. | Time intervals of change are often long with children with disabilities, but developmental progress will usually occur more quickly at younger rather than older ages, making early intervention important. |

**IQ** or an **intelligence quotient** through the use of "statistical techniques that compare responses of subjects at different ages." The fact that these scores are correlated "across ages and across different tests" is used to support the notion that intelligence does not change much with age or training or experience (Gardner, 1993:15).

The cultural bias of IQ tests has been a controversial issue in the use of IQ tests to determine access to and positions within various social institutions like schools, the military, and the workplace. *Cultural bias* refers to the perceived advantage gained by persons taking intelligence tests who are members of the same dominant culture as the persons creating the test. In addition, this bias works to the disadvantage of persons not from the dominant culture who take the test. For example, Stephen Jay Gould in his book, *The Mismeasure of Man,* argued that IQ tests served to continue and to exacerbate the historic exclusion of many lower social-economic status (SES) persons, especially many African Americans (in Herrnstein and Murray, 1994:11–12).

A controversial traditional approach to IQ is that put forth by Herrnstein and Murray in the book *The Bell Curve*. They support the notion of "g" or general intelligence. In addition, they argue that IQ tests do not necessarily reflect cultural bias. They argue that when "properly administered, IQ tests are not demonstrably biased against social, economic, ethnic, or racial subgroups" (1994:23). In Chapter 6, we will further explore the notion of intelligence as a factor in individual development and we will examine an alternative perspective on intelligence offered by Gardner and referred to as multiple intelligence that challenges the traditional notion of IQ.

## Developmental Paradigms and Social Work

Like the need for variety in transportation modes for moving from one place to another, knowledge of a wide range of different developmental theories and perspectives is essential for effective social work practice. Knowledge of diverse theories can provide us with multiple tools for multiple applications. This is especially true given the rich and varied range of people and experiences with which social workers deal. The worldviews or paradigms from which our perspectives on human behavior and development emerge must adequately recognize the dramatic developmental variations among individuals. These variations may include the very nature of the specific tasks to be accomplished, the timing of those tasks, the means used to accomplish tasks, and the historical and current patterns of resource availability or lack of availability for use in accomplishing tasks. In other words, we must recognize that such differences as race, class, sexual orientation, and gender have significant impact on the nature of our developmental experiences.

If these variations are not recognized or if differences are only narrowly recognized, the theories and approaches we use to guide our social work practice will offer helpful guidance for only some persons and will be confusing, frustrating, and even damaging to others. Theories or perspectives that neglect to take into account variations in individuals' characteristics, histories, and environments render those individuals at variance as developmentally inadequate (abnormal) or entirely invisible. If traditional developmental theories or perspectives reflect only the developmental experiences of white, middle-class, heterosexual, males, for example, it is extremely likely that people of color, low-income persons, gay men or lesbians, and women will either be ignored completely by the theories or they will be found to be inadequate or abnormal according to the criteria of the traditional theories.

**Test your understanding of Normal and Abnormal: Traditional and Alternative Perspectives by taking this short Quiz.**

## The Traditional Theories: Why do I need to know?

Chapter 6 will focus on exploration of alternative approaches to understanding human behavior and development. However, in order to understand these alternative approaches, we need to be cognizant of the more traditional theories about human behavior and development. Traditional theories are incomplete, they exclude many people, and they reflect biases due to the value assumptions and historical periods out of which they emerged. However, these inadequacies do not decrease the powerful influences these traditional theories have had in the past, currently have, and will continue to have on the construction and application of knowledge about human behavior and development. Traditional approaches provide a departure point from which we may embark on our journey, in Chapter 6, toward more complete, more inclusive, and less biased visions (or visions in which bias is recognized and used to facilitate inclusiveness) of development to improve all our efforts to reach our fullest potential. Many of the alternative models of development we will explore began as extensions or reconceptualizations of traditional theories.

There is another very practical reason for learning about traditional theories of human behavior and development. The practice world that social workers inhabit and that you will soon enter (and we hope transform) is a world constructed largely on traditional views of human behavior and development. To survive in that world long enough to change it we must be conversant in the discourse of that world. We must have sufficient knowledge of traditional and dominant paradigms of human behavior and development to make decisions about what in those worldviews we wish to retain because of its usefulness in attaining the goal of maximizing human potential, and what we must discard or alter to better serve that same core concern of social work.

## Reductionism and Determinism

In order to make appropriate decisions about the traditional approaches we explore we must recognize their limits. The developmental models we have historically used are not representative of even most people when we compare the race, gender, and class diversity of the people with whom social workers work and the race, class, and gender reflected in traditional models. This is to say nothing of differences in sexual orientation, age, and disabling conditions completely ignored or specified as abnormal in many traditional models. Traditional developmental models emphasize almost exclusively the experiences of white, young, middle-class, heterosexual men who have no disabling conditions.

Many traditional theories of human development are also limited because they present people as if they can be reduced simply to the specific elements focused on by the theory. This reductionism, for example, is evident in Erikson's much-used theory of the life cycle. Erikson's theory of development is often presented as if the human is composed entirely of, and behaves and develops solely as a result of, ego dynamics put into place or determined as a result of life experiences occurring during infancy and very early childhood. The same reductionist and deterministic tendencies can be found in the focus on infantile sexuality of Freudian developmental theory, on cognition and young children in Piaget's theory, and on the development of moral judgment in the theory of Kohlberg.

Erikson was aware of these tendencies in his own and in Freud's approaches and cautioned against them: "When men concentrate on an uncharted area of human

## Human Behavior

**Practice Behavior Example:** Critique and apply knowledge to understand person and environment.

---

**Critical Thinking Question:** After you read the following sections about traditional perspectives on human behavior and development, choose one theory or perspective and determine one limitation you would need to be aware of if you were to apply elements of the theory or perspective in practice. This activity will also require use of your critical thinking skills.

---

existence, they aggrandize this area to become the universe, and they reify its center as the prime reality" (Erikson, 1963:414–15). When we do this we are left with tremendous voids in our knowledge about human development upon which to base our practice. We will attempt to be aware of this tendency as we explore traditional and dominant perspectives in this chapter. We will also try to guard against this tendency as we explore alternative perspectives in the next chapter.

The reader should be alert to the exclusive use of male pronouns and exclusive references to males in direct quotations of traditional developmental theorists used in this book. This reflects the writing style of the time when the work was done. References to males were considered universal and inclusive of females. An exclusive reference to males also reflects actual populations on which many traditional models were based. These models were in fact much more about men's developmental experiences than they were about those of women. They, in effect, rendered women invisible both figuratively and literally.

## TRADITIONAL AND DOMINANT DEVELOPMENTAL THEORIES

The following sections offer summaries of several prominent and influential traditional/dominant theories or models for understanding or explaining individual human behavior and development. The approaches presented have been chosen for several reasons. These models represent not the totality of traditional approaches to understanding individual behavior and development, but they are models that have had powerful influences on social work education and practice related to individuals. They have been extremely influential determiners and reflectors of traditional and dominant paradigm thinking in social work and in many other disciplines. Considered together they offer perspectives that address human behavior through the lifespan. In sum, they also articulate many of the most basic, almost universally used concepts for attempting to understand individual behavior and development. Finally, they are presented here because they have been influential departure points for a number of the alternative approaches to understanding individual behavior and development that we will explore in the next chapter.

The traditional models we will explore are those put forward by Freud, Erikson, Piaget, Kohlberg, and Levinson. While certainly not the only traditional perspectives on individual development, these theories represent some of the most influential thinking about individual human behavior and development during the 20th century. As we review the fundamentals of these traditional approaches, we will continually evaluate them in terms of their consistency with the dimensions of the traditional and dominant paradigm.

### Freud

#### Historical perspective

Freud was born in Moravia (a part of what was, prior to the redivision of the Soviet Union and Eastern Europe, Czechoslovakia) in 1856. He attended medical school in

Vienna, a place of prominence in medical science at the time. He was trained according to the traditional/dominant paradigm as a medical scientist. His initial scientific research was focused on the physiology and neurology of fish. Freud maintained a scientific perspective in his research later on. His research approach focused on observation rather than experimentation and was reflected later in his development and practice of psychoanalysis. Freud was also influenced by what in his time was called psychic healing, a much more intuitive, less traditional approach to understanding and intervening in human behavior, from which emerged hypnotism (Green, 1989:33–35; Loevinger, 1987:14–19). Freud's research and practice in psychoanalysis led him to conclude that the causes of his patients' symptoms could always be found in early childhood traumas and parental relationships (Green, 1989:36–37; Loevinger, 1987:15–16).

Freud developed techniques of free association and dream interpretation to trace and intervene in the early traumas and parental relationships that he believed were the source of his patients' distress. Free association is a process in which the patient is encouraged to relax and report any ideas that come to mind. The notion is that all ideas are important and if sufficiently studied and pursued can be connected back to the unconscious and early sources of their symptoms. Dream interpretation consists of studying the content of patients' dreams in order to detect symbolic and hidden meanings that are then used to interpret and help the patient to work through the troubling early experiences in order to resolve their presenting symptoms. (Green, 1989; Loevinger, 1987).

## The model

Freud's conclusions about often unconscious (unremembered) early experiences as a primary cause of later life troubles and his pursuit of psychoanalysis as a means of intervention in those troubles led him to construct a system through which he explained individual human behavior and development. In 1930, Healy, Bronner, and Bowers presented a summary of many of the basic concepts, processes, and structures that constituted Freud's system. Their work is helpful from a historical perspective because it was written contemporary with much of Freud's actual work and writing. Their approach is also helpful because rather than interpret Freud's work from their own perspectives, they relied heavily on Freud's words and works. This is important because so many different people have interpreted and reinterpreted Freud's work over time, it is often difficult to discern what is really Freud's perspective and what is the adaptation of his ideas by others. Such varied interpretations are understandable given the influence and revolutionary nature of his paradigm at the time, but it is important to have some sense of his original constructs and ideas. Freud's work is also an example of how a paradigm now considered traditional and limited in many ways was at the time of its development and introduction considered quite alternative, even radical.

Healy, Bronner, and Bowers presented Freud's psychoanalysis as a structure that was a synthesis of psychology and biology. They referred to it as a "structure erected within the field of psychobiologic science" (1930:xviii). They summarized this synthesis of biology and psychology:

a. Biological and psychological development are inseparably interrelated.

b. The essential nature of the individual consists in strivings and urges, innate or unlearned, which originally are quite independent of environment.

c. Whatever the individual is or does at any given moment is very largely predetermined by his earlier experiences and his reactions to them.

**d.** The earliest years of life represent the period when biological and mental experiences most profoundly influence the individual because he is then less pre-formed or conditioned.

**e.** Existing actively in the mental life of the individual there is a vast amount of which he is unaware.

**f.** The biological and consequently the psychological constitution varies in different individuals. (1930:xx)

Healy, Bronner, and Bowers suggest that to understand Freud's psychoanalytic paradigm we must first understand what they referred to as the "cardinal formulations" upon which it is based. Their cardinal formulations serve as a useful summary of the basic concepts of this paradigm. *Libido* is "that force by which the sexual instinct is represented in the mind." Libido or eros is "the energy . . . of those instincts which have to do with all that may be comprised under the word 'love.'" The suggestion here is that the concept of libido has a much wider meaning than simply "sex drive." It also incorporates love of self, of others, friendships, and love for humanity in general (1930:2–4).

Green provides a more recent but similar interpretation of this cornerstone of psychoanalytic thought, calling it instinctual or psychic energy (also referred to as nervous energy, drive energy, libido, or tension). Each person is born with a fixed amount of instinctual energy of two types. *Eros*, the "positive energy of life, activity, hope, and sexual desire," and *thanatos*, the "negative energy of death, destruction, despair, and aggression" (1989:36, 38–39).

*Cathexis* "is the accumulation or concentration of psychic energy in a particular place or channel, libidinal or non-libidinal" (Healy et al., 1930:8). This notion of cathexis is somewhat similar to the notion of energy we explored earlier in our discussion of social systems thinking (see Chapter 3). *Polarities* represent aspects of mental life that operate in opposition to one another. This principle of opposites emphasized the polarities of activity–passivity, self–outer world (subject–object), pleasure–pain, life–death, love-hate, and masculine–feminine (Healy et al., 1930:18). Thinking in terms of such polarities as these has much in common with our earlier discussion of the binary or competitive nature of much dominant or traditional paradigm thinking from Chapter 2. *Ambivalence* is the "contradictory emotional attitudes toward the same object" (Healy et al., 1930:20). *Ambivalence* represents an unhealthy or problematic tendency, according to Freudian theory. However, it has some similarity with the concept of ambiguity we discussed in Chapter 3 as a reality of human behavior that social workers must appreciate. *Ambivalence* suggests a negative condition; *ambiguity* suggests an alternative real and necessary aspect of human behavior.

Among the most important formulations of psychoanalysis is what Healy et al. (1930:22) refer to as the "divisional constitution of mental life." Mental life is made up of the conscious, the preconscious, and the unconscious. These notions are indeed essential to understanding Freud's approach. The **unconscious** element of our mental lives is much more powerful than the conscious as an influence on our behavior, according to psychoanalytic thinking. This is a very active part of our being and has much influence on our conscious thought and behavior. The unconscious may either have never been at a conscious level or it may contain once-conscious thought that has become repressed or submerged in the unconscious (Healy et al., 1930:24–28). The **preconscious** "is that part of mental life which in appropriate circumstances, either through an effort of the will or stimulated by an associated idea, can be brought up into consciousness." The preconscious has more in common with the conscious part of our mental selves but can at times function to bring memories from the unconscious to a conscious level. The *conscious* level is the smallest of the three levels and contains thought and ideas of which we are "aware at any given time." The content of the conscious mind is extremely transitory and is constantly changing (Healy et al., 1930:30–32).

Freud found the division of our mental life into *conscious, preconscious,* and *unconscious* helpful but insufficient for explaining human behavior. To more fully explain human behavior he later developed another three-part construct for conceptualizing our mental selves. This construct consisted of id, ego, and superego. He believed that this structure complemented his earlier construct of conscious, preconscious, and unconscious, rather than replacing it (Healy et al., 1930:34). The *id* is the source of instinctive energy. It contains libido drives and is unconscious. It seeks to maximize pleasure, is amoral, and has no unity of purpose (Healy et al., 1930:36). The *ego* represents that part of our mental life that results when id impulses are modified by the expectations and requirements of the external world. Ego emerges out of the id and represents what is commonly thought of as "reason and sanity." Ego strives to be moral and represses tendencies that might give free reign to our unmoral id impulses. The ego is in constant struggle with three influences upon it: "the external world, the libido of the id, and the severity of the superego" (Healy et al., 1930:38). The *superego* grows out of the ego and has the capacity to rule it. It is mostly unconscious and represents what we commonly think of as conscience. It is heavily influenced by our parents. It can evoke guilt and "exercise the censorship of morals" (Healy et al., 1930:44–46).

Green's (1989) summary of Freud's conceptualization of psychosexual stages through which humans develop is somewhat consistent with the historical summary of Healy et al. (1930:80ff). Green suggests five discrete stages, however, while Healy et al. refer to three basic stages, of which the first, infancy, contains three substages (oral, anal, and genital). For clarity here we use Green's model. However, it is helpful to understand that Healy et al. reflect the dominant emphasis in traditional Freudian thinking placed on infancy and infantile sexuality by subsuming several substages under infancy.

Freud's developmental stages focus on critical developmental periods and on the role of sexuality in development from infancy on. Much traditional developmental thinking has its source in this linear, deterministic, and reductionist stage-based model. The first stage is the *oral stage* (birth to about age one). Its focus is on the mouth as a conflicting source of both pleasure (as in taking in nourishment) and pain (denial of nourishment on demand) and on parents as pivotal actors in gratification or denial of oral needs. The second stage is the *anal stage* (about age one to three). The focus of psychic energy shifts at this stage from the mouth to the anus and to control of the elimination of waste and is associated with sexual pleasure, personal power, and control. Conflict over the child's struggle for power and control during the anal stage is most often depicted in toilet training conflicts. These conflicts center on issues of independence and self-control, Freud believed. The third stage, the *phallic stage* (about three to six), is critical in development of sexual identity and sex roles. Instinctual energy is focused on the genitals in this stage and its conflict is around love/hate relationships with parents. Young boys compete for the affection of their mothers with their fathers in the *oedipal complex* that moves the boy through fear of castration by the father in retribution for the boy's desire for the mother, to a compromise in which the boy identifies with the more powerful father and accepts his values, attitudes, behaviors, and habits, resulting in the birth of the superego.

Freud describes a similar, though much less clearly articulated, process for girls that has come to be referred to as the *Electra complex* that takes the girl through penis envy symbolic of the power of the father and males, blaming the mother for depriving her of a penis, to recognition of the impossibility of attaining a penis and a resulting identification with the mother. According to Freud, out of this identification emerges a girl socialized to female sex roles. At this point she has a superego, albeit a weaker superego than that of males, because her lack of a penis prevents castration anxiety and the concomitant psychic strength (superego) that comes from the more intense repression struggles on the part of boys. Regarding women and the development of the superego or conscience, "their Super-ego is never so inexorable, so impersonal, so independent of its emotional origins, as we require it to be in men" (Freud in Healy et al., 1930:51). Healy et al. (1930:51) note that other psychoanalysts of Freud's day agreed "on the more infantile character of the Super-ego in the woman."

Agreement was not universal, however. Healy et al. reported, in their 1930 work on Freud, the important contention of Karen Horney (a female psychoanalyst, we might emphasize) "that the belief in 'penis envy' has evolved as the result of a too exclusively masculine orientation." Horney countered that "the girl has in the capacity for motherhood 'a quite indisputable and by no means negligible physiological superiority.'" She further claimed that there was sufficient data "for believing that 'the unconscious of the male psyche clearly reflects intense envy of motherhood, pregnancy, childhood'" (1930:161). According to Horney, "the whole matter has been approached too much from the male point of view" (1930:163). We shall see in the following chapter that many alternative paradigm thinkers have taken these observations seriously and seek to redefine human behavior and development in ways that more appropriately and adequately incorporate the realities of girls' and women's developmental experiences.

The fourth stage is *latency* (about five or six to puberty). This stage includes the child's movement out of the family to influences of the larger society, primarily in the company of same-sex peers. Sexual instincts and energy are channeled to sports, school, and social play. Freud gave little attention to this stage because of lack of intense sexual conflict characteristic of the previous and following stages. The fifth stage is the *genital stage* (puberty to adulthood). The focal conflict of this stage is the establishment of mature heterosexual behavior patterns through which to obtain sexual pleasure and love (Green, 1989:42–49).

Another influential component in traditional Freudian developmental thinking was that of defense mechanisms. *Defense mechanisms* are automatic patterns of thinking aimed at reducing anxiety (Green, 1989:49). Healy et al. (1930:198) refer to defense mechanisms as "dynamisms" that are "very specific processes by which the unconscious Ego attempts to take care of, or to defend itself against, Id urges, desires, wishes." Thinking of these mechanisms as dynamisms or dynamic forces helps communicate their process or active nature. Some major defense mechanisms include *repression,* the submergence of memories and thoughts that produce anxiety; *regression,* reversion to an earlier, less anxiety-provoking stage of development; *projection,* attributing one's anxiety-provoking thoughts or feelings to someone else; *reaction formation,* behaving in a way that is the extreme opposite of the anxiety-producing behavior; *displacement,* unconsciously shifting anxiety-producing feelings away from threatening objects or persons (Green, 1989:49–51).

## Conclusion

The picture of individual development that emerges from Freud's influential model is one consistent in many ways with traditional paradigm thinking. It is linear and stage-based. Although it has been applied and interpreted very broadly, its focus is relatively narrow in its predominant concern for intrapsychic structures and processes. It is constructed on a scientific, positivistic foundation. It is based on masculinist and patriarchal perspectives that assume male experience as central. Gilligan provides evidence that the tendency to use male life as the norm for human development has a long history that goes at least back to Freud (Gilligan, 1982:6). Female developmental experiences are described only in terms of their difference from normal or modal male experience. The standards of white Eurocentric culture from which the model emerged are considered universal. It reflects the white European experiences of its founder and of the patients upon which Freud's findings were based. The model reflects an individualistic bias that places primacy on separateness and autonomy as necessary end points for mature development. It is binary, with its emphasis on polarities. Implicit also in the model is the dimension of privilege. This dimension incorporates some of the other dimensions of the traditional/dominant paradigm, and from this synthesis emerges the profile of privilege that characterizes a person who is young, white, heterosexual, Judeo-Christian, male, able-bodied, with sufficient resources and power (Pharr, 1988).

### Freud: A paradigm shift from the social environment to individual behavior

Freud's model has had, as noted earlier, significant influences on social work. Ann Weick (1981:140) refers to psychoanalytic theory, for example, as perhaps "the most important development in shaping the evolution of social work." A fundamental element in this evolution was the shifting of focus in social work's approach to addressing problems toward individual functioning and internal or "intrapsychic phenomena . . . as the critical variables." Such a fundamental shift toward the individual was accompanied by a shift away from environmental concerns as foremost in understanding and addressing issues of well-being. A result of this shift was a medical or pathology (illness) perspective on people's problems rather than a social change or strengths perspective.

A medical or pathology perspective also was historically significant in that it redefined human behavior as predictable according to determinable laws consistent with traditional paradigm thinking, rather than as unpredictable and contextually emergent, which would have been more consistent with alternative paradigm perspectives. Thomas Szasz, in his book *The Myth of Mental Illness*, argues that this trend in psychiatry had significant political meaning. It attempted to obscure the relationship between personal troubles and political issues. It suggested that an individual's problems were solely a result of "genetic-psychological" factors (Szasz, 1961:5). On the other hand, Szasz argues, more consistent with alternative paradigm thinking (and more consistent with core concerns of social work), that "psychological laws are relativistic with respect to social conditions. In other words, *the laws of psychology cannot be formulated independently of the laws of sociology*" (1961:7). We cannot understand human behavior unless we simultaneously attend to and seek understanding of the social environment.

To suggest that we consider, in our choices about perspectives for understanding human behavior and the social environment (HBSE), these criticisms of Freud's model of individual development and behavior is not to suggest that we discard it wholesale. Much about Freud's approach offered new insight into the complexities of human behavior. Its suggestion that our later mental lives are influenced by the experiences of our earlier lives alone was extremely important, even revolutionary. We must, however, recognize the contradictions between Freud's approach and our attempt to develop holistic, inclusive perspectives consistent with the core concerns of social work. Thus, the recommendation here, as with all models whether traditional or alternative, is to approach this model critically, cautiously, and analytically. It is also important to note that traditional psychoanalytic theory is being questioned and revised in light of concerns about its exclusion of the experiences of many people, especially those of women. Miller (1986:28) notes, for example, that the emphasis of traditional psychoanalytic theory on autonomy and independence as central to healthy growth and development is being challenged by some theorists who say that the ability to form and maintain interdependent relationship with others is of equal importance in healthy growth and development. Miller suggests that the new call to place equal emphasis on relationship and interdependence is emerging from efforts to look at human development from the perspective of women rather than solely from the perspective of men (1986).

## Piaget

### Historical perspective

Piaget, like Freud, began his study and research from a traditional scientific approach. Piaget focused on biology before turning to psychology and human behavior. He became interested in the study of snails and at age twelve he published his first of some twenty papers on snails. Piaget's first work in psychology was in the laboratory begun by Binet, originator of the intelligence test (IQ test) for quantitatively measuring intelligence. Piaget's interest was, however, qualitative rather than quantitative in that he was interested in why the children gave the answers they did to questions rather than in the quantity of their correct answers. His studies were carried out using complex qualitative interviews with young children, including his own three children. His research resulted in a hierarchical stage model of the development of thinking in children that has, like Freud, had a far-reaching impact on traditional thinking about how humans develop (Loevinger, 1987:177–182).

### The model

Piaget's cognitive developmental model includes four major developmental periods of thinking—sensorimotor, preoperational, concrete operational, and formal operational thought. The **sensorimotor period** is made up of six different stages that constitute "the precursors and first rudimentary stage of intelligence." First, are *impulsive and reflex actions* unconnected with "each other and for their own sake" (sucking). Second, are *circular or repetitive actions* (kicking, grasping a blanket) that are gradually combined into two or more schemes (grasping and looking at a blanket simultaneously). To Piaget, a **scheme** (the term scheme is often translated as *schema*) is a pattern of stimuli and movements that together form a unity and result in sensorimotor coordination. Third, *practicing circular or repetitive actions for their consequences* (kicking to shake the crib) reflects the beginning of concentration. Fourth, the baby *"coordinates schemes and applies them to new situations."* This represents the beginning of intentionality or experimentation in using one scheme to accomplish another (pulling a handkerchief to reach a toy underneath). This stage occurs near the end of the first year. The fifth stage *continues experimentation* *but with more novelty and variation of patterns.* The sixth sensorimotor stage *allows the baby to invent new means of doing things by thinking* rather than only by groping. At this point the baby also learns **object permanence,** which refers to understanding that when an object is out of sight it does not cease to exist (Loevinger, 1987:182–183).

The next three periods involve the development of **operational thought (preoperational, concrete operations, formal operations).** In *preoperational thought* the child learns to use signs and symbols to think about and do things with objects and events that are absent. This period begins with the acquisition of language at about 18 months to two years and continues to ages six or seven. Preoperational thought is focused on concrete, external features of an object or situation and centers on the child (is egocentric) (Loevinger, 1987:183).

The next period is *concrete operational thought* (about 7 to 14, but may last through adulthood (Green, 1989:178). The child reasons correctly about concrete things and events and can do so within "a coherent and integrated cognitive system" for organizing and manipulating the world (Falvell in Loevinger, 1987:183). The child also begins the development of the ability to perceive what Piaget called conservation. *Conservation* refers to the ability to understand that objects can change in some respect but remain the same object. Conservation of volume refers to the ability to understand that the quantity of liquid remains the same even when it is poured from one container of a given shape into a container of a different shape. For example, pouring a cup of water from a tall slender glass into a short wide glass. The sophistication of the child's understanding of conservation to this point occurs late in this period. The final period is that of *formal operations* (14 through adulthood). During this stage the person reasons relatively correctly about hypothetical situations. Important for Piaget was the realization that as the child develops, thinking is not simply a collection of unconnected pieces of information, it is a system of construction. New learning is fitted into what is already known. Piaget referred to this ability as *equilibration.*

## Conclusion

Piaget's model is less traditional in its more qualitative emphasis, but it reflects a developmental world very consistent with traditional paradigm thinking. It is positivistic or empiricist in its focus on knowledge based on direct observation as "real" knowledge. It is linear in its accent on specific progression of stages. It does not recognize differences in developmental experiences emerging from differing experiences resulting from gender. Piaget's model reflects no differentiation in developmental experiences based on race and class. It generally gives no recognition to social or environmental conditions that may impinge on individual development. Thus, it offers little guidance for connecting the personal and the political or on the interrelationships between individual and social change.

As with Freud's model, it is important to recognize that a critical approach such as that taken here is not a suggestion that we completely discard this model. It is to suggest, however, that we examine the model with a critical eye for its consistency with social work concerns. Piaget's work has been extremely influential and helpful in increasing our understanding of how some children learn to think and to think about their experiences of their worlds. His focus on understanding *how* children learn what they learn offers an important alternative to emphasizing only *how much* they learn based on quantifying *how many* correct answers they get on objective tests. To recognize these strengths we need not deny the limitations of this model and of the research upon which it is based.

## Kohlberg

### Introduction

Kohlberg's research focuses on the development of moral judgment and is in part an outgrowth of Piaget's work. Kohlberg's method involved presenting subjects with a series of moral dilemmas to which they were asked to respond. Piaget's study of moral judgment included only children under twelve or thirteen years of age. Kohlberg extended the ages of his subjects beyond those studied by Piaget by interviewing a large number of adolescent boys (Loevinger, 1987:193ff).

### The model

Based on his research, Kohlberg found moral judgment to exist on *"three general levels—preconventional,* characterized by a concrete individual perspective; the *conventional,* characterized by a member-of-society perspective; and the *postconventional,* or principled, characterized by a prior-to society perspective" (Kohlberg in Loevinger, 1987:194). Within each of the three general levels are two stages. Thus, Kohlberg's model consists of six distinct stages distributed across three more general levels of judgment.

Stage 1 is characterized by "a punishment-and-obedience orientation." Stage 2 is characterized by "hedonism." Stage 3 is focused on "maintaining good relations and the approval of others." Stage 4 is focused on "conformity to social norms." Stage 5 is characterized by "a sense of shared rights and duties as grounded in an implied social contract." At stage 6 "what is morally right is defined by self-chosen principles of conscience" (Loevinger, 1987:194–195).

### Conclusion

Kohlberg's model reflects consistency with the dimensions of the traditional/dominant paradigm. It is based on scientific, positivistic, and objectivistic assumptions. The research upon which the model was based included exclusively male subjects. It reflects no recognition for differing developmental experiences based on color or class. It places a premium on development of autonomy, separateness, or individuality. It, like the other models we have explored thus far, portrays development from the perspective of privilege—the assumption of sufficient resources and power to fulfill developmental imperatives.

### Analysis/Criticism: "Women's place" in Freud, Piaget, and Kohlberg

Carol Gilligan (1982) examined the developmental theories of both Jean Piaget and Lawrence Kohlberg for their inclusion and treatment of the developmental experiences of women. These theories have much to say, you may recall from the summaries given earlier in this chapter, about the development of moral judgment and a sense of justice. Gilligan also discussed the treatment women received in Freud's theories in relation to these two fundamental developmental tasks. She noted that Freud found women's sense of justice "compromised in its refusal of blind impartiality" (1982:18).

According to Gilligan, in "Piaget's account (1932) of the moral judgment of the child, girls are an aside, a curiosity to whom he devotes four brief entries in an index that omits 'boys' altogether because 'the child' is assumed to be male." Kohlberg's research does not include females at all. His six stages "are based empirically on a study of eighty-four boys whose development Kohlberg followed for over twenty years." Kohlberg claimed that his model fit humans universally, but Gilligan pointed out, "those groups not included in his original sample rarely reach his higher stages." Women's judgment, for example, rarely goes beyond stage 3 on this six-stage scale. At stage 3 morality is seen in interpersonal terms; goodness is equivalent to helping and pleasing others. Kohlberg implied that only by entering the typically male arenas will women develop to higher stages where relationships are subordinated to rules (stage 4) and rules to universal principles of justice (stages 5 and 6). The paradox presented in Kohlberg's model is that characteristics that traditionally define "goodness" in women—care for and sensitivity to others—are also those that mark them as deficient in moral development. The problem in this paradox of positive qualities perceived as developmental deficiencies, Gilligan suggested, is that the model emerged from the study of men's lives (Gilligan, 1982:18). Karen Horney made a very similar assessment many years ago, we might recall from our earlier discussion of Freudian theory and Horney's criticism of its treatment of women.

## Erikson

### Introduction

The stage-based model derived by Erik Erikson may be the model most often used to teach individual development in HBSE courses in social work curricula and in developmental psychology courses. It is difficult to understate the influence that Erikson's eight-stage model has had on the way individual development through the lifespan is perceived in this society.

Concepts associated with Erikson's model are used almost universally in the language of traditional human development approaches. Erikson's model is also often the departure point or base from which alternative models and theories of development emerge. Such basic concepts as developmental stage, psychosocial or developmental crisis, and the epigenetic principle all emerge from, and are central in Erikson's approach to individual development. These concepts are often used to describe central developmental processes from alternative paradigm perspectives as well. These concepts have become so central to developmental thinking that we will briefly describe them here. However, as you read the excerpts from Erikson later in this chapter, you are encouraged to take note of his discussion and use of these central developmental concepts as he summarizes his eight-stage model.

For Erikson, human development takes place according to a series of predetermined steps through which the person proceeds as he or she becomes psychologically, biologically, and socially ready. The unfolding of these steps allows the individual to participate in social life in increasingly wide-ranging and sophisticated ways. The model assumes that the environment in which development takes place provides the necessary resources and presents the necessary challenges at the proper times for the individual to move through each step. This process of orderly development through a series of steps is guided by what Erikson refers to as the epigenetic principle. The *epigenetic principle* holds that each step takes place as part of an overall plan made up of all the necessary steps or parts. Each particular developmental step emerges out of the context of the overall plan and each step comes about when the internal and external conditions exist to make the individual especially ready to do what is necessary to take the step. This time of readiness is referred to by Erikson as *ascendancy* (Erikson, 1968:92–93).

The necessary steps are referred to as developmental stages. A *developmental stage* is a critical period during which an individual struggles to address and resolve a developmental crisis. Resolution of each crisis enables the individual to proceed to the next stage. This process continues until the individual has progressed through all eight developmental stages. For Erikson, *developmental crisis* did not mean an impending catastrophe as much as it meant "a turning point, a crucial period of increased vulnerability and heightened potential" (Erikson, 1968 in Bloom, 1985:36). See Table 5.2 for an overview of Erikson's eight developmental stages and related ego strengths, crises, and explanations.

### Analysis/Criticism: "Women's place" in Erikson

Erik Erikson's influential theory of eight developmental stages portrays male development and experience as the norm. Gilligan and others (Berzoff, 1989; Miller, 1991) analyze and provide critiques of Erikson's theory specifically in terms of the developmental theme of relationship and connectedness and generally in terms of its treatment or representation of women.

Gilligan finds Erikson, when outlining the developmental journey from child to adult, to be talking about the male child. Much of Erikson's model focuses on the development of identity, a sense of who we are. For Erikson the normal steps to development of identity are steps requiring specifically an identity marked by primacy of separateness and autonomy. Gilligan points out, for example, that after the initial stage of establishment of a sense of trust which requires the establishment of a bond, a relationship initially with the infant's caregiver (usually mother), the focus of development shifts to individuation.

The stages of autonomy versus shame and doubt, initiative versus guilt, industry versus inferiority, and identity versus identity diffusion all call for resolutions weighted toward separateness, individual drive and competence, and identity as a separate self in adolescence. The individual, then, in Erikson's male model, arrives at the adulthood crisis of intimacy versus isolation having spent all the previous years, with the exception of the establishment of trust in infancy, honing developmental skills that place a premium on separateness. But what is not indicated is that such a model is most likely to result in men who are poorly prepared for incorporating and appreciating the intimacy required of adults.

Erikson does recognize differences in the developmental experiences of women to some extent, but he describes these differences in his work virtually as afterthoughts or asides from the normal male model he presents. In his book *Identity: Youth and Crisis* (1968), for example, he addresses women's different developmental issues and experiences in the second-to-last chapter, "Womanhood and the Inner Space." The last chapter addresses, interestingly, "Race and Wider Identity." Neither of these chapters, based on lectures and papers written in 1964 and 1966 long after his original outline of the eight stages in 1950, resulted in changes or revision in the model. In his 1950 work, *Childhood and Society*, he mentions that, in the initiative versus guilt stage, boys' forms of initiative development activities focus on "phallic-intrusive modes" while girls focus on "modes of 'catching' in more aggressive forms of snatching or in the milder form of making oneself attractive and endearing" (Erikson, 1950). In his 1968 work, Gilligan notes, Erikson finds identity development in adolescence for girls different from that in boys. However, these differences did not result in changes in his original outline of life cycle stages (Gilligan, 1982:12).

## Table 5.2   Erikson's Psychosocial Stages of Development

| Stage | Developmental Crisis | Successful Dealing with Crisis | Unsuccessful Dealing with Crisis |
|---|---|---|---|
| 1. Infant<br>Birth to 1 year old | **Trust Versus Mistrust**<br>Babies learn to trust or mistrust others based on whether or not their needs—such as food and comfort—are met. | If babies' needs are met, they learn to trust people and expect life to be pleasant. | If babies' needs are not met, they learn not to trust. |
| 2. Toddler<br>1 to 3 years old | **Autonomy Versus Shame and Doubt**<br>Toddlers realize that they can direct their own behavior. | If toddlers are successful in directing their own behavior, they learn to be independent. | If toddler's attempts at being independent are blocked, they learn self-doubt and shame for being unsuccessful. |
| 3. Preschool Age<br>3 to 5 years old | **Initiative Versus Guilt**<br>Preschoolers are challenged to control their own behavior, such as controlling their exuberance when they are in a restaurant. | If preschoolers succeed in taking responsibility, they feel capable and develop initiative. | If preschoolers fail in taking responsibility, they feel irresponsible, anxious, and guilty. |
| 4. Elementary School Age<br>5 to 12 years old | **Industry Versus Inferiority**<br>When children succeed in learning new skills and obtaining new knowledge, they develop a sense of industry, a feeling of competence arising from their work and effort. | When children succeed at learning new skills, they develop a sense of industry, a feeling of competence and self-esteem arising from their work and effort. | If children fail to develop new abilities, they feel incompetent, inadequate, and inferior. |
| 5. Adolescence<br>13 to early twenties | **Identity Versus Role Confusion**<br>Adolescents are faced with deciding who or what they want to be in terms of occupation, beliefs, attitudes, and behavior patterns. | Adolescents who succeed in defining who they are and finding a role for themselves develop a strong sense of identity. | Adolescents who fail to define their identity become confused and withdraw or want to inconspicuously blend in with the crowd. |
| 6. Early Adulthood<br>Twenties and thirties | **Intimacy Versus Isolation**<br>The task facing those in early adulthood is to be able to share who they are with another person in a close, committed relationship. | People who succeed in this task will have satisfying intimate relationships. | Adults who fail at this task will be isolated from other people and may suffer from loneliness. |
| 7. Middle Adulthood<br>Forties and fifties | **Generativity Versus Stagnation**<br>The challenge is to be creative, productive, and nurturant of the next generation. | Adults who succeed in this challenge will be creative, productive, and nurturant, thereby benefiting themselves, their family, community, country, and future generations. | Adults who fail will be passive, and self-centered, feel that they have done nothing for the next generation, and feel that the world is no better off for their being alive. |
| 8. Late Adulthood<br>Sixties and beyond | **Ego Integrity Versus Despair**<br>The issue is whether a person will reach wisdom, spiritual tranquility, a sense of wholeness, and acceptance of his or her life. | Elderly people who succeed in addressing this issue will enjoy life and not fear death. | Elderly people who fail will feel that their life is empty and will fear death. |

## Levinson: Adult Development

### Introduction

Daniel Levinson recognized that most developmental research began with and focused on the developmental experiences and tasks of very early life. Most traditional models would then apply the concepts and patterns observed or emerging from studies of children to later points in the life cycle. The target of his research, unlike that of the others we have explored thus far, was the developmental experiences and stages of adulthood, primarily what he defined as middle adulthood. Like the other traditional models we have explored, Levinson's model, described in his book, *The Seasons of a Man's Life* (1978), talks about development only in terms of the experiences of men.

### The model

Levinson et al. (1978:18) concluded that generally the life cycle moves through a series of four partially overlapping eras, each of which lasts approximately 22 years. Their research also concluded that the cycle can be further broken down into developmental periods that "give a finer picture of the dramatic events and the details of living" (1978:19). Levinson claims a fairly high degree of specificity regarding the ages at which each era begins and ends. The range of variation is, he believes, "probably not more than five or six years." A central concept in Levinson's model is that of transition between eras. Transitions between eras last four or five years and require "a basic change in the fabric of one's life" (1978:19). The eras and transition periods are listed below:

> **Era 1.**  *[Preadulthood] Childhood and Adolescence: 0–22 years*
> *Early Childhood Transition: 0–3*
> *Early Adult Transition: 17–22*
>
> **Era 2.**  *Early Adulthood: 17–45*
> *Early Adult Transition: 17–22*
> *Mid-life Transition: 40–45*
>
> **Era 3.**  *Middle Adulthood: 40–65*
> *Mid-life Transition: 40–45*
> *Late Adult Transition: 60–65*
>
> **Era 4.**  *Late Adulthood: 60–?*
> *Late Adult Transition: 60–65 (Levinson et al., 1978:20)*

In Preadulthood (Era 1) the social environment includes family, school, peer group, and neighborhood. Developmental tasks include becoming disciplined, industrious, and skilled. Puberty occurs at approximately 12 or 13 and acts as a transition to adolescence, "the culmination of the pre-adult era." The Early Adult Transition (approximately age 17 to 22) acts as a bridge from adolescence to early adulthood. Levinson says, "during this period the growing male is a boy-man" and experiences extraordinary growth but remains immature and vulnerable as he enters the adult world (1978:21).

Early Adulthood (Era 2) "may be the most dramatic of all eras" with mental and biological characteristics reaching their peaks. This era includes formation of preliminary adult identity and first choices "such as marriage, occupation, residence and style of living." The man during this era typically begets and raises children, contributes his labor to the economy, and moves from a "novice adult" to a "senior position in work, family and community" (1978:22). This is a demanding and rewarding time filled with stress, challenges, and accomplishments according to Levinson.

Middle Adulthood (Era 3), with its Mid-life Transition from about 40 to 45, Levinson refers to as "among the most controversial of our work" (1978:23). The controversy around discovery of this transition involves its lack of any clear cut universal event such as puberty in marking the transition from childhood to adolescence and early adulthood. This transition period includes more subtle, evolutionary, and thematic changes in biological and psychological functioning, the sequence of generations, and the evolution of careers and enterprises (1978:24).

This era is marked by some decline in "instinctual energies" and biological functions such as sexual capacity. Levinson describes this not necessarily as a deficit, since "the quality of his love relationships may well improve as he develops a greater capacity for intimacy and integrates more fully the tender, 'feminine' aspects of his self. He has the possibility of becoming a more responsive friend to men as well as women" (1978:25). Levinson notes differences in intensity of changes and in individual men's responses to them during this time. "The Mid-life Transition may be rather mild. When it involves considerable turmoil and disruption, we speak of a mid-life crisis." This transition involves a recognition of one's mortality and loss of youth for most men that is not completed here but continues for the remainder of life (Levinson et al., 1978:26).

A key concept in Levinson's model is that of generation. We will also explore other definitions and discussions of the concept, generation, in Chapter 7. He describes a generation in this way: "Members of a given generation are at the same age level in contrast to younger and older generations. With the passing years, a young adult has the sense of moving from one generation to the next and of forming new relationships with the other generation in his world." A generation "covers a span of some 12–15 years" (1978:27). Levinson uses Jose Ortega Y Gasset's conception of generations as a guide:

1. Childhood: 0–15;
2. Youth: 15–30;
3. Initiation: 30–45;
4. Dominance: 45–60;
5. Old age: 60+. (1978:28)

Levinson's notion of evolving career and enterprises calls on "every man in the early forties . . . to sort things out, come to terms with the limitations and consider the next step in the journey." Men around 40 often experience some culminating event representing a significant success or failure in terms of movement along the life path. Levinson also describes this time of life as a period of "individuation," "a developmental process through which a person becomes more uniquely individual. Acquiring a clearer and fuller identity of his own, he becomes better able to utilize his inner resources and pursue his own aims. He generates new levels of awareness, meaning and understanding" (1978:31–33).

Late Adulthood (Era 4) is not the focus of Levinson's work, but he does give some attention to describing its tasks. He believes this era lasts from 60 to 85. The developmental tasks include balancing the "splitting of youth and age" in order to sustain his youthfulness in a new form appropriate to late adulthood, terminating and modifying earlier life structure, moving off "center stage of his world," finding "a new balance of involvement with society and with the self," to gain a sense of integrity of his life, finding meaning in his life in order to come to terms with death, and making peace with enemies inside the self and in the world—not to stop fighting for his convictions but "to fight with less rancor, with fewer illusions and with broader perspective" (1978:36–38).

Levinson very briefly describes an additional era of Late Adulthood beginning at around 80. Development at this point in life, while virtually unexplored (in 1978 when Levinson's work was first published), involved, he believed, such fundamental developmental tasks as "coming to terms with the process of dying and preparing for his own death," preparing himself for afterlife if he believes in immortality of the soul or, if not, concern for the fate of humanity and his own part in human evolution, and gaining meaning from life and death generally and his own specifically. "He must come finally to terms with the self—knowing it and loving it reasonably well, and being ready to give it up" (1978:38–39).

After publication of *The Season's of a Man's Life,* Levinson continued to explore adult development. In some of his later work, he stressed the need to develop models that appreciate and incorporate multiple and complex influences on the lives of humans. He emphasized the need to maintain an emphasis on the mutual influences of the individual and the social environment as development unfolds (Levinson, 1986). Levinson also extended his theoretical position to include the developmental experiences of women. This extension to include women was based on a study of adult women and development he conducted subsequent to the original work that focused solely on the adult development of men. He concluded that the original model, with very little adaptation, fits equally the experiences of men and women. According to Levinson, "women and men go through the same sequence of periods in adult life structure development, and at the same ages" (Levinson and Levinson, 1996:413). However, Levinson found that women's experiences, as they go through the same sequences of periods in adult development, differ from those of men. The major concept used to describe these differential experiences was that of gender splitting. *Gender splitting* is "a rigid division between female and male, feminine and masculine, in all aspects of life" (Levinson and Levinson, 1996:414). Levinson found gender splitting to be especially apparent in the male and female experiences of public occupational and domestic spheres of life—"women's work and men's work, feminine and masculine within the self." Levinson posited that gender splitting "is encouraged by the existence of a patriarchal society in which women are generally subordinate to men, and the splitting helps maintain that society" (Levinson and Levinson, 1996:414). However, as women increasingly enter the public sphere of work outside the home, Levinson concluded the "lives and personalities of women and men are becoming more similar" (Levinson and Levinson, 1996:414). Levinson's perspective on the inclusion of the developmental experiences of both males and females in his model is quite different from that offered by Gilligan (1982) in her critique of Levinson's theory. Berzoff (1989) also questioned the ability to make generalizations about the patterns of adult development for men and women. (See "Analysis / Criticism" sections in the next page.)

## Disengagement Theory of Aging

Another traditional approach to understanding adult development, especially later adulthood, is *disengagement theory.* Achenbaum and Bengtson claim that "disengagement theory . . . represents the first truly explicit, truly multidisciplinary, and truly influential theory advanced by social science researchers in gerontology" (1994:756). The "disengagement theory of aging" was originally conceptualized by Cumming and Henry (1961) in their book, *Growing Old*. The central argument of the theory was that "**Disengagement** is an inevitable process of aging whereby many relationships between the individual and society are altered and eventually severed. [It] could be seen in both psychological (ego mechanism) and sociological (role and normative) changes. It was also manifest in loss of morale" (Achenbaum and Bengtson, 1994:758).

### Challenges to disengagement

Disengagement theory was challenged by researchers who suggested very different and much more varied views of the experiences of persons as they aged. According to Achenbaum and Bengtson, Havighurst, in 1957, in putting forth his theory of "the social competence of middle-aged people . . . emphasized that most people ably adjusted their social roles well into their late sixties. Furthermore, he suggested that life satisfaction depended, indirectly at least, on social activity" (1994:759). They also note that in 1968 Smith "challenged both the universality and the functionality in assumptions about 'disengagement' by failing to confirm their propositions in surveys of African Americans, the chronically ill, and poor people." Tallmer and Kutner in 1969 suggested "it is not age which produces disengagement . . . but the impact of physical and social stress which may be expected to increase with age" (in Achenbaum and Bengtson, 1994:760).

Bengtson reported in 1969 that there appeared to be "more *variation* than *uniformity* in retirement roles and activities across occupational and national groups. . . . there was little evidence for the 'universality' of disengagement" (Achenbaum and Bengtson, 1994:760). In a similar manner in 1968 and 1969 Neugarten "stressed *diversity* in patterns of aging, and the *variations* in the aged's personalities" (Achenbaum and Bengtson, 1994:759). More recently, Tornstam (1999/2000) has reexamined this theory. As a result of his research, he has put forth an alternative theory of "gerotranscendence." See Chapter 6 for more on Tornstam's theory and other alternative theories of aging.

### Analysis/Criticism: "Women's place" in adult development

Neugarten, in her research on the process of aging, argued for looking at adult development and aging from multiple perspectives in order to appreciate the diversity in the experience of aging for different people. For example, she noted that in her research she found that individuals' experiences of aging process varied considerably according to both gender and social class. Neugarten was basically arguing against the notion of "biology as destiny" that had been put forth by traditional researchers in the area of adulthood and aging (Achenbaum and Bengtson, 1994:759–60).

TOM CARTER / PHOTOEDIT

*Does this photo communicate an image consistent with or inconsistent with Disengagement Theory of Aging? In what ways is the image consistent or inconsistent with this theory?*

Achenbaum and Bengtson (1994:759) note, "Neugarten established her eminence in several domains of aging research. "First, she stressed" the importance of sex-and gender-based differences in biological and social time clocks." Second, she urged that researchers "look at the entire life course in addressing processes of aging, she never assumed invariant continuities in behavioral patterns." Bernice Neugarten laid the foundation for much on the later feminist and alternative approaches to considering diversity, gender, and class in research on adulthood rather than assuming only biological determinants of the aging process.

Carol Gilligan's (1982) research on women also informs adult developmental perspectives. She addresses specifically the exclusively male-based adult developmental model depicted by Levinson and the stages of adult development outlined in Erikson's male-focused model. Gilligan finds that the exclusion of the developmental experiences of women from these models results in incomplete portrayals of human development. The portrayals of the men emerging from these models lack what she considers to be some essential capacities. In existing traditional models of adult development, Gilligan finds "that among those men whose lives have served as the model for adult development, the capacity for relationships is in some sense diminished and the men are constricted in their emotional expression" (1982:154). Existing models display "a failure to describe the progression of relationships toward a maturity of interdependence [and] . . . the reality of continuing connection is lost or relegated to the background where the figures of women appear" (Gilligan, 1982:155).

In adolescence and young adulthood, male and female voices reflect quite different central developmental experiences. For men "the role of separation as it defines and empowers the self" seems central. For women, "the ongoing process of attachment that creates and sustains the human community" is focal (Gilligan, 1982:156). Gilligan notes that by listening to the previously unheard voices of women in thinking about adult development, one is pressed to re-envision notions of adult development.

Perhaps as important as the implications of the treatment or neglect of women in traditional developmental thinking that Gilligan speaks of is the need for adult developmental perspectives that allow women to speak and to be heard in order to begin to develop true models of *human development*. As Gilligan points out, "Among the most pressing items on the agenda for research on adult development is the need to delineate *in women's own terms* the experience of their adult life." To listen to and learn from the developmental experiences of women is to include over one half of humanity in models of human development that has traditionally been neglected. It is also essential to realize, as Gilligan suggests earlier, that to listen to the voices of women is to learn a great deal about what is necessary for more completely understanding the meaning of individual development for both women and men.

### Analysis/Criticism: "Lesbians' place" in adult development

According to Furst (in Wheeler-Scruggs, 2008:45), "Levinson's universal developmental age-linked model of adult development disregarded culture, historical, and gender differences." Wheeler-Scruggs (2008) conducted research to assess the "goodness of fit" of lesbian adult development with Levinson's model. In her research she found, "there did seem to be the same basic ordering of structure-building and structure-changing periods" for the lesbians in her research study. She notes also, though, "how tasks are accomplished should be addressed differently for lesbians" (Wheeler-Scruggs, 2008:45) She suggests, for example:

> a model of adult development for lesbians, transitional figures for separation from family, such as husbands or partners, may need to be replaced by feelings of independence, differentiation from parents, and solitary decision-making needs. Additionally, components that relate directly to being lesbian need to be considered as foundational in lesbian life structures. For example, coming out must be reflected in any adult development theory concerning lesbians. The family component also takes on different dimensions for this population. Although society does not generally recognize the monogamous relationship between two lesbians as a family unit, lesbian couples themselves do. Friends also play an important role in the sense of family that lesbians construct. The societal nonrecognition [sic] of being a family unit and the role friends play in the makeup of that family unit will need to be considered in adult development theories for lesbians (Wheeler-Scruggs, 2008:45).

## Analysis/Criticism: Traditional Developmental Approaches and People of Color

### Race in developmental research/Erikson

According to Erikson successful human development depends on resolution of intrapsychic conflict about membership in the following groups:

1. Gender
2. Religion
3. Age
4. Occupation
5. Political ideology
6. Sexual orientation (Helms, 1994:287)

Consideration of race or ethnicity is conspicuously absent from the list above. Helms notes that Erikson saw "racial-group membership as a significant aspect of negative identity development in African Americans, he had no notion of racial-group membership as a significant aspect of White people's identities. Nor did he have a postulate by which identification with one's racial group could have positive implications for personality adjustment for members of any racial group. . . . Yet in the United States, of the many collective identity groups to which a person might belong, race is the most salient, enduring, recognizable, and inflammatory" (1994:287).

Parks et al. point out the neglect of diversity and the resulting image of diversity as abnormal in much of the individual development literature. They note that "until fairly recently, the literature was essentially comparative and was critical of those who differed from the White male 'norm.' Theories of normal psychological functioning and development in a wide range of areas were developed by studying groups of White men . . . and women and Blacks were seen as deficient when differences between their experiences and those of White men emerged . . . the general image of psychological health was developed from an essentially racist, sexist, and heterosexist frame of reference" (1996:624).

## Themes Regarding People of Color in Traditional Developmental Approaches

Spencer (1990:267–269) summarizes some of the themes in traditional approaches to the study of development and people of color. She outlines several characteristics of traditional or dominant approaches that have resulted in inadequate and inaccurate portrayals of the developmental experiences of people of color. She argues that these portrayals have been detrimental to the African American, Asian American, Hispanic American, and American Indian people they exclude or inaccurately and incompletely depict. These traditional themes include the following:

1. Traditional-paradigm researchers have often been trained to view race and socioeconomic status as "nuisance" variables to be controlled for.

2. Study of minorities has too often been conducted from the approach of considering minorities as "deviant" from majority-based norms. The "deviance" approach neglected the often creative adaptation of people of color to the developmental barriers placed before them by hostile environments.

3. "Normative" development has too often been defined according to Eurocentric standards, excluding from the norm all but the most assimilated minorities. Cultural differences and structural explanations that recognize inequality and discrimination have often been largely ignored.

4. "The color-blind view of 'people as people' runs counter to unique cultural values, hypothesized cultural learning styles, and associated untoward social experiences. For example, the Western values of individualism and competition are in direct conflict with cooperation and collaboration, values of some minority cultures, notably American Indians, Asian Americans, and African Americans."

5. Treatment of minority group members as if they are invisible, portraying them only in a negative light (e.g., crime suspects) or providing only stereotyped, narrow portrayals (e.g., sports figures) result in a very limited and very limiting set of role models for minority children.

6. Many traditional portrayals reflect a "melting pot" perspective that was suggested over 20 years ago and that did not exist then, does not exist now, will not likely come about in the future, and is not desirable.

7. Such exclusionary and inaccurate portrayals are disadvantageous to the broader culture. Their neglect of minority experiences and problem-solving patterns deny the broader culture the opportunity to "be enriched by the talents, creativity, and intelligence of minority youngsters who have been provided an opportunity to reach their potentials" (1990:267–269).

These themes reflect many of the dimensions of traditional and dominant paradigm thinking. They clearly reflect the need for the creation and application of perspectives on the development of people of color based on the dimensions of alternative paradigms. As is the case with understanding traditional paradigm thinking generally, recognizing the weaknesses of traditional approaches to the study of the development of people of color is important for us as social workers if we are going to be advocates for more inclusive, strengths-based perspectives. The alternative

**Test your understanding of Traditional Theories of Individual Development by taking this short Quiz.**

perspectives on development and people of color described in the following chapter offer a number of other perspectives to help increase our understanding of HBSE and upon which to base our practice.

## SUMMARY/TRANSITION

This chapter introduced a critical perspective from which to view traditional thinking about individual human development. It described the importance for social workers of applying this critical perspective to traditional thinking about individual development in order to recognize its limitations. It also explored the necessity of appreciating the importance, power, and usefulness of traditional paradigm thinking about individual development for effective social work practice.

This chapter then presented several of the most prominent traditional models of individual development. The models explored included the psychoanalytic approach of Freud; the cognitive developmental approach of Piaget; Kohlberg's extension of Piaget's work to the development of moral judgment; the developmental stage-based model of Erikson so often used to guide social workers; the adult development model of Levinson; and the disengagement theory of aging. Each of these models was subjected to analysis and criticism from the perspective of women's developmental experiences to illustrate their neglect and misrepresentation of women. In addition, a number of limitations of the approaches of traditional paradigms to the treatment of people of color were presented.

In the next chapter we continue our analytic/critical approach to thinking about individual development. In addition, we explore a number of alternative perspectives, some of which emerge as extensions of the traditional models explored in this chapter. These alternative perspectives allow us to think about the developmental experiences of the many individuals (women, people of color, persons with disabilities, gay men, and lesbians) neglected or omitted entirely from traditional paradigmatic thinking about individual human development. While the models we explored in this chapter are likely to have been familiar to many of us from other courses, our travels in the next chapter are likely to take many of us to destinations quite new to us.

**Recall what you learned in this chapter by completing the** Chapter Review.

KAYTE DEIOMA/PHOTOEDIT

# Alternative and Possible Perspectives on Individuals

## INTRODUCTION

In this chapter we focus on extending and deepening our understanding of individuals' developmental experiences and the social environments in which these experiences take place. We want to learn to integrate the strengths inherent, but often unrecognized, in the diverse developmental realities, experiences, and strategies of different individuals so we can do better social work.

## DESTINATIONS

The destination of our journey in this chapter is not some static and final point at which we arrive upon a complete or absolute understanding of "proper individual behavior and development." In fact, our goal in this chapter is not any one destination at all. Our paramount concern is that during the journey we learn about multiple models to use as resources—tools, information, awareness, ways of thinking about developmental issues—to help us recognize the developmental commonalities shared by us all as humans and to recognize and respect how different humans develop differently. In addition, the information provided in this chapter is intended to provide a base from which to continue learning about human behavior throughout our lives. If there were a single destination it would be that place at which we attain sufficient knowledge upon which to base action to remove barriers to achieving the full human potential of any person with whom we work.

Themes receiving special emphasis in this chapter include diversity, diversity within diversity, multiple diversities, and multiple perspectives on understanding differences. We explored the notion of developmental universals or commonalities in Chapter 4. In this chapter we will be much more concerned with developmental variation as not only acceptable, but as necessary for healthy individual human development and essential for a healthy society as well.

## ALTERNATIVE AND POSSIBLE DEVELOPMENTAL THEORIES

The alternative/possible models we will explore focus on developmental approaches that include persons and conditions left out of or only peripherally addressed by traditional models. These approaches also reflect dimensions of the alternative paradigm for understanding human behavior and the social environment (HBSE) outlined in Chapter 2.

We must recognize that no one alternative approach offers a model incorporating all the dimensions of alternative paradigms. Each, however, provides an alternative to traditional models along at least one, if not several, of the alternative paradigmatic dimensions. This diversity of focuses is in keeping with our search for multiple models and approaches that reflect the differing developmental experiences of diverse persons. Rather than any one alternative offering some complete and final answer, the alternatives we will explore reflect a variety of attempts to develop multiple answers to the developmental questions emerging from different persons, experiences, and conditions of concern to social workers.

Although the alternatives discussed differ from one another in many ways, they share some important dimensions and themes. They offer voices and visions that are important in responding to the exclusion of many persons from traditional paradigms. They address historical conditions of oppression. Other themes that emerge from some of the alternative perspectives we will explore include:

1. Differences in experiences in carrying out the common developmental process of identity formation.

2. A lack of developmental mentors or role models for many oppressed and excluded persons.

CLEO PHOTO/ALAMY

*Reflecting on this multiracial, multigenerational family what might be some examples of the parents and grandparents' success in fostering ego strength, supporting biracial labeling, and providing a multiracial environment to support the children's positive identity development?*

3. Impact on an individual's development of deficit or abnormal status often accorded excluded or oppressed persons by traditional models or by dominant society.

4. Explicit attention to social environmental (SE) influences on individual development.

Another important structural characteristic of many of the alternative approaches is their *nonlinear, contextual quality*. This characteristic is most obvious in the non-stage-based nature of some of the alternatives we are about to explore. Even the models that emerge from or are adaptations of traditional stage-based models tend to be contextual and nonchronological. The approaches and models explored in this chapter attempt to include and reflect the dimensions (to varying degrees) of alternative paradigm thinking. They have also been chosen to address alternative perspectives on individual development throughout the Life Course. The alternative approaches that we explore, you will notice, often have their roots in traditional or dominant models, but they seek to transcend the limits of the traditional models in order to embrace diversity.

## The Larger Environment and Individual Development

One of the themes especially significant in considering alternative perspectives on development is the role played by the larger social environment. As we noted in Chapter 5, few traditional theories of individual development attend to the significant influence of social environmental factors on development, yet the nature of interaction with the larger environment (e.g., experiences of racism, homophobia, or sexism) has a significant influence on development throughout the Life Course. In addition, the availability of needed resources from the larger social environment for optimum development is a critical factor in developmental outcomes (nutrition, health care, housing, education, etc.). For example, Andrews and Ben-Arieh describe the critical importance of both positive interaction in and the availability of necessary material resources from the larger environment for optimal development. They point out that "material resources such as food, safe water, clothing, and housing are necessary but insufficient for holistic development. Stable, nurturing social relationships and safe, stimulating environments are essential" (Andrews and Ben-Arieh, 1999:110).

## Poverty and Individual Development

Poverty, especially as it affects children and women of childbearing years, often has a profound impact on individual development. Poverty results in a reduction of the resources available in the child's and the mother's environment necessary to provide for positive child development. *Poverty* is, of course, determined by income and "includes money income before taxes." The U.S. Department of Health and Human Services uses "poverty guidelines" to determine eligibility for many of its services and policies. Those guidelines for 2012 are included in Table 6.1 for the 48 contiguous states and the District of Columbia.

Research indicates that poverty is not usually a continuous state for most people. For most people "spells of poverty are fairly brief." However, for those households only slightly above poverty, a fall back into poverty can happen quickly with the loss of a job or the exit of one of the breadwinners from the family. As a result many families will move in and out of poverty over time. Studies of these data also reveal significant differences between African Americans and white Americans. African Americans "were more likely to be touched by poverty and more likely to be exposed to poverty for substantially longer periods" than whites (Rank and Hirschl, 1999:202).

Rank and Hirschl argue that since most of us will experience poverty during adulthood (to say nothing of the likelihood of childhood poverty) and since poverty underlies so many of the problems confronted by social workers, we should all take a very keen interest in reducing poverty. Rank and Hirschl point out, "for the majority of Americans, it is in their direct self-interest to have programs and policies that alleviate . . . the ravages of poverty." They point out that "for the majority of American adults, the question is not if they will experience poverty, but when" (1999:213–14).

## Food Insecurity in the United States and Globally

Among the most basic effects of poverty are hunger and malnutrition. Hunger and malnutrition play multiple and complex roles in human developmental outcomes. Adequate nutrition is necessary for a healthy and productive life.

### Food Insecurity

According to the World Health Organization (WHO) there are three components of food security:

- Food availability: Sufficient quantities of food available on a consistent basis.
- Food access: Having sufficient resources to obtain appropriate foods for a nutritious diet.
- Food use: Appropriate use based on knowledge of basic nutrition and care, as well as adequate water and sanitation. (WHO, 2011)

**Watch the video** *"Employed but Still Homeless, Working Poor"* **to see how see the impact of poverty even on many people who work fulltime.**

**Critical Thinking Question:** What are two ways social workers might intervene to help move working poor people out of poverty?

---

**Practice Contexts**

**Practice Behavior Example:** Continuously discover, appraise, and attend to changing locales, populations, scientific and technological developments, and emerging societal trends to provide relevant services.

**Critical Thinking Question:** Why is it important, as a professional social worker, to understand current and emerging trends in global food insecurity, even though you are working in an affluent community in the United States? How might you use your current practice context to reduce global food insecurity?

### Table 6.1

#### 2012 Poverty Guidelines for the 48 Contiguous States and the District of Columbia

| Persons in family/household | Poverty guideline |
| --- | --- |
| 1 | $11,170 |
| 2 | 15,130 |
| 3 | 19,090 |
| 4 | 23,050 |
| 5 | 27,010 |
| 6 | 30,970 |
| 7 | 34,930 |
| 8 | 38,890 |

For families/households with more than 8 persons, add $3,960 for each additional person.

#### 2012 Poverty Guidelines for Alaska

| Persons in family/household | Poverty guideline |
| --- | --- |
| 1 | $13,970 |
| 2 | 18,920 |
| 3 | 23,870 |
| 4 | 28,820 |
| 5 | 33,770 |
| 6 | 38,720 |
| 7 | 43.670 |
| 8 | 48,620 |

For families/households with more than 8 persons, add $4,950 for each additional person.

#### 2012 Poverty Guidelines for Hawaii

| Persons in family/household | Poverty guideline |
| --- | --- |
| 1 | $12,860 |
| 2 | 17,410 |
| 3 | 21,960 |
| 4 | 26,510 |
| 5 | 31,060 |
| 6 | 35,610 |
| 7 | 40,160 |
| 8 | 44,710 |

For families/households with more than 8 persons, add $4,550 for each additional person.

Source: *Federal Register*, Vol. 77, No. 17, January 26, 2012, pp. 4034–4035

According to the U.S. Department of Agriculture (USDA), the agency with the most responsibility for measuring food security, there are four levels of food security:

- High food security—Households had no problems, or anxiety about, consistently accessing adequate food.
- Marginal food security—Households had problems at times, or anxiety about, accessing adequate food, but the quality, variety, and quantity of their food intake were not substantially reduced.
- Low food security—Households reduced the quality, variety, and desirability of their diets, but the quantity of food intake and normal eating patterns were not substantially disrupted.
- Very low food security—At times during the year, eating patterns of one or more household members were disrupted and food intake reduced because the household lacked money and other resources for food. (USDA, September 2013)

The USDA considers household food insecurity to exist if three or more of the following conditions exist:

- Worry of running out of food before getting money to buy more;
- The food supply did not last and there is no money to buy more;
- Unable to afford food to make balanced meals;
- Adults felt they ate less than they should, or
- Adults reduced the size of their meal or skipped meals for 3 or more months. (USDA, September 2013) (Hoefer & Curry, 2012, pp. 61–62)

Food insecurity, especially long-term insecurity, has many negative effects on individuals and families. Food insecurity damages both physical and mental development. This is especially true for infants and toddlers because their brains and bodies are developing so rapidly at many levels and need sufficient and continuous nutrition to provide the energy necessary for growth. For these young children food insecurity, even at moderate levels, results in lifelong risks in critical areas of development including cognitive, social, behavioral, and emotional development (Hoefer & Curry, 2012, p. 62). One of the most common results of malnutrition for infants is low birth weight. "Low birth-weight babies often do not survive, but if they do survive, their impaired immune systems make them more vulnerable to infection and disease" (Seipel, 1999:420–1).

**Test your understanding of Alternative and Possible Developmental Theories by taking this short** Quiz.

# BASIC CONCEPTS FOR UNDERSTANDING INDIVIDUAL DEVELOPMENT

## Identity Development

Spencer and Markstrom-Adams (1990) remind us that according to Erikson, *identity development* is a major developmental task for which the stage is set during childhood and then played out during adolescence. Spencer and Markstrom-Adams (1990:290) suggest that the complexity of identity development increases "as a function of color, behavioral distinctions, language differences, physical features, and long-standing, although frequently not addressed social stereotypes."

In order to acknowledge this complexity, they believe that "new conceptual frame-works shaped by models of normal developmental processes are needed (i.e., as opposed to deviance- and deficit-dependent formulations)." New conceptual paradigms are necessary because "racial and ethnic groups have heretofore been examined through pathology-driven models" (Spencer and Markstrom-Adams, 1990:304). In addition, traditional developmental theories often ignore the interplay of external societal factors with internal cognitive factors.

Sanders Thompson addresses the complexity of African American identity development. She notes the multiple levels of identity that must be considered in efforts to understand African American identity and identity formation. In doing so, she calls for a "multidimensional approach to racial identification." She defines *racial group identification* as "a psychological attachment to one of several social categories available to individuals when the category selected is based on race or skin color and/or a common history, particularly as it relates to oppression and discrimination due to skin color." However, not all members of a group identify to the same extent with all elements of the group's identity (Sanders Thompson, 2001:155). We will look more closely at the issues related to individual and group identity later in this chapter.

## Sexuality

A core element of our identity as human beings is our sexual orientation. *Sexual orientation* is typically defined by researchers as *the sexual attraction, identity, arousals, fantasies, and behaviors individuals have for one sex, the other sex, or both sexes.* In addition, each of these characteristics is seen as existing on a continuum in terms of the degree or frequency the focus is on one sex, the other sex, or both sexes. Traditionally though, people's sexual orientations are divided into two—heterosexual and homosexual or three—heterosexual, bisexual, or gay/lesbian—separate and static categories. In other words, if a man's sexual orientation is gay he is sexually attracted and fantasizes about men, not women. In addition, his sexual and romantic relationships will be with men only (no women) (Vrangalova & Savin-Williams, 2012:85).

Traditional perspectives also tend to assume sexuality is synonymous with sexual behavior. In addition, traditional paradigm thinking makes the assumption that one's sexuality and the nature of its expression remain constant throughout an individual's life span. Many researchers in the area of sexuality have found significant evidence of a much greater variability among humans in terms of sexuality than indicated by traditional paradigm thinking in this area. Researchers have discovered wide ranges of sexual behaviors, sexuality expressed in many ways in addition to sexual behaviors or activities, and variations in sexual orientation at different points in the life span of many people.

### The Kinsey Scale

Alfred Kinsey (1948:638) categorized the wide variations in sexual orientation as a continuum from exclusive interest in same-sex relationships to exclusive interest in opposite-sex relationships. Kinsey created a scale, graduated between heterosexuality and homosexuality, to rate individuals on actual experiences and psychological reactions. The ratings are as follows:

0–Entirely heterosexual.
1–Predominantly heterosexual, only incidentally homosexual.

2–Predominantly heterosexual, but with a distinct homosexual history.

3–Equally heterosexual and homosexual.

4–Predominantly homosexual, but with a distinct heterosexual history.

5–Predominantly homosexual, only incidentally heterosexual.

6–Entirely homosexual.

Recent research suggests (similar to that of Kinsey) rather than two (heterosexual, homosexual) or three categories (heterosexual, bisexual, or gay/lesbian) a five-category classification more effectively describes the complexity and range of sexual orientations. The five categories are:

1. Heterosexual

2. Mostly heterosexual

3. Bisexual

4. Mostly gay/lesbian

5. Gay/lesbian (Vrangalova & Savin-Williams, 2012:85)

Increasingly, scholars of sexual identity and sexual orientation are giving more attention to understanding the needs and realities faced by transgender persons. We will address transgender in the later section of this chapter—Focus: Sexual Orientation.

## Multiple Intelligences

Like sexuality, the concept of *intelligence* is also a significant influence on individual identity development and plays a significant role in the way others define us. We explored traditional notions of intelligence in Chapter 4. Now we will turn to an alternative perspective on intelligence put forth by Gardner (1983, 1993). Gardner's theory of intelligences has important implications not only for understanding variation in individual development but for analyzing schools and other socializing institutions through which people learn. Gardner suggests that, rather than unitary IQ tests, we should "look instead at more naturalistic sources of information about how peoples around the world develop skills important to their way of life" (1993:7).

### Gardner's alternative definition of intelligence

Gardner alternatively defines intelligence as "the ability to solve problems, or to fashion products, that are valued in one or more cultural or community settings" (1993:15). Gardner and his colleagues believe that "human cognitive competence is better described in terms of a set of abilities, talents, or skills . . . call[ed] 'intelligences.' All normal individuals possess each of these skills to some extent; individuals differ in the degree of skill and in the nature of their combination" (1993:15).

Gardner's approach is consistent with alternative paradigm thinking and some postmodern approaches in that rather than focusing only on the "norm" or "center," it focuses on people at the margins in an effort to develop new ways to understand the concept of intelligence and it emphasizes the notion of appreciating local or culture-based knowledge. Gardner notes that in his research he looks at special populations such as "prodigies, idiot savants, autistic children, children with learning disabilities, all of whom exhibit very jagged cognitive profiles—profiles that are extremely difficult to explain in terms of a unitary view of intelligence" (1993:8).

As a result of his research Gardner has posited a set of seven intelligences or "multiple intelligences." He suggests there may be more than seven and that the seven he has discovered are of equal value and not rank ordered in terms of importance (1993:8–9). The seven are:

1. *Linguistic Intelligence:* Ability to use language as a form of expression and communication (e.g., poets).

2. *Logical-mathematical Intelligence:* This is logical and mathematical ability as well as scientific ability. Much of the current IQ testing is based on skills in the areas of linguistic and logical-mathematical intelligence through its testing of verbal and mathematical skills.

3. *Spatial Intelligence:* The ability to form a mental model of a spatial world and to be able to maneuver and operate using that model (e.g., sailors, engineers, surgeons, sculptors, and painters, he suggests have high spatial intelligence).

4. *Musical Intelligence:* The ability to appreciate and use music as a form of expression (e.g., singers, composers, musicians).

5. *Bodily-kinesthetic Intelligence:* The ability to solve problems or to fashion products using one's whole body, or parts of the body (e.g., dancers, athletes, surgeons, craftspeople).

6. *Interpersonal Intelligence:* The ability to understand other people: what motivates them, how they work, how to work cooperatively with them (e.g., successful salespeople, politicians, teachers, clinicians, religious leaders. We might add social workers to this list as well.).

7. *Intrapersonal Intelligence:* a capacity to form an accurate, veridical [truthful] model of oneself and to be able to use that model to operate effectively in life (Gardner, 1983:8–9).

## Creativity

Much of the alternative thinking about multiple intelligences is related to the notion of creativity. **Creativity** can be defined as the ability to solve problems in innovative ways. However, creativity is a multifaceted concept involving much more than simply problem solving. These notions of creativity reflect a number of the dimensions of alternative paradigm thinking including interrelatedness, intuitiveness, heuristic approaches, and multiple ways of knowing. These multiple perspectives can help us appreciate the multidimensional nature of creativity. Through this appreciation we can increase our ability to recognize and nurture creativity in ourselves and in the people with whom we work.

### Stages of creativity

Scholars generally agree there are several stages of the creative process. One model suggests these stages include:

1. Preparation

2. Incubation

3. Insight or illumination

4. Manifestation (Goswami, 1996:56)

*Preparation* and *incubation* focus on "information gathering, theorizing, and unconscious processing." In other words the process begins with collecting information about a new concept or idea, next we try to arrange that information into a possible explanation of the new concept or idea, then there is a period where the information and possible explanation "floats around" in what some people call "the back or our mind." The **insight** or *illumination* stage (think of what we often think as the "lightbulb coming on" or what some refer to as the "aha!" experience) results from our thinking about the idea, both consciously and unconsciously. The final stage, *manifestation*, allows us to concretely articulate and communicate the new concept or idea to others.

It is important to recognize, as we have elsewhere, these stages appear quite linear—1, 2, 3, 4. However, the creative process is really fairly "tangled" or interwoven. For example, the light bulb going (illumination) may lead us to gather more information and allow it to "float around the back or our mind" for another undetermined length of time. This may in turn allow us to develop additional insight about the concept or idea or "polish" it allowing us to more effectively or completely communicate our new, refined, concept or idea (Goswami, 1996:56).

The following sections dealing with alternative perspectives on individual development and behavior are organized according to several "focuses"—people of color, women, sexual orientation, people with disabilities, elders, and men. These focuses are intended to highlight developmental issues and tasks faced by different groups but that are not focused on in traditional paradigm research. The concepts and issues dealt with within the specific "focus" sections, however, are not intended to apply exclusively to the persons or groups discussed in a specific section. As we have stressed, there is much overlap, interrelatedness, and similarity among developmental issues, conditions, and experiences of the groups discussed. We must also be extremely aware of *"diversity within diversity."* There are wide ranges of variability among members of specific groups. Unless we are aware of diversity within diversity, we risk denying the uniqueness of individuals. It is very important also to recognize the special developmental complexities faced by persons who are simultaneously members of more than one diverse group.

The division into "focus" sections that follow is simply intended to assist us in organizing the materials. It cannot be overstated, though, that we must not allow this organizational convenience to hide the interconnections among the individuals, groups, and experiences we explore. We do not want to obscure or oversimplify the reality that issues related to color, gender, sexual orientation, class, age, disabling conditions, and religion interact in powerful ways that influence the developmental experiences of different individuals in countless complex and different ways.

**Test your understanding of Basic Concepts for Understanding Individual Development by taking this short** Quiz.

# FOCUS: PEOPLE OF COLOR

## Introduction

This chapter, and later chapters as well, present the work of a number of scholars from a variety of disciplines and perspectives who are people of color as well as dominant group scholars. In some cases these perspectives give an alternative voice to existing and traditional developmental models, and in some cases entirely alternative perspectives on development are suggested.

Often alternative perspectives on existing models and completely alternative models offered by these scholars are marked most notably by differences in themes running throughout and transcending developmental stages, phases, periods, or eras. The differences in theme seem to indicate the complex nature of differential life experiences of people of color and whites in U.S. society. Equally important, perhaps, are the similarities marked by shared conceptions of the developmental needs and milestones so fundamentally a part of the developmental journeys of all who are members of the human community. Once again we experience commonality and difference as simultaneous and inseparable elements of humans' developmental experiences. Before we look at specific alternatives, it may be helpful to consider some basic information about people of color in the United States.

## Developmental Perspectives and People of Color

Identity development theory, especially regarding African Americans, has progressed through several reconceptualizations over the past 15 to 20 years. However, this has not been a linear progression. Existing conceptualizations can overlap and complement each other. This reflects the complexity and multidimensional nature of attempts to fully understand how identities are formed. For example, Sanders Thompson notes four different types of identity regarding African Americans. *Physical identity* refers to "a sense of acceptance and comfort with the physical attributes of African Americans." *Psychological identity* refers to "the individual's sense of concern for and commitment to and pride in the racial group." *Sociopolitical identity* refers "to the individual's attitude toward the social and political issues facing the African American community." Finally, *cultural identity* refers to "an individual's awareness and knowledge of as well as commitment to the cultural traditions of African Americans" (2001:159).

In addition, she describes three prominent conceptualizations of African American identity development: Nigrescence models, Africentric models, and group or social identity models (Sanders Thompson, 2001). We will explore Nigrescence and Africentic models in the following sections.

## Nigrescence/Black Identity Development Models

The most influential model of African American identity development was conceptualized by Cross. Cross's original model of African American identity development "emphasized that African Americans differ in their degree of identification with African American culture" (Parks, Carter, Gushue, 1996:624). This differential identification was tied to stages of identity development.

Sue and Sue (in Parks et al., 1996:624–625) have suggested the catalyst propelling individuals through the stages was societal oppression. Helms noted the "crucial role that the experience of the difference in 'social power' plays in the process of racial identity development" (in Parks et al., 1996:625). The above authors suggest that given the central place of oppression by the dominant group of non-dominant group members, the model can be applied to other non-dominant groups.

Cross's four stages, Pre-encounter, Encounter, Immersion-Emersion, and Internalization, are described in more detail below.

1. *Pre-encounter:* The individual views the "world from a White frame of reference" and devalues or denies her/his Blackness in thinking, actions, and behaviors. The person's frame of reference is referred to as "deracinated" and is characterized by a white normative standard in which attitudes are "pro-White and anti-Black."

2. *Encounter:* The individual experiences significant events or situations, such as housing discrimination because of skin color, that dramatically call into question previous attitudes and frames of reference. This stage involves the realization that his or her previous frame of reference is inappropriate and results in the decision to "develop a Black identity."

3. *Immersion-Emersion:* This involves a transition to a new Black identity in which the old frame of reference is discarded. This stage involves immersion in "Blackness" through intense attachment to elements of black culture and withdrawal from interactions with other ethnic groups. The tendency here is to glorify African American people and to denigrate white people.

4. *Internalization:* The person at this stage achieves a "sense of inner security and self-confidence with his or her Blackness." At this point there is a general decline of strong anti-white feelings, although African American is the primary reference group. "This person moves toward a more pluralistic, nonracist perspective" (Parham, 1989:189–190; Cross, 1971).

Parham stresses the importance of recognizing the highly individualized nature of racial identity development. He emphasizes:

recognizing that within-group variability is an important element in understanding Black people cannot be overstated. Tendencies to make between-group comparisons (Black vs. White) and/or to overgeneralize (all Blacks are alike) provides little, if any, conceptual clarity and should be avoided, or at least used with caution. (1989:223)

## Africentric/African-Centered Models

Bent-Goodley (2005) provides a framework for approaching African American identity development at individual, family, and community levels based on an African-centered worldview that recognizes both the history of oppression and the strengths and principles of African-centered culture reflecting "the best of Africa." This approach is consistent with the definition of African-centered social work as "a method of social work practice based on traditional African philosophical assumptions that are used to explain and to solve human and societal problems" (Schiele, 1997:804 in Bent-Goodley, 2005:199).

Bent-Goodley presents eight principles central to this perspective in a linear fashion, but stresses that "they are connected as part of the larger African-centered paradigm." She further explains this connectedness, "collectively, the principles help individuals 'understand and respect the sameness of self and of other individuals, and to have a high sense of responsibility for the well-being and harmonious interconnection between self and community'" (Harvey and Hill, 2004:68 in Bent-Goodley, 2005:199). The principles guiding this perspective are:

1. *Fundamental Goodness:* An important principle of the African-centered paradigm is that each person is fundamentally good.

2. *Self-Knowledge:* A fundamental social work principle is to begin where the client is. However, the African-centered principle of self-knowledge encourages the practitioner to begin where the practitioner is.

3. *Communalism* is defined as "sensitivity to the interdependence of people and the notion that group concerns transcend individual strivings" (Harvey, 2001:227 in Bent-Goodley, 2005:199).

4. *Interconnectedness:* The principles of interconnectedness and collective struggle are evident throughout the African American experience. Interconnectedness "recognizes that people 'are dependent upon each other; they are, in essence, considered as one'" (Graham, 1999:258 in Bent-Goodley, 2005:199).

5. *Spirituality* is another critical component of the African-centered paradigm. Spirituality can be defined as "the sense of the sacred and divine" (Martin and Martin 2002:1 in Bent-Goodley, 2005:200).

6. *Self-reliance:* Another essential component of the African-centered paradigm is self-reliance. . . . Although the collective experience is always at the center, members of the community are expected to make a contribution to the community and society.

7. *Language and the Oral Tradition* are also a part of the African-centered paradigm. Language brings people together and develops a basis of understanding. . . . The flow of communication or rhythm is also a part of the oral traditions.

8. *Thought and Practice:* The principle of thought and practice is primarily from the Black feminist tradition. . . . However, this principle is relevant to the African-centered perspective in that it emphasizes combining knowledge with social action. The idea of having knowledge of an injustice without engaging in planned change to eradicate the problem is antithetical to the African-centered paradigm (Bent-Goodley, 2005:198–200).

## Multidimensional Model of Racial Identity

Another alternative model developed to help us understand the complexity of the development experiences and their influence on identities and behaviors of African Americans and potentially other groups with minority status (women, lesbians, gay men, and bisexuals) is the *Multidimensional Model of Racial Identity* (MMRI). "The MMRI defines *racial identity* in African Americans as the significance and qualitative meaning that individuals attribute to their membership within the Black racial group within their self-concepts" (Sellers et al., 1998:26–27). The MMRI is based on four assumptions that are the foundation of the model and four dimensions of racial identity that encompass the level of importance and the meaning of race for individual African American racial identity.

The four assumptions:

1. Identities are situationally [environmentally] influenced as well as being stable qualities of the person.

2. Individuals have a number of different identities and these identities are hierarchically ordered.

3. Individuals' perception of the racial identity is the most valid indicator of their identity.

4. MMRI is primarily concerned with the status of an individual's racial identity as opposed to its development. . . . [The focus is on] the significance and the nature of an individual's racial identity at a given point in time in the individual's life as opposed to placing an individual in a particular stage along a particular developmental sequence [stage] (Sellers et al., 1998:23).

Using the earlier four assumptions as a foundation, MMRI proposes four dimensions, along with subcategories in dimensions of *regard* and philosophies related to *ideology.* Two of the dimensions are *racial salience* and *the centrality of the identity.* These two dimensions focus on the importance of race as part of an individual's personal definition of self. The second two dimensions are *the regard in which the person holds the group associated with the identity* and *the ideology associated with the identity* (Sellers et al., 1998:24).

The four dimensions are described as follows, along with subcategories:

1. *Salience* refers to the extent to which one's race is a relevant part of one's self-concept at a particular moment in a particular situation.

2. *Centrality* refers to the extent to which a person normatively defines himself or herself with regard to race. Unlike salience, centrality is, by definition, relatively stable across situations.

3. *Regard* . . . is the extent to which the individual feels positively about his or her race (Sellers et al., 1998:25–26).

   a. *Private regard* refers to how positively or negatively an individual feels toward other African Americans and about being an African American.

   b. *Public regard* is "defined as the extent to which individuals feel other view African Americans positively or negatively" (Sellers et al., 1998:26).

4. *Ideology* . . . represents the person's philosophy about the ways in which African Americans should live and interact with society (Sellers et al., 1998:27).

   a. *Nationalist ideology* focuses on the "uniqueness of being Black." This "ideology posits that African American should be in control of the own destiny with minimal input from other groups." A person with this ideology is "more likely to participate in African American organizations" (Sellers et al., 1998:27).

   b. "The *oppressed minority ideology* emphasize the similarities between the oppression that African Americans face and that of other groups." A person with this ideology is keenly aware of oppression toward African Americans, but also sees a link between this oppression and that faced by other minority groups. This person "is more likely to view coalition building as the most appropriate strategy for social change" (Sellers et al., 1998:27–28).

   c. The *assimilationist ideology* focuses on the "similarities between African Americans and the rest of American society." A person with this ideology "can be an activist for social change; however, he or she is likely to feel that African Americans need to work with the system to change it" (Sellers et al., 1998:27).

   d. "The *humanist ideology* emphasized the similarities among all humans. . . . [Persons with this ideology] are likely to view everyone as belonging to the same race—the human race. A humanist ideology is often concerned more with 'larger' issues facing the human race (such as the environment, peace, and hunger)" (Sellers et al., 1998:28).

## Invisibility and Microaggressions

Work, especially by professionals and scholars of African descent such as that described in the previous sections, continues to expand our understanding of the complexities of identity development for African Americans. Work by Franklin (1999) conceptualizing one source of challenge and opportunity influencing African American male identity development is that of an *invisibility syndrome*. Franklin defines **invisibility** as "a psychological experience wherein the person feels that his or her personal identity and ability are undermined by racism in a myriad of interpersonal circumstances" (1999). Franklin further explains that invisibility is "an inner struggle with the feeling that one's talents, abilities, personality, and worth are not valued or even recognized because of prejudice and racism." He suggests that understanding this concept is essential to understanding the lifelong developmental struggles faced by men of African descent. He further suggests that this concept can be applied to women of African descent as well. Franklin (1999) believes that racial identity development theory is important and complementary to the invisibility syndrome. However, he believes:

> the scope of the invisibility syndrome paradigm is broader . . . than the racial identity model because it allows for interpretation of greater domains of human experiences that make up one's personal identity, as impacted by encounters of racism. In addition, the paradigm is intended to help assess personal self-efficacy and resilience in the face of encounters with racialized environments.

Specifically, the invisibility syndrome includes seven dynamic and interacting elements that represent intrapsychic processes experienced by African American men when faced with either a single racist encounter or the accumulation of racist encounters over time. Franklin uses Pierce's (1988, 1992 in Franklin, 1999) concept of microaggressions to further clarify the nature of these encounters. According to Pierce, *microaggressions* are:

> verbal offensive mechanisms and nonverbal, sometimes kinetic offensive mechanisms that control 'space, time, energy, and mobility of the Black, while producing feelings of degradation, and erosion of self-confidence and self-image' (1988:31), which, in their pervasiveness, have a cumulative deleterious psychological effect over time.

To take a closer look at themes, specific examples, messages through racial microaggressions, see Table 6.2.

According to Franklin, when these encounters occur:

1. One feels a lack of recognition or appropriate acknowledgment;
2. One feels there is no satisfaction or gratification from the encounter (it is painful and injurious);
3. One feels self-doubt about legitimacy—such as "Am I in the right place; should I be here?";
4. There is no validation from the experience "Am I a person of worth?"—or the person seeks some form of corroboration of experiences from another person;
5. One feels disrespected (this is led to by the previous elements and is linked to the following);

## Table 6.2 Examples of Racial Microaggressions

| Theme | Microaggresion | Message |
|---|---|---|
| *Alien in own land* When Asian Americans and Latino Americans are assumed to be foreign-born | "Where are you from?" <br> "Where were you born?" <br> A person asking an Asian American to teach them words in their native language | You are not American. <br> You are a foreigner. |
| *Ascription of intelligence* Assigning intelligence to a person of color on the basis of their race | "You are a credit to your race." <br> "You are so articulate." <br> Asking an Asian person to help with a math or science problem | People of color are generally not as intelligent as Whites. <br> It is unusual for someone of your race to be intelligent. <br> All Asians are intelligent and good in math/sciences. |
| *Color blindness* Statements that indicate that a White person does not want to acknowledge race | "When I look at you, I don't see color." <br> • "America is a melting pot." <br> • "There is only one race, the human race." | Denying a person of color's racial/ethnic experiences. <br> Assimilate/acculturate to the dominant culture. <br> Denying the individual as a racial/cultural being. |
| *Criminality/assumption of criminal status* A person of color is presumed to be dangerous, criminal, or deviant on the basis of their color | A White man or woman clutching their purse or checking their wallet as a Black or Latino approaches or passes <br> A store owner following a customer of color around the store <br> A White person waits to ride the next elevator when a person of color is on it | You are a criminal. <br> You are going to steal/ You are poor/ You do not belong. <br> You are dangerous. |
| *Denial of individual racism* A statement made when Whites deny their racial biases | "I'm not racist. I have several Black friends." <br> • "As a woman, I know what you go through as a racial minority." | I am immune to racism because I have friends of color. <br> Your racial oppression is no different than my gender oppression. I can't be a racist. I'm like you. |
| *Myth of meritocracy* Statements which assert that race does not play a role in life successes | "I believe the most qualified person should get the job." <br> "Everyone can succeed in this society, if they work hard enough." | Assimilate to dominant culture. |
| *Pathologizing cultural values/communication styles* The notion that the values and communication styles of the dominant/White culture are ideal | Asking a Black person: "Why do you have to be so loud/animated? Just calm down." <br> To an Asian or Latino person: "Why are you so quiet? We want to know what you think. Be more verbal." "Speak up more." <br> Dismissing an individual who brings up race/culture in work/school setting | Leave your cultural baggage outside. |

*(Continued)*

## Table 6.2 Continued

| Theme | Microaggresion | Message |
|---|---|---|
| *Second-class citizen* <br> Occurs when a White person is given preferential treatment as a consumer over a person of color | Person of color mistaken for a service worker <br> Having a taxi cab pass a person of color and pick up a White passenger <br> Being ignored at a store counter as attention is given to the White customer behind you <br> "You people . . ." | People of color are servants to Whites. They couldn't possibly occupy high-status positions. <br> You are likely to cause trouble and/ or travel to a dangerous neighborhood. <br> Whites are more valued customers than people of color. <br> You don't belong. You are a lesser being. |
| *Environmental microaggressions* <br> Macro-level microaggressions, which are more apparent on systemic and environmental levels | A college or university with buildings that are all named after White heterosexual upper class males <br> Television shows and movies that feature predominantly White people, without representation of people of color <br> Overcrowding of public schools in communities of color <br> Overabundance of liquor stores in communities of color | You don't belong/ You won't succeed here. There is only so far you can go. <br> You are an outsider/ You don't exist. <br> People of color don't/ shouldn't value education. <br> People of color are deviant. |

Source: Sue et al. (2007). Racial microaggressions in everyday life: Implication for clinical practice, *American psychologist*. Washington D.C.: American Psychological Association.

6. One's sense of dignity is compromised and challenged;

7. One's basic identity is shaken, if not uprooted.

Franklin and others (Parham, 1999; Yeh, 1999) caution that, while these feelings cause confusion and alienation in the person experiencing them, they can also provide opportunities for growth, resolution, and increasing resiliency. However, they must be recognized, and support, knowledge, and understanding on the part of culturally competent professionals or community members are often needed. For example, Franklin points out that, "Embracing the recognition and supportive identity attachments in the brotherhood of other African American men would be an example of a positive counterweight determining visibility." Development of a bicultural identity and worldview so important to the survival and thriving of people of color in a predominantly white environment is

> prevented by invisibility . . . because of racism's rejection and intolerance of the group of origin's defining attributes (e.g., skin color, intelligence, language, spiritual beliefs). Racism's unconditional rejection of people puts the individual's task of identity development in a quandary. There are social pressures on the individual, as a member of a minority group, to assimilate, and 'tolerance'—not acceptance—is the normative code of behavior of the dominant group.

Positive outcomes are influenced by three types of racial socialization
Protective, proactive, and adaptive racial socialization are identified as three distinct views of the world that Black male adolescents can acquire from messages and experiences given by caregivers.

1. Those having protective racial socialization beliefs view the world as distrustful and filled with racially hostile intents; they learn caution and are encouraged to succeed despite these circumstances.

2. Those who experience more proactive racial socialization are encouraged to focus on personal talent and cultural heritage, and less on racial hostility. Within proactive racial socialization are three important factors: spiritual and religious coping, cultural pride reinforcement, and extended family caring.

3. Adaptive racial socialization is represented as an integration of protective and proactive beliefs (Stevenson 1997 in Franklin 1999).

In commenting on Franklin's invisibility construct, Parham (1999) stressed the importance of a social change perspective, respect for spirituality and the importance of community in achieving positive outcomes leading to "visibility" in response to experiences of invisibility. He suggests that a powerful means of positively addressing invisibility is the development of a social advocacy or change perspective on the part of both the worker and the person experiencing the impact of invisibility to address the causes of racist encounters and environments. In addition, Parham (1999) points to the importance of a spiritual perspective:

> Still, there are dynamics associated with the energy and life force of African descent people that demand that the model address the spiritual dimension of the self as well. The African-centered worldview conceptualizes the world as a spiritual reality, where the manifestation of spiritness is the essence of one's humanity. From this viewpoint, it is therefore reasonable to believe that therapeutic healing must include a deliberate focus on the spiritness that permeates the cognitive, affective, and behavioral parts of the self.

## Multiracial Identities

Jackson and Samuels point out that "according to the 2010 U. S. census, approximately 9 million individuals report multiracial identities" and by 2050 up to 20 percent of Americans could identify as multiracial (Jackson & Samuels, 2011).

Fong, Spickard, & Ewalt (1995:726) stress the significant benefits and strengths that can accrue from positive identity as a multiracial person. They note that "At the individual level, psychological benefits may accrue to a multiracial individual from opportunities to adopt a multiracial consciousness. For individuals of mixed parentage, it is generally healthful and empowering to embrace both, or all, parts of themselves." Other members of communities of color do not always share the potential benefits at the individual level of identifying oneself as a multiracial person.

### Competing individual and community values

Fong et al. note the complex and often conflicting concerns about multiracial identity for communities of color. They note that

> Some African American civic leaders, for example, worry that if "biracial" and mixed become accepted ethnic identities, individuals with dual heritages will cease to identity as African American and that their numbers and talents will become unavailable to the African American community. Mass (1992) echoed this concern, reporting that there is fear in the Japanese American Community that it may "disappear" because mixed people may "hasten assimilation into mainstream culture." (Fong, et al. 1995: 726)

## Biracial and Multiracial Identity Development

Given the complexities, ambiguities, and competing concerns about biracial and multiracial identify at the community level, it is nevertheless important to explore the processes and struggles individuals must contend with in the development of positive multiracial identity. We will first explore a model for understanding the processes of biracial identity development across the lifespan. Then we will look at some processes and issues of specific concern for biracial and multiracial children and their parents.

Aldarondo (2001) suggests that the model of biracial identity development provided by Kerwin and Ponterotto (1995) is helpful, especially given that it is based on empirical research and incorporates a number of prior models. This model is outlined in the box below

### Parenting biracial children

Parents can help children develop a positive biracial or multiracial identity by providing "their children the structure and the words that help them make sense of their experiences as they develop their self-concept and self-esteem. . . . Providing open communication about race and an interracial label validates and fosters the child's rudimentary interracial self-concept." ". . . In valuing each of the child's racial and ethnic heritages, parents structure emotional safety and confidence through a positive interracial label and through modeling an ability to discuss racial and ethnic differences openly" (Kich, 1992:308).

### A strengths-based approach

Parents of biracial children need special understanding of several important factors to help their child build a positive biracial self-concept:

1. *Fostering ego strength:* Early ego-enhancing treatment of the child in the family including building "secure attachments, the support of individuation,

---

## Biracial and Bicultural Identity Development

### A Model of Biracial Development

1. Preschool Stage: Individuals become aware of racial and ethnic differences. The timing of awareness may be influenced by whether or not biracial children have exposure to multiple racial groups and whether or not their parents discuss racial and ethnic differences.

2. Entry to School: Biracial children face questions about their identity from other children in school. The child begins to place him or herself into racial or ethnic categories. This experience is highly influenced by such contextual issues as the level of school integration or diversity and the availability of role models from different racial or ethnic groups.

3. Preadolescence: The biracial individual becomes sensitive to differences such as physical appearance, language, and culture.

4. Adolescence: This is often a difficult time for biracial persons "because of the external pressure to choose one group over another."

5. College/Young Adulthood: "During this time period identification is still primarily with one culture, but individuals are more likely to reject others' expectations for a singular racial identity and instead move toward appreciation of their multiple heritages" (Aldarondo, 2001:243).

6. Adulthood: "During this time individuals continue to integrate the disparate pieces of their own background to form their racial identity" Aldarondo, 2001:243. As is the case with many linear stage theories, Aldarondo suggests that successful integration of a complete biracial identity depends on successful resolution of the prior stages.

the fostering of social and physical competencies, and encouragement of self-assertion."

2. *Biracial labeling:* Presentation of a biracial label to the child by the parents assists in developing a biracial identity. This is not always necessary but is helpful often since the child "must assimilate a racial and ethnic label that is more complex and less readily available outside of his or her family than the labels of Black, White, Asian, Chicano, and so on."

3. *Ambivalence and racial material:* Parents need to realize that "their children's racial ambivalence is a developmental attainment that allows the continued exploration of racial identity."

4. *Multiracial environment for parents and children:* A multiethnic community and social environment seems basic to positive biracial identity development. This is probably even more important for a biracial child than for either an African American or white child. (Jacobs, 1992:204–205)

## FOCUS: WHITENESS/WHITE IDENTITY

As we learned from exploring the notion of paradigms and in our discussion of Whiteness in Chapter 2, the dominant group tends to measure and value worth in terms of standards of whiteness. However, the concept of whiteness itself is such a "taken for granted" dimension of the traditional paradigm that as a racial construct it is largely unexamined.

Helms suggests that whites often deny "that a White *racial* group exists that benefits from White privilege" (1994:305).

Recognition of the importance of including content about whiteness and white privilege in social work education, specifically, is increasing. However, the importance of this content was recognized earlier by other disciplines, such as education and psychology. As a result, this content is available and can be adapted to social work education. For example, Abrams and Gibson (2007) have used content and educational approaches from other disciplines, as well as past models of social work diversity education, to argue for the importance of giving more attention to white privilege, white racial identity development, and whiteness in social work education.

Abrams and Gibson (2007:148) suggest:

teaching about White privilege is fundamental to understanding the systematic oppression of people of color and raising self-awareness about practitioners' roles and responsibilities with culturally diverse clientele and communities. An additional benefit of this alternative model is the opportunity for the majority group of social work students (namely White students) to explore the meaning of their own ethnic and racial identities in relation to those whom they will encounter in their fieldwork and future professional practice.

They remind us of the social work profession's history of attempts to address diversity and oppression in education for practice. They describe three models used to attempt to provide content in this area. First, was the "assimilation" model that is considered by most to be outdated and has been largely rejected. This model "viewed ethnic racial minorities as deviant and encouraged them to acculturate to culturally dominant Anglo-Saxon norms." Second, the "culturally sensitive practice" model, popular in the 1980s, "targeted change in workers and agencies because of their ethnocentricity." In this model, the focus of changes shifted from the client to workers as well as their agencies. Third, was the "anti-racism" model. This model was more radical and proposed that "individuals in positions of power play a role in perpetuating the institutionally racist practices that systematically disadvantage ethnic and cultural minorities" (Abrams and Gibson, 2007:149). They suggest, however, that none of these models incorporate the importance of white privilege and "its relationship to racial oppression, power, and inequities in access to resources" (Abrams and Gibson, 2007:150). White privilege was defined and discussed at length in Chapter 2. In addition, these models did not address whiteness. Abrams and Gibson argue:

> The inclusion of content on oppression and social justice without mention of White privilege creates an imbalance in content as it silently maintains an assumption about the "hidden center" of White privilege. . . . In addition, the absence of content on Whiteness deprives White students of the opportunity to reflect on their own ethnic and cultural identities . . . or sift through ideas about how racism affects their own lives. (2007:150)

Further, they note, "in fact, most White people typically deny belonging to any racial or ethnic group and are unable to pinpoint how Whiteness occupies a center or mainstream position in society or even in their own personal lives" (Abrams and Gibson, 2007:151). As a result, it is very important that significant attention to whiteness, white privilege, and white racial identity theory be included in our effort to more fully understand the complexities of human behavior and the social environment.

## White Identity Development Models

Based on the same structural and developmental approach as identity development for people of color and women, white identity models are receiving more attention. Table 6.3 provides a helpful comparison of several models of white racial identity development.

# FOCUS: WOMEN

As in the case of accounting for the developmental experiences of people of color, traditional approaches to research on human development have too often neglected or inaccurately portrayed women. However, a growing body of research on the developmental experiences and themes of women is emerging as a result of the work of a number of individuals and groups from a variety of disciplines and perspectives. The work of Sandra Harding, Evelyn Fox Keller, and others in the natural sciences (Harding, 1986; Keller, 1985); Nancy Chodorow in psychiatry and psychoanalysis (Chodorow, 1978); Jean Baker Miller and her colleagues at the Stone Center for Developmental Services and Studies at Wellesley College in development and psychology (Jordan et al., 1991; Miller, 1986); Mary Belenky and her coresearchers with the Education for Women's Development Project in education (Belenky et al., 1986); Carol Gilligan's work to increase our understanding of women's developmental experiences (Gilligan, 1982); Patricia Hill Collins's work in the area of African American feminist thought (Collins, 1990); and many others have created

### Table 6.3 White Racial Identity Models

| Author | Component | Description |
|---|---|---|
| Helms (1990) | Stage 1: Contact | Unaware of own racial identity |
| | Stage 2: Disintegration | First acknowledgment of White identity |
| | Stage 3: Reintegration | Idealizes Whites: denigrates Blacks |
| | Stage 4: Pseudoindependence | Intellectualized acceptance of own and others' race |
| | Stage 5: Immersion/Emersion | Honest appraisal of racism and significance of Whiteness |
| | Stage 6: Autonomy | Internalizes a multicultural identity |
| Sue and Sue (1990) | Stage 1: Conformity | Ethnocentric, limited knowledge of other races |
| | Stage 2: Dissonance | Inconsistencies in belief system |
| | Stage 3: Resistance and Immersion | Person challenges own racism |
| | Stage 4: Introspection | Acceptance of being White |
| | Stage 5: Integrative Awareness | Self-fulfillment with regard to racial identity |
| Scott (1997) | Type I: Noncontact | Status quo; denies racism; seeks power and privilege |
| | Type II: Claustrophobic | Other races are "closing in" on him; disillusionment with the American dream; feels power and privilege are going to other races |
| | Type III: Conscious Identity | Dissonance between existing belief system and reality |
| | Type IV: Empirical | Questioning their role in racism and oppression and their struggle for unrealistic power from oppression |
| | Type V: Optimal | Person understands how his struggle for power and privilege has caused racism and oppression |

Source: Adapted from Helms, J. (1990), Sue and Sue (1990), and Scott (1997).

tremendously helpful resources to begin to include and understand the alternative perspectives of women. The work of these researchers and many others is unfolding and very much in process. We will look at a number of these efforts in the sections that follow.

## Women and Development: A Different Voice

In current discussions of women's development, perhaps most influential has been the work of Carol Gilligan (1982). It is important to recognize as we explore the work of Gilligan and other researchers working in the area of women's development that there is a great deal of mutual influence and integration of one another's work among many of the scholars working in the area of women's development. This cooperation, interconnectedness, and interrelatedness are consistent with the alternative paradigm generally. It also reflects a recurring theme or pattern in women's development itself. Through her own research and the integration of research of others, such as Jean Baker Miller and Nancy Chodorow, for example, Gilligan offers an alternative perspective on human development that seeks to focus on and include women's developmental issues to a much greater extent than the traditional developmental approaches of Freud, Erikson, Piaget, Kohlberg, and Levinson.

As a result of her research and that of others, Gilligan suggests the need for a paradigmatic shift that includes rather than excludes the perspectives, experiences, and views of the world of women. In her work she extends developmental paradigms to include and reflect the unique experiences of women. The importance of this extension of developmental paradigms to include women is underscored by the reality that women constitute between 52 percent and 53 percent of the population. As we have noted before, women are hardly a minority, although they have minority status in the United States and most other societies due to their unequal power and access to resources.

Gilligan's work to include and better understand women's development resulted in her discovery of a "different voice" that she found was characterized not necessarily by gender but by theme. She found this theme originally as a result of her efforts to understand the development of moral decision making among women. The voice, Gilligan asserts, is not necessarily exclusively male or female but reflects two different modes of thought. One mode focuses on individualization and rights, the other on connectedness and responsibility. In other words, one mode reflects the dimension of separateness and impersonality consistent with traditional paradigm thinking. The other mode reflects the dimension of interrelatedness and the value of personal experiences and relationships characteristic of alternative paradigm thinking. Although these themes are not necessarily tied to gender, according to Gilligan, they do seem to reflect the different developmental experiences of males and females. The theme of relatedness and connection has also been found by a number of other researchers working in the area of women's development. The work of Jean Baker Miller (and her colleagues), published in 1976, reported that "women's sense of self becomes very much organized around being able to make and then maintain affiliation and relationships" (1976:83). Miller and her colleagues at the Stone Center for Developmental Services and Studies at Wellesley College came to refer to this significant and recurring theme in the developmental experiences of women as "self-in-relation theory" (Jordan et al., 1991:vi).

Gilligan's work and the work of others takes us beyond traditional paradigms of development by presenting evidence that "normal" development may very well be different for females than for males for a variety of reasons. Gilligan suggests that traditional models and scales of human development based almost exclusively on the study of white males do not readily or necessarily apply to the development of females. She suggests that these differences in developmental experiences and patterns between males and females often result in depictions of females in traditional developmental models as developing "less normally" than males. Rather than women developing less normally, this alternative approach posits that "the failure of women to fit existing models of human growth may point to a problem in the representation, a limitation in the conception of human condition, an omission of certain truths about life" (Gilligan, 1982:2). In other words, the problem is one of model not femaleness.

## Women and Identity Development

Gilligan's work focuses on women's identity formation and moral development. Her research focuses on adolescence and adulthood. However, she extends her approach to include assumptions about development during infancy and childhood as well. Gilligan's work is especially helpful in expanding understanding of the concepts of identity formation and moral development. These are central concepts in the traditional developmental models of Erikson and Kohlberg. As we will see, a shift in perspective, in this case from male to female, can result in dramatic shifts in the meanings attached to such apparently universal developmental issues as identity formation and moral development.

Gilligan reminds us that traditional models for explaining human development are often put forth as resulting directly from scientific, objective, and value-neutral processes. When we find that many of these models are based exclusively on the experiences of males, although their assertions about development are applied equally to females, the assumptions of objectivity and neutrality must be questioned. We are reminded of our earlier assertions about paradigms as human constructions subject to the limitations of the perspectives held by the humans creating them. This is essentially the case Gilligan makes about seeing life, specifically identity formation and moral development, through men's eyes only. As is the case with virtually all researchers concerned with individual development—both traditional and alternative—a primary concern of Gilligan's is that of identity formation. How do we come to see ourselves as we see ourselves? How we see ourselves has countless implications for how we behave.

Research on gender differences is not new. However, such research becomes problematic when "different" becomes defined as "better or worse than." When women do not conform to a standard based on men's interpretation of research data, the conclusion all too often is that there is something wrong with women, not with the standard (Gilligan, 1982:14). In the case here of individuation and relatedness, the perspective of the observer has a good deal to do with the value accorded developmental experiences and behaviors of the observed. From Freud's and Erikson's male-centered perspective, identity constructed around attachment is ultimately a source of developmental weakness; from Chodorow's female-centered perspective, it is a source of developmental strength.

## Women and moral development

Another core concern of researchers attempting to understand human behavior both from traditional and alternative perspectives is that of *moral development*. How do we come to define what is right and wrong and how do we come to base our decisions and actions on our definitions of what is right and what is wrong? Gilligan's approach to moral development emerged from looking at women's lives. Her alternative model is marked not by age-based developmental stages as are most traditional models— Kohlberg's for example—but by themes or principles. Her model integrates the following principles or themes:

1. Moral problems arise out of conflicting responsibilities rather than competing rights.

2. Moral problems require resolution through thinking that is contextual and narrative rather than formal and abstract.

3. Morality centers on the activity of care; it centers around responsibilities and relationships in the same way that morality as fairness centers on understanding rights and rules.

This framework's emphasis on context, relationship, and interrelatedness has much in common with several of the dimensions of alternative paradigm thinking that we explored earlier (Chapter 2).

In contrast, Kohlberg's is a morality focused on a reflective understanding of human rights. A morality of rights differs from a morality of responsibility in that it emphasizes separation rather than connection and sees the individual rather than the

relationship as primary. Gilligan believes that a perspective on morality that emphasizes responsibility and relationship does not mutually exclude a sense of individuality
or autonomy. She suggests, as Loevinger does, that we see autonomy in the context of
relationship. Loevinger urges us to move away from traditional either/or dichotomous
thinking about morality and suggests we replace this thinking with "a feeling for the
complexity and multifaceted character of real people in real situations" (Loevinger in
Gilligan, 1982:21).

The responsibility perspective focuses on the limitations of any particular resolution and is concerned with the conflicts that remain. This conception does not focus
on single solutions to single moral problems but focuses instead on the connectedness
of any solution to an interdependent network of other problems and other solutions.
In other words, it is an integrative, holistic, contextual approach consistent with one of
the basic dimensions of our alternative paradigms and with social work purposes and
values.

The gender implications of the two very different views of moral development are
significant, Gilligan believes. Women's moral judgments show difference between the
sexes but also give an alternate conception of maturity. Women bring to the life cycle a
different and valuable point of view and a different and valuable ordering of priorities.
For Gilligan (1982:23) "the elusive mystery of women's development lies in its recognition of the continuing importance of attachment in the human life cycle." Certainly such
a perspective is an important one for social workers.

Gilligan cautions, though, that these different themes of moral development are not
"gendered" in any absolute sense and should not result in generalizations about women's
or men's development. Indeed, some women's sense of morality may be rights-focused
and some men's may be responsibility-focused. However, given the differing findings of
her work with female subjects and Kohlberg's work with male subjects, it is understandable that these differing notions of morality would be sources of uncertainty, confusion,
and fear for any person whose sense of determining what is correct and "right" behavior comes from the other perspective. She suggests, for example, that it is understandable that a morality of rights and noninterference may appear unsettling to women in
its potential justification of indifference and unconcern. It is also clearly understandable that from a male perspective, a morality of responsibility appears inconclusive and
diffuse, given its insistent contextual relativism (Gilligan, 1982:23 and 123ff).

Another significant perspective that emerges from Gilligan's research is her notion
of an *ethic of care*, more clearly delineated within women's identities and sense of
morality. This ethic of care emphasizing relationship and responsibility for others
is interconnected with the concept of "integrity" discussed by traditional paradigm
researchers such as Erikson. *Integrity*, a focus of much adult developmental thinking,
has a different (and richer, more complex) meaning for women, "because women's
sense of integrity appears to be entwined with an ethic of care . . . to see themselves as women is to see themselves in a relationship of connection . . . the ethic
or responsibility can become a self-chosen anchor of personal integrity and strength"
(Gilligan, 1982:171).

Gilligan believes that an "ethic of care" has significant implications for such societal concerns as aggression and hierarchy or inequality. She suggests that "women's
development delineates the path not only to a less violent life but also to a maturity
realized through interdependence and taking care." She points out that "just as the
language of responsibilities provides a weblike imagery of relationships to replace a

hierarchical ordering that dissolves with the coming of equality, so the language of rights underlines the importance of including in the network of care not only the other but also the self." She believes that "in the different voice of women lies the truth of an ethic of care, the tie between relationship and responsibility, and the origins of aggression in the failure of connection" (1982:172–173). Such a perspective on care, relationship, and responsibility has much in common with the historical mission and values of social work, with their emphases on inherent human worth and dignity and with social change to achieve social and economic justice and maximize individual and collective human potential.

> **Human Behavior**
>
> **Practice Behavior Example:** Critique and apply knowledge to understand person and environment.
>
> **Critical Thinking Question:** How might Carol Gilligan's *ethic of care* perspective on women's development be applied to men's development? Give one strength and one limitation of its application to men?

The "ethic of care" is also consistent with our alternative paradigm's concern for integration and interrelatedness. The commonality is perhaps most evident in Gilligan's suggestion that it is essential to begin to integrate the two disparate voices reflected in traditional models and in her alternate model of human development. She believes the two voices are not mutually exclusive: "While an ethic of justice proceeds from the premise of equality—that everyone should be treated the same—an ethic of care rests on the premise of nonviolence—that no one should be hurt. In the representation of maturity, both perspectives converge in the realization that just as inequality adversely affects both parties in an unequal relationship, so too violence is destructive for everyone involved" (1982:174).

### Criticisms

Critics of Gilligan's approach and other researchers investigating interconnections among race, class, and gender in developmental experiences suggest that the experiences of the males and females in Gilligan's research can be assumed to reflect the experiences of persons who are white and relatively well-off financially (middle-class). These scholars are critical of Gilligan's work for not adequately addressing the diversity of characteristics, experiences, and environmental contexts among women. These criticisms have often focused also on the necessity of recognizing the interlocking nature of oppressions resulting from gender, class, and race in the United States and Western society.

Stack (1986:322), for example, finds that "the caste and economic system within rural southern communities creates a setting in which Black women and men have a very similar experience of class, that is, a similar relationship to production, employment, and material and economic rewards." Her suggestion is that in many cases women and men of color may have more in common with each other than do many white and black women because of the overriding impact of race and class. She suggests that for many African Americans "under conditions of economic deprivation there is a convergence between women and men in their construction of themselves in relationship to others, and that these conditions produce a convergence seen in women's and men's vocabulary of rights, morality, and the social good" (Stack, 1986:322–323). However, Stack does not suggest that such work as Gilligan's should be discounted because of its lack of incorporation of factors of race and class along with gender. She suggests that future research should build upon this work by adding dimensions such as race and class (1986:324). Gilligan's later work reflects a very conscious attempt to integrate race, class, sexuality, and gender.

**Models of women's identity development**

In addition to the work of Carol Gilligan, Jean Baker Miller, and others concerned with understanding more fully the development and identity formation of women are models of women and development proposed by Conarton and Kreger-Silverman. The model developed by Conarton and Kreger-Silverman was influenced by the work of Carol Gilligan as well as Jung and Dabrowski (Wastell, 1996).

## Adult Women and Developmental Experiences

As with traditional studies of women's development, studies of women's midlife experiences have been relatively few and have been too often generalized from studies of men at midlife done by men. McQuaide suggests that earlier studies of women's midlife experiences are also limited because women's experiences have changed radically as a result of the women's movement, feminism, greater reproductive choices, and more women entering the workforce. In addition, McQuaide argues that studies of women have been "problem-based" rather than "strengths-based." McQuaide's study of midlife, white women living in the New York area found that "midlife, for white, middle-class and upper middle-class women, at least, is not a time of torment" (McQuaide, 1998:21–29). The reader should note that McQuaide clearly identifies the narrow scope of the population she used in her research. What are the limitations of this sample in terms of race and geographic representation? McQuaide also found that well-being for the women she studied was increased by having a "confidante or a group of women friends, as well as having positive role models" (1998:29). She also found that for the women she studied, having a positive and strong self-concept in the face of a society marked by the social devaluation of midlife women was important (McQuaide, 1998:30).

## FOCUS: SEXUAL ORIENTATION

Next we turn our attention to alternative models for understanding the special developmental issues and tasks faced by gay men, lesbians, bisexual, and transgender persons. Several different models of identity development are offered from a variety of perspectives for helping us develop a more holistic perspective on the development of persons with diverse sexual orientations and identities.

In addition to the significant number of gay men, lesbians, bisexual and transgender persons in the population, the significance of increasing our understanding of the developmental and environmental experiences of gay men and lesbians is underscored by the intensity of controversy surrounding many issues related to sexual orientation. Central to these controversies is the question of whether gay men and lesbians should have the same rights and protections as heterosexuals in all spheres of personal and social life. The rights in question include such basic ones as parenthood, the right to form and have legal recognition of gay- and lesbian-headed families (the right to marry), the right to serve in the military *openly* and other social institutions, the right to have access to housing

### Human Rights & Justice

**Practice Behavior Example:** Understand that each person, regardless of position in society, has basic human rights, such as freedom, safety, privacy, an adequate standard of living, health care, and education.

**Critical Thinking Question:** As you read this section, describe one societal barrier to LBGT persons' freedom, safety, and privacy.

without discrimination, and the right to have partners and family members covered by health insurance and other job-related benefits (domestic partnership rights) taken for granted by heterosexual workers and their families.

It is difficult to accurately determine the number of gay, lesbian, and bisexual persons in the general population. Part of this difficulty relates to how one defines gay, lesbian, or bisexual (see Kinsey continuum of sexual orientation earlier in this chapter). However, according to the American Community Survey, there "are an estimated 8.8 million gay, lesbian, and bisexual (GLB) persons in the U.S." (Gates, 2006:1). According to Burgess, "the number of transgendered people is unknown" (in Burdge, 2007:244). Burdge notes, however, that a 2003 report "suggested that self-identified transgendered people account for 2 percent to 3 percent of the overall lesbian, gay, bisexual, and transgender (LGBT) community" (Burdge, 2007:244).

While traditional and dominant forces in society continue to struggle with discrimination, oppression, and social injustice in contrast to full acceptance at both personal and policy levels of persons with diverse sexual orientations and sexual identities, other cultures have historically been more successful in achieving full inclusion, as well as the provision of respected statuses for these persons. For example, in an article addressing caregiving practices among American Indians, the authors point out:

> Native LGBTQT-S (lesbian, gay, bi-sexual, transgender, queer, or two-spirit; hereafter referred to as two-spirit) people often have specific cultural roles and responsibilities tied to caregiving in indigenous communities. . . . Moreover, these roles are intimately tied to their identities as Native LGBTQ or "two-spirit" people (Evans-Campbell et al., 2007:78).

The authors further note:

> Many indigenous societies in North America have historically acknowledged and incorporated the existence of diverse gender and sexual identities among community members. . . . Although there were exceptions, these community members tended to be well integrated with Native communities and often occupied highly respected social and ceremonial roles (Evans-Campbell et al., 2007:78).

## Sexual Orientation and Biology

In addition, many questions remain about the origins and causes of homosexuality itself and about whether homosexuality is an orientation beyond the control of the individual or whether being gay or lesbian is a preference or a choice one makes. There is significant new evidence emerging from research in the natural sciences suggesting that biological factors operate in the determination of sexual orientation. These findings suggest that being a gay or lesbian person is no more chosen than being left-handed or brown-eyed is chosen. This is one of the reasons that the term *sexual orientation* is now preferred over the term *sexual preference*. *Preference* suggests one can choose to be or not be gay or lesbian. While one may choose not to openly acknowledge to self or to others one's homosexual identity, one's sexual *orientation* does not appear to be so clearly a matter of choice. This is perhaps best explained as the difference between acceptance of one's homosexuality and the choice not to accept or act on one's sexual feelings. The process of acknowledging gay or lesbian feelings and identity to self and/or others is often referred to as **coming out**.

In one study of gay men with twin and adopted brothers, substantial genetic influences in male sexual orientation were suggested. In this study homosexuality occurred among both brothers 52 percent of the time for identical twins who share their genes and 22 percent of the time among fraternal twins who share half the same genes. Among brothers with different biological parents but adopted into and raised in the same home, only 6 percent of the time did both brothers have a homosexual orientation (Bower, 1992:6). In another study, significant differences in the hypothalamus of the brain were found between gay men and nongay men, again suggesting a biological link in sexual orientation, but this time through a study using physiological evidence rather than the more sociological evidence in the study of twins and brothers (Bowers, 1992:6). These studies are, of course, not proof in any final sense, but they do raise important questions about biology and sexual orientation. Since both of these studies included only gay men and excluded lesbians, the biological origins of lesbian orientation are even less certain. Even given the uncertainties about the biological origins of gay or lesbian orientation, there are a number of theoretical models available that can help us understand the developmental experiences and environments of gay men and lesbians. We explore some of these models next.

## Perspectives on Lesbian, Gay Male, Bisexual, and Transgender Development

According to D'Augelli, perspectives on lesbian, gay male, and bisexual persons have changed dramatically "from mental illness to alternative life-style to sexual variation to diverse minority" (1994:328). D'Augelli suggests a human development model for understanding the development of gay men, lesbians, and bisexual persons. The phases of this model are outlined below.

1. *Exiting Heterosexual Identity:* "involves personal and social recognition that one's sexual orientation is not heterosexual. . . . Exiting from heterosexuality also means telling *others* that one is lesbian, gay, or bisexual. This 'coming out' begins with the very first person to whom an individual discloses and continues throughout life, decreasing only to the extent that the person is consistently and publicly identified with a non-heterosexual label."

2. *Developing a Personal Lesbian-Gay-Bisexual Identity Status:* "An individual must develop a sense of personal socioaffectional stability that effectively summarizes thoughts, feelings, and desires . . . such an initial status may be subject to revision as more experience is accumulated. . . . To a large degree, they cannot confirm their sexual-orientation status without contact with others."

3. *Developing a Lesbian-Gay-Bisexual Social Identity:* "This involves creating a large and varied set of people who know of the person's sexual orientation and are available to provide social support. This, too, is a lifelong process that has a profound effect on personal development."

4. *Becoming a Lesbian-Gay-Bisexual Offspring:* "Parental relationships are often temporarily disrupted with the disclosure of sexual orientation. . . . Generally, families show patterns of adaptation, with parents, siblings, and members of the extended family coming to overlapping, but not identical approaches."

5. *Developing a Lesbian-Gay-Bisexual Intimacy Status:* "The psychological complexities of same-sex dyadic relationships are made much more problematic by the invisibility of lesbian and gay couples in our cultural imagery. . . . The lack of cultural scripts directly applicable to lesbian, gay, and bisexual people leads to ambiguity and uncertainty, but it also forces the emergence of personal, couple-specific, and community norms, which should be more personally adaptive."

6. *Entering a Lesbian-Gay-Bisexual Community:* "This set of identity processes involves the development of commitment to political and social action. For some who believe their sexual orientation to be a purely private matter, this never happens. . . . To be lesbian, gay, or bisexual in the fullest sense—to have a meaningful identity—leads to a consciousness of the history of one's own oppression. It also, generally, leads to an appreciation of how the oppression continues, and commitment to resisting it" (1994:324–328).

## Life Course Theory and Sexual Orientation

As discussed in Chapter 3 (with additional attention in Chapter 7), Life Course theory is increasingly considered a significant alternative theory for understanding the complexities of human development because it is more contextual and fluid than traditional stage-based theories. In other words, it helps provide a more complete view of human behavior and the social environment. Hammack (2005) suggests that Life Course theory also offers an alternative and helpful approach to understanding developmental processes related to gay, lesbian, and bisexual persons, especially in terms of the impact of context, such as historical context, on the developmental trajectories experienced by different birth cohorts of gay, lesbian, and bisexual persons. He presents "A Model of Sexual Orientation Development in the Life Course Perspective." Using this perspective Hammack defines sexual orientation:

> as the biologically based affective disposition of sexual desire which motivates behavior and assumption of identity. There are three important propositions embedded in this definition: (1) that individuals possess a biological disposition to respond affectively to members of a particular sex; (2) that this disposition is reflected in sexual desire, and (3) that a subjective understanding of one's desire in the context of a specific cultural model of human sexuality leads to behavioral practice and identity assumption (2005:276).

He also differentiates between the meanings of sexual orientation and sexual identity in terms of a Life Course developmental sexual orientation perspective. He notes:

> The conceptual distinction between sexual orientation and sexual identity is made explicit in this perspective. In contrast to the definition of sexual orientation, gay or lesbian identity is defined as a sexual identity category describing individuals who, by and large, have sex exclusively with members of the same sex. In making this terminological distinction, it is posited that biology, psychology, and society all assume pivotal roles in the formation of individual selves within a particular cultural context. In addition, the salience and significance of interpersonal relationships in the formation of a gay, lesbian, or bisexual identity cannot be underestimated (Hammack, 2005:277).

In describing the impact of historical context on development of gay, lesbian, and bisexual persons in the United States, Hammack refers to "recent work on sexual orientation by Cohler and colleagues" that describes "the importance of birth cohort in the development of gay men and lesbians in the United States." These researchers identify "at least five cohorts with unique developmental experiences" (2005:275):

1. *Pre-War (World War II):* Gay persons' lives during this period were "characterized by massive secrecy, furtive sex, and the inevitability of marriage and reproduction."

2. *Post-War:* Persons in this cohort experienced "the post-War urban culture, increasingly populated by hordes of soldiers who had engaged in homosexual behavior, witnessed the birth of urban gay communities, with more gay men choosing to live a non-heterosexual lifestyle."

3. *Post-Stonewall:* Persons' experiences during this period were significantly influenced by "the Stonewall Inn riots of 1969 [which] provided significant maturation and momentum to the Gay Civil Rights Movement . . . [and marked] the political and social involvement of a generation."

4. *AIDS:* "With the discovery of AIDS in the early 1980s, this generation (along with the previous one) began to die en masse. . . . Those who came of age in the 1980s became highly educated about AIDS, and a cultural shift from promiscuity to monogamy occurred among gay men."

5. *Post-AIDS:* "Those who came of age in the mid and late 1990s witnessed the effectiveness of AIDS treatments, began to view HIV as a chronic, manageable illness (rather than the death sentence it was in the 1980s), and began to engage in unsafe sex in increasing numbers." In addition, the social climate, especially in the popular media, for many gay, lesbian, and bisexual persons in this cohort has become more accepting and inclusive. (Hammack, 2005:274–275).

Through a Life Course perspective on development and sexual orientation, we are able to better understand the many complex developmental experiences by more carefully considering both the person and the environment.

## Multiple Meanings of Lesbianism

Rothblum (1994:630) asks the question: "What is a lesbian?" She notes, "Burch has differentiated between 'primary lesbians,' who have never had sexual relations with men, and 'bisexual lesbians,' who self-identified as heterosexual and had sexual relations with men before they had sexual relations with women. Very few women have had exclusively same-gender sexual experiences" (Rothblum, 1994:630). Rothblum suggests, "Once women come out as lesbians, the lesbian community presumes that this will be permanent; in fact some lesbians subsequently become sexual with men" (1994:630). Rothblum also asks the important and often controversial question: "Is sexual orientation a choice or is it predetermined (e.g., genetic, hormonal)?" She indicates the varied perspectives on the answer to this question even between lesbians and gay men by noting that "generally, lesbians view sexual orientation as a choice (e.g., they state they became lesbians because it was more congruent with radical feminism), whereas gay men are more likely to view it as predetermined" (Rothblum, 1994:630).

According to Rothblum, traditional definitions "of sexual activity, both the hetero-sexual and the lesbian/bisexual versions, focus on genital activity and thus ignore other, nongential sexual experiences that women may have had" (1994:633). She specifically points out that

> We have no terminology for the early sexual crushes that some girls develop on other people, usually a female friend or female teacher. We have no language for the sexual feelings that arise between adult friends, even when both friends are in sexual relationships with other people. In contrast, if the friends engage in genital sexual activity with each other, we immediately have language; they are having an affair. . . . In the lesbian communities, ex-lovers often remain friends and friends often become lovers . . . closeted lesbians may introduce their lovers to their family or co-workers as their friends. . . . Lack of language for sexuality that is not focused on genital contact means that such experiences are forgotten or cannot clearly be articulated (Rothblum, 1994:633).

### What is a lesbian relationship?

Rothblum points out that "the sex-focused definition of what constitutes a lesbian relationship" is extremely limited because it "ignores the reality of women's ways of relating" (1994:634). According to Rothblum, "for centuries, women have felt strong love, affection, and intimacy for other women, even when both women were married to men. When two unmarried women lived together as spinsters, they were considered to be in a '**Boston marriage**,' [emphasis added] a term that reflected the presumed asexual nature of the relationship (the word Boston usually referred to Puritan values)" (1994:635). Lillian Faderman (in Rothblum, 1994:335) has described the passion and love between women in the 19th century:

> It became clear that women's love relationships have seldom been limited to that one area of expression, that love between women has been primarily a sexual phenomenon only in male fantasy literature. "Lesbian" describes a relationship in which two women's strongest emotions and affections are directed toward each other. Sexual contact may be a part of the relationship to a greater or lesser degree, or it may be entirely absent.

## Bisexualities

Many of the issues about sexuality as a continuum and as expressed in multiple ways (see earlier section on sexuality) can be applied to thinking about bisexuality. For example, bisexual identity and bisexual behavior are not necessarily the same thing.

### Bisexual myths and stereotypes

Eliason (1996) points out a number of myths and stereotypes about bisexual persons. These myths and stereotypes reflect the complexities of a non-binary notion of sexual orientation. While there are few models and relatively little research on strengths-based approaches to understanding sexual orientation in relation to gay men and lesbians, there are even fewer resources available to assist us in understanding the complexities of bisexuality both individually across the lifespan and socially in terms of group and community attitudes and perspectives concerning bisexual persons. According to Eliason "Most people appear to have even more negativity and bewilderment about bisexuals than gay men or lesbians" (1996:131).

**Stereotypes**

- Bisexuals are just confused—they cannot decide whether to be homosexual or heterosexual.
- Bisexuals are promiscuous and must always have a partner of each gender.
- Bisexuals are afraid to admit that they are really lesbian or gay.
- Bisexuals are incapable of sustaining a long-term relationship and will always leave one person for someone of the other gender (Eliason, 1996:131).

According to Eliason (1996:131), traditional myths and stereotypes about bisexual persons have more recently been exacerbated by misconceptions about the interrelationship of bisexuality and AIDS:

> There is also a strong feeling among some people that bisexuals are responsible for bringing AIDS into the heterosexual community. Centers for Disease Control researchers found that risk behaviors, not risk groups, are the important variable. The lesbian, gay, and bisexual communities are among the most knowledgeable about HIV transmission and safer sex techniques. The greatest risk appears to be the large number of men who identify themselves as heterosexual but regularly engage in sex with men and do not inform their female lovers or do not engage in safer sex practices.

**Bisexual research**

Contrary to the misunderstandings and myths described earlier, there is some research that does help inform our understanding of the variation and complexity of bisexuality. Eliason (1994:131) points out, for example:

> Weinberg, Williams, and Pryor found that there were many different ways to experience bisexuality. Some were more attracted to women than to men (i.e., rarely is there a 50–50 distribution of sexual attractions); a few were simultaneous bisexuals (at any given time, having a lover of each gender), but most were serial bisexuals with one lover at a time. Bisexuals were no more confused about their identities than were lesbians or gay men, and even heterosexuals often experienced some confusion (70% of bisexuals, 65% of lesbians and gay men, and 28% of heterosexuals were confused about their sexual identity at some time in their lives).

Bisexuality may be much more common than most people think. According to Gates (2011:1), "An estimated 19 million Americans (8.2%) report that they have engaged in same-sex sexual behavior and nearly 25.6 million Americans (11%) acknowledge at least some same-sex sexual attraction."

## Transgender

As Burgess points out, since the 1990s persons who self-identify as transgender have begun to unite politically and socially "to demand the rights and respect" they deserve. As a result, transgender persons are increasingly visible in general society. This often results in a backlash from important external influences on transgender persons, including "families, schools, peer groups, places of employment and other institutions" (Burgess, 2000:36). For social workers (or soon-to-be social workers), providing effective and respectful services to members of this population is increasingly important. However, Burgess suggests that we are often "ill-equipped with accurate knowledge" about the transgender population (Burgess, 2000:36).

In an earlier chapter, we discussed the importance and power of language and words in helping or hindering the well-being and quality of life of groups of people who face discrimination and oppression. We also noted the constantly changing nature of terms viewed as appropriate by members of these groups. In addition, the importance of accepting and respecting the self-definition of terminology by members of the groups themselves was discussed as an element of empowerment of group members. As is the case with other groups facing oppression and discrimination, a significant impediment to working effectively and respectfully with members of the transgender population is lack of knowledge of basic terms and definitions for describing and understanding this population. The following text box includes basic terms and definitions related to the transgender community.

**Watch the video** "Intersex" **for a view of one family's experience with the medical system and their son born with ambiguous genitalia (hermaphrodism).**

**Critical Thinking Question:** Defend the positions for and against surgery at birth for intersex persons.

## Cass's Model of Homosexual Identity Formation

Cass (1984:143) presents a model of homosexual identity formation that focuses "on the homosexual situation as experienced and perceived by homosexuals themselves." Themes common in a variety of models of homosexual identity development include change and growth as central to identity development. This is true of Cass's model as well. Her model differs from some others in that it takes a strengths perspective and does not operate from the assumption "that people perceive the acquisition of a homosexual identity in a negative light." It also differs from some other models in that it applies to identity formation for both gay men and lesbians.

Cass perceives identity development for homosexuals to proceed through six stages according to a variety of cognitive, behavioral, and affective dimensions (1984:147). At each stage, however, the decision not to proceed any further in the development of a homosexual identity may occur. Identity formation at any stage may take either a negative path away from acceptance and integration of a positive identity or a positive path toward acceptance and integration of a positive homosexual identity as part of one's total self-image. *Identity foreclosure* is the choice by an individual at any stage of homosexual identity development not to proceed any further. However, choosing identity foreclosure does not mean that homosexuality itself can be simply chosen or rejected. It simply means choices are made not to act upon feelings or continue to explore those feelings. Cass's model has significant limitations according to some researchers because it has not been thoroughly empirically tested. However, recent research on the model indicates an empirical base for various aspects of the model (Greene & Britton, 2012:203–205). It is presented here because it is the most widely used model of gay identity formation. Cass's stages of homosexual identity formation are:

Stage 1: *Identity Confusion.* Persons at this stage face considerable confusion. Their previous identities in terms of sexual orientation are questioned as they perceive that their behaviors "(actions, feelings, thoughts) may be defined as homosexual."

Stage 2: *Identity Comparison.* The person accepts the possibility of a homosexual identity. He or she faces feelings of alienation with the recognition of clear differences between one's self and nonhomosexual others. If identity foreclosure does not occur, the individual may choose to make contacts with other homosexuals as a way of lessening feelings of alienation.

Stage 3: *Identity Tolerance.* Tolerance rather than acceptance of a homosexual self-image is characteristic of this stage. Increasing commitment to homosexual identity results in seeking out companionship of other homosexuals. Disclosure of one's homosexuality to heterosexuals or "coming out" is rare during this stage. The tendency is to maintain two identities, a public identity shared with heterosexuals and a private identity shared with homosexuals.

Stage 4: *Identity Acceptance.* "Increased contact with the homosexual subculture encourages a more positive view of homosexuality and the gradual development of a network of homosexual friends." One attempts to both fit into society and retain a homosexual life-style. "Passing" or pretending heterosexuality is practiced in some contexts while there is also likely to be some selective disclosure to heterosexual others, especially friends and relatives.

Stage 5: *Identity Pride.* Feelings of pride in one's homosexuality, strong "loyalty to homosexuals as a group," and devaluing heterosexuality is characteristic of this stage. This stage also often includes intense anger about society's stigmatization of homosexuals. This anger is often turned to disclosure to and confrontation with heterosexuals in attempts to gain validity and equality for homosexuals.

Stage 6: *Identity Synthesis.* Positive contacts with non-homosexuals helps create a sense of not being able to simply divide the world into good homosexuals and bad heterosexuals. With this comes a sense of "people having many sides to their character, only one part of which is related to homosexuality." One develops a way of life in which homosexuality is no longer hidden and public and private selves are integrated into a positive identity (1984:147–153).

**Test your understanding of Development and Sexual Orientation by taking this short** Quiz.

---

## Basic Terms and Definitions Related to the Transgender Community

**Transgender:** A term for people whose gender identity, expression or behavior is different from those typically associated with their assigned sex at birth. Transgender is a broad term and is good for non-transgender people to use. "Trans" is shorthand for "transgender." (Note: Transgender is correctly used as an adjective, not a noun, thus "transgender people" is appropriate but "transgenders" is often viewed as disrespectful.)

**Transgender Man:** A term for a transgender person who currently identifies as a man (see also "FTM").

**Transgender Woman:** A term for a transgender person who currently identifies as a woman (see also "MTF").

**Gender Identity:** An individual's internal sense of being male, female, or something else. Since gender identity is internal, one's gender identity is not necessarily visible to others.

**Gender Expression:** How a person represents or expresses one's gender identity to others, often through behavior, clothing, hairstyles, voice or body characteristics.

**Transsexual:** An older term for people whose gender identity is different from their assigned sex at birth who seek to transition from male to female or female to male. Many do not prefer this term because it is thought to sound overly clinical.

**Cross-dresser:** A term for people who dress in clothing traditionally or stereotypically worn by the other sex, but who generally have no intent to live full-time as the other gender. The older term "transvestite" is considered derogatory by many in the United States.

**Queer:** A term used to refer to lesbian, gay, bisexual, and sometimes also transgender people. Some use queer as an alternative to "LGBT" in an effort to be more inclusive. Depending on the user, the term has either a derogatory or an affirming connotation, as many have sought to reclaim the term that was once widely used in a negative way.

**Genderqueer:** A term used by some individuals who identify as neither entirely male nor entirely female.

**Gender Non-conforming:** A term for individuals whose gender expression is different from societal expectations related to gender.

**Bi-gender:** One who has a significant gender identity that encompasses both genders, male and female. Some may feel that one side or the other is stronger, but both sides are there.

**Two-Spirit:** A contemporary term that refers to the historical and current First Nations people whose individual spirits were a blend of male and female spirits. This term has been reclaimed by some Native American LGBT communities in order to honor their heritage and provide an alternative to the Western labels of gay, lesbian, bisexual, or transgender.

**FTM:** A person who transitions from "female-to-male," meaning a person who was assigned female at birth, but identifies and lives as a male. Also known as a "transgender man."

**MTF:** A person who transitions from "male-to-female," meaning a person who was assigned male at birth, but identifies and lives as a female. Also known as a "transgender woman."

**Sex Reassignment Surgery:** Surgical procedures that change one's body to better reflect a person's gender identity. This may include many different procedures, including those sometimes also referred to as "top surgery" (breast augmentation or chest reconstruction) or "bottom surgery" (altering genitals). Contrary to popular belief, there is not one surgery; in fact there are many different surgeries. These surgeries are medically necessary for some people, however not all people want, need,

or can have surgery as part of their transition. "Sex change" is considered a derogatory term by many.

**Sexual Orientation:** A term describing a person's attraction to members of the same sex and/or a different sex, usually defined as lesbian, gay, bisexual, heterosexual, or asexual.

**Transition:** The time when a person begins living as the gender with which they identify rather than the gender they were assigned at birth, which often includes changing one's first name and dressing and grooming differently. Transitioning may or may not also include medical and aspects, including taking hormones, having surgery, or changing identity documents (e.g. driver's license, Social Security record) to reflect one's gender identity. Medical and legal steps are often difficult for people to afford.

**Intersex:** A term used for people who are born with a reproductive or sexual anatomy and/or chromosome pattern that does not seem to fit typical definitions of male or female. Intersex conditions are also known as differences of sex development (DSD).

**Drag Queen:** Used to refer to male performers who dress as women for the purpose of entertaining others at bars, clubs, or other events. It is also sometimes used in a derogatory manner to refer to transgender women.

**Drag King:** Used to refer to female performers who dress as men for the purpose of entertaining others at bars, clubs, or other events.

Source: National Center for Transgender Equality • 1325 Massachusetts Avenue NW, Suite 700, Washington, DC 20005 (202) 903-0112 • ncte@nctequality.org www.nctequality.org

# FOCUS: ELDERS

## Theories of Aging

In Chapter 4 we addressed the disengagement theory of aging as a very traditional approach to theories of aging. Here we will address some of the less traditional approaches to understanding aging. Schroots provides a summary of major theories of aging that have been developed since World War II (Schroots, 1996:742).

First, regarding disengagement theory (see Chapter 4), Schroots argues that it presents "a one-sided view of the aged, given the significant proportion of older people who do not lose interest in life and do not withdraw from society" (1996:744). Baltes and colleagues attempted to take a more holistic or balanced view of human aging by presenting seven propositions to explain human aging and its variability:

1. There are major differences between normal, pathological, and optimal aging, the latter defined as aging under development enhancing and age-friendly environmental conditions;

2. The course of aging shows much interindividual variability (heterogeneity);

3. There is much latent reserve capacity in old age;

4. There is aging loss in the range of reserve capacity or adaptivity;

5. Individual and social knowledge (crystallized intelligence) enriches the mind and can compensate for age-related decline in fluid intelligence (aging losses);

6. With age, the balance between gains and losses becomes increasingly negative; and finally,

7. The self in old age remains a resilient system of coping and maintaining integrity. (cited in Schroots, 1996:745)

As a counterpoint to disengagement theory, Havighurst suggested *activity theory*, which states, "in order to maintain a positive sense of self, elderly persons must substitute new roles for those lost in old age. As such, activity theory presents a more realistic view of older people" (cited in Schroots, 1996:744). While both of these theories have had significant influence on the study and perception of human aging, a newer, alternative, and somewhat more balanced theory it that of *gerotranscendence*. This theory, developed by Tornstam, suggests that as we move through old age, we experience "a shift in metaperspective from a materialistic and rational vision to a more cosmic and transcendent one, normally followed by an increase in life satisfaction." Gerotranscendence is related to "three levels of age-related ontological change." Remember from Chapter 3 that ontology refers our perspective about what is real. These three levels of ontological change, according to Tornstam, are:

1. *Cosmic level* —changes in the perception of time, space and objects, increase of affinity with past and coming generations, changes in the perception of life, disappearing fear of death, acceptance of the mystery dimension in life, and increase of cosmic communion with the spirit of the universe;

2. *Self*—discovery of hidden (both good and bad) aspects of the self, decrease of self-centeredness, self-transcendence from egoism to altruism, rediscovery of the child within, and ego-integrity;

3. *Social and Individual relations* —less interest in superficial relations, increasing need for solitude, more understanding of the difference between self and role, decreasing interest in material things, and increase of reflection (cited in Schroots, 1996:746–747).

Clearly, gerotranscendence offers an alternative to both disengagement and activity theory. It synthesizes elements of both, while adding significant attention to less concrete but important alternative notions of aging processes involving changing perceptions at the cosmic level (time, space, and objects), continuing self-discovery, and changes in perceptions of the importance of social and individual relations.

# FOCUS: PERSONS WITH DISABILITIES

## The Americans with Disabilities Act as Amended (ADAAA)

The Americans with Disabilities Act (ADA), which became law in 1990 is a significant piece of legislation and has multiple implications for social workers whether we are working at the individual, family, group, organizational, or community level. The act was amended in 2008 as the Americans with Disabilities Act as Amended (ADAAA). The amended act broadened and clarified both the definition and intent of the original act. The act is based on the principle that "physical or mental disabilities in no way diminish a person's right to fully participate in all aspects of society, yet many people with physical or mental disabilities have been precluded from doing so because of discrimination; others who have a record of a disability or are regarded as having a disability also have been subjected to discrimination" ADAAA, 2008. The box below offers ADAAA definitions, explanations, and a list of the covered major life activities.

In addition, the amended act sought to clarify how disabilities were to be defined by giving additional instructions: "The definition of disability in this Act shall be construed in favor of *broad coverage of individuals* under this Act, to the maximum extent permitted by the terms of this Act" (emphasis added). Three significant elements of the amended act were clarification that "An impairment that substantially limits one major life activity need not limit other major life activities in order to be considered a disability"; "An impairment that is episodic or in remission is a disability if it would substantially limit a major life activity when active"; and "being regarded as having such an impairment" resulting in discriminatory treatment. Orlin points out, for example, that people with severe burns may not regard themselves as impaired, but encounter discrimination because others "regard" them as having a disability (1995:235).

---

### Important Definitions

"(1) DISABILITY.—The term 'disability' means, with respect to an individual—

"(A) a physical or mental impairment that substantially limits one or more major life activities of such individual;

"(B) a record of such an impairment; or

"(C) being regarded as having such an impairment (as described in paragraph (3)).

"(2) MAJOR LIFE ACTIVITIES.—

"(A) IN GENERAL.—For purposes of paragraph (1), major life activities include, but are not limited to, caring for oneself, performing manual tasks, seeing, hearing, eating, sleeping, walking, standing, lifting, bending, speaking, breathing, learning, reading, concentrating, thinking, communicating, and working.

"(B) MAJOR BODILY FUNCTIONS.—For purposes of paragraph (1), a major life activity also includes the operation of a major bodily function, including but not limited to, functions of the immune system, normal cell growth, digestive, bowel, bladder, neurological, brain, respiratory, circulatory, endocrine, and reproductive functions.

Source: ADA AMENDMENTS ACT OF 2008
**PL 110-325 (S 3406)**
**September 25, 2008**

Episodic or disabilities in remission include:

Chronic impairments with symptoms or effects that are episodic rather than present all the time can be a disability even if the symptoms or effects would only substantially limit a major life activity when the impairment is active. . . . Examples of impairments that may be episodic, including epilepsy, hypertension, asthma, diabetes, major depressive disorder, bipolar disorder, and schizophrenia. An impairment such as cancer that is in remission but that may possibly return in a substantially limiting form will also be a disability under the ADAAA and the final regulations.

Source: http://www.eeoc.gov/laws/regulations/ada_qa_final_rule.cfm

## What does ADAAA cover?

The kinds of facilities and activities covered by the act include:

- Places of lodging;
- A restaurant, bar, or other establishment serving food or drink;
- A motion picture house, theater, concert hall, stadium, or other place of exhibition or entertainment;
- An auditorium, convention center, lecture hall, or other place of public gathering;
- A bakery, grocery store, clothing store, hardware store, shopping center, or other sales or rental establishment;
- A laundromat, dry-cleaner, bank, barber shop, beauty shop, travel service, shoe repair service, funeral parlor, gas station, office of an accountant or lawyer, pharmacy, insurance of fire, professional office of a health care provider, hospital, or other service establishment;
- A terminal, depot, or other station used for specified public transportation;
- A museum, library, gallery, or other place of public display or collection;
- A park, zoo, amusement park, or other place of recreation;
- A nursery, elementary, secondary, undergraduate, or postgraduate private school, or other place of education;
- A day care center, senior citizen center, homeless shelter, food bank, adoption agency, or other social service center establishment; and
- A gymnasium, health spa, bowling alley, golf course, or other place of exercise or recreation. (Department of Justice, 2010, p. 32)

Orlin also explains the concept of *"reasonable accommodation"* (1995:236). This concept means the employer must make individualized accommodation "based on the specific needs of a qualified individual with a disability to enable that person to perform the essential functions of a job, unless such accommodation would be an 'undue hardship.'" *Undue hardship* is defined as "an action requiring 'significant difficulty or expense'" (ADA, 1990). Any accommodation that would be unduly costly, extensive, substantial, or disruptive or that would fundamentally alter the nature or operation of the business or organization would be an undue hardship. Assessment of undue hardship existence varies from situation to situation depending on such factors as the resources of the organization available to make accommodation, for example, a small agency versus a large academic medical center (Orlin, 1995:236). Often accommodations can be inexpensive and reasonably simple.

**ADA protections for family, volunteers, and social workers**

Family members or people otherwise associated with people with disabilities are also protected by ADA, "because discrimination against a person with an association or relationship with a person with a disability is also prohibited" (Orlin, 1995:238). Examples are:

- A person who does volunteer work with people with AIDS is protected from discrimination by his/her employer because of the association.
- A person with a spouse with a disability cannot be refused a job by an employer concerned that the spouse's impairment will cause the person to miss too much work.
- A child with a sibling who has AIDS cannot be denied admission to a day care center.

The protection provided in ADA in the above areas is especially important to social workers and other professionals who provide services to persons with disabilities. It is intended to prevent discrimination against these professionals in the course of carrying out their professional responsibilities.

## Social Work, Developmental Disabilities, and Children

Increasing federal mandates require social workers to be knowledgeable and effective in working with children and families with or at risk of developmental disabilities. Malone et al. (2000) note that the Education of the Handicapped Act Amendments of 1986 (P L 99-457) required services not only to children with developmental disabilities or at risk for them but required family-centered services as well. Other related federal legislation includes the Developmental Disabilities Assistance and Bill of Rights Act. They note specifically that "we have moved to a definition of developmental disabilities that is inclusive of any number of conditions oriented to functional abilities and sensitive to family issues." Federal mandates also cover "young children with developmental concerns." This includes children from birth to five years old with a condition that without services "will likely result in substantial functional limitations in three or more major life activities." These life activities include the following:

- self care,
- receptive and expressive language,
- learning,
- mobility,
- self direction,
- capacity for independent living, and
- economic self-sufficiency if services are not provided.

Malone et al. point out:

Developmental concerns experienced by children can challenge typical development in the key domains: cognition, social and emotional growth, language and communication, and physical growth and skill. These concerns may be due to inherited genetic influences, environmental influences (or a combination of genetic and environmental factors) and have their genesis during the prenatal, perinatal, or postnatal period.

Malone et al. include both genetically or inherited conditions as well as environmental conditions that might result in developmental delays or disability.

**Genetically based concerns:**

- Down syndrome
- Fragile X syndrome
- Phenylketonuria (PKU)
- Tay-Sachs disease

**Environmentally based concerns:**

- Encephalitis
- Meningitis
- Rubella (German measles)
- Fetal alcohol syndrome
- Lead poisoning
- Poor nutrition
- Child abuse (Malone et al., 2000)

## Persons with Disabilities and Social and Economic Justice

Kopels points out that in its research prior to passage of the ADA, "Congress found that the 43 million Americans who have one or more physical or mental disabilities, are, as a group, severely disadvantaged due to discrimination in the critical areas of employment, housing, public accommodations, education, transportation, communication, recreation, institutionalization, health services, voting, and access to public services" (1995:338). Kopels also reminds us, "People with disabilities are statistically the poorest, least educated, and largest minority population in America." This extreme poverty results from both the types of jobs traditionally available and the lack of access to training and education: "Individuals with disabilities, however, have traditionally been employed in low-status, low-paying jobs. They have not had equal access to educational and training opportunities that could have prepared them for more gainful employment" (Kopels, 1995:338).

## ADA and Advocating for Social and Economic Justice

Kopels urges social work students to ask questions about the physical and policy environments in their field placement agencies. You might also adapt these questions to the colleges and universities you attend.

*Physical*

- Does agency have stairs, ramps, doorways, water fountains, restrooms, telephones, and other amenities that are accessible to clients with differing levels of abilities?
- What environmental modifications should be made?
- If the student became disabled while in field placement, would he or she be able to continue to work at the agency, or would "reasonable accommodations" need to be made?

*Policy*

- Does the agency provide sign language interpreters, if necessary, during counseling sessions?
- Can clients with visual impairments read their records?
- Is there a uniform policy for maintaining the confidentiality of client records, or do records of certain clients, like those with HIV/AIDS, illegally contain special, identifying notations? (1995:343)

# FOCUS: MEN

Kimmel and Messner (1995:xiv–xv) point out that just as "white people rarely think of themselves as 'raced' people [and] rarely think of race as a central element in their experience. . . . men often think of themselves as genderless, as if gender did not matter in the daily experiences of our lives." They note though, that researchers have been studying masculinity for many years. These studies traditionally have focused on three models:

1. *Biological models* have focused on the ways in which innate biological differences between males and females programed different social behaviors.

2. *Anthropological models* have examined masculinity cross-culturally, stressing the variations in the behaviors and attributes associated with being a man.

3. *Sociological models* have [until recently] stressed how socialization of boys and girls included accommodation to a "sex role" specific to one's biological sex. (Kimmel and Messner, 1995:xv)

**Test your understanding of Development and People with Disabilities by taking this short** Quiz.

## Men, Masculinity, and Identity

Kimmel and Messner (1995:xix–xx) argue that the traditional models for studying masculinity have increasingly come into question for assuming the definition of masculinity is universal across cultures; for omitting historical realities; and for failing to account for issues of power that are central to getting a fuller understanding of male identity development. Research on masculinity has undergone significant change in the last twenty years and has become more inclusive of elements and realities of masculinity omitted from earlier traditional perspectives. Newer alternative models have been heavily influenced by feminist research directed toward understanding the relationship between males and females. Most significant among the results of newer alternative approaches to studying masculinity was the realization that "power dynamics are an essential element in both the definition and enactment of gender." Traditional sex role research had ignored both the reality of power relations and of the reality that men held the dominant position within the power relations between genders. In addition, alternative models "looked at 'gender relations' and understood how the definition of either masculinity or femininity was relational, that is, how the definition of one gender depended, in part, on the understanding of the definition of the other" (Kimmel and Messner, 1995:xix).

Kimmel and Messner believe:

the research on masculinity is entering a new stage in which the variations among men are seen as central to the understanding of men's lives. The unexamined assumption in earlier studies had been that one version of masculinity—white, middle-age, middle-class, heterosexual—was the sex role into which all men were struggling to fit in our society. Thus, working-class men, men of color, gay men, and younger and older men were all observed as departing in significant ways from the traditional definitions of masculinity (1995:xix).

### Masculinities

Newer alternative approaches see masculinity as multiple and present the newer notion of *masculinities* "the ways in which different men construct different versions of masculinity" (Kimmel and Messner, 1995:xx). Kimmel and Messner suggest that more complete understandings of maleness and masculinity can be found through *social constructionist* approaches which seek to understand that one's identity as man "is developed through a complex process of interaction with the culture in which" one learns "the gender scripts appropriate to our culture, and attempt[s] to modify those scripts to make them more palatable"; through approaches that recognize "the experience of masculinity is not uniform and universally generalizable to all men in our society"; and through *Life Course* approaches which "chart the construction of these various masculinities in men's lives, and . . . examine pivotal developmental moments or institutional locations during a man's life in which the meanings of masculinity are articulated" (Kimmel and Messner, 1995:xx–xxi).

## NOMAS: An Alternative Vision of Maleness

An alternative perspective on masculinity and maleness is presented in the principles of the organization called National Organization for Men Against Sexism (NOMAS). NOMAS is an organization dedicated to enhancing men's lives and recognizes that:

> "The traditional male role has steered many men into pattern of existence that include isolation from children, denial of feelings, lack of close relationships, competitiveness, aggressiveness, preoccupation with work and success. NOMAS believes that men can live happier, healthier and more fulfilling lives by challenging stereotypes and opting for new masculinity – one that embraces children, spouses and friends in positive and holistic fashion." (NOMAS, n.d.)

## Men and Violence

A key area of concern for understanding and changing traditional notions of masculinity is that of violence. Here we will explore violence as a key issue and problem with which men must struggle, be accountable for, and address. Rothblum stresses:

> Sex and violence against women are strongly associated in our society. . . . Most women, consciously or unconsciously, engage in a number of activities in order to avoid being raped by men (e.g., not listing their first name in the telephone directory, using a male voice on their telephone answering machine, not going out or driving or walking alone at night, taking self-defense courses, etc.). . . . Sex and fear of violence are so intertwined for most women that it is difficult to conceive of living a life free from that fear (1994:628–629).

Levy contends:

Society must redefine what normal masculinity is so that violent behavior toward women is seen as pathological and unacceptable. This change does not require categorization of violent behavior as a medically diagnosable pattern or disease but as behavior for which the perpetrator is held responsible. For example, young men in high school are generally ignored when they are seen pushing or hitting their girlfriends and are often surprised when accused of date rape. Their concepts of normal masculinity are shaken when confronted with the criminality of their behavior (1995:320).

Levy calls upon "Social work intervention in the 21st century [to] be guided by a definition of rape and battering as hate crimes against women, rather than seeing them exclusively as acts by 'a sick person.'" Further, she suggests, "Feminist social work practice that aims to eliminate violence against women must address the problem as a violation of human rights" (1995:321).

## SUMMARY/COMMONALITIES

Myers et al. (1991) suggest that there are a number of important commonalities in developmental frameworks and models that address the experiences of members of diverse groups such as persons of color; women; gay men, lesbians, and bisexual persons, elders, persons with disabilities, and white men. Common developmental processes include:

a. A denial, devaluation, or lack of awareness of their oppressed identity;

b. A questioning of their oppressed identity;

c. An immersion in the oppressed subculture;

d. A realization of the limitations of a devalued sense of self; and

e. An integration of the oppressed part of self into their whole self-identity (1991:54–55).

It is important to note also as we conclude this chapter that developmental issues and alternative perspectives on other diverse persons and groups and the interrelationships of multiple diversities will continue to be dealt with as we proceed through the other chapters. This will be especially the case in relation to family as a major context of individual development, but diversities will continue to be a thread as well in regard to groups, organizations, communities, and globally as contexts in which individual developmental issues and tasks are played out.

**Recall what you learned in this chapter by completing the** Chapter Review.

JANINE WIEDEL PHOTOLIBRARY / ALAMY

# Perspectives on Familiness

## FAMILINESS

You may be wondering about the term *familiness* used in the title of this chapter. Why not "Perspectives on Family" or "Perspectives on *the* Family"? In this chapter, as throughout this book, our goal is to develop the most inclusive and varied set of perspectives that we can to think about family. To accomplish this we need to accept at the outset that *family* comes in many different shapes and sizes and accomplishes many different things for many different people. In order to respect this rich diversity, it is helpful to think not of *family* in the sense that there is one universal "best" or "most appropriate" family structure or set of family functions. Instead we want to begin with an expanded notion of *family* as multiple and diverse in both its forms and its functions.

The concept of *familiness* allows us to broaden what is often (traditionally) a quite limited notion of family. This concept reminds us as individuals and as members of particular families to think always about possible alternate structures and sets of functions that constitute *family* for others. The notion of familiness allows us to continue to respect the central role that family plays in virtually all our lives, but it also allows us room to accept that the family tasks fulfilled, the family needs met, the family structures (forms) used, and the environmental contexts in which family exists for us and for others are all subject to great variability and difference.

154

Our goal here is twofold. We want to develop more flexible, fluid, and multifaceted perspectives from which to learn about alternate family forms and structures. We also want to more fully understand traditional family structures and functions. Perhaps the most important implication of this somewhat unconventional term, *familiness*, is its use as a reminder to us that *family* as a social institution and *families* as the intimate and individualized arenas in which we carry out so much of our lives can and do change.

*Familiness* includes the traditional functions and responsibilities assigned by societies to families, such as childbearing, child rearing, intimacy, and security. It also recognizes the great diversity in structures, values, and contexts that define family for different people. In addition to traditional concerns when thinking about family, such as structure and function, *familiness* includes consideration of culture, gender, sexual orientation, age, disabling conditions, income, and spirituality.

This part of our journey toward understanding human behavior and the social environment (HBSE) within the context of familiness is not separate from, but is quite interconnected with, the concerns, issues, and perspectives we have explored in the previous chapters. The content of this chapter will be interwoven with the perspectives and information we explore in the chapters to come. Familiness, our focus in this chapter, is a major context for and has far-reaching influences on the developmental experiences and challenges of individuals. Individual members of families simultaneously have far-reaching and intense influences on the structure and functioning of families. Families and family issues simultaneously influence and are influenced by the groups, organizations, communities, and, increasingly, the global arena with which they interact and of which they are a part. This perspective is consistent with the systems perspective we explored in Chapter 4.

It is contended here, in fact, that familiness is a kind of intersection in our journey to more comprehensive understanding of HBSE. At this intersection our individual lives and experiences meet and are influenced by other individuals and other systems around us. Familiness has significant consequences for the choices we make about the travels we take later in life and for the quality of our experiences on those journeys. At the same time the issues related to familiness become major elements in our continuing developmental journeys.

In many ways, especially when we include alternative notions of *family* in our thinking, the boundaries between systems are blurred. It is often difficult to tell where family stops and group, organization, community, and the rest of the world begin. *Family* is sometimes considered a specific type of small group, for example. This interweaving should not be seen as troublesome, however. It is yet another example of the ambiguity that threads its way along our journey to understanding HBSE. We will attempt to use this ambiguity to appreciate the interdependence of these system levels and as a means of further developing a sense of strength in the ambiguous and interdependent nature of family and other system levels.

We will find, as we explore the various models of family in this chapter, that many of those approaches operate from similar assumptions to those of the approaches to understanding individual behavior and development. Many perspectives on family, for example, assume a stage-based, chronological, often linear progression of development. For example, in some cases we will find notions of family development to be strikingly similar to and consistent with Erikson's stage-based model for individual development. This is especially true of traditional perspectives on family. It is true to some extent also for some alternative approaches to family. As in the case of alternative models of individual development, we will find that alternative notions about family often begin with traditional models as departure points from which to then alter, expand upon, or offer contrasting perspectives on family functions and structures. Before exploring traditional and alternate perspectives on family we will consider some of the implications for social workers of how *family* is defined and some current issues and realities facing families today.

## SOCIAL WORK AND FAMILIES

### Social Work Implications

Hartman and Laird stress the importance to social workers of how *family* is defined. They note that the definitions of *family* that we use have a direct impact on the nature of the practice models we use for working with families. The definition of *family* also directly influences the kind of policies we have at local, state, national, and international levels regarding families. For example, as we noted in an earlier chapter, if the definition of *family* does not include gay and lesbian families or other persons living together as families but who are not legally recognized, the members of these families will not be eligible for benefits and rights typically available to family members. This can include such wide-ranging benefits and rights as covered by health and life insurance policies or family visitation policies in hospitals. Hartman and Laird also stress how our personal definitions of *family* and our own experiences in families can be strong influences on how we deal with family issues in our practice of social work (1983:26).

---

**Policy Practice**

**Practice Behavior Example:** Understand that policy affects service delivery and social workers actively engage in policy practice.

---

**Critical Thinking Question:** Do you think the family unit should drive so many of the policies that impact service to enhance human well-being and quality of life? Why? Why not?

---

### Current Influences on Families

Perhaps the most significant reality facing families today is that of change. What this means for increasing numbers of families is that the so-called normal **nuclear family**—the husband as breadwinner, wife as homemaker, and their offspring all living in a residence apart from their other relatives—does not apply. Some examples of current influence within this climate of change include:

- More adults are single today than in the past, including 38 percent of U.S. adults ages 25–64 years (Lofquist, et al., 2012). In 2010, less than half of all households (48 percent) were husband-wife households, which is a drop from 52 percent in 2000. This is the first time this type of household has dropped below 50 percent since 1940 when data were first collected by the Census (Blocklin et al., 2012:2).
- Overall, the unmarried partner population numbered 7.7 million in 2010 and grew 41 percent between 2000 and 2010, four times as fast as the overall household population (10 percent) (Lofquist et al., 2012:3).

- In 2000, multigenerational households made up 3.7 percent of all households, while in 2010 they made up 4.4 percent of all households.
- In 2010, almost 7 percent of married couple households included a householder and spouse of different races.
- There were 358,000 same-sex unmarried partner households in 2000, increasing to 646,000 in the 2010 Census. In 2000, same-sex unmarried partner households accounted for 0.3 percent of all households, doubling in proportion to 0.6 percent of all households in 2010.
- Overall, at least 80 percent of all same-sex spousal households reported a status of "married" in 2008, 2009, and 2010 (Lofquist et al., 2012:7-17).

**Watch the video** *"The Changing Face of Aging in America"* **for a view of the influence of income and educational disparities on aging in America.**

**Critical Thinking Question:** What should the role of social work be in reducing these disparities?

## Family and Child Poverty

According to the American Family Report Card for 2012, in the United States large numbers of children in families experience poverty and its many accompanying risks and vulnerabilities. While family poverty cuts across race and ethnicity, whites are less likely than other groups to be poor. African American and Hispanic heritage families are about three times more likely to live in poverty than white families (Staveteig and Wigton, 2000).

See Figure 7.1 on the next page and note the "grades" received for meeting the needs of children and families in poverty.

**Test your understanding of Social Work and Families by taking this short** Quiz.

# FAMILY AND GLOBAL ISSUES: IMMIGRATION

Immigration to the United States is considered in this chapter concerning families because the majority of people who immigrate do so in the context of families. According to the American Immigration Lawyers Association (AILA), "most legal immigrants, about 8 out of 11, come to join close family members." According to AILA, "family-sponsored immigrants enter as either immediate relatives—spouses, unmarried minor children, parents of U.S. citizens, or through the *family preference system*, for relatives of permanent residents and siblings of U.S. citizens." The AILA notes, "it is easy to see that family reunification is the cornerstone of our legal immigration policy. It is truly one of the most visible areas in government policy in which we support and strengthen family values. We acknowledge that family unification translates into strong families who build strong communities." The second priority is to allow in a relatively small number of immigrants with skills needed by businesses and industries when citizens with those skills are not available. The third priority of immigration policy is to allow oppressed persons fleeing religious and political persecution a haven. The intent is to offer protection to persons facing "ethnic cleansing, religious oppression, torture, and even death" because of their beliefs or practices (American Immigration Lawyers Association, 1999).

### Human Rights & Justice

**Practice Behavior Example:** Recognize the global interconnections of oppression and have knowledge about theories of justice and strategies to promote human and civil rights.

**Critical Thinking Question:** Should the immigration priority be focused on oppression by higher than the third priority in U.S. immigration policy? Why or why not? What rationale would you use to defend your response (use your critical thinking skills!)?

## Immigrants and Oppression/Discrimination

Given the intent to address oppression through immigration policy, it is unfortunate that immigrants may actually face discrimination and oppression in this country because of their immigrant status. Immigration has become a divisive issue among many kinship

| CHILDREN LIVING IN POVERTY | D |
|---|---|
| • In 2011, 24.5 percent of children under age 5 were living in poverty.* | |
| • In 2011, 21.9 percent of children under age 18 were living in poverty.<br>* The Federal Poverty Level (FPL) is an annual salary for a family of four at or below $22, 811. | |
| • In 2011, 14.5 percent of Caucasian, Non-Hispanic/Latino children under age 5 and 11.9 percent of children under age 18 were living in poverty. | |
| • In 2011, 35.3 percent of Hispanic/Latino children under age 5 and 33.7 percent of children under age 18 were living in poverty. | |
| • In 2011, 42.4 percent of African-American children under age 5 and 38.6 percent of children under age 18 were living in poverty. | |
| CHILDREN LIVING IN LOW-INCOME FAMILIES | D |
| • In 2011, 47.4 percent of children under age 6 were living in low-income families.* | |
| • In 2011, 43.9 percent of children under age 18 were living in low-income families.[1]<br>* A family is considered low-income when it is living at or below 200 percent of the FPL, an annual salary for a family of four at or below $45,622. | |
| CHILDREN WITH UNEMPLOYED PARENTS | C− |
| • In 2011, 7.7 percent of parents with related children were unemployed.[2] | |
| FOOD INSECURITY | C− |
| • In 2011, more than 8.5 million children lived in households where one or more child was food insecure.[3] | |
| STABLE HOUSING | D |
| • In 2010, 67 percent of low-income households with children spent more than 30 percent of their income on housing costs.[4] | |
| • In the 2010–2011 school year, out of 49.5 million children enrolled in the public school system, 1.1 million were identified as homeless by the U.S. Department of Education.[5] | |

America's report card 2012: children in the U.S.

**Figure 7.1**
Report Card for Meeting the Needs of Children and Families in Poverty

1. U.S. Census Bureau (2012), 2011 Current Population Survey, Annual Social and Economic Supplement, Age and Sex of All People, Family Members and Unrelated Individuals Iterated by Income-to-Poverty Ratio and Race.
2. U.S. Department of Labor (2012), Bureau of Labor Statistics, Current Population Survey, Employment Characteristics of Families 2011.
3. U.S. Department of Agriculture (2012), Economic Research Service, Household Food Security in the United States in 2011.
4. The Annie E. Casey Foundation (2011), KIDS COUNT Data Center, 2010 Analysis of the U.S. Census Bureau, American Community Survey.
5. U.S. Department of Education (2012), Student Achievement and School Accountability Programs, Education for Homeless Children and Youth Programs, 2010–2011 Data Collection Summary.

(First Focus, 2012, pp. 6–7)

individuals and groups in the United States. Even though the United States is in many ways a nation of immigrants, many people tend to be fearful and suspicious of immigrants. As is the case so often with prejudice and discrimination, many of the assumptions about immigrants are based on little fact. For example, some people argue that immigration should be reduced or ended because immigrants are a drain on the economy and public services. In fact, "immigrants pay more in taxes than they receive in public services, and are less likely to be on public assistance than U.S. born residents" (Hernandez and McGoldrick, 1999:169). According to Hernandez and McGoldrick, "legal and undocumented immigrant families pay an estimated $70 billion a year in taxes while receiving $43 billion in services" (1999:169).

Others believe the majority of immigrants are in the United States illegally. AILA reports that "undocumented immigrants constitute only 1 percent of the total U.S. population and, contrary to popular belief, most of these immigrants do not enter the United States illegally by crossing our border with Canada or Mexico. . . . [Of those] here illegally, 6 out of 10 enter the U.S. legally with a student, tourist, or business visa and become illegal when they stay in the United States after their visas expire" (Hernandez and McGoldrick, 1999).

## Impact of Immigration on Families and Children

The process of immigration is stressful for all immigrant families and, depending on the circumstances that led to immigration, may be a challenge to the very survival of family members. Hernandez and McGoldrick point out that

> People immigrate for many reasons: for work, study, political and economic survival, or increased life options. Families may migrate to escape oppression, famine, or life without a future. Although migration has become the norm for many people worldwide, it is still a stressful and long-lasting transition and one that is generally not recognized by our society as a whole (1999:170).

The stresses that accompany immigration vary according to the family member and the point in the Life Course of family members. For example, "acculturation processes can threaten the family's structural composition by reversing hierarchies and family roles." Young children may acculturate more quickly than older family members. As children move out of the family into school and community, they may move away from both their parents and their original culture. In addition, as children move into the new culture more quickly than their parents do, they may "take on the task of interpreting the new culture for the parents," and parental leadership may be threatened (Hernandez and McGoldrick, 1999).

Given both the complexities and the potential for oppression as immigrant families make the transition to the United States, it is important for social workers to recognize and understand the impact of this social environmental context on the human behavior of family members. Mather defines children in immigrant families as "those under age 18 who were born outside of the United States or who reside with at least one foreign-born parent." In addition, she notes, "people are classified as 'foreign-born' if they are not U.S. citizens or if they are U.S. citizens by naturalization" (Mather, 2009:2).

## APPROACHES TO UNDERSTANDING FAMILINESS

Social workers are expected to understand the concept of family-centered practice, so it is addressed first in the following sections. Next we explore both traditional and alternative approaches to defining and understanding family.

## Key Elements of Family-Centered Practice

**A**ccording to the U.S. Administration for Children and Families, elements of family-centered practice, "can be incorporated into the work of diverse systems, including child welfare, early childhood development, the courts, and other community-based systems of care."

Key components of family-centered practice include:

- Working with the family unit to ensure the safety and well-being of all family members.
- Strengthening the capacity of families to function effectively.

- Engaging, empowering, and partnering with families throughout the decision- and goal-making processes.
- Providing individualized, culturally responsive, flexible, and relevant services for each family.
- Linking families with collaborative, comprehensive, culturally relevant, community-based networks of supports and services.

(U. S. Department of Health & Human Services Administration for Children & Families, n.d.)

### Family-Centered Practice

An alternative approach to thinking about and working with families is referred to as a *family-centered approach*. Rounds et al. point out that "In a family-centered approach, family members, not professionals, determine who constitutes the family" (1994:7). In addition, they explain that, "A family-centered approach stresses family-professional collaboration, which requires a high degree of trust, mutual respect, and participation by both parties" (Rounds, Weil, Bishop, 1994:9). Often associated with a family-centered approach to practice is a family preservation perspective.

We will continue, as we proceed on our journey to understanding both traditional and alternative notions of family, to consider the social work practice implications of current influences and changes occurring in families.

## TRADITIONAL MODELS

The notion of family development as a series of predictable stages through which families pass is perhaps the oldest and most common framework for organizing traditional models for understanding family behavior and development. Duvall (1971:113–114) notes that some early stage models were quite simple. One early model consisted only of two stages:

1.  the expanding family stage, taking the family from its formation to the time its children are grown; and
2.  the contracting family stage, during which children leave the home and only the parents remain.

Duvall also describes a 1931 four-stage model. This model consisted of:

1.  married couples just starting out;
2.  couples with one or more children;
3.  couples with one or more adult self-supporting children; and
4.  couples growing old.

Another four-stage model she described focused on the formal education system as a major determiner of family developmental stages. This model consisted of:

1. preschool family;
2. grade school family;
3. high school family; and
4. all-adult family (Kirkpatrick et al. in Duvall, 1971:114).

Some later stage-centered models of family life cycle included as many as 24 stages (Duvall, 1971:114–115).

As noted earlier, many models of family development bear a striking resemblance to stage-based, chronological models of individual development, such as Erikson's model of individual psychosocial development. This similarity is not coincidental. Traditional approaches to family development are child-focused or *child-centered*. The developmental stages that an individual child passes through, according to many traditional models, in effect drive the development of the family. The family is pressed to change or react as a result of changes in the individual developmental stages of the child, usually the eldest child (Devore and Schlesinger, 1991:274). For example, the birth of a child—the onset of the first stage of individual development—results in a shift from one developmental stage to another for the family. As we explore models of family development keyed to developmental stages of children, we will question the assumptions and inclusiveness of such models. For example, if all conceptualizations of family are premised on the bearing and rearing of children, are childless individuals or couples by definition excluded from having family (familiness)? We shall further explore this issue later in this chapter.

## Traditional Definitions

Before exploring in more detail some models of family that are consistent with traditional paradigm thinking, it is perhaps helpful to define what is meant by *traditional family*. Traditional definitions of family have generally focused either on structure or function. Structural definitions focus on relationship among members that are based on marriage, blood, or adoption. Functional definitions focus on tasks performed by family for its members or for society, such as child rearing, meeting affectional needs of adults, and transmitting the values of the larger society (Hartman and Laird, 1983:27–28).

## Duvall and Hill: National Conference on Family Life Model

Evelyn Duvall and Reuben Hill (in Kennedy, 1978) co-chaired a committee for the National Conference on Family Life in 1948 out of which emerged a model consisting of a sequence of eight stages. This model is child-centered and has been widely used and adapted since its creation. A major assumption of this model is that parenting children is the central activity of adult family life (Kennedy, 1978:70).

This model of a family life cycle incorporated three criteria into eight stages. The three criteria included: 1) a major change in family size, 2) the developmental age of the oldest child, and 3) a change in the work status of "father." The eight stages of the original model (Kennedy, 1978:70) are as follows:

**Stage 1:** Establishment (newly married, childless)

**Stage 2:** New Parents (infant—3 years)

**Stage 3:** Preschool family (child 3–6 years and possible younger siblings)

**Stage 4:** School-age family (oldest child 6–12 years, possible younger siblings)

**Stage 5:** Family with adolescent (oldest child 13–19, possible younger siblings)

**Stage 6:** Family with young adult (oldest 20, until first child leaves home)

**Stage 7:** Family as launching center (from departure of first to last child)

**Stage 8:** Post-parental family, the middle years (after children have left home until father retires).

This model was adapted slightly by Hill in an article appearing in 1986. The passage of almost forty years resulted in virtually no substantive changes in the model itself (Hill, 1986:21), although, as we shall see, significant changes were occurring in the form and function of family for many members of society. The most substantive change between the two models is perhaps the recognition in the final or eighth stage of the 1986 adaptation of the model that the producer of family income (breadwinner) is not necessarily the father as was the implication in the earlier model.

### Family developmental tasks

The family life cycle approach, of which the Duvall and Hill model earlier is perhaps the most used example, was also influenced a great deal by the concept of developmental tasks. The notion of developmental tasks, if you recall from our earlier discussion of individual models of development, was a fundamental element used by Erikson and others to describe the activities individuals engaged in and struggled with as they moved through their various developmental stages. This concept was also a central organizing element used by family developmentalists to describe the activities and struggles faced by whole families as they moved along their developmental journeys. Eleanor Godfrey as early as 1950 defined family developmental tasks as "those that must be accomplished by a family in a way that will satisfy (a) biological requirements, (b) cultural imperatives, and (c) personal aspirations and values, if a family is to continue to grow as a unit" (in Duvall, 1988:131). Duvall describes these basic family tasks as:

1. providing physical care;
2. allocating resources;
3. determining who does what;
4. assuring members' socialization;
5. establishing interaction patterns;
6. incorporating and releasing members;
7. relating to society through its institutions; and
8. maintaining morale and motivation (Duvall, 1988:131).

These basic tasks, according to family developmentalists, are addressed by every family at every stage of its life cycle. However, each family accomplishes these tasks in its own ways. If it does not, society steps in the form of some agent of social control (including social workers) to try to ensure the accomplishment of the necessary tasks (Duvall, 1988:131).

## Changes in Traditional Family Life Cycle Models

Carter and McGoldrick, in their book, *The Expanded Family Life Cycle*, note the impact of discrimination and oppression on families: "vast differences in family life cycle patterns are caused by oppressive social forces: racism, sexism, homophobia, classism, ageism, and cultural prejudices of all kinds" (1999: xv). This recognition is reflected in increased attention to families of color, gay and lesbian families, and single adults. In an earlier edition of their book, they recognized many changes had occurred in the family in the recent past and more and more families, even American middle-class families, were not fitting the traditional model. Among the influences resulting in changes in the family life cycle were a lower birthrate, longer life expectancy, the changing role of women, and increasing rates of divorce and remarriage (1989:10–11). In addition to these influences, Carter and McGoldrick asserted that while in earlier periods "child rearing occupied adults for their entire active life span, it now occupies less than half the time span of adult life prior to old age. The meaning of the family is changing drastically, since it is no longer organized primarily around this activity" (1989:11). This recognition of movement away from a solely child-centered focus on family life is especially significant in light of our observations about this as a central feature of virtually all traditional models of family.

### Divorce, remarriage, and stepfamilies

As divorce rates have climbed, remarriage rates and the number of persons living in stepfamilies have risen dramatically as well. A *stepfamily*, also referred to as a *blended family*, is broadly defined as "a household containing a child who is biologically related to only one of the adults." In response to changes taking place in family configurations and processes as a result of increasing divorce and remarriage rates, Carter and McGoldrick present what they refer to as a new family life cycle stage for divorcing families and a stage model for new step- or blended families. See Tables 7.1 and 7.2.

**Table 7.1   An Additional Stage of the Family Life Cycle for Divorcing Families**

| Phase | Emotional Process of Transition *Prerequisite* Attitude | Developmental Issues |
|---|---|---|
| The decision to divorce | Acceptance of inability to resolve marital tensions sufficiently to continue relationship | Acceptance of one's own part in the failure of the marriage |
| Planning the breakup of the system | Supporting viable arrangements for all parts of the system | **a.** Working cooperatively on problems of custody, visitation, and finances **b.** Dealing with extended family about the divorce |
| Separation | **a.** Willingness to continue cooperative coparental relationship and joint financial support of children **b.** Work on resolution of attachment to spouse | **a.** Mourning loss of intact family **b.** Restructuring marital and parent-child relationships and finances; adaptation to living apart **c.** Realignment of relationships with extended family; staying connected with spouse's extended family |
| The divorce | More work on emotional divorce: Overcoming hurt, anger, guilt, etc. | **a.** Mourning loss of intact family: giving up fantasies of reunion **b.** Retrieval of hopes, dreams, expectations from the marriage **c.** Staying connected with extended families |

**Table 7.1    An Additional Stage of the Family Life Cycle for Divorcing Families (*Continued*)**

Post-divorce family

| Single-parent (custodial household or primary residence) | Willingness to maintain financial responsibilities, continue parental contact with ex-spouse, and support contact of children with ex-spouse and his or her family | **a.** Making flexible visitation arrangements with ex-spouse and his [her] family<br>**b.** Rebuilding own financial resources<br>**c.** Rebuilding own social network |
| --- | --- | --- |
| Single-parent (noncustodial) | Willingness to maintain parental contact with ex-spouse and support custodial parent's relationship with children | **a.** Finding ways to continue effective parenting relationship with children<br>**b.** Maintaining financial responsibilities to ex-spouse and children<br>**c.** Rebuilding own social network |

Source: Carter, B., and McGoldrick, M., *The Expanded Family Lifecycle.* Copyright © 1999 by Allyn & Bacon. Reprinted/adapted by permission.

**Table 7.2    Remarried Family Formation: A Developmental Outline***

| Steps | Prerequisite Attitude | Developmental Issues |
| --- | --- | --- |
| **1.** Entering the new relationship | Recovery from loss of first marriage (adequate "emotional divorce") | Recommitment to marriage and to forming a family with readiness to deal with the complexity and ambiguity |
| **2.** Conceptualizing and planning new marriage and family | Accepting one's own fears and those of new spouse and children about remarriage and forming a stepfamily<br>Accepting need for time and patience for adjustment to complexity and ambiguity of:<br>**a.** Multiple new roles<br>**b.** Boundaries: space, time, membership, and authority<br>**c.** Affective Issues: guilt, loyalty conflicts, desire for mutuality, unresolvable past hurts | **a.** Work on openness in the new relationships to avoid pseudomutuality.<br>**b.** Plan for maintenance of cooperative financial and coparental relationships with ex-spouses.<br>**c.** Plan to help children deal with fears, loyalty conflicts, and membership in two systems.<br>**d.** Realignment of relationships with extended family to include new spouse and children.<br>**e.** Plan maintenance of connections for children with extended family of ex-spouse(s). |
| **3.** Remarriage and re-constitution of family | Final resolution of attachment to previous spouse and ideal of "intact" family<br>Acceptance of a different model of family with permeable boundaries | **a.** Restructuring family boundaries to allow for inclusion of new spouse-stepparent.<br>**b.** Realignment of relationships and financial arrangements throughout subsystems to permit interweaving of several systems.<br>**c.** Making room for relationships of all children with biological (noncustodial) parents, grandparents, and other extended family.<br>**d.** Sharing memories and histories to enhance stepfamily integration. |

*Variation on a developmental scheme presented by Ransom et al. (1979)

Source: Carter, B., and McGoldrick, M., *The Expanded Family Lifecycle.* Copyright © 1999 by Allyn & Bacon. Reprinted/adapted by permission.

There can be a wide range of responses to divorce on the part of family members. This range still includes the possibility of severe problems for some family members, but it also includes recognition of the potential for divorce and remarriage to bring quite positive results as well. For example, divorce may result in relief from intense conflict and life-threatening abuse for some people. Remarriage for many may present opportunities for forming satisfying and harmonious new relationships. Even when choosing to remain single, for many persons divorce provides an opportunity for personal growth and development (Hetherington, Law, and O'Connor, 1993:208–209).

It is clear that the structures and dynamics of families are rapidly changing. Among the significant change occurring in families is the increasing number of grandparents resuming parental responsibility for their grandchildren.

## Grandparents as Parents

AARP notes, "an increasing [number] of grandparents are also beginning their second round of parenting. As of 2010, 2.5 million older Americans across the nation reported being both the householder and caretaker to their grandchildren" (American Association of Retired Persons, 2012).

- 4.9 million children (7 percent) under age 18 live in grandparent-headed households. That's up from 4.5 million living in grandparent-headed households ten years ago.
- Approximately 20 percent of these children (964,579) have neither parent present and the grandparents are responsible for their basic needs. This is a decrease from 2000, when approximately one-third lived without parents. This is most likely because of the increase in multigenerational homes headed by grandparents that include grandparent, parent, and grandchild, and another likely result of economic conditions.
- 51 percent of grandparents who have grandkids living with them are white (up from 46 percent in 2000); 24 percent are Black/African American (down from 28 percent in 2000); and 19 percent are Hispanic/Latino (down slightly from 20 percent in 2000).
- For grandparents reporting responsibility for grandchildren 67 percent are under age 60, which is down from 71 percent in 2000. And 20 percent live in poverty; up from 18.8 percent in 2000 (Goyer, 2010).

Grandparents provide regular care for grandchildren or assume other parental roles either formally through court orders or decisions or informally where the grandchild lives with or spends a regular portion of his/her day with a grandparent (Jendrek, 1994:206). The grandparent-as-parent role is a form of kinship care (see discussion of kinship care later in this chapter).

### Parental roles

The role of parent from a legal perspective includes both legal and physical custody:

- Legal custody is "the right or authority of a parent, or parents, to make decisions concerning the child's upbringing" (Schulman and Pitt in Jendrek, 1994:207). For example, decisions about medical care, education, discipline.
- Physical custody is "the right to physical possession of the child, i.e., to have the child live with the . . . parent" (Schulman and Pitt in Jendrek, 1994:207).

**Watch the video** "Grandparents Raising Kids" **to explore this growing phenomenon.**

---

**Critical Thinking Question:**
While viewing the video, determine the type of custody described in the text that you believe these grandparents are likely to have.

Combining the traditional parent roles regarding legal and physical custody results in three possible categories of *grandparents-as-parent* roles:

1. *Custodial grandparents:* "A legal relationship with the grandchild (adoption, full custody, temporary custody, or guardianship). . . . These grandparents assume the functions typically linked to parenthood in our society; they become the grandchild's physical and legal custodians." Grandparents typically assume custodial care of grandchildren because of severe problems in the grandchild's nuclear family including financial, emotional or mental health, and substance abuse problems (Jendrek, 1994:207).

2. *Day-care grandparents:* These grandparents "are not casual baby-sitters; they provide grandchildren with daily care for extended periods. Day-care grandparents assume responsibility for the physical care of their grandchildren but assume no legal responsibility" (Jendrek, 1994:207).

3. *Living-with grandparents:* These grandparents "assume a parenting role that falls between that of the custodial and day-care grandparent. Living-with grandparents do not have legal custody but provide some, if not all, of the daily physical care for the grandchild." Two categories of living-with grandparents:
   - those who have one or more of the grandchild's parents living with them; and
   - those who have neither parent in their household (Jendrek, 1994: 207–208).

**Test your understanding of Traditional Models of familiness by taking this short** Quiz.

In the remainder of this chapter we will explore differences in familiness as alternatives to, as well as variations on, traditional models of family. Whenever possible we will present alternative notions on familiness from the perspective of the persons who represent those alternatives.

## THE ALTERNATIVE/POSSIBLE

As indicated earlier in this chapter, many alternative approaches to understanding familiness are extensions or adaptations of traditional models or perspectives. Other alternative approaches include perspectives that offer striking contrasts to traditional approaches. The alternative approaches to understanding familiness that we are about to explore will provide us with a number of concepts important for understanding human behavior in the social environment more generally, in addition to their usefulness in helping us to expand our understanding of familiness.

The alternative approaches we are about to explore tend to be more flexible and more pluralistic than are traditional approaches to thinking about families and familiness. They tend to accept that changes occurring in the environment often require changes in the structures and functions of families. They do not assume that all families do or should look and behave the same or that the same family will or should look and behave the same way at different times. These approaches tend to place greater emphasis on the environmental and social forces that influence family structures and functions. A number of the models also stress the interdependence of families with other related systems—individuals, groups, organizations, and communities.

### Alternative Definitions

We are often presented with images that suggest that the only viable definition of family is one consistent with the traditional two-parent, child-centered, nuclear, white heterosexual, stage-based portrayals we visited in the preceding sections. While this perspective on family is an accurate portrayal of many families (though, as we noted earlier, the number of families fitting this definition is rapidly decreasing), there are many, many families not reflected in this portrayal. These ways of defining family and familiness are more likely to include or reflect dimensions of alternative paradigm thinking that we have been exploring throughout this book, such as recognition of a diversity of family forms.

If multiple or diverse definitions of family forms are not available, great numbers of very real functioning families can be rendered invisible. Some examples of the variety of family definitions present a more balanced view of the range of perspectives on what we and others may mean when we think and talk about "family."

"The family is the natural and fundamental group unit of society and is entitled to protection by society and the State" (United Nations, 1948).

"Society's definition of 'family' is rapidly expanding and has come to include single parents, biracial couples, blended families, unrelated individuals living cooperatively, and homosexual couples, among others" (Crawford, 1999:271).

"Ultimately, I define 'family' as the smallest, organized, durable network of kin and non-kin who interact daily, providing domestic needs of children and assuring their survival" (Stack, 1996:31).

"There are diverse types of families, many of which include people related by marriage or biology, or adoption, as well as people related through affection, obligation, dependence, or cooperation (Rothausen, 1999:820)."

"We define family as any group of people related either biologically, emotionally, or legally. That is, the group of people that the patient defines as significant for his or her well-being" (McDaniel et al., 2005:2).

"A group of people who love and care for each other" (Seligman in Scanzoni and Marsiglio, 1991:117).

"…the National Institute of Mental Health (NIMH) adopted the definition of a 'network of mutual commitment' to connote the new structures that are the reality of families in the 1990s" (Pequengnat & Bray, 1997:3).

The quality of the relationships that constitute family is central to many definitions of family. Quality of relationships, for example, was a primary consideration in a court ruling regarding the definition of family in a case supporting gay rights. In this case the judge concluded: "It is the totality of the relationship, as evidenced by the dedication, caring, and self-sacrifice of the parties which should, in the final analysis, control the definition of family" (Stacey in Walsh, 2003). The following three family types are commonly used in scholarly literature on families.

Family Types:

Family of origin: The family into which you were born. It is your original biological family.

Family of procreation: the family a person forms through marriage and/or childbearing (Mosby's Medical Dictionary, 2009).

Family of choice: Persons or group of people an individual sees as significant in their life. It may include none, all, or some members of their family of origin. In addition, it may include individuals such as significant others, domestic partners, friends, and coworkers (UC Berkeley Gender Equality Resource Center, n.d.).

**Family structure and diversity**

The diversity of family structures combined with variations in structure according to the race/ethnicity of families is another clear example of "diversity within diversity" (see discussion of diversity within diversity and multiple diversities in Chapter 2).

As we continue our journey toward more comprehensive ways to understand familiness, we will keep in mind these multiple and flexible notions of family. The following exploration of alternative notions of familiness is organized according to several "Focus" areas. This arrangement is similar to that used in Chapter 6 for alternative perspectives on individual development. The cautions suggested in that chapter concerning false divisions and oversimplification of multidimensional and interacting factors apply here as well.

## Life Course Theory and Familiness

Life Course theory, as an independent and evidence-based theory, has also often been considered an important approach to understanding more fully family development and the intersections of family development with the developmental patterns of the individuals who make up the family along with the larger environmental contexts that have significant influence on family development and well-being. We explore the family-focused application of Life Course theory here. We consider terms and concepts central to the theory and four contexts: temporal, sociostructural, process and change, and family diversity that provide the organizing framework for the theory.

*Life Course* theory is a contextual, processual, and dynamic approach. It looks at change in individual lives and in family units over time by tracing individual developmental *trajectories* or paths in the context of the development of family units over time. Life Course theory is concerned with the interconnections between personal biographies or life stories and social-historical time (Bengston and Allen, 1993:469-499). Glen Elder, one of the early leaders in research that resulted in the development of Life Course theory, defines another central concept of the theory: human agency. According to Elder, the "principle of . . . *human agency* states that *individuals construct their own Life Course through choices and actions they take within the opportunities and constraints of history and social circumstances*" (1998:4).

**Temporal context**

The *temporal context* is used to describe the multiple timeclocks that affect family life. Life Course theory itself reflects a timeclock that is *sociogenic* in that it is concerned with the entire lifetime of individuals and families as they develop in the context of the larger society. Another sense of timeclocks within family development is referred to as ontogenetic time and ontogenetic events. The term *ontogenetic* describes the developmental levels of individuals as they grow, change, and age from birth to death and is indexed most simply but quite inexactly by chronological years. As we have noted elsewhere, some psychologists (Piaget, Kohlberg, Erikson, and Valliant) use age period or level or stages that describe that the behavior of individuals in families is in part a function of the individual's ontogenetic development level and of other family members' ontogenetic levels. *Ontogenetic time* and *ontogenetic events* are ways of describing that the

---

### Human Behavior

**Practice Behavior Example:** Know about human behavior across the Life Course; the range of social systems in which people live; and the ways social systems promote or deter people in maintaining or achieving health and well-being.

**Critical Thinking Question:** How does Life Course theory assist us in gaining, organizing, and using this critical knowledge? How is Life Course theory different from traditional life-span theories?

behavior of individuals in families is in part a function of the individual's ontogenetic development level and of other family member ontogenetic levels (Bengston and Allen, 1993:470–472; 480–481).

Another temporal or time-related concept that is important in understanding Life Course theory is that of generation. *Generation* refers to the position of individuals in the ranked descent within a biosocial family of procreation and succession. Related concepts are *generational time* and *generational events*, which are a way of depicting that the behavior of individuals in families is also a function of generational placement with attendant roles and expectation. Generational time is also called family time. *Generational* or *family time* is indexed not only by biogenetic statuses within families (grandparent, parent, child), but also by the roles, expectations, and identities related to those statuses (Bengston and Allen, 1993:471; 481). The concept of generation is addressed in more detail in a later section of this chapter.

Still another temporal context helpful in understanding Life Course theory is historical time and place events. Elder notes, *"empirical research findings . . . affirm the principle of . . . historical time and place: that the Life Course of individuals is embedded in and shaped by the historical times and places they experience over a lifetime"* (Elder, 1998:3). The concepts of **historical time** and **historical events** reflect that the behavior of individuals and families, and of families as units, is also a function of secular or period events, especially geopolitical or economic events. This temporal context is usually indicated in terms of events, periods, or eras dominated by watershed geopolitical or economic events: the Civil War Period, the Depression, the Vietnam era (Bengston and Allen, 1993:481–482). We should note, though, that some alternative theorists would argue that "real" historical impact is best understood in terms of the impact of these watershed events on the individual and family. In other words, the local or personal consequences of these events on day-to-day life must be considered central.

## Sociostructural context

The *sociocultural context* is a way of understanding the social ecology of families in terms of several dimensions. Sociostructural context includes the concept of **social structural location** or the location of families in the broader social structure. This location of the family within the larger society influences the events they experience as the family and its members develop and interact over time. The sociostructural context also includes the **social construction of meaning** in that families and their members attach meaning to events that occur and interact at multiple levels: individual life span, generational, and historical events are interpreted through meanings adapted from social structure location and developed through family interaction (Bengston and Allen, 1993:482–483).

Examples of the social construction of meaning might include: norms about the right time to marry, give birth, become a grandparent, and retire. The meanings attached to events also are influenced within families by their *cultural context*. Shared meanings reflected in cultural values both create and interpret life span, generation, and historical events as they impinge on families. Cultural values give meaning to change in families and those meanings may be quite different from one cultural context to another (Bengston and Allen, 1993:483).

## Continuity and change

Life Course theorists see families influenced significantly by both stability and change which are often referred to as homeostasis and adaptability or the dialectics of continuity and change. Families and members respond over time to individual developmental, generational, and historical events and their responses to this range of events reflect both change (adaptability) and continuity (homeostasis), or innovation and transmission. The concept of *diachronic analysis of families* is a process of analyzes of processes over time—focusing on dynamic, as contrasted with static, elements of phenomena. Family processes are examined in addition to family structure. The notion of simultaneously attending to both continuity and change also implies that we cannot understand or explain development from just one point in time. Interactions among age, period, and cohort phenomena influence behaviors of families and individual members over time. Life Course theorists stress the dynamic, nonlinear notion of change and its impact. For example, individual, generational, and historical changes combined with the social context of those changes mutually effect members, families and the larger community, or social context (Bengston and Allen, 1993:483–484).

### Heterogeneity and diversity among families

Life Course advocates also emphasize diversity among families and note that there is considerable diversity in the ways families react to and give meaning to individual developmental, generational, and historical events. These theorists also suggest that heterogeneity or diversity in families increases over time. They note that, for example, a family kinship network is increasingly diverse over time, adding and changing members through birth and marriage. In addition, Life Course theory recognizes there is considerable variation in family structure as a result of differences in location within the social structure: gender, race/ethnicity, or socioeconomic status (Bengston and Allen, 1993:484).

### Generation

The concept of generation, addressed briefly earlier, has been defined in a number of ways. Probably the most traditional way of defining a generation is based on biological or kinship relationships such as "my generation," "my parents' generation," or "my grandparents' generation." A broader notion of generation includes people who are born during a specific period of time, for example, the Baby Boomer generation is considered to be the group or cohort of people born roughly between 1946 and 1964. However, consistent with Life Course theory, the notion of generation has been expanded to include other shared characteristics and experiences. From this perspective a generation is, "an identifiable group that shares birth years, age location [experiences the same historical events], and significant life events at critical development stages" (Espinoza, 2012:31–32).

### An Example: Gen Y/Millennials

If you are reading this there is a good possibility that you are a member of the Millennial generation (also referred to as Gen Y). There are different opinions about the specific time period and age range of the Millennial generation as is also the case with other generations. According to a Pew Research Center study conducted in 2010, the millennial generation consists of people born during the period of roughly 1977–1992 or people in the age range of approximately 18–33 (Pew Research Center, 2010).

Millennials or Gen Ys are considered to have a number of characteristics that differentiate them from prior generations. The most distinguishing characteristic of Millennials is that they are considered *digital natives*. Gen Ys have grown up with technology and have integrated it into their everyday life at many levels. Baby Boomers are *digital immigrants* because they grew up in an analog world (Evans & Forbes, 2012:398).

Some researchers suggest, because of the integration of technology throughout daily life almost from birth, Millennials' brains are actually wired differently than previous generations. A Time Inc. study released in 2012, includes among its findings that: "This study strongly suggests a transformation in the time spent, patterns of visual attention and emotional consequences of modern media consumption that is rewiring the brains of a generation of Americans like never before." The study also found a high degree of multi-tasking: "Digital Natives switch their attention between media platforms (i.e. TVs, magazines, tablets, smartphones or channels within platforms) 27 times per hour, about every other minute" (Time Inc., 2012).

The results and implications of the impact of technology on Millennials are still emerging. However, current data suggests a number of interesting characteristics in the behavior and environments of digital natives, especially students. Millennials, for example, practice what might be called an integrated life where traditional boundaries between different activities are blurred. They tend to "see school life, work life, and social life as one. They will do work at school, school at work, social life at school and work. Work and social life blend seamlessly, since technology affords the ability access both "work and play in real time simultaneously" (Espinoza, 2012:35–36).

Other characteristics include: celebrating diversity; an intense life style almost 24/7 due to instant internet access of mobile technology; very close relationships with parents to the point that parents of Millennials have been referred to as "helicopter" parents given their hovering tendencies; intense investments in friendships; considering friends as family in many ways, given their constant and instant connectivity; investment of time and energy in group and community projects; and preference for collaborative work with clear and worthwhile goals. The Pew Research Center notes "today's students are the first generation that has not needed an authority figure to access information." In summary, the Center "predicts that this generation will be nimble, quick-acting multitaskers, with the internet serving as their 'external brain'" (Espinoza, 2012:29–40; Evans & Forbes, 2012:398–400; Lichy, 2012:103; Young, 2012).

**Test your understanding of Life Course Theory and Familiness by taking this short** Quiz.

## FOCUS: PEOPLE OF COLOR

Harrison et al. use an ecological framework as a departure point for developing an alternative approach to familiness. This approach emphasizes the interaction of individuals with the social environment. Harrison et al. focus on the ecological challenges faced by the families of color in their interactions with social systems and institutions in the larger environment (1990:347). Others have stressed the importance of using a strengths-based approach to dealing with families of color (Attneave in McGoldrick, Pearce, and Giordano, 1982:81–82; Boyd-Franklin in Walsh, 2003:268–269). A strengths-based perspective for understanding families of color is consistent with the principles of the strengths-based perspective on social work described in Chapter 4. Central to a strengths-based approach to families of color is the notion of adaptive strategies.

### Adaptive Strategies

Families of color develop a variety of adaptive strategies to overcome environmental barriers to their (and their members') well-being and development (Ho, 1987). Harrison et al. describe *adaptive strategies* as observable social behavioral "cultural patterns that promote the survival and well-being of the community, families, and individual members of the group" (1990:350). Adaptive strategies recognize the interdependence of community, individual, and family systems. This interdependence offers an example of family as the intersection at which a variety of systems come together and interact with one another.

A strengths-based adaptive-strategies approach to studying and understanding families of color and their children offers an alternative to traditional deficit- or pathology-focused approaches. The specific groups with which we are concerned include African Americans, American Indians/Alaskan Natives, Asian/Pacific Americans, and Latino Americans (Harrison et al., 1990:348).

An adaptive-strategies approach highlights the interconnectedness of the status of families of color, adaptive strategies, socialization goals, and child outcomes (Harrison et al., 1990:348). Through this approach we can delineate a number of contextual or environmental issues that interact to result in the need for adaptive strategies on the part of these families and their members. Specific issues addressed through this approach include racism and oppression, extendedness of families, role flexibility within families, biculturalism, and spirituality and ancestral worldview. While there are some differences in the nature of these strategies from one group to another, the strategies themselves seem to be strikingly similar across the groups (Boyd-Franklin in Walsh, 2003; Harrison et al., 1990:350; Ho, 1987).

### Response to racism and oppression

A number of statuses or conditions interact in the social environments of families of color and result in the need to create adaptive strategies to respond effectively to those conditions. Basic among these is the status of minority group itself. As you may recall, minority group status is not necessarily determined by size of group, but by subordinate status ascribed to members of the group by majority or dominant groups in society. Harrison et al. remind us that a crucial variable "in majority-minority relations is the differential power of one group relative to another" (Yetman in Harrison et al., 1990:348).

In addition to the variable of differential power, ethnocentrism and competition for resources to meet human needs combine to form systems of ethnic stratification (Harrison et al., 1990:348).

Another important concept is ethnic stratification. *Ethnic stratification* is "a system or arrangement where some relatively fixed group membership (e.g., race, religion, or nationality) is used as one of the standards of judgment for assigning social position with its attendant differential rewards" (Noel in Harrison et al., 1990:348). In other words, ethnic stratification is a system of differential treatment based on minority or majority group status.

Caste or castelike status is a specific form of ethnic stratification. Caste and class are often compared and contrasted in discussion of social status. Caste and class are similar in that they both represent social positions held by persons or groups in a society. They differ, however, in that social class implies a position or status from which one can move as various conditions change. For example, increasing a family's educational level, income, or moving from one neighborhood to another may result in movement from a lower social class to a middle-class status. Caste status, however, is not nearly as amenable to such movement. An *ascribed status* is permanent and based on characteristics or conditions not subject to the control of the individual, such as skin color, or, as Ogbu notes, historic conditions of slavery, conquest, or colonization.

For Ogbu, castelike groups in the United States may differ in many ways, but all have in common the element of being treated as exploitable resources. Examples of this treatment for specific groups include:

a. The enslavement of Africans and, after emancipation, their segregation and perceived inferior status based on race;

b. Military conflicts over land and territory between American Indians and European Americans, and the forced removal and transfer of Indians to reservations;

c. Asian Americans whose recent immigrants from Indochina sometimes suffer from the same subordination and exploitation endured by earlier immigrants from China, Philippines, and Japan (the latter were incarcerated during World War II); and

d. Hispanics who were incorporated through conquest and displacement (Harrison et al., 1990:348).

Again, we see that while specific experiences vary considerably among different groups in this society, many conditions that result from these experiences are often shared by the members of different groups. Underlying these conditions is a theme of racism and oppression.

Effective adaptive strategies for families of color include recognition of the realities of racism and oppression for members in a society in which the traditional/dominant paradigm prevails in the existing social hierarchy (Boyd-Franklin in Walsh, 2003; Harrison et al., 1990:347–348). Harrison et al. stress, for example, "historically, ethnic minority children were not included in samples of subjects studied for establishing normative trends or investigating theoretical questions. Most often data on ethnic minority children came from comparative studies with a controversial deficit explanation" (1990:348). Such findings offer dramatic examples of the invisibility or "abnormality (pathology)" accorded diverse persons (non-European descended) in much traditional paradigm research we explored in Chapter 2. Boyd-Franklin stresses that dealing with racism and oppression is central to family life for African Americans. For African-American parents "normal family development" is a complex process that involves educating their children to recognize and deal with racism, discrimination, and negative messages from society about African Americans. African-American parents must simultaneously help their children not to internalize the negative messages from society, but to be proud of who they are and believe that they can achieve in spite of racism and discrimination (Walsh, 2003:262).

The challenges faced by ethnic minority families result from long and shared histories of oppression and discrimination. The impact of these conditions on social and economic well-being of ethnic minority families has very real consequences in poverty, high unemployment, substandard or no housing, and poor health. All of these are of intense concern to social workers, for they present major barriers to families and their members reaching their fullest human potential. These obstacles, however, do not prevent ethnic minority families from pursuing goals of "educational achievement, economic development in the community, political power, affordable housing, and maintaining cultural and religious traditions" (Harrison et al., 1990:349). One significant source of strength and support for pursuing these goals is the extended family.

### Extended and augmented or "fictive" family networks

The specific nature or makeup of extended families differs considerably among ethnic minority groups. This family type is, however, found as an adaptive strategy and a strength across all the ethnic minority groups discussed here. The concept of extended family refers to multiple dimensions of familiness. *Extended family* as we use the term refers to more than traditional definitions of extended family as the nuclear family plus grandparents, aunts, uncles, and other kin related by blood or marriage. Included as members are not only parents and their children, but other relatives related by blood or marriage as well as non-blood or non-marriage-related persons who are considered by other family members, and consider themselves, family. Extended family for many families of color is really an "extensive kinship network." This network helps family members survive "by providing support, encouragement, and 'reciprocity' in terms of sharing goods, money, and services" (Boyd-Franklin in Walsh, 2003:268–269).

For many African-American families this network "might include older relatives such as great-grandparents, grandmothers, grandfathers, aunts, uncles, cousins, older brothers and sisters, all of whom may participate in child- rearing, and 'non-blood relatives' such as godparents, babysitters, neighbors, friends, church family members, ministers, ministers' wives, and so forth" (Boyd-Franklin, 1993:368). African-American extended familiness expand family into community relationships through fictive kinship. *Fictive kinship* is "the caregiving and mutual-aid relationship among nonrelated blacks that exists because of their common ancestry, history, and social plight" (Martin and Martin, 1985:5). Andrew Billingsley (1968) referred to this extended family form as *augmented family*. Billingsley (1992) more recently referred to this arrangement as *"relationships of appropriation."*

For many Native American families, extended family consists of a "collective, cooperative social network that extends from the mother and father union to the extended family and ultimately to the community and tribe" (Harrison et al., 1990:351). In many traditional Native American families, parenting is shared by several adults. In these traditional extended families "uncles and aunts often had particular disciplinary responsibilities toward their nieces and nephews, freeing biological parents for a much looser, more pleasure-oriented association with offspring" (Attneave in McGoldrick, Pearce, and Giordano, 1982:72–73).

"The traditional Asian/Pacific-American family is characterized by well-defined, unilaterally organized, and highly interdependent roles within a cohesive patriarchal vertical structure" in which "prescribed roles and relationships emphasize subordination and interdependence . . . and esteem for . . . the virtue of filial piety" (Harrison et al., 1990:351). *Filial piety* is an intense sense of respect for and obligation to one's parents and ancestors.

Latino family extendedness emphasizes "strong feelings of identification, loyalty, and solidarity with the parents and the extended family" and involves "frequent contact and reciprocity among members of the same family." It has some similarities with the African-American family "in that it is bilaterally organized and includes nonrelative members (e.g., *compadres*)" (Harrison et al., 1990:351–352).

All of these forms of extended family offer a variety of sources of strength and support in addition to that offered by one's most immediate or nuclear family. It is crucial to recognize that there is great variation within groups (diversity-in-diversity) in the importance placed on extended family. These variations might be related to the number of generations a family has lived in the United States or whether or not one has access to extended family members. Some Native Americans who have moved to urban areas from their reservation communities to find employment, for example, may have great difficulty gaining access to their extended family support networks. Many first-generation or recent Asian and Latino(a) immigrants may have had to leave their extended family in their country of origin.

### Kinship care

Closely associated with the adaptive strategy of extended family networks described earlier is the concept of **kinship care**. *Kinship care* has been defined as "the full-time nurturing and protection of children who must be separated from their parent by relatives, members of their tribes or clans, godparents, step-parents, or other adults who have a kinship bond with a child" (Child Welfare League of America in Wilhelmus, 1998:118).

The history of kinship care is connected to the strong history of extended kinship in African and African-American history: "The primary family unit in West Africa at the time of slavery in the United States was the extended family, which incorporated the entire community. Children belonged to, and were the responsibility of, the collective community" (Scannapieco and Jackson, 1996:191). In West Africa, according to Yusane, "'kinship relations were the foundation of social organization' and the 'extended family system is based on interdependent functions' that also serve as protection from calamities. African children were valued and viewed as an investment in the future" (Scannapieco and Jackson, 1996:191).

Scannapieco and Jackson also note that "Africans saw children as part of their immortality, and there were no 'illegitimate' children. All children were the shared concern of the community, and children were expected to care for their parents when the parent got old (respect for elders in the family and community continues as an African tradition" (1996:191).

Kinship care can be structured in three different ways:

1. Formal kinship care is a legal arrangement in which the child welfare agency has custody of a child being placed with relatives.

2. Informal kinship care is when the child welfare agency facilitates the placement of a child but does not seek custody.

3. Private kinship care is a voluntary agreement between biological parents and family members without the involvement of the child welfare system (Ayala-Quillen, 1998; Geen, 2000; Dubowitz, 1994; Winokur et al., 2008, p. 339).

### Social role flexibility/fluidity of roles

This concept applied to ethnic minority families, means that "familial social roles can be regarded as flexible in definition, responsibility, and performance. Parenting of younger siblings by older siblings, sharing of the breadwinner role among adults, and alternative family arrangements" are examples of this role flexibility (Harrison et al., 1990:352). Freeman (Logan, Freeman, McRoy, 1990:57ff) refers to this flexibility as *fluidity of roles* and suggests that it has historically been a significant source of strength for African-American families as they faced survival in a hostile environment that often required family members to shift from one family role to another.

Pinderhughes points out that the flexibility of roles, although a source of strength and survival for many African-American families, has often been viewed as a deficit "because it was different from the White middle-class nuclear family model" of very specific role expectations for males and females (McGoldrick, Pearce, and Giordano, 1982:112–113). Hines and Boyd-Franklin suggest that role flexibility results in a greater sense of equality for African-American couples. They suggest that the emphasis put on equality between men and women by the women's movement has long been a reality for many African-American women. Having a working mate is much less threatening for many African-American men than for many white men because of this history of role flexibility (McGoldrick, Pearce, and Giordano, 1982:89–90).

### Biculturalism

We explored this concept briefly in Chapter 5 as it related to individual development. This important concept carries even more significance in the context of family. *Biculturalism* is "the ability to function in two worlds" (Pinderhughes in McGoldrick, Pearce, and Giordano, 1982:114). However, Harrison et al. stress the complexity of this process for people of color because of the devaluing of their original cultures by the majority group in U.S. society. People of color and their families are put in the position of accommodating or changing behaviors or beliefs to make them consistent with those of the majority culture, and simultaneously engaging in a complex process of keeping and giving up parts of the culture of origin. The result is a person who learns to "function optimally in more than one cultural context and to switch repertoires of behaviors appropriately and adaptively as called for by the situation" (Laosa, 1977 in Harrison et al., 1990:352). Freeman refers to the virtual requirement of biculturality on the part of African-American families as the "dual perspective." She notes that African-American parents have the double responsibilities of socializing their children "to adapt to and function well in a larger society that often views their racial and cultural background in a derogatory manner." However, at the same time parents must focus on retaining "a positive racial identity and meet expectations of their racial group that may be in conflict with expectations of the society" (Logan et al., 1990:61).

Biculturality is not an option for social workers, it is a necessity. To be able to enter into the culture of another person is an essential skill for social workers living in a multi-cultural pluralistic society. Biculturality is very similar at the cultural level to empathy at the interpersonal level. Empathy at the cultural and at the interpersonal level should not be considered separate skills but two components of the same essential skill necessary for competent practice on the part of any social worker.

### Spirituality and ancestral worldviews

As we learned in Chapter 1, worldviews are extremely influential in the way we see ourselves, others, and the world around us. Our worldviews are also strong influences on our families. We discovered, in our earlier exploration of worldviews, that the dominant worldview or paradigm was characterized by an emphasis on individualism and separateness in which every person is separate from every other person and is solely responsible for her or his own well-being. This Eurocentric individualistic worldview is contrary to the ancestral worldviews of many ethnic minority groups. For many minority groups a worldview emphasizing the interrelatedness of the self or the individual with other systems in the person's environment such as families, households, communities, and the ethnic group as a whole is held (English, 1991:20–24; Harrison et al., 1990:353; Martin and Martin, 1985).

Ancestral worldviews are reflected throughout the institutions responsible for imparting the beliefs and values of the group. In addition to and in conjunction with the family, religious and spiritual institutions hold and pass along the philosophical standpoints or worldviews of the people. Many African Americans hold a worldview with roots in an African philosophical position that stresses collectivism rather than individualism. The worldviews of many Native Americans perceive all aspects of life as interrelated and of religious significance although there is no single dominant religion among the many Native American cultures. Asian/Pacific American families stress a belief system in which harmony is a core value. Latino religious beliefs reinforce a belief system in which familism is a central tenet (Harrison et al., 1990:354). Such worldviews as these have much more in common with the core concerns of social work; with the principles of social systems and ecological thinking and with the growing emphasis in social work on the roles of spirituality and religion in understanding the lives of the people with whom we work.

The church often plays an important and supportive role for families of color. Church provides a sense of community and interrelatedness for many families. Family and church are so interrelated for some African Americans, for example, that church members may refer to other members as their "church family." One's church family may provide such important supports as role models for young family members and assistance with child rearing. For families trying to survive in what is likely a hostile environment, "churches often provide an alternative network for friends, junior choir, after school and summer activities, babysitting, and male and female adult role models." These role models are likely to include "the minister, minister's wife, deacons, deaconesses, elders, and trustee boards" (Boyd-Franklin, 1993:369). Social workers need to be aware that such sources of strength and support as the "church family" may be available to assist African-American families. Boyd-Franklin (1993:369–370) suggests that social workers need to become "acquainted with the ministers in African-American communities as these individuals have a great deal of power and influence" and can often provide a wide range of support for families.

Even for African-American families that do not belong to a formal church, spirituality may play a significant role. This spirituality can be quite distinct from a "religious orientation." Consistent with an Afrocentric worldview that sees reality as both spiritual and material at the same time, spirituality is a part of every person (Myers, 1985:34–35). This spirituality "is often a strength and a survival mechanism for African-American families that can be tapped, particularly in times of death and dying, illness, loss, and bereavement" (Boyd-Franklin, 1993:370).

## Islam: family and spirituality

The events of 9/11/2001 and the subsequent wars in Iraq and Afghanistan have reinforced the importance of having accurate information about members of the populations with which we work, in this case the Muslim/Arab population. This is especially true of this population because of the tendency of many, post-9/11, to see all persons who are Muslim or of Arabic ancestry as terrorists or supporters of terrorism because of their adherence to fundamentalist Islam. This is certainly not the case for the great majority of persons who are Muslim.

The Muslim population is growing rapidly around the world and in the United States. There are between 6 and 8 million Muslims living in North America (Rehman and Dziegielewski, 2003:32). In addition, as noted earlier in this chapter, "special immigrant status" may now be granted to some citizens of Iraq and Afghanistan who have worked for the U.S. government in connection with the wars. Yet as social workers and in general we know little about Muslim culture or religion. In Chapter 11, we will look more closely at Muslim culture and community. Here we address Islamic spirituality in relation to its influence on family.

The term "'Islam' . . . refers to the religion based on the doctrine that Muslims believe was revealed in the year AD 610 to the Prophet Muhammad in the city of Mecca. People who adhere to the religion of Islam are called Muslims. . . . The basis of Islam is the Koran, a Holy Book . . . 'it is the eternal, uncreated, literal word of God, sent down from heaven, revealed . . . to the prophet Muhammad as a guidance for human kind.' . . . A second valid religious authority is the *Hadith*, the tradition of the Prophet Muhammad's words and deeds as well as those of many of the early Muslims" (Al-Krenawi and Graham, 2000:82).

Values recognized by the Koran include the following:

- Hospitality and generosity in giving and spending;
- Respect for elders and parents;
- Wealth and preeminence of male children;
- Subordination of women to men;
- Modesty;
- Intensive religiosity;
- Equality of all human beings; and
- Health and strength (Hall and Livingston, 2006:144).

These basic values are central influences on the organization and behaviors of Muslim families.

Arab families place high value on spirituality in the form of Islam. The patriarchal arrangement is its traditional family structure. Both recent and not so recent Arab immigrants who follow Islam conform to a hierarchical organization of authority that extends to roles, obligations, and status. The welfare of the family supersedes the welfare of the individual, making the family the basis of identity. . . . Furthermore, family is a reference point for behavior and spiritual directives (Hall and Livingston, 2006:143).

In addition, "in Arab families, where Islam is the spiritual tradition, reverence for the patriarch, as well as concern for the family's status, provides a strong sense of solidarity and loyalty" (Hall and Livingston, 2006:144).

However, it is very important to understand that Muslim/Arab families are quite diverse in terms of which and to what extent values and behaviors within Islam are emphasized. As a result, it is crucial that social "workers should be aware that no particular set of beliefs and values exists that is representative of all Muslims" (Hodge, 2005:164).

As indicated earlier:

The basic social unit for Muslims is the family. . . . However, "family" is often conceptualized broadly to include relatives or even the whole Islamic community. It is the family, most specifically the husband and wife, that is understood to be responsible for reproducing spiritual and social values. Thus, family, both nuclear and extended, is essential to the spiritual and social health of the broader ummah [community] (Hodge, 2005:165).

As noted earlier, we will look more closely at Muslim community and culture in Chapter 11.

In summary, Al-Krenawi and Graham suggest that social workers who work with Muslim families should:

1. Have an understanding of Muslim family arrangements as more hierarchical and less flexible.

2. Have an understanding of the implications of gender construction within Muslim society, which limits women's movements outside the home.

3. Appreciate that the client may be reluctant to work with a practitioner of the opposite sex.

4. Have a basic understanding of Islam . . . and Islamic movement traditions, as well as their common practices and implications (2000:299).

## Familiness and Multiracial Realities

As we discovered in Chapter 5, as U.S. society becomes more diverse the boundaries between and among diversities are becoming more and more blurred. One example of this is the growing population of biracial and multiracial people. The issue of multiracial identity and heritage has special implications for families, both in the area of adoption/foster care and in the area of special challenges for parenting multiracial children.

### Multiracial adoption and foster care

Fong et al. note that the existence of substantial numbers of racially mixed people "suggests that social workers may have to recast the dialogue about what have been regarded as 'transracial' adoptions" (1996:22). *Transracial adoptions* are also referred to as "interracial," "interethnic," or "transethnic" adoptions (Hollingsworth, 1998:104). They point out that the position taken by social work since the 1970s has been that children should be placed for adoption with parents of like ancestry. National Association of Black Social Workers [NABSW] advocated for this policy initially and most strongly. The formal position, put forth in 1974 by NABSW was: "Only a black family can transmit the emotional and sensitive subtleties of perception and reaction essential for a black child's survival in a racist society" (Smith in Fong, Spickard, Ewalt, 1996:22). "Similar arguments can be made for placement of American Indian, Mexican American, and Asian American children" (Fong et al., 1996:22). The Indian Child Welfare Act of 1978 recognized the importance of maintaining cultural and community relationships as well as family relationship decisions about the welfare of Native American children. It gave "tribal courts exclusive jurisdiction over American Indian child custody proceedings" (Hollingsworth, 1998:105).

Policy and practice in the area of multiethnic and multiracial adoption and foster care have remained unsettled. Since passage of the Multiethnic Placement Act of 1994, social workers and others concerned with child welfare have continued to struggle with fundamental issues about how to achieve what is best for children of color who may need out-of-home placement either temporarily (foster care) or permanently (adoption). Hollingsworth found five themes that have emerged from the ongoing struggle among organizations concerned with child welfare and transracial adoption:

1. That ethnic heritage is important;

2. That children be raised preferably by their biological parents or, when not possible, by other biological relatives;

3. That economic need alone is not an acceptable reason for children to be deprived of their biological parents;

4. That efforts should be made to ensure that adoptive parents of the same race as the child are available and systemic barriers should not interfere; and

5. That placement with parents of a different race is acceptable and even preferable when the alternative means a child is deprived of a permanent home and family (Hollingsworth, 1998:113).

Clearly the issue of multiethnic adoption is complex and must be considered from multiple perspectives. Hollingsworth argues, "seeking to solve the problems associated with the overrepresentation of children of color in the child welfare system by protecting transracial adoption is simplistic and fails to protect those who are most vulnerable in this society—the children dependent on that society." She suggests, "a more responsible approach is to understand and eliminate the circumstances that constitute the cause of the situation" (Hollingsworth, 1998:114).

*Multiracial adoption and foster care* The Multiethnic Placement Act of 1994 (P.L. 103-382) challenges the traditional practice of using race and ethnicity as the deciding factor in adoption. The act bans discrimination in placement decisions based solely on race, color, or national origin. . . . It allows agencies to consider the cultural, ethnic, or racial background of children and the capacity of the prospective foster or adoptive parents to meet the needs of the children based upon their background; and stipulates that agencies engage in active recruitment of potential foster or adoptive parents who reflect the racial and ethnic diversity of the children needing placement (Smith in Fong et al., 1996:23).

**Test your understanding of familiness and People of Color by taking this short Quiz.**

## FOCUS: WOMEN

### Feminist Perspectives on Families and Familiness

The family arena has traditionally created and enforced very different and often confining, oppressive, and exploitative roles and expectations for women members at the same time that women are central figures in virtually all traditional (and most alternate) notions of family.

Consistent with our attempts to explore alternatives to traditional approaches to thinking about familiness and its implications for understanding HBSE, the alternatives we explore here reflect efforts to recognize the often complex and oppressive forces emerging from traditional family arrangements. This part of our journey represents another point at which we can rethink or revision familiness in ways that empower all members of families, in this case specifically women members, to reach their full human potential. This, of course, has important implications for social workers' concerns about and responsibilities for assisting all humans in reaching their fullest human potential.

Ferree's synthesis of feminist thinking about the family sphere reflects several dimensions of alternate paradigm thinking in addition to the feminist dimension. It critically examines a number of the dimensions of traditional paradigm thinking. Her synthesis addresses issues of separateness versus interrelatedness; diversity; oppression; privilege; and masculinity/patriarchy.

Ferree describes a number of common themes of feminist premises in thinking about women and familiness. She notes, "male dominance within families is part of a wider system of male power." This patriarchal family arrangement is damaging to women and "is neither natural nor inevitable" (1990:866). Feminist analyses of family question the notion of family as separate from other social institutions such as political and economic institutions. They question notions of family as a "separate sphere" that is a safe and private haven unconnected to the public or outside world. On the other hand, feminist analyses remind us that violence and inequality characteristic of the public world also permeate in significant ways the family sphere. Feminist perspectives suggest that there are very different and often conflicting interests inside families that are associated with gender. Feminist critiques of traditional perspectives on the family suggest "a new approach that (a) defines families as fully integrated into wider systems of economic and political power and (b) recognizes the diverging and sometimes conflicting interests of each member" (1990:867). With this perspective in mind we will explore a number of issues and concepts important for understanding familiness and that have significant consequences for women in the context of family. These issues and concepts will include gender or sex roles, family work, and dual-wage-earner families.

### Gender or sex role?

Traditional notions of sex roles in families emerge out of and along with traditional notions of family and of the "proper" roles of family members, especially the roles of males and females. The traditional notion of family was based largely on the observations by social scientists of "white, middle-class suburban families of the 1950s." As we discovered earlier, what emerged was the nuclear family structure portrayed as the ideal or the norm. Within this structure men were to play the instrumental/breadwinner/leader role and women were to play the socioemotional/homemaker/supportive role (Walsh, 2003:10).

ROBIN NELSON / PHOTOEDIT

*How might the experiences of the woman in this photo reflect the concept of "second shift" described in the narrative? Might this woman need a "wife" in the sense described by Ferree in the discussion of "dual-wage-earner" families?*

Subsequently, we have begun to realize that this model of family caused significant problems for families and their individual members. Wives and mothers were overburdened with responsibilities for the well-being of husbands and fathers, as well as children, at the same time that society undervalued (and in monetary terms attached no value to) their contributions. Fathers and husbands, on the other hand, were seen as head of the household but were in fact on the margins of the family as a result of the demands of their breadwinner role. This placed even more responsibility for the family on wives and mothers. What appeared functional from the perspective of the masculine-focused dominant perspective "proved quite dysfunctional for women in families. . . . The disproportionate responsibility for maintaining the household and the well-being of husband, children, and elders, while sacrificing their own needs and identities, proved detrimental" to women's physical and mental health (Walsh 1993:20; 2003:14–16).

The traditional perspective on sex roles as equal and complementary made invisible the very real power differentials inherent in the perspective. The failure to recognize power differentials built into traditional notions of sex roles—men as strong and women as weak, for example—supported the continuing oppression of women within the structure of family. The analysis of power inequalities within traditional definitions of family has helped to recognize and bring into the open the abuses and inequalities of power and conflict that result in wife battering, marital rape, and incest (Walsh, 1993:380). Not only do narrow, inflexible, and inequitable sex role definitions result in threats to the health of many women, but we also know from the all-too-familiar cases of sexual and physical assault within the context of families that the result for many women can be fatal.

We have noted at a number of points in our journey that issues related to power and inequality are essential to understanding the complexities of HBSE. A gender model is helpful in this regard because it focuses on issues of domination, categorization, and stratification—all fundamental and necessary concepts for understanding power.

### Family work

The term *family work* is a helpful concept for thinking about work in the context of family. **Family work** refers to "the household chores and childcare tasks that must be performed by families to maintain the household and its members" (Piotrkowski and Hughes, 1993:191). Family work is "free" work in that regardless of who does the work, there is no monetary payment for doing it. Traditional views of family see men as the only paid workers in the family and therefore men are seen as the "providers" for the other dependent family members—women and children. Women, on the other hand, are responsible for family work.

Several theories are used to explain the way family work is distributed within families. The *time availability theory* suggests that in two-partner opposite sex households, who does family work is based on rational decision-making; the partner with the most time available assumes greater responsibility for family work. The *economic* or *relative resources theory* also involves rational decision-making, but assumes the male partner brings in the most financial resources and the female partner exchanges her unpaid family work for the economic resources earned by the male partner. The *gender display perspective* posits that men with traditional attitudes about gender will do less family work and men with more alternative or egalitarian attitudes will do more. Using the same perspective, women with more traditional attitudes about gender will do more family work than women with less traditional views of gender.

Scholars have carried out research on which of these theories is the best predictor of who assumes responsibility for family work. Findings of this research suggest the most powerful predictor among the three is the gender display perspective. Men with more traditional gender attitudes did less family work than men with more egalitarian gender attitudes. Women with more traditional gender attitudes did more family work than women with more egalitarian gender attitudes. In relation to the other two rational and income driven perspectives, researchers found that "gender trumps money" (Chesters, 2013:78-92; Wight, Bianchi, & Hunt, 2013).

### Dual-wage-earner families and family work

For many women, entering the work force has resulted in what some writers have referred to as a "second shift." As more and more women have entered the full-time work force to share breadwinning responsibilities, there has not been a corresponding sharing of family work responsibilities by their husbands. Another and seldom discussed aspect of family work is the role of children in performing unpaid labor when both mothers and fathers work for pay outside the household. The division of labor among children in the household is also gendered in that "daughters are still more likely to be given housework than sons, and among sons and daughters who do housework, daughters do more hours of work" (Ferree, 1990:874–875).

More recent research on the division of family work in dual-wage-earner families comparing data for 1986 through 2005 indicates changes in the distribution of household work are occurring. While overall, women continue to do more family work than men regardless their outside earnings status, men are doing more than in the past and women are doing less (Chesters, 2013: 92; Wight et al., 2013: 395-398). However, the shift is not sufficient to have overcome the long-term disparities in family work between men and women. Figure 7.2 illustrates the convergence of typical household duties and gender of the person carrying them out between 1965 and 2011.

Social policy continues to be driven by the implausible assumptions that all family members are equally well off, that above-poverty-line household incomes imply no below-poverty-line individuals within them, and that increasing total family income has the same effect if it derives from a rise in male or female income (Ferree, 1990:878). For us as social workers, this perspective helps us appreciate the implications for women and families in the areas of HBSE, practice, research, and policy.

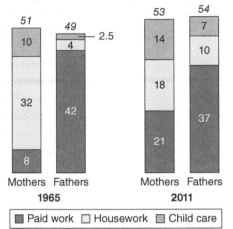

*Average number of hours per week spent on …*

**Paid work**  ☐ **Housework**  ■ **Child care**

Note: Based on adults ages 18–64 with own child(ren) under age 18 living in the household. Total figures (at the top of each bar) may not add to component parts due to rounding.

**Figure 7.2**
Moms and Dads, 1965-2011: Roles Converge, but Gaps Remain

(Parker & Wang, 2013)

**Test your understanding of Women and familiness by taking this short** Quiz.

## FOCUS: SEXUAL ORIENTATION

### Familiness from a Lesbian/Gay Perspective

Traditional approaches to family not only assume a nuclear, two-parent, white, child-centered family form; they also assume a heterosexual pairing/partnership as the foundation upon which family is built. Slater and Mencher (1991) and other scholars point out that such assumptions neglect a significant portion of the population and deny legitimacy to the family forms and functions that exist among gay and lesbian families.

Like a number of other diverse family types, gay and lesbian families have for the most part been treated as if they were deviant and dysfunctional or as if they did not exist at all. Our notion of familiness, along with our search for inclusiveness consistent with our notions of alternative paradigms, recognizes the need to understand family issues related to gay and lesbian families.

Laird suggests that gay and lesbian families must be included in efforts to understand familiness. She suggests further that lesbian and gay families can "teach us important things about other families, about gender relationships, about parenting, about adaptation to tensions in this society, and especially about strengths and resilience" (1993:284). Gay and lesbian families are both similar and different in many ways from heterosexual families.

Like heterosexual families, gay and lesbian families are not a monolithic group. They display a wide range of diversities. As Laird points out, gay men and lesbians vary in terms of race, class, sex, age, religion, political affiliation, and all the other differences displayed among any group of individuals. As a result, gay and lesbian families reflect this wide array of individual differences as well (Laird, 1993:286). However, the general movement for gay liberation has been criticized by many of its diverse members for its lack of diversity and inclusiveness. Carrier, for example, suggests that gay liberation in the United States has been primarily a white, middle-class movement (Laird, 1993:291).

Traditional models of family are also child-centered (see earlier discussion of traditional models). Slater and Mencher note that while some lesbians have and wish to have children, lesbian life is not as child-centered as traditional models of family life. They remind us that childless heterosexual couples also experience this lack of a place in traditional models. Childless couples and lesbian and gay couples do nevertheless "establish and maintain a family unit which passes through discrete stages with their attendant stresses, transitions, and accomplishments" (1991:376).

QUEERSTOCK, INC. / ALAMY

*How might these partners and their families reflect diversity and "diversity within diversity" in some of the ways discussed in this chapter?*

## A need for multiple approaches

Traditional family theories tend to stress clarity of stages and linear progression through them, clarity of roles, and clarity of family boundaries. They tend to see ambiguity in these areas as inherently problematic. They have neglected, however, to consider that the gay and lesbian families who struggle with ambiguities in these areas may result in creating "new ways of relating that are positive for postmodern family functioning" (Demo and Allen 1996:426).

## Defining Gay and Lesbian Families

While gay and lesbian families have much in common with heterosexual families, they are also difficult to define because of their differences from traditional notions of family. Laird (1993:294) suggests that gay and lesbian families might be best referred to as *families of choice* (see definition earlier in this chapter). Gay and lesbian families are "formed from lovers, friends, biological and adopted children, blood relatives, stepchildren, and even ex-lovers, families that do not necessarily share a common household. In fact, in some lesbian communities, the boundaries between family, kinship, and community become quite diffuse." Given all these variations we must recognize that there is no "uniform or normative definition for 'gay family' any more than there is for 'American' family." In addition, Laird argues, "definitions of family are political and ideological, created and recreated in social discourse and shaped in social relations of power" (Laird in Walsh, 2003:178). However, this lack of a single or clear definition of gay and lesbian family may suggest some significant strengths from which heterosexual family studies and social workers working with families might benefit:

> With their relatively fluid boundaries and varied memberships, their patterns of nonhierarchical decision making, their innovative divisions of labor, and the relative weight given to friendship as well as blood relatedness, such families offer further challenge to dominant notions of family structure and function and present an opportunity for mental health professionals to assess the limitations in current definitions of family and kinship (Laird in Walsh, 2003:179).

## Contested Terrain: Gay and Lesbian Marriage

As I write this, intense political and social debates are taking place concerning the rights of gay men and lesbians to form families through marriage or civil unions that provide the same benefits and responsibilities as those accorded heterosexual couples and their families. The context of these debates in terms of outcomes to date has been primarily at the state level, though the debates themselves are also taking place at a national level. In addition, the Supreme Court recently (March 2013) heard arguments concerning the constitutionality of laws recognizing marriage as between a woman and a man only. This case is based on a May 2008 California State Supreme Court ruling declaring it illegal to discriminate against same-sex couples by denying them the right to marry, "after which 18,000 gay and lesbian couples got married there." However, in November 2008 California voters "approved Proposition 8, which amended the state constitution to ban gay marriage" (CNN, 2009). The 18,000 couples who married prior to the passage of Proposition 8 were allowed to retain their marital status. In addition, the Court heard arguments concerning the constitutionality of the federal Defense of Marriage Act (DOMA) passed by Congress and signed by President Clinton in 1996. This law restricts federal benefits only to opposite sex marriages. Since signing the law former President Clinton has reversed his position and now publicly supports same-sex marriage. In addition, the Obama administration has refused to defend DOMA in any court.

In the last several years, many people have changed their position on allowing gay marriage. An NBC/Wall Street Journal poll found the following significant shifts in positions on gay marriage among a variety of groups in the past four years.

- African-American voters have gone from 53 percent opposing gay marriage to 51 percent in favor.
- Blue-collar workers have gone from 80 percent opposed with 18 percent in favor to 47 percent in favor and 43 percent against.
- Voters 65 and older have gone from 80 percent opposed and 16 percent in support to 54 percent opposed and 32 percent in favor.
- Southern voters have gone from 71 percent opposed and 20 percent in favor to 50 percent opposed and 42 percent in favor.

Source: NBC/Wall Street Journal. http://tv.msnbc.com/2013/03/29/african-americans-blue-collar-workers-do-an-about-face-on-gay-marriage-poll/Accessed March 30, 2013.

There have been dramatic shifts among the overall population as well according to a survey by the Pew Research Center conducted between March 13 and March 17, 2013. This research was compared to polling conducted in 2003. According to the findings, in 2003 58 percent of Americans opposed gay and lesbian marriage and 33 percent were in support Within 10 years the percentages have shifted to 44 percent opposed and 49 percent in support (Pew Research Center, 2013).

The map shown in Figure 7.3 on the next page shows the status of gay marriage across the United States.

Note to reader: Use the Source URL for Figure 7.3 to see if the map has changed in the time since it was included here. ©2014 National Conference of State Legislatures. All Rights Reserved. Accessed on March 6, 2014.

## Parenting

The American Academy of Pediatrics offers guidance to gay and lesbian parents about how to answer children's question appropriately for the child's current stage of development. Most important, according to the Academy, is that the parent be honest when responding to children's questions. To prepare parents to respond in age-appropriate ways to their children's questions they suggest the following:

- **Preschool-aged children** often are very curious about their family background, so they may ask many questions about a mother or a father whom they don't know or who isn't always around. It's best to answer their questions simply and honestly. Expect more questions as new ideas occur to your child.
- **School-aged children** will become more aware that their family is different and may want to know about their family background. They may think of new questions as they meet other children from different family backgrounds.
- **Young and older teens** are aware that they are different. Some teens who didn't care before may become self-conscious and even embarrassed about their parents. Some teens may become concerned about their own sexual orientation but may be reluctant to talk with others for fear of being teased or criticized. This may be a good time to talk more about your sexual orientation and life choices (Healthychildren.org, 2005).

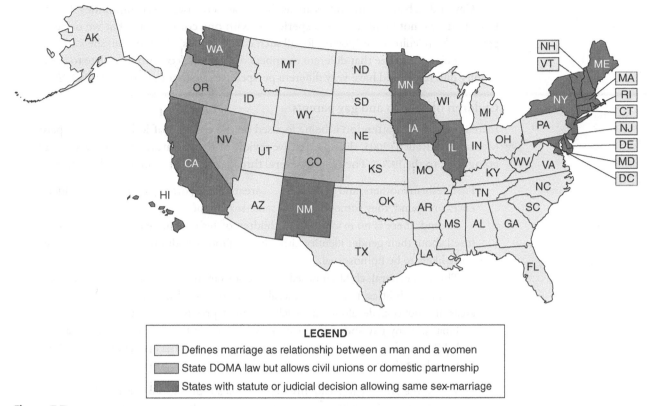

**Figure 7.3**
State Defense of Marriage Acts and Same-Sex Marriage Laws

Source: http://www.ncsl.org/issues-research/human-services/same-sex-marriage-overview.aspx

Adoption and foster care by gay or lesbian families have also been areas of significant debate. For example, the American Academy of Pediatricians has endorsed adoption by gay and lesbian persons (Laird in Walsh, 2003:182). Again in 2013 the Academy reinforced its support: "When marriage of their parents is not a viable option, children should not be deprived of the opportunity for temporary foster care or adoption by single parents or couples, irrespective of their sexual orientation" (Perren & Siegel, 2013).

### Family and community

As noted earlier, the lesbian community has created many innovative and positive responses to the general hostility and lack of support for lesbian familiness in the society at large. The lesbian community may often "offer the lesbian family its only source of positive public and social identity" (Slater and Mencher, 1990:380). The lesbian and gay community allows members to discover and to communicate with each other and among families what is normal and typical for lesbian or gay families and individuals. The community allows members to begin to identify common experiences in meeting challenges and accomplishing family developmental tasks. Lesbian and gay communities are also a source of family rituals specific to the experiences and needs of lesbian and gay families. The community may, for example, offer a context for carrying out rituals borrowed from heterosexual culture, such as exchanging rings or anniversary cards. The lesbian community has also created its own unique validation rituals in recognition of the contextual issues faced by lesbian individuals and families. These include rituals to recognize "coming out" and lesbian commitment ceremonies.

Gay and lesbian communities are as diverse as heterosexual communities. Laird cautions that "we not assume, from experiences with one community, that we understand gay or lesbian 'culture' or 'norms' for all such communities." In addition, she stresses that we must also recognize that different members of the same community relate to the community differently and have very different perspectives on that community (1993:293).

### Children of lesbian and gay parents

Increasing research attention is being focused on the children of lesbian and gay parents. Meezan and Rauch (2005) did an extensive review of the literature on same-sex parenting going back to the 1970s. They found several threads running through the literature.

> First, lesbian mothers, and gay fathers . . . are much like other parents. Where differences are found, they sometimes favor same-sex parents.
>
> Second, there is no evidence that children of lesbian and gay parents are confused about their gender identity, either in childhood or adulthood, or that they are more likely to be homosexual.
>
> Third, in general, children raised in same-sex environments show no differences in cognitive abilities, behavior, general emotional development, or such specific areas of emotional development as self-esteem, depression, or anxiety.
>
> Finally, many gay and lesbian parents worry about their children being teased, and children often expend emotional energy hiding or otherwise controlling information about their parents, mainly to avoid ridicule.

Similarly, the American Academy of Pediatrics reports, "children with gay and/or lesbian parents are ultimately just as happy with themselves and their own gender as are their friends with heterosexual parents." In addition, research comparing children raised by homosexual parents to children raised by heterosexual parents has found no developmental differences in intelligence, psychological adjustment, social adjustment, or peer popularity between them (Healthychildren.org, 2005).

## FOCUS: FAMILIES AND DISABILITY

Social workers are expected by federal mandates as well as our values and ethics to provide services to families and their members with disabilities. In order to do so effectively it is important to understand a range of issues facing these families with whom we work. In addition, we must develop a keen understanding of social environmental issues influencing these families and their members. Some of these issues include culture, income or poverty, and accessibility of services. All these factors can be interrelated for many families of children with disabilities.

Harry (2002) provides a helpful historical overview of approaches used in working with families with children with disabilities. She notes that

> prior to the 1970s, the emphasis was on psychoanalytic approaches to parents, particularly mothers, an approach that for the most part presented the mother as a victim or patient in severe psychological crisis who needed to go through certain stages of reaction before a point of 'acceptance' could be reached.

Harry (2002) notes that this approach may have had some relevance in its attempt to help parents come to terms with their child with a disability. However, she also points out that this approach was limited in several ways. It "focused almost totally on White, middle-class families who could access the kinds of services offered by the psychoanalytic model." It promoted a "pathological view of families of children with disabilities," and it totally ignored cultural differences in the ways families may react to and deal with a child with a disability.

The passage of P.L. 99-457 in the 1986 Education of the Handicapped Amendments brought us to the present point where parents were to be partners or collaborators with service providers for their children. As noted in Chapter 5 and elsewhere, the fundamental approach was to be family-centered practice (Harry, 2002). This approach has also reinforced the importance for social workers of culturally competent practice with families.

Harry (2002) contrasts the current approach to the early years of the disability movement, which she refers to as highly ethnocentric. The primary concern of the leaders of this movement was the fight for recognition by people with disabilities as a minority group or culture with distinct needs and issues. As a result, Harry posits that adding a multicultural focus would have diluted the movement's drive for recognition of its own.

Bailey et al. (1999) point out that "almost all parents experience challenges in learning about and gaining access to services if they have a child or family member with a disability." These challenges for parents include:

1. learning about their child's disability,
2. becoming aware of their child's educational and therapeutic needs,
3. identifying the range of services that potentially could help support them and their child, and
4. gaining access to those services.

Additional interacting factors include:

1. characteristics of the child (e.g., severity of disability, specialization of needs for services or equipment, known features of the disability),
2. characteristics of the family (e.g., education of parents, knowledge of services, advocacy efforts), and
3. characteristics of the community (e.g., availability of resources, attitude of professionals, interagency collaboration) (Bailey et al., 1999).

Bailey et al. (1999) studied Latino/a access and use of the service system provided through P.L. 99-457. They noted that for Latino/as, like parents of many nondominant ethnic groups, there were special challenges to successfully accessing and using services for their children. Some of these challenges included:

- difficulties due to language barriers,
- lack of familiarity with cultural expectations for appropriate help-seeking behavior, or
- professionals who do not understand or appreciate fully the implications of cultural and ethnic variation in values, goals, and behavior.

With the passage of P.L. 99-457 in 1986 and its call for family-centered practice, cultural differences among families of children with disabilities became a significant concern of both researchers and practitioners. For example, in 1993 Weisner studied the differences between European American families and East African families in concerns about caring for their children with disabilities and found that European American parents were very concerned about the difficulty of maintaining equality of treatment toward the siblings and felt discomfort with allotting 'undue' responsibility to the nondisabled siblings. By contrast, such matters were found not to be a cause for concern among the East African parents, in whose family systems sibling equity was not a predominant value and for whom responsibility for younger or less competent siblings was a matter of tradition (Weisner in Harry, 2002).

Additional research on diverse families in the United States has produced four themes important for understanding and working with families of children with disabilities:

1. the fact that social groups construct disability differently from one another and from professionals,

2. the differential expectations for childhood development and differential interpretations of the etiology and meaning of disabilities,

3. the role of culture in parental coping styles, and

4. the effects of any of the foregoing factors on parental participation in the special education process (Harry, 2002).

Harry urges professionals to be cautious of stereotyping that may result from overgeneralizing cultural patterns of constructing disability when working with individual families. For example, she notes that

it is well known that traditional cultural patterns have been described for particular groups, such as the attribution of disability to spiritual retribution or reward among many Asian groups, an emphasis on the wholeness of the spirit within a disabled body among Native American groups, and the belief that conditions such as epilepsy are reflections of spiritual phenomena within the individual (Fadiman 1997 in Harry, 2002).

However, the degree to which these constructions are held by any one family is subject to great variation. Harry also calls for service providers to develop an understanding of the disability perspective of the family with whom they are working, rather than impose their own perspective on the family. For example, Atkin (1991) pointed out that, "Service provision for disabled people [persons with disabilities] usually embodies the views of the provider rather than the user" (p. 37), and called for research and service provision policies that are informed by "an account of disability in terms of black people's perceptions without these perceptions being seen as pathological" (p. 44 in Harry, 2002).

Harry (2002) describes six challenges professionals face in providing effective services to culturally different families:

1. cultural differences in definitions and interpretations of disabilities;

2. cultural differences in family coping styles and responses to disability-related stress;

3. cultural differences in parental interaction styles, as well as expectations of participation and advocacy;

4. differential cultural group access to information and services;

5. negative professional attitudes to, and perceptions of, families' roles in the special education process; and

6. dissonance in the cultural fit of programs.

Malone et al. (2000) provide a helpful list of the types of services social workers can provide to families with children or other members with disabilities:

1. conduct home visits to assess living conditions, patterns of parent–child interaction, and special instruction to child and family;

2. conduct psychosocial developmental assessment of the child in the family context;

3. assess and provide services related to basic family needs and problems in family functioning;

4. investigate allegations of child neglect and maltreatment;

5. provide individual and family counseling;

6. plan and implement family services such as parent support groups and appropriate social-skills building activities for child and parent;

7. identify, mobilize, and link families to available supports;

8. help families to interface necessary social systems (conduct "boundary" work);

9. facilitate linkages among home, school, and community;

10. evaluate community resources or supports and factors that contribute to risk;

11. advocate for family rights and access to community resources;

12. provide information and education to families and professionals;

13. assist with transition planning;

14. serve as a family liaison or negotiator on the assessment and evaluation team;

15. consult with other professionals on family issues.

In addition to delivering culturally competent services in the areas above, social workers must also understand the impact of poverty on these families. Recent studies have found a significant link between poverty and risk for disability in children (Fujiura and Yamaki, 2000; Kaye et al., 1996; Seelman and Sweeney, 1995 in Park, Turnbull, Turnbull III, 2002). In addition, "among children with disabilities aged 3 to 21 in the United States, 28% are living in poor families. By contrast, among the children without disabilities in the same age range, only 16% are living in poverty" (Fujiura and Yamaki, 2000 in Park et al., 2002).

Park et al. (2002) note:

the fact that households with a family member with developmental disabilities have significantly lower income and greater dependence on means-tested income support indicates that poor families of children with a disability will be affected by poverty more severely than either poor families of non-disabled children or affluent families of children with a disability (Fujiura and Yamaki, 1997).

## SUMMARY/TRANSITION

In this chapter we explored some significant current influences on families. We have considered some social work implications of familiness. Traditional perspectives on family were examined, including definitions, historical perspectives on the family, family developmental tasks, life cycle notions of family, and some changes that have occurred in traditional perspectives on family. Divorce, remarriage, and stepfamilies were explored as traditional because of the number of individuals and families struggling with divorce and remarriage. It was recognized, though, that for the individuals struggling with the challenges of divorce, remarriage, and the formation of stepfamilies, these family constellations are in all likelihood considered alternative.

In this chapter we also explored alternative perspectives on familiness. We surveyed some alternative definitions of *family* or *familiness* and examined multifaceted definitions of *familiness* that attempt to integrate both traditional and alternative aspects. We explored a number of issues related to families and people of color. We employed an ecological approach to better understanding families of color. This approach included investigation of adaptive strategies employed by people of color to deal with the consequences of racism and oppression. Among the adaptive strategies explored were family extendedness, social role flexibility, biculturalism, and spirituality and ancestral worldviews. We also explored the impact of migration and immigration on families.

This chapter addressed issues and concerns related to women in families. This included a feminist perspective on family and familiness. Within the feminist perspective we explored gender and sex roles, the concept of family work, family violence, and issues of concern in dual-wage-earner families. In this chapter we explored the issues of familiness from the perspectives of gay and lesbian families. We struggled with definitions of gay and lesbian families. We looked at family roles, gay and lesbian couples and relationships, and the place of gay and lesbian community in considerations of familiness. We also examined some of the findings of research on the status of children of gay and lesbian parents.

**Recall what you learned in this chapter by completing the** Chapter Review.

Finally, we explored the importance of understanding and competently working with families with members who have disabilities. The next chapter will focus on traditional and alternative notions about small groups. We will also consider the social work implications of a variety of approaches to understanding small-group structures and dynamics.

# 8

# Perspectives on Groups

## INTRODUCTION

Knowledge about small groups is essential for social workers. Much of social work practice takes place in the context of small groups. Whether your practice is directed primarily toward individuals, families, organizations, or communities, much of what you do on a day-to-day basis will be done in the context of small groups. Addressing the needs of individuals and families will almost certainly require work in the context of some type of team. Medical social workers working with individuals and families, for example, are often members of multidisciplinary care teams made up of physicians, nurses, dieticians, physical therapists, and others. These teams are small groups and require understanding of the dynamics of small groups. Social workers practicing in an administrative or management context carry out much of their day-to-day practice through such small groups as work groups and committees. If your practice setting is at the community level, you are almost certain to be involved in task forces and consumer groups.

Certainly if you practice as a generalist social worker, you will be involved in small-group efforts at many levels, including any combination of those described earlier. Practice in a public social services setting, for example, may require you to be involved in interdisciplinary teams, staff work groups, support groups for clients, community task forces, and any number of other types of groups.

Our involvement as social workers in such a variety of group settings as those described earlier will require sufficient knowledge about small groups to be effective as both a group member and a facilitator or leader.

## DEFINITIONS

A very basic definition of a group is *"a small, face-to-face collection of persons who interact to accomplish some purpose"* (Brown, 1991:3). Another definition suggests that a group is *"two or more individuals in face-to-face interaction, each aware of his or her membership in the group, each aware of the others who belong to the group, and each aware of their positive interdependence as they strive to achieve mutual goals"* (Johnson and Johnson, 1991:14). Both of these definitions' concern for shared purpose and common interaction clearly differentiate a group from what is often referred to as an aggregate or a mere collection of individuals with no common purpose and little or no mutual interaction. An example of an aggregate or mere collection of people is the people with whom you might ride an elevator. These definitions also suggest a compatibility with the core purposes and values of social work and the assumptions we make about ourselves, others, and social work in this book.

## HISTORICAL PERSPECTIVE

The small group as an important context for understanding and influencing human behavior has a multidisciplinary history. It has roots in the disciplines of education, psychology, sociology, and social work. Concern for understanding the influences of groups on individual and collective behavior is primarily a product of the 20th century, although through much of modern history important questions about the place of groups in our individual and collective lives have been raised.

### History of Group Theory and Practice

Twentieth-century researchers' concerns have been multi-focused, including the role of groups in democracy, leadership, decision-making, work, leisure, education, and problem solving. Social workers have focused their interests in small-group behavior in a range of areas from social reform to the role of groups in education, leisure, therapy, and citizenship.

An early institution through which the influences of groups on individual and community life were studied and used for problem solving was the settlement house movement of the early 20th century. Later on social workers turned their interests in groups to the therapeutic or treatment potential of groups for dealing with mental illness and other problems in living. More recently, social workers have extended their interests in and work with groups to their use as a means of self-help and support for the persons with whom we work. Self-help and support groups are used to address a great variety of issues, from increasing political awareness, as in consciousness-raising groups in the women's and civil rights movements, to groups for dealing with addictions, physical or sexual abuse, and other personal difficulties that can benefit from the assistance of others with similar experiences (Brown, 1991; Johnson and Johnson 1991; Worchel, Wood, and Simpson, 1992).

### Professional Identity

**Practice Behavior Example:** Know the profession's history.

**Critical Thinking Example:** Give an example of how group work history adds to our body of knowledge about the profession's overall history?

## History with a Group

Just as it is important to have some sense of the emergence in history of concern for small groups as a unit of study and as an important environment within which human behavior occurs, it is important to recognize the impact of historical factors on the development of any particular small group. Every small group with which we deal or to which we belong is heavily influenced by the past experiences of the members of the group. Group members do not enter group situations from a vacuum. We come to groups having had past experiences in groups—both positive and negative. We come to groups with perspectives on other people based on our past experiences with others. Depending on the quality of our past individual and group experiences, it is possible that two different people can join the same group at the same time and have diametrically opposed perceptions about what their shared experience in the new group will be like. Maleka can enter a group for the first time and see in the faces of the other group members rich and exciting possibilities for new friendships, new ideas, and new solutions to her problems. Anthony can look at the same faces and see a terrifying collection of strangers and potential enemies waiting to create many more problems for him than they could ever solve. It is out of this diversity of perceptions, based on radically different pasts, that the challenge of groupness emerges. As social workers, we are often charged with guiding these very different people to share their differences in an attempt to confirm the hopes of Andrea and to allay the anxiety and the fears of Mitchell so both can benefit from each other's experiences and come closer to fulfilling both their potentials as humans. We cannot hope to do this unless we are aware of the history and experiences we bring to the group ourselves. What, then, is this mysterious entity called the small group?

Before we explore specific approaches and concepts for understanding small groups, it may be helpful to recognize some similarities among models and concepts used for understanding human behavior in group environments and approaches to understanding human behavior at other levels with which we are concerned in this book. Models for understanding small-group development, for example, share a number of things with models for understanding individual and family development. Perhaps the most apparent similarity is that of stage-based models of group development. Many approaches to understanding the development of any particular group include some framework based on developmental stages. Many of the concepts for explaining small-group structures and functions also can be applied to organizational and community levels of human behavior. Such concepts as leadership, roles, norms, and socialization are examples of concepts used for understanding small groups that we will see again as we explore organizations and communities.

**Test your understanding of Definitions and History of Groups by taking this short** Quiz.

# TRADITIONAL AND ALTERNATIVE PERSPECTIVES

## Basic Concepts

We will examine a number of basic dimensions and concepts commonly used to explain small-group structures and dynamics, whether discussing traditional or alternative perspectives on groups. As we explore these basic dimensions and concepts we will examine the different emphasis placed on the concepts in traditional and alternative paradigm thinking.

## Product and Process Dimensions

One way of thinking about a group is to consider whether the group is product or process focused. Some students of groups have emphasized the product or outcome dimension, while others have been primarily concerned with internal group processes that occur during the life of a group. The dimensions of outcome and process are also sometimes referred to as *task* and *maintenance*, or *instrumental* and expressive (Anderson and Carter, 1990; Napier and Gershenfeld, 1985; Worchel et al., 1992). All these terms suggest that groups operate simultaneously on two levels. The *task level* is concerned with the accomplishment of the concrete goals of the group—a task force must complete a grant application to begin a service to people with AIDS or who are HIV positive, for example. The *process dimension* is concerned primarily with the nature of the relationships among the members and their impact on the functioning of the group. For example, this dimension includes the socioemotional needs of the task force members—task force members must develop effective processes for relating to one another and for addressing their individual feelings related to AIDS and HIV in the group context in order to effectively complete the task. The members must be able to work together.

## Goals and Purposes

Most researchers and practitioners agree that all groups must have elements of both outcome and process. There is a good deal of disagreement, however, on which element of this dimension should be of primary concern. The amount of attention to task or process is influenced by the goals or purposes of the group. A *group goal* is most simply defined as *a place the group would like to be* (Napier and Gershenfeld, 1985:181–225).

Traditional perspectives would suggest that a task-oriented group such as the one discussed earlier might give precedence to accomplishing its goal of completing the grant application over concerns for how well the group members were able to "get along" with each other. Alternative perspectives would suggest, however, that the group is not driven exclusively by its stated goal or purpose at all times. The group cannot accomplish its task unless members can get along with each other well enough to unite in their efforts to accomplish the task and unless they are comfortable enough as individuals with the group's goal to invest their individual energies in pursuit of that group goal. These are process and socioemotional dimensions that cannot be separated from the product or task dimensions.

Some groups have purposes or goals that are more process or socioemotionally oriented than task or outcome oriented: a men's consciousness-raising group formed to address members' concerns for developing ways of relating to and behaving toward each other and to women in ways that are nonsexist, for example. Such a group is concerned primarily with changing members' ways of thinking, relating, and behaving. Its focus is process oriented. However, it also requires that the group accomplish concrete tasks as well. Members will need to determine tasks they will undertake to operate the group—when, where, and how often they will meet, for example. However, the task dimension is clearly secondary to the process concerns of the group for focusing on socioemotional and relationship dimensions.

Goals and purposes of groups, whether process or product focused, may be determined externally or internally. The task force goal to develop a grant application for AIDS/HIV services may have resulted from an agency board of directors' decision to develop services in this area and the board's direction to the staff to form a task force to implement its directive. It might have emerged as a result of external concerns raised by persons in the community who were HIV positive, who had AIDS, or who provided care for persons with AIDS. It might also have emerged from discussions among the persons who were members of the task force about the needs for such services and about the possible mechanisms for funding services. The men's consciousness-raising group's goals or purposes may also have been determined externally or internally. The group might have been created by agency management as a result of complaints by women coworkers, for example, of sexist behavior and sexual harassment by their male colleagues. The group might also have emerged out of its members' own recognition of their difficulties in relating to and behaving toward the women in their lives in nonsexist ways.

Whether groups' goals and purposes come about as a result of external or internal forces has important consequences for the ways groups will operate. As social workers we are likely to find ourselves in the position of facilitating or being a member of groups with externally imposed as well as internally determined goals and purposes.

## Membership

The examples of external and internal determination of goals for a group also suggest that members of groups come to be members in different ways. The different sources of goal setting for the AIDS/HIV task force and the men's group illustrate that membership might be voluntary or involuntary. The task force members called upon by the board of directors of their agency and the men required to be members of the consciousness-raising group because of their coworkers' complaints probably felt very different about being a part of their respective groups than did the task force members and the men's group members who decided among themselves that they wanted to become members of their group.

Membership describes the quality of the relationship between an individual and a group. Group members, whether they are in the group voluntarily or involuntarily, know they are members of the group. How we come to be a group member and how we feel about our membership in a group influences the level of membership we will have in the group. It influences how much of ourselves we will invest in the group.

Group membership can be differentiated by levels. *Formal or full psychological membership* suggests that we have invested ourselves significantly in the group and its goals; we feel a high degree of commitment to the group's goals and to the other group members. The other members of the group likewise see and accept us as full members of the group. When we are voluntarily a member of a group, and when we participate directly in determining the group's goals, we are more likely to experience full psychological membership.

We do not have this degree of membership in all groups to which we belong. We might be a marginal member of some groups. *Marginal members* are not willing to invest themselves fully in the group. They may do what is necessary to remain a member of the group, but only what is minimally necessary. Marginal members do make contributions to groups, but to a much lesser degree than full psychological members. There are a number of factors that result in marginal membership. We may be in the group involuntarily. We may not feel that we were a part of the process of forming the goals of the group. If the goals of the group were determined externally, for example, we may feel less ownership in its goals and therefore be more marginal as a member. We may also be a marginal member if we simply do not have time to become a full member but wish to support the goals of the group and contribute what we can in support of the group goals. In other words, marginal membership is not necessarily negative for the group or member. Marginal members can provide valuable services to groups.

Another level of membership in groups that is worthy of note is aspiring membership. An *aspiring member* is one who is not formally a member of a group but wishes to be a member. As an aspiring member we might identify strongly with the goals of the group, but we may not be able to become a formal member of the group for a variety of reasons. The group may not have room for us or we may not meet membership criteria for the group (Napier and Gershenfeld, 1985:74–111).

As group facilitators and members, social workers need to be particularly aware of this level of membership. Aspiring members offer a rich potential source of new group members who are likely to invest a great deal of energy in helping the group to achieve its goals. As social workers, we should also be concerned that aspiring members are not being excluded from membership in a group because of barriers that deny them access. If an aspiring member has a disability that makes it impossible for her or him to get to the group meetings and therefore does not apply for formal membership, we must act to move that aspiring member to full membership. If a member aspires to be a part of a group but finds or believes that her or his gender, sexual orientation, income, or other difference prevents him or her from being a full member, we must act to remove such barriers to membership.

## Leadership, Followership, and Decision-Making

Bass (in Gastil, 1994:954–955) provides a *general definition of leadership* as "an interaction between two or more members of a group that often involves a structuring or restructuring of the situation and the perceptions and expectation of the members. . . . Leadership occurs when one group member modifies the motivation or competencies of others in the group. Any member of the group can exhibit some amount of leadership." Gastil argues that leadership is "only *constructive* behaviors aimed at pursuing group goals" (1994:955). One traditional approach to leadership put forth by Lewin suggests three styles of leadership:

1. *Democratic leadership* focuses on group decision-making, active member involvement, honest praise and criticism, and comradeship. (We will examine in more detail democratic leadership later in this section);

2. *Autocratic leadership* characterized by domineering and hierarchical leader behavior; and

3. *Laissez-faire leadership* characterized by an uninvolved, non-directive approach to leading (in Gastil, 1994:955).

### Practice Contexts

**Practice Behavior Example:** Provide leadership in promoting sustainable changes in service delivery and practice to improve the quality of social services

**Critical Thinking Question:** After reading the section, "Leadership, Followership, and Decision-Making," which of the type or style of leadership do you think is the most consistent with social work values and principles?

Other traditional notions of leadership tend to frame this element of group life as a set of inborn traits, as the product of the situation or environment, or as emerging from the position of leadership held by the person. The *trait* notion suggests that leaders are born. It implies that leadership is possible only for people who have the traits of leadership and that these people (leaders) are somehow destined for greatness or influence well above the rest of us. *Situational leadership* suggests that leaders emerge out of the requirements of a particular situation. If a person has the necessary expertise required to solve a particular problem, the requirements of the situation create the leader. *Positional leadership* suggests that leaders are created by the positions they hold. The position of chair or president will evoke from its holder the qualities necessary to lead. The authority or influence necessary for leadership comes out of the position or title. Trait, situational, and positional notions of leadership are incomplete or either/or perspectives. You either have the magical traits of leadership or you do not; either you find yourself in a situation requiring your expertise or you do not; either you end up in a leadership position or you do not. These traditional notions are incomplete and leave out some important considerations. They suggest that leaders and followers are mutually exclusive roles (Napier and Gershenfeld, 1985:227–296). In Chapter 8 we will address traditional and alternative types and styles of leadership in the context of organizations.

### Functional leadership

An alternative perspective on leadership suggests that leaders and followers are not so dichotomous or separate from each other. A *functional* definition of leadership suggests that leadership is simply behavior that assists a group to achieve its goals. Such a definition recognizes the potential for anyone in the group to be a leader. Leadership is demonstrated simply by doing what is necessary to help the group reach its goals, whether they be process or product related. Such a definition recognizes that sometimes people have the necessary characteristics or traits to lead in a particular context. One member's temperament may allow him or her to more readily lead the group in efforts to resolve conflict than others in the group, for example. A functional definition also suggests that a person with a leadership position such as chair or president may more readily lead the group in some formal activities—convening or adjourning the group, for example. A functional perspective also suggests that there are times when the environment or situation may call upon the expertise of a particular member to lead the group, such as a group facing a financial crisis calling upon a member with accounting skills to lead it through the crisis. Functional leadership offers an alternative notion of leadership that recognizes leadership within a group as mobile and flexible. A functional definition makes it difficult to distinguish leaders from followers, because everyone is viewed as having the potential for leadership. Functional leadership might be effectively practiced through a rotating rather than a fixed structure of leadership in groups. Rotating leaders also reduces tendencies toward hierarchical and positional group structures. Alcoholics Anonymous groups are examples of group efforts in which functional and nonhierarchical forms of leadership are emphasized.

The potential for leadership on the part of all group members, however, may not necessarily be realized. Unless group members recognize the existence of this potential in each other and unless they allow each other to act on their potential, it will not be realized. In effect, this alternative notion of leadership suggests that, contrary to traditional notions, leaders are not simply born or created by positions or situations; leaders are created by followers. Other members of the group allow leaders to lead by accepting the leadership behavior of the member who leads (Napier and Gershenfeld, 1985:227–296).

Some researchers suggest that the concept of leadership as traditionally understood, especially trait or "great person" notions, is alienating. Gemmill and Oakley (1992: 120) suggest that by accepting the necessity of a leader or of a hierarchy with leaders at the top, we "de-skill" everyone else in the group. We relinquish our potential for developing our own "critical thinking, visions, inspirations and emotions" when we define leadership as a special quality or set of qualities held only by some special person (or select group of persons) other than ourselves. By turning over decision-making and power to someone else through traditional ways of defining leaders we *are* able, however, to remove much of the uncertainty and ambiguity we are likely to experience in small groups with functional, rotating, or nonhierarchical leadership approaches. In doing so we—the followers—are relieved of making risky, sometimes frightening decisions. In turning ourselves over to a leader, we are, unfortunately, also relieved of the opportunity to participate equally in addressing issues that directly affect us (Gemmill and Oakley, 1992:117–123).

This notion of leadership is compatible with the dimensions of alternate paradigm thinking. It replaces hierarchy with equality. It incorporates a feminist perspective in redefining power from "power over" to "power as the ability to influence people to act in their own interests, rather than induce them to act according to goals and desires of leaders" (Gemmill and Oakley, 1992:124). It "re-visions" or reconceptualizes leadership as supportive and cooperative behaviors rather than impersonal and competitive behaviors. It redefines leadership as "people taking the initiative, carrying things through, having ideas and the imagination to get something started, and exhibiting particular skills in different areas" (Bunch and Fisher, 1976 in Gemmill and Oakely, 1992:124–125).

## Democratic Groups

As has been the case with other alternate or "new" perspectives, this alternative view of leadership has a great deal in common with what we historically have defined—although we have rarely practiced it—as democracy or democratic decision-making. This reconceptualization also is more compatible with the core concerns of social work. It emphasizes several elements of what has been defined as **unitary democracy**—cooperation, common ground, relationship, and consensus (Gastil, 1992:282).

Gastil (1992:278–301) defines small-group democracy and the decision-making processes that must take place in democratic groups. According to Gastil, **democratic groups** have power and they distribute that power among members equally. They are inclusive and their members are fully committed to democratic process. They are based on relationships among members that acknowledge their individuality while also recognizing mutual responsibilities as group members. Democratic groups operate through processes that ensure each member equal and adequate opportunities to speak and participate. These opportunities are coupled with a willingness on the part of members to listen to what others have to say. The element of listening is perhaps harder to ensure than that of guaranteeing the opportunity to speak. One is meaningless, however, unless the other is present. This decision-making process also protects a member's right to speak and be heard in dissent from a position taken by the group as well (Gastil, 1992).

### Democratic leadership/followership

A definition of **democratic leadership** is "behavior that influences people in a manner consistent with and/or conducive to basic democratic principles and processes, such as self-determination, inclusiveness, equal participation, and deliberation" (Gastil, 1994:956). Gastil specifies that "leadership is behavior, not position" (1994: 957). A democratic group is called a **demos**.

Three primary functions of democratic leadership behavior:

1. *Distributing responsibility:*
   - "Seeks to evoke maximum involvement and the participation of every member in the group activities and in the determination of objectives"
   - "Seeks to spread responsibility rather than to concentrate it" (Krech et al. in Gastil, 1994:958).

2. *Empowerment:*

- Requires a politically competent membership skilled at speaking, thinking, organizing, and many more tasks.
- Democratic leaders avoid behaviors associated with a "great man" [*sic*] model of leadership.
- Democratic leaders show genuine care and concern for members without being paternalistic.
- Democratic leaders seek to make members into leaders; seek to make themselves replaceable.

3. *Aiding deliberation:*

- Through constructive participation, facilitation, and maintenance of healthy relationships and a positive emotional setting
- Through careful listening and respectful acknowledgment of others' views (Gastil, 1994:958–961).

**Facilitation** The term "facilitator" typically refers to someone with multiple roles and responsibilities in the group. These may include leader, mediator, conflict manager, or content expert. Most researchers agree that facilitation involves attention to both the task/product and the process/relationship dimensions (Kolb, Jin, & Song, 2008: 118–120). Gastil, (1994:961) differentiates the concept of facilitation from participation. *Facilitation*, according to Gastil, is a form of ***metacommunication***, which is communication *about* the group's deliberation. Facilitation involves:

1. Keeping deliberation focused and on track
2. Encouraging free discussion and broad participation, sometimes needing to discourage verbosity and draw out shy or marginalized voices (at the community level this may mean outreach to isolated or marginalized groups who have not, but should have a voice in public debate)
3. Encouraging "members to observe the norms and laws that the demos has adopted"
4. Maintaining a healthy emotional setting, positive member relationships, and a "spirit of congeniality" (Gastil, 1994: 961).

Another somewhat similar perspective on group facilitation focuses on five primary competencies needed for effective facilitation. These include:

1. **Communication.** Listens actively. Uses body language and nonverbal communication effectively. Asks and uses questions effectively.
2. **Relationship (Process)** Creates a climate that supports interaction and discussion. Manages intragroup conflict and difficult or disruptive members effectively.
3. **Task (Product).** Assists in developing/implementing goals and establishing ground rules (Norms) along with other members.
4. **Organization.** Plans meeting and does follow-up.
5. **Professional ethics.** Of course underlying the entire facilitation process is attention to professional social work values and ethics. (Adapted from Kolb et al., 2008: 128)

The researchers carrying out research on facilitator competencies found "listens actively" to be the highest ranked competency (Kolb et al., 2008: 127). Facilitation and leadership are often considered the same thing; however, they are not synonyms.

**Distribution of leadership**  Gastil stresses that democratic leadership should be distributed widely among the group members. He believes that diffusing leadership does not make a group "leaderless," instead it makes the group "leaderful." This "leaderful" or diffused leadership is reflected in the suggestions below:

- In the ideal demos, more than one person serves every leadership function, no individual does an inordinate amount of the leading, and every group member performs leadership functions some of the time.
- In most cases it is possible to rotate leadership functions among the membership so that individual members become capable of serving a variety of leadership functions. (Gastil, 1994:962)

**Follower responsibilities**  The wide distribution of democratic leadership behaviors among all members requires significant follower responsibilities. *Followers*:

1. Must take responsibility for the well-being of the demos
2. Must be accountable for their actions and decisions
3. Are ultimately responsible for maintaining their autonomy (independence)
4. Recognize ways they can function as leaders
5. Must be willing to work with those leading (Gastil, 1994:963–964).

When is democratic leadership not appropriate?

This alternative approach to democratic leadership is not appropriate for all group settings. Democratic leadership is not appropriate:

- When the problem is clearly defined and has an obvious technical solution, e.g., setting a broken bone
- When an "executive" or "judge" is needed to interpret a decision of the demos, but judge/executive must remain accountable to demos
- If group is indifferent to a problem
- When the problem is not within the jurisdiction of the group (Gastil, 1994: 964–965).

Why do people reject democratic leadership?

- Because the democratic structure threatens their undemocratic authority. To move toward democracy would cost status, power, money.
- Some people have authoritarian values and have a strong belief in "the justness and efficiency of powerful, directive authorities."
- "Most people have, to some degree, an unconscious and conscious desire for a hero, a charismatic figure capable of solving our problems and sweeping away confusion."
- Some people reject the very notion of leadership and do not believe in the necessity of leaders (anarchic). (Gastil, 1994:970)

This decision-making process is very different from traditional autocratic approaches to decision-making based on hierarchical structures in which leaders have sufficient power and authority to impose their position and will on members. It is also quite different from traditional notions of democratic leadership styles of decision-making in which only majority rule is emphasized. This model's emphasis on high degrees of participation and efforts to achieve consensus seeks decisions that respect the concerns and standpoints of all members. It does not suggest that every member will agree equally with every decision made by the group, but that every member will feel sufficiently heard to abide by the decision of the group. Such decision-making processes take considerably more time than traditional autocratic or simple majority rule processes, but both process and product are beneficiaries of the responsible participation and resources of all members rather than of a few in leadership positions (Gastil, 1992).

Implementing alternative models of leadership, followership, and decision-making is quite challenging and demands a great deal from group members. These models require a high degree of self-awareness on the part of all members. Members must be aware, for example, of limits on the group's time. Members must be careful to ensure that others have time to speak and be heard. Members are challenged through these processes to be as concerned with the collective good as they are with their individual well-being. These cooperative, collective, and highly participative processes are often very difficult to learn and to implement. This is especially the case for many of us who have been socialized into competitive, individualistic, and hierarchical structures and processes for group decision-making.

While cooperative, collective, and participative leadership and decision-making processes seem at odds with the competitive, individualistic, and hierarchical leadership and decision-making approaches consistent with the dominant paradigm, alternative approaches have a long history of use by many American Indian tribes in North America. Attneave reminds us that for many of these tribes:

> Tribal histories never suggested the impatient solution of majority vote so revered by "democracies." If a sizable portion of the band, tribe, or village dissented, discussion continued until some compromise could be reached. Except when asked specifically to do so, no one spoke for anyone else, and each was expected to participate. Discussions could last for hours, even days, until all were heard and a group decision was reached (Attneave in McGoldrick, Pearce, and Giordano, 1982:66–67).

Attneave (1982:67) notes that even today the influence of the old alternative approaches can be seen and that "tribal meetings still last for hours, and tensions can be high as one faction seeks consensus while another pushes for a majority vote." This is an indication of the challenges to be faced when alternative perspectives and traditional ones meet.

## Roles and Norms

Other basic concepts that help us to understand human behavior in the context of groups include roles and norms. *Roles* are expectations about what is appropriate behavior for persons in particular positions. Roles may be formally assigned, such as president or recorder, or they may be informal and based on the interests and skills of individuals such as harmonizer (someone the group looks to keep the peace) or summarizer (someone skilled in restating the key elements from a discussion).

As members of groups we play multiple roles, depending on the current needs and demands of the group. Sometimes our multiple roles tend to contradict each other.

**Human Behavior**

**Practice Behavior Examples:** Know about human behavior across the life course; the range of social systems in which people live; and the ways social systems promote or deter people in maintaining or achieving health and well-being.

**Critical Thinking Question:** Give one example of how a specific group might promote and one example of how a specific group might deter people (group members, others influenced by the group, the group's purpose, etc.) in maintaining or achieving health and well-being.

When we find ourselves in this situation we are experiencing role conflict. *Role conflict* "refers to the disparity which an individual experiences among competing roles" (Brown, 1991:75). We are likely to experience role conflict, for example, if we are assigned by our agency administrator to facilitate a group and we attempt to play roles to facilitate a functional, democratic, and consensus-oriented leadership style, but we are given a very short time to accomplish the goal set for the group by the administrator. We experience a conflict between the demand of the alternate roles required to be a consensus builder and the traditional and more time-saving leadership roles based on majority rule or even autocratic leadership.

Such conflicts are often not easily resolved. In most instances resolution requires a compromise between what we would prefer ideally and what is possible practically. For example, if there is insufficient time to reach complete consensus, we can still emphasize the need for everyone to participate in discussions and decision-making to the maximum extent possible. We can also look to the other group members for ways to make the process as participative as possible, given the time constraints, rather than shifting entirely to an autocratic approach.

*Norms* are the "group's common beliefs regarding appropriate behavior for members." Norms guide group members' behaviors in their interactions with each other (Johnson and Johnson, 1991:16–17). They help members know what to expect of others and what is expected of them. Roles and norms are important concepts for understanding both traditional and alternative perspectives on groups. The specific nature of the roles and norms that structure a group may serve either to maintain power inequality and restrict diversity or they may serve to guide groups to ensure that power is shared equally and that diversity is sought and respected. Norms for a specific group emerge over time and must be learned by new members entering the group. This process of learning the norms of the group is referred to as socialization. We have discussed socialization processes previously in the context of individual development and as a process through which families transmit to their children the values and rules of behavior of the family and the society in which the family lives.

## Conformity and Deviance in Groups

Two factors related to roles and norms important to consider in groups, both as a leader or facilitator and as a group member, are the concepts of conformity and deviance in groups. Conformity refers to "bringing one's behavior into alignment with a group's expectations" (Sabini, 1995:A3). *Deviance* is defined as violation of "norms or rules of behavior" (Curran and Renzetti, 1996:10). We will explore these concepts by looking more at the related concepts of idiosyncrasy credit, groupthink, and team think.

### Idiosyncrasy credit

Hollander defines idiosyncrasy credit as "the potential for individuals to behaviorally deviate from group norms without being sanctioned," and also as the "'positively disposed impressions' a person acquires as a member of a group" (Estrada, Brown, Lee, 1995:57). Idiosyncrasy credit or the ability to deviate from group norms without negative sanction from other group members can be gained in a number of ways. It can be gained by importing it from external sources (you secure outside funding for your group to reach its goals); by being assigned a high-status role within the group (your status as group chair); by displaying competence (your negotiating skills allowed you to settle a troubling conflict within the group); by conforming to group norms (you almost always adhere to group norms, so you are occasionally allowed to violate a norm, with the group trusting that based on your history you will return to adhering to the norms); or by being group-oriented in your motivation (the group trusts that your deviance will be good for the group because you have in the past worked for the good of the group). Hollander noted that there are limits to the extent and use of idiosyncrasy credits that group members will allow. Hollander posited that "members will only allow them to act differently in a manner that is consistent with their high-status roles" (Estrada et al., 1995:58–59).

## Individual and Group Aspects

Traditionally, some researchers have directed their interest toward the individuals who constitute groups, while others have concentrated on the group as an entity in itself, separate in many ways from the individuals who make it up (Johnson and Johnson, 1991:15; Worchel et al., 1992:2). Alternative perspectives on groups suggest that we must recognize the importance of groups both for the individuals who make them up and the group as a whole.

Process and outcome, goals and purposes, and levels of membership may all look very different, depending on whether one is looking at the dimension from the perspective of the individual group member or from that of the group as whole. Much of what must happen in a group involves striking a balance between what is best for the individuals who make up the group and what is best for the group as a whole. At all levels groups must struggle to achieve an optimum balance between meeting the individual needs of the members and the needs of the group as an entity.

As social workers who will be responsible for facilitating and practicing in groups, we must recognize the need to help blend the goals of individual members with the purposes of the group in such a way that one does not constrain the other but actually complements the other. All the concepts and dimensions of groups we have explored thus far must be considered in our efforts to help individual members and the group as a whole to accomplish their goals. We must recognize that whether a group's goals are set internally or externally and whether its membership is voluntary or involuntary will influence how well individuals who constitute the group can come together as a group and operate as a unit. A group in order to be a group must create a bond among its members, often referred to as cohesiveness. This is a complex and difficult task that cannot be accomplished without the support of group members.

As we discussed in our examination of membership, individuals come to groups with a range of levels of commitment and investment in the group. Individuals come to groups with their own goals for being there. For involuntary members, the goal may be simply to put up with and put into the group enough to survive until they can leave. For voluntary, full psychological members the individual goal may be to do whatever is necessary to see the group's purposes fulfilled. Their individual goal may be virtually the same as the group's goal. This is of course more likely if the members feel they have a part in fashioning the group's goal and if they can therefore see themselves and their individual goals reflected in the group's goal. Alternative perspectives on groups that place a premium on process and participation, cooperation, consensus decision-making, and shared or functional leadership tend to be more able to blend individual and group interests and needs.

### Agendas

Achieving a balance between the needs of the individual and those of group, however, cannot be achieved effectively unless members feel able to state and make known to other members their own goals, interests, and reasons for participating in the group. This process is sometimes referred to as agenda setting in groups. If individuals are able to voice their individual agendas for the group, the members can then work to effectively blend members' individual agendas with the purposes or goals of the group to create more integrated *surface agendas*. When agendas are not brought to the surface in this manner they are referred to as *hidden agendas*. You have probably heard this term in reference to groups with which you have been associated. One member may suggest to another (usually outside the context of the group meeting) that one of the other members has a hidden agenda. What they really mean is that that member has individual goals he or she wishes to achieve through the group that have not been brought to the surface and shared with the other members of the group. A hidden agenda is not necessarily damaging to the group, but hidden agendas often create difficulties for groups. They are often sources of confusion and interfere with group progress in setting and moving toward shared group goals. On the other hand, if a member has an unspoken individual goal that he or she wishes to achieve through the group that is not contrary to the goals of the group, it need not be problematic. For example, in the men's group we discussed earlier, if a member has as an individual and unspoken goal, improving his ability to use what he learns in the group to help him socialize his young son to behave in nonsexist ways, this hidden agenda will not likely interfere with the group's overall goal of reducing its members' sexist behaviors.

Just as individual and group goals must be blended and can become problematic if they conflict, roles played by members in groups may serve to advance the interests and needs of the group or they may serve to further individual interests and needs and conflict with the well-being of the group. Napier and Gershenfeld (1985:238–244) discuss individual and group roles in their discussion of leadership behavior in groups. They suggest that any member may exercise leadership by assuming roles conducive to the group's accomplishment of its tasks. They differentiate between group task (or product) and group maintenance (or process) focused roles. They also suggest that roles that serve the individual's interests over those of the group tend to create problems in the group's functioning.

### Product-focused roles

Napier and Gershenfeld list a number of task- or product-oriented roles that serve to help the group select and move toward common outcomes. The *initiator* gets the ball rolling by proposing tasks or goals to the group. The *information* or *opinion seeker* requests facts and seeks relevant information about a group concern. The *information* or *opinion giver* offers information about group concerns. The *clarifier* or *elaborator* interprets and reflects back to the group ideas and suggestions to clear up confusion and offer alternatives. The *summarizer* pulls together related ideas and restates the suggestion after the group has discussed them and offers a decision or conclusion for the group to accept or reject. The *consensus tester* checks with the group periodically to see how much agreement there is to find out how close the group is to reaching a consensus. The product-oriented roles can be found to differing degrees in different groups. Not all groups are characterized by all of these roles (1985:238–244).

## Process-focused roles

Group maintenance, process, or socioemotional roles that help the group move forward as a group are also suggested by Napier and Gershenfeld (1985). The encourager demonstrates warmth, friendliness, and responsiveness to others and gives recognition and opportunities for others to contribute to group efforts. The *expressor of group feelings* attempts to feed back to the group his or her sense of the mood or affective climate of the group. The *harmonizer* attempts to reconcile differences and reduce tensions by helping group members to explore their differences. The *compromiser* is willing to try to reconcile their differences. The *gatekeeper* attempts to keep channels of communication open by helping to bring all members into participation to help the group solve its problems. The *standard setter* suggests standards for the group to use and tests group efforts against the standards of the group. It is important to restate here that these different roles do not necessarily represent separate members of groups (Napier and Gershenfeld, 1985:239–244, 279–280). Our functional definition of leadership implies that different members of the group demonstrate or play these roles at different times depending on the needs of the group and its individual members. As in the case with product-oriented roles, not all groups display all of these process-oriented roles.

## Individual-focused roles

Individual roles represent sets of behaviors that serve the needs of individuals, often at the expense of the well-being of the group. Individuals playing these roles are concerned with meeting their own needs and interests. Napier and Gershenfeld (1985: 241–242) suggest several individual roles that interfere with a group's ability to reach its goals. The aggressor tends to attack and belittle the positions and contributions of others, often sarcastically. The *blocker* suggests why a suggestion will not work and why his or her position is the only one worthy of attention. The *self-confessor* uses the other group members to ventilate about personal problems and to seek sympathy. The *recognition seeker* offers his or her personal response to a problem as exemplary of what should be done in the current group situation. The *dominator* attempts to take over the proceedings of the group by interrupting others, by flattering other members, or by asserting his or her superior status. The *cynic-humorist* uses double-edged humor to remind the group of the pointless nature of its efforts. The *special interest pleader* attempts to sway the group to his or her individual preference by suggesting that his or her position is representative of an entire group of similarly minded people outside the confines of the group.

It is important to recognize that some of the behaviors associated with individual roles described earlier are not inherently harmful to the group's efforts. Certainly at times confrontation, conflict, discussion of personal problems, comparing a current group predicament to similar past individual experiences, humor, and reminding group members of the interests of persons outside the immediate group can be quite helpful to groups. These roles and their associated behaviors become harmful only when they are played at the expense of the good of the group and serve to help individuals gain power over the group for their individual interests and needs.

**Test your understanding of Group Norms and Roles by taking this short** Quiz.

### Groupthink

The concept of idiosyncrasy credit is an example of groups allowing members to deviate from their norms or rules. Group researchers have also noted the power of groups to press members to conform to group decisions, even when the group's decision may not be the best possible decision. Neck and Manz note that "excessive emphasis on group cohesiveness and conformity can interfere with effective thinking processes" (1994: 933). Janis (1982) called this phenomenon *groupthink*. **Groupthink** is "a mode of thinking that people engage in when they are deeply involved in a cohesive in-group, when the members' striving for unanimity override their motivation to realistically appraise alternative courses of action . . . a deterioration of mental efficiency, reality testing, and moral judgment that results from in-group pressures" (Janis, 1982:9).

Janis (1983) and others (Manz & Sims, 1982; Moorhead, Ference, & Neck, 1991) expanded the concept of groupthink to encompass work groups, as well as political groups. They found that the principles were equally applicable to both types of groups. Janis enumerated the following six antecedent conditions contributing to the occurrence of groupthink:

    **a.** group cohesiveness,

    **b.** insulation of the group,

    **c.** lack of a tradition of impartial leadership,

### Symptoms of Groupthink

1. Direct social pressure placed on a member who argues against the group's shared beliefs
2. Members' self-censorship of their own thoughts or concerns that deviate from the group consensus
3. An illusion of the groups' invulnerability to failure
4. A shared illusion of unanimity
5. The emergence of self-appointed mind guards that screen out adverse information from outside the group
6. Collective efforts to rationalize
7. Stereotyped views of enemy leaders as weak or incompetent
8. An unquestioned belief in the group's inherent morality (Neck and Manz, 1994:932–933).

### Decision-Making Defects

1. Incomplete survey of alternatives
2. Incomplete survey of objectives
3. Failure to examine the risks of the preferred choice
4. Failure to reappraise initially rejected alternatives
5. Poor information search
6. Selective bias in processing information at hand
7. Failure to work out contingency plans

### How to Avoid Groupthink

1. Assignment of role of critical evaluator to each member
2. Leader impartiality in setting goals and directions for group
3. Setting up of several independent policy-planning and evaluation groups to work on the same problem
4. Periodic division into separate outside groups and reconvening to work out differences
5. Member discussion and deliberations outside the group with trusted colleagues and reporting back of their findings (This suggestion does not apply to groups with a norm of confidentiality within the group.)
6. Invitation of one or more outside experts (non-core group members) to each meeting
7. Assignment of one member to the role of devil's advocate at each meeting
8. Spending time attending to interrelationships among group members
9. After consensus is reached, holding a "second chance" meeting to express doubts and rethink as necessary. (Janis, 1982: 262–271)

   **d.** lack of norms requiring methodical procedures,

   **e.** homogeneity of members' social background and ideology,

   **f.** high stress from external threats with low hope of a better solution than the leader's, and

   **g.** low self-esteem, temporarily induced by recent failures that make members' inadequacies salient, excessive difficulties on current decision-making tasks that lower each group member's sense of self-efficacy, or moral dilemmas. (Mitchell & Eckstein, 2009: 163–164)

### Avoiding Groupthink

There are seven suggested ways to avoid groupthink. While all seven approaches may not be possible in every group, it is important to use as many of the approaches possible to effectively avoid groupthink. The seven suggestions are:

1. Leaders should assign each member the role of "critical evaluator." This allows each member to freely air objections and doubts.

2. Higher-ups should not express an opinion when assigning a task to a group.

3. The organization should set up several independent groups, working on the same problem.

4. All effective alternatives should be examined.

5. Each member should discuss the group's ideas with trusted people outside of the group.

6. The group should invite outside experts into meetings. Group members should be allowed to discuss with and question the outside experts.

7. At least one group member should be assigned the role of Devil's advocate. This should be a different person for each meeting. (developed by Irving Janis) (Harris, 2010)

Teamthink and avoiding groupthink If we are aware of the symptoms and the faulty decision-making processes that lead to groupthink, we can work to avoid it in our work in groups.

    Other mechanisms for avoiding groupthink included using **methodical decision-making procedures** to "ensure that the group adheres to a highly structured and systematic decision-making process . . . [and make groupthink less likely] by promoting constructive criticism, nonconformity, and open-mindedness within the decision-making group" (Neck and Moorhead, 1995:549). Miranda suggests that the effective use and management of **conflict** in a group can help prevent groupthink: "Productive conflict leads to group satisfaction with outcomes and a perception that the conflict has been useful. Productive conflict also leads to an improved group climate and greater group cohesion and is likely to enhance the quality of the group's decision" (1994:124).

> **Test your understanding of Basic Concepts for understanding groups by taking this short** Quiz.

## Stage Theories and Models

Johnson and Johnson (1991:19) note that there are many different approaches that incorporate the notions of stages or phases through which groups pass. These approaches, they suggest, can be divided into two types. "*Sequential-stage theories* specify the 'typical' order of the phases of group development" and "*recurring-phase theories* specify the issues that dominate group interaction which reoccur again and again" (Johnson and Johnson, 1991:19). Sequential theories are more prescribed and less flexible approaches to the study of groups. They are more consistent with traditional paradigm thinking. Recurring-phase theories are more emergent and fluid and are more compatible with alternative notions of groups.

Hare (1994:441) addresses the diversity of opinions about groups evolving through a series of predictable phases or stages. "Even when phases can be identified, group members may need to recycle through the initial phases several times before they are ready to deal with the task at hand" (Hare, 1994:441).

### Sequential-stage theories

Traditional notions of group life have much in common with traditional notions of individual development. This is especially the case in their conceptualization of groups as a relatively fixed sequence of stages, each of which the group must pass through in a fixed order as it develops and pursues its purposes or goals. There are a number of different models of groups based on sequential-stage theories.

A common sequential-stage model of groups is that of Tuckman and Jensen (1977 in Johnson and Johnson 1991:395; Napier and Gershenfeld 1985:467). They based their model on an extensive review of the literature on group development. This model includes five stages referred to as forming, storming, norming, performing, and adjourning.

1. *Forming* is a stage of uncertainty and some discomfort as new group members come together for the first time in a new situation.

2. *Storming* occurs as group members raise questions and display resistance to the demands of the group. This is a period of conflict and rebellion.

3. *Norming* is the group's establishment of mechanisms for resolving conflict, working together as a group, and accomplishing the group purpose. Order is established.

4. *Performing* is the actual carrying out on the part of the group and its members of the tasks necessary to accomplish its purpose.

5. *Adjourning* is the termination phase of the group. It occurs as the task is completed and the group members make preparations to end their work together.

Another sequential-stage model posits seven stages through which groups pass during their development (Johnson and Johnson, 1991:395):

1. defining and structuring procedures and becoming oriented;

2. conforming to procedures and getting acquainted;

3. recognizing mutuality and building trust;

4. rebelling and differentiating;

5. committing to and taking ownership for the goals, procedures, and other members;

6. functioning maturely and productively; and

7. terminating.

Brown (1991:69–74) synthesizes the work of a number of researchers on small groups, including a number of social work researchers (Garland, Jones, and Kolodny, 1973; Hartford, 1971; Sarri and Galinsky, 1985 in Brown, 1991). His model also incorporates some aspects of the Tuckman and Jensen model outlined earlier. Brown's synthesis is summarized below:

1. *Origin Stage:* This is also referred to by some as a pre-group stage. This stage occurs as an idea for a group, and the sharing of that idea with others is transformed into the decision to create a group.

2. *Formation:* This phase includes people's feeling of uncertainty upon entering a group situation. This phase recognizes that people bring to a new group their past experiences—both positive and negative—with groups.

3. *Power and control:* Differences and conflicts emerge during this stage as people struggle to maintain their personal interests and values at the same time that they are asked to submit to the needs and purposes of the group. An informal structure begins to form, with members taking a variety of task and mainte- nance or socioemotional roles.

4. *Intimacy:* This stage occurs when the socioemotional climate of the group is able to incorporate the differences in personality and experiences of the members. Norms or accepted patterns of behavior begin to take shape. Also, an informal status hierarchy may emerge as people demonstrate leadership behavior that assists the group in achieving its purposes.

5. *Maturation:* Not all groups progress to this stage because of their inability to negotiate the differences necessary to problem-solve or because of insufficient time within which to accomplish the necessary tasks. Groups that reach this stage experience a balance of socioemotional and task activities. They are able to effectively attend both to the product and process dimensions of the group in order to get the work of the group done. People feel able to express their dif- ferences and have them respected. At this stage conflict is likely to occur, but it is not counterproductive to the group's continuance as it was in the power and control phase. There is a high degree of cohesiveness or feelings of connected- ness to each other on the parts of group members.

6. *Separation:* This is the termination or ending phase. This phase may not be expe- rienced by all groups or it may not be experienced by all group members at the same time in any final sense. Separation occurs most noticeably in time-limited groups that meet for a specified purpose or purposes and then disband. In groups that are not time limited, but are ongoing, members come and go in a more fluid way. Separation may be occurring for some members at the same time that other members are newly joining the group in such open-ended groups. Ambivalence characterizes the group or members undergoing termination.

## Recurring-stage alternatives

Many alternative notions of groups accept that groups tend to develop in stages. However, alternative perspectives place much more emphasis on circular or looping patterns within the overall framework of stages or phases. Alternative perspectives are less linear than traditional notions and they are more multidimensional. They accept and even expect that developmental stages are subject to recurrence throughout the life of a group.

Recurring-stage perspectives accept that change and movement are ongoing and necessary in groups. These alternative approaches, however, accept that often for groups to progress they must return to previous stages and revisit past issues. Going forward

often means going backward. Conflict may recur periodically in the group's development, for example. Changes in the larger environment may cause the group to change its
goals or its membership. These external changes may in turn cause the group to return
to internal issues of origin, or conflict. External changes may also cause the group to
jump ahead to consider termination or separation issues.

Both external and internal changes make it necessary for a group to revisit previous
phases or to jump ahead nonsequentially to new stages. These many uncertainties are
part of the reality of change that groups must face and they raise important questions
about the reliability of a traditional, linear, fixed-stage perspective on groups. They suggest that an alternate recurring-phase perspective might be more appropriate.

## Social Systems/Ecological Perspectives

Social systems or ecological perspectives on groups offer another often used alternative
approach to groups. As we discussed in Chapter 3, social workers have found social systems or ecological perspectives helpful frameworks for incorporating some of the important social and environmental influences on human behavior. A systems framework
is helpful in our attempts to understand group behavior more completely for this same
reason. It recognizes the dynamic nature of groups and the interrelatedness of the larger
environment, the group itself, and the members of the group.

Small groups can be viewed as social systems (Anderson and Carter, 1990; Brown,
1991). In doing so we are able to take advantage of the emphasis in social systems thinking on recognizing the interrelatedness and mutual influence of one entity, in this case
the small group, with entities or systems in the larger environment. Systems thinking
also allows us to look inside the system of concern or focal system, the small group in
this context, to see the interrelatedness and mutual influences of the component parts or
subsystems on one another. This is especially helpful in thinking about small groups because it provides us a framework within which to place a number of things we have been
learning during this part of our journey toward more comprehensive understanding of
human behavior and the social environment (HBSE).

For example, a social systems framework allows us to fit the personal and historical
experiences gained by group members in their interactions with the larger environment
prior to joining a group with the impact of these experiences on the person's perceptions
and behaviors inside the group. The impact of racism or sexism that a member experiences outside the group is very likely to influence the behavior of the member inside
the group. A systems approach also recognizes the influence of events that occur in the
larger environment or suprasystem during the life of a group on the behavior of the
group. If cutbacks in agency funding cause the layoff of one or more members of the
task force seeking funds to create services for people who are HIV positive and people
with AIDS, that small group will be forced to respond in some way. Reducing the scope
of its goals, reorganizing responsibilities or tasks within the group, spending time processing the confusion and disruption caused by the change in membership, or perhaps
even terminating for lack of sufficient human resources to continue its work are all possible responses within the group to the change occurring in the environment external to
the group. This environmental change in turn has a major impact on the subsystems or
component parts of the task force. Some individuals not only must leave the group, but
they are now out of work entirely. Other members are faced with additional work and
attendant stress as a result of the loss of other members.

Other concepts from systems thinking can also help us to understand small groups. The concept of *holon* (Anderson and Carter, 1990) appropriately applies to small groups. It defines a critical characteristic of systems as being both a whole and a part at the same time. Certainly our task force on AIDS/HIV and our men's group can be seen as simultaneously whole entities and parts of other systems—agencies, communities, professions. Energy and linkage (Anderson and Carter, 1990) are other helpful concepts in thinking about small groups. Energy, defined as the "capacity for action," (Anderson and Carter, 1990) aptly describes the potential for groups to act and move to solve problems and to develop. Linkage or the ability to connect with other systems to exchange or transfer energy is another helpful way of understanding how small groups do their work. The subsystems, the individual members, of small groups connect with each other and exchange energy as they attempt to define issues, acquire resources, and bring about desired changes. At the same time small groups link with systems in the larger environment to exchange energy. The very goal of the AIDS/HIV task force was to link with other systems external to it in order to acquire funding. The purpose of the men's group was to allow group members to more effectively link or interact with women in the larger environment in nonsexist and nonexploitative ways.

Anderson and Carter (1990) also describe organization as an essential characteristic of social systems. *Organization* is the ability of a system to put its parts together into a working whole. Certainly the characteristics of leadership, followership, membership, and roles and norms all reflect the efforts of small groups to organize or structure themselves to achieve their goals.

Traditional perspectives on small groups and alternate approaches when considered together offer us a great deal of information from which to choose as we attempt to lead, facilitate, and be members of groups. In addition to these perspectives, it is essential that issues of diversity and oppression be considered in conjunction with any perspective or framework for understanding human behavior in a group environment.

## Diversity, Oppression, and Groups

### Groups: Oppression and social and economic justice

Understanding group behavior in the social environment requires serious attention to issues of diversity. Successful group membership or group facilitation requires knowledge of and respect for the differences that we and other group members bring to the group. Groups also can be effective contexts for addressing oppression.

Garvin (in Sundell et al., 1985:461ff) suggests a number of group formats that might be helpful in efforts to empower oppressed people. Groups can be appropriate for addressing needs of members of such diverse groups as gay men and lesbians, elderly persons, persons with disabilities including persons with mental illnesses, and persons living in poverty. The history of social work with groups has its origins in social reform and the settlement house movement (see historical perspective section at the beginning of the chapter). This history reflects the potential for social work in group contexts to address the needs of oppressed persons.

WALTER HODGES/GETTY IMAGES

*As a member of or facilitator for the group in this photo, what are some of the areas discussed by Davis, in 'Groups and People of Color' (next page) you would need to consider?*

## Types of Groups

Garvin describes a number of group formats for use in working with oppressed persons. These formats illustrate more generally the kinds of groups social workers use in their work. We have mentioned some of these group types previously. They include:

1. *Consciousness-raising groups*: Time limited groups that help members share their experiences and explore their feelings about their oppressed status. These groups also help members explore possible avenues to empowerment.

2. *Treatment groups*: Groups that attempt to modify dysfunctional behaviors, thinking, and feelings. For example, a treatment group for gay men might assist the members to deal with feelings of depression and low self-esteem that can result from harassment and other forms of discrimination. It is essential that the group facilitator have a positive perspective on gay and lesbian sexual orientation. This reinforces again the need for social workers to be self-aware and to address our own tendencies toward homophobia (fear of homosexuality).

3. *Social action groups*: Groups directed to bringing changes in the larger environment in order to reduce oppression. Such groups can also teach members valuable skills in working with others and can help members increase their self-esteem.

4. *Network and support groups*: These groups can assist members in reducing feelings of social isolation and in recognizing their strengths by helping members to connect with others in similar situations to provide mutual support and to seek resources.

5. *Skill groups*: These groups have as goals development of members' empowerment skills. Empowerment skills learned and practiced in these groups might include group leadership, social change, communication, and networking (Garvin in Sundell et al., 1985:466–467).

### Groups and people of color

Davis (1985) outlines a number of important considerations both for persons of color and white persons as group members and as facilitators. Davis (1985:325) stresses that issues of color affect all group contexts and perspectives. He urges that "those practitioners who believe their particular group work orientation transcends race and culture would perhaps do best by minorities to refrain from working with them" because race and culture are such powerful forces in this society.

Davis outlines a number of areas related to group dynamics in which race or color plays an important part. These areas include:

1. *Group composition*: Should groups be racially homogeneous or heterogeneous? The purpose of the group should be considered carefully in answering this question. Traditionally, groups purposefully composed of racially similar persons have been formed to enhance ethnic identity. Groups composed of people of different racial and ethnic backgrounds have often been formed to reduce racial prejudice. Davis suggests that a more complex

### Diversity in Practice

**Practice Behavior Examples:** Gain sufficient self-awareness to eliminate the influence of personal biases and values in working with diverse groups.

**Critical Thinking Question:** Identify a personal bias and value you need to be aware of or eliminate in order be more effective as a leader or member of diverse groups?

question of racial composition is raised when race is unrelated to the group's purpose. Preferences of group members vary markedly by color. African Americans have been found to prefer group composition to be approximately half white and half nonwhite. Whites appear to prefer African Americans to compose no more than 20 percent of the members. These findings suggest that for African Americans it is important to feel, in the context of the small group, that they are not in the minority. Whites, on the other hand, appear to be threatened when they are not in the majority. Davis (1985:328–332) suggests that because neither minority persons of color nor majority whites prefer to be in a minority, workers should attempt racial balance in group composition.

Racial balance will also help avoid tokenism in group composition. *Tokenism* is the practice of giving the appearance of representation and access to resources or decision-making without actually doing so. For example, one low-income-neighborhood person is placed on a task force to decide whether a potentially lucrative convention center project should be allowed to displace residents of the low-income neighborhood. All the other task force members are wealthy business executives and land developers who are likely to benefit financially from the project. While the task force composition might give the appearance that the neighborhood is represented, it is highly unlikely that the neighborhood person will be able to counter the interests of the other members. The low-income-neighborhood resident is a token (Davis, 1985:328–332).

2. *Culture and communication*: It is important to recognize that cultural communication styles are important influences in any group. Davis illustrates the contrast between the high value placed on restraint and humility by Asian culture and the value placed on confrontation as a means of testing the validity of one's point of views by many African Americans. Davis suggests that such differences do not mean that different cultures should avoid being mixed in small groups, but that these differences must be taken into account in group process (1985:332).

3. *Trust*: Issues of trust among members and between members and facilitators must receive special attention when dealing with groups composed of whites and persons of color. Experiences brought to the group from the external environment often result in persons of color hesitating to disclose information about themselves to whites out of feelings of distrust based on discriminatory treatment by whites in the larger society. Persons of color also assume, often justifiably so, that white persons know so little about them because of segregation in society that whites have little of value to offer in understanding or solving their problems. On the other hand, whites often are unwilling to accept or trust that minority persons of color, even when in the position of expert, have anything of value to offer (Davis, 1985:332–334).

4. *Status and roles*: Groups composed of persons of color and of whites must attend carefully to issues of status and roles in the group. There is often a tendency to attach statuses and roles within groups according to the patterns of minority/majority relations in the larger society. This is especially problematic when white group members are unaware of changes in status in the larger society of many persons of color who have overcome obstacles and barriers to attain statuses and roles equal to those of whites (Davis, 1985:334).

### Diversity and creativity in groups

Concerns are often raised about the difficulties and problems that flow from diverse groups, especially racially mixed groups. McLeod et al. remind us, to the contrary, that the theme of "'value-in-diversity,' rests on a hypothesis that ethnic diversity, at least when properly managed, produces tangible, positive effects on organizational outcomes" (1996:249). In the corporate context for example, scholars "suggest that ethnic diversity may be related to increased organizational creativity and flexibility . . . [and] that the insights and sensitivities brought by people from varying ethnic backgrounds may help companies to reach a wider variety of markets" (McLeod, Lobel, Cox, 1996:249).

A key argument underlying the notion of diversity as a positive factor in small groups "is that the variety of perspectives and experiences represented on heterogeneous teams contributes to the production of high-quality ideas. Moreover, the variety in perspectives can stimulate further idea production by group members" (McLeod et al., 1996:250). In other words, diversity in perspectives and thought processes results in increased creativity in problem solving in groups. McLeod et al. note that Kanter refers to this as *kaleidoscope thinking*, "twisting reality into new patterns and rearranging the pieces to create a new reality. . . . Having contact with people from a variety of perspectives is one condition necessary for kaleidoscope thinking" (1996:250).

The conflict that may emerge in groups as a result of member diversity may also be an asset. Nemeth, for example, suggests that "minority dissent appears to stimulate exactly what theorists have recommended for improved performance and decision-making, that is, a consideration of the issue from multiple perspectives" (McLeod et al., 1996:250).

McLeod et al. concluded that their findings supported the hypothesis "that diverse groups will have a performance advantage over homogeneous groups on a creativity task requiring knowledge of different cultures. On the other hand, . . . [they] also found evidence suggesting that members of heterogeneous groups may have had more negative affective reactions to their groups than did members of homogeneous groups" (1996:257).

The researchers in this study suggest therefore that diversity in groups is complex and that both increased numbers (quantity) of diverse members and quality of the interaction among members or "proper management of diversity" are equally important in reaping the potential benefits of an increasingly diverse workforce (McLeod et al., 1996:260–261).

Researchers have continued to attempt to unravel the complexity of diversity in the context of work with small groups. Attempts have been made to better understand the interplay of diversity with product or outcome dimensions of groups and the process or socioemotional dimensions. For example, Knouse and Dansby (1999) studied the impact of work-group diversity and work-group effectiveness. While their findings were similar in some ways to previous research, they also posited some additional issues regarding diversity in small groups. They found as others have (Kanter, 1977; Mcleod et al., 1996), that group effectiveness seems to decline and conflict is more likely to increase in groups that include over 30 percent membership from diverse groups. However, they suggest that effectiveness or group product is likely related to other more complex factors, such as status and power differences as Davis (1985) has suggested. They note, "groups that contain powerful higher status minorities or women tend to have less conflict than those with less powerful members of subgroups" (Tolbert et al. in Knouse and Dansby, 1999). These authors suggest that, rather than looking only at the physical proportion of diverse members in a group, we need to seek a more sophisticated overall measure of diversity that also considers such factors as status, power, differences in ability, and psychological differences. Time together as a group may also be an important factor. They note, for example, that Harrison, Price, and Bell (1998, in Knouse and Dansby, 1999) "found that as the time increased that group members worked together, the effects of surface-level diversity decreased. . . . Group members had greater opportunities over time to interact and thus better understand each other and form interpersonal relationships."

In another recent study, Oetzel (2001) found that an independent or interdependent self-image (belief and comfort in working individually versus collectively, often connected to cultural background) and communication processes (participation, cooperation, respect) are important elements of understanding diversity in small groups. Oetzel found that the self-image of group members in terms of having an individualistic or collectivistic perspective was more explanatory of group communication processes than group composition. He also found that interdependent perspective was positively associated with participation and cooperation in small groups. In addition, he found that equal participation and respect resulted in a member giving more effort to achieving group outcomes and more group member satisfaction.

Research in the area of groups and diversity continues to produce both interesting and sometimes conflicting results. Thomas et al. conducted research on creativity and group enjoyment related to heterogeneous and homogeneous groups. The task before their groups was to develop a creative ending to an open-ended short story (Thomas, 1999). Their findings were both interesting and confounding. For example, they found, "teams composed primarily of ethnic minorities resulted in more positive emotions and fewer negative ones" (1999:145). However, Thomas also found that "there was no significant difference in creativity between groups composed mainly of ethnic minorities and those composed mostly of Caucasians" (1999:145). This finding contradicts the findings of McLeod et al. (see previous page), who concluded that diverse groups did have an advantage over homogeneous groups on a creativity task that required knowledge of different cultures. It is important to recognize there are many factors that influence groups and diversity. For example, the tasks required in these two studies were quite different. Another interesting finding of the Thomas study was that "teams composed mainly of ethnic minorities reported having a better time [group enjoyment] than teams composed mostly of Caucasians" (1999:152). Thomas further notes that while "there were no advantages in creativity, there were no disadvantages either. This suggests that greater group enjoyment was not achieved at the cost of performance on the task" (1999:152).

Thomas concludes that his "research findings are important both theoretically and practically. They provided evidence for the overall effects of ethnic composition regardless of individual race/ethnicity. Ethnic composition can truly be more than the sum of its individual members. Asians, non-Asian ethnic minorities, and Caucasians all enjoyed working in minority-dominated teams more. . . . All other things (like performance) being equal, it seems that groups dominated by minorities are more enjoyable for everyone" (1999:152).

### Practice implications of diversity in groups

Davis et al. stress that "race is such an emotionally charged area of practice that leaders may fail to identify and deal with racial issues because they wish to avoid racial confrontations, are anxious, or perhaps are unsure about how to proceed" (1996:77). Davis et al. stress that the "color blind" approach that says race is transcended when different people come together in a group for a common purpose denies the significance of race (1996:78). These scholars point out, instead, that "whenever people of different races come together in groups, leaders can assume that race is an issue, but not necessarily a problem" (Davis, Galinsky, Schopler, 1996:77). However, due to the history of race relations, individuals' perceptions of racial difference, and issues in the larger environment, race can be a significant source of tension in these groups. Both leaders and members need to be prepared to understand and address racial tensions in racially mixed groups.

Davis et al. (1996:83) suggest there are three basic sources of racial tension within racially mixed groups of people of color and white people. These sources of tension are from:

1. Within individual group members
2. The nature of the group itself
3. The environment of the group

In order to deal with racial tensions, Davis et al. (1996:83–84) suggest the leader needs "trifocal" vision. This trifocal vision requires leaders to:

1. Consider issues related to individuals such as:
   - Have general knowledge of how different populations tend to view power, authority, status, interpersonal boundaries, typical cultural and family expectations, but must be careful not to overgeneralize in these areas.
   - Be sensitive to the specific racial makeup of the group and the number of persons from each group: unequal numbers can lead to subgrouping and domination by members of one group; equal numbers may not be perceived as balanced on the part of group members used to being a majority (e.g., whites).
2. Consider issues related to the group itself such as:
   - Group purpose and goals, especially if different members from different races have different expectations of focus or purpose.
   - Norms that promote recognition and respect for differences, member equality, and open discussion of racial issues can help prevent members from being cautious, mistrustful, and guarded.
3. Consider issues related to the larger environment such as:
   - Climate of society.
   - Events in the members' neighborhoods.
   - The sponsoring organization's reputation for responsiveness to racial concerns.
   - The way member's significant others view the group.

Within racially mixed groups, according to Davis et al. (1996:85), problems concerning racial issues can occur at three levels:

1. *Between members and leaders:* If the leader is the only representative of a particular race, he/she can feel isolated; leaders can be insensitive; members can doubt the leader's ability due to race; leaders who are people of color may find their competence challenged by whites and members of other races.

2. *Between members:* Racist behaviors/comments leading to verbal or physical attacks; subgroup formation by race to dominate; members who avoid discussing sensitive topics; members don't participate because they feel isolated or under attack because of their race.

3. *Between member and environment:* Institutional racism in community and society; member's reluctance to attend meetings in unfamiliar territory; sponsoring organizations perceived as unresponsive.

## Groups and gender

Just as the patterns of interaction and treatment in larger society impact small-group dynamics around issues of race and color, group behavior is influenced powerfully by issues related to gender. Social workers must respect and understand the impact of gender on group dynamics. Rosabeth Moss Kanter has studied the interactions of males and females in small group and organizational contexts extensively.

Kanter has found evidence that "the presence of both men and women in the same group heightens tension and may put women at a disadvantage" (1977:372). She also suggests that power and status differentials between men and women in society tend to be replicated in small mixed-gender groups. Since "males have generally higher status and power in American society than females . . . when men and women are ostensible peers, the male's external status may give him an advantage inside the group. . . . In mixed groups of 'peers' men and women may not, in fact, be equal, especially if their external statuses are discrepant" (1977:373).

Kanter also describes differential impacts of gender in leadership of work groups. Kanter (1977:374) suggests that "even if women have formal authority, they may not necessarily be able to exercise it over reluctant subordinates." She cites the example of a case in which a woman "had formal leadership of a group of men, but the men did not accept this, reporting informally to her male superior."

Kanter suggests a number of strategies for reducing the inequalities and difficulties faced by women in mixed-gender work groups. She suggests that the most important means of addressing this problem is to "change the sex ratio in the power structure of organizations, to put more women in positions of visible leadership" (1977:381).

She suggests, more importantly, and similar to Davis's observation about the racial composition of groups, that the relative proportion of men and women in work groups and training groups should . . . be taken into account in designing programs. Whenever possible, a 'critical mass' of females should be included in every working group—more than two or three, and a large enough percentage that they can reduce stereotyping, change the culture of the group, and offer support without being a competitive threat to one another. If there are only a few women in the sales force, for example, this analysis suggests that they should be clustered rather than spread widely. (1977:383)

Only if we attend carefully to issues of diversity in the groups we create, those we facilitate, and those to which we belong will our efforts result in effective groups.

## Relationship of feminist perspectives and social work with groups

Researchers studying groups through a feminist lens focus primarily on the gender composition of groups. Some focus on the proportion of men and women in groups and the notion of a "tipping point" when the proportion of men and women leads to cultural change in the group. Still other researchers focus on the actual numbers of men and women in a group to ascertain the level of "tokenism," for example, what are the dynamics if there is only one woman or one man in a particular group (Scott, Hollingshead, McGrath, Moreland, & Rohrliaugh, 2004). Lewis notes that principles of social work with groups have a number of commonalities with principles of feminism (1992:273):

1. A *common consciousness* of the embedded details of victimization.

2. The systematic *deconstruction* of negative and disadvantaging definitions of reality.

3. The process of *naming,* of identifying the consequences of established structures and patterns.

4. Trust in the *processes within the group* to reconstruct a new reality and to provide the context within which to test and practice new language, behaviors, expectations, and aspirations.

5. A belief in the *power of the group,* united to bring about desired changes in the context, however small these may be.

6. A *sense of community* through the experience of reaching out and discovering allies and "same-thinkers and doers" in the wider social context.

### Groups and persons with disabilities

As we noted in elsewhere, there are 43 million persons with disabilities in the United States. Given the number of persons with disabilities in the population and given the special needs of this group, it is very likely that social workers will work with persons with disabilities in virtually all kinds of small-group situations. As a result it is important to be sensitive to the needs, feelings, and strengths of persons with disabilities. Resources Centers for Independent Living provides a "Bill of Rights for People with Disabilities" (See Box) This Bill of Rights can help us make sure we are respectful and inclusive of persons with disabilities in our work in groups.

Helpful suggestions for insuring that persons with disabilities are able to exercise their full rights within group contexts are included in what Patterson et al. (1995:79) refer to as:

### Disability etiquette for groups

1. It is appropriate to acknowledge that a disability exists, but asking personal questions is inappropriate unless one has a close relationship with the person with the disability.

2. It is important to speak directly to the person with a disability, even when a third party (e.g., attendant, relative, interpreter) is present.

3. It is appropriate to use common words such as *look* or *see,* for individuals with visual impairments, as well as *running* or *walking* with people who use wheelchairs.

4. It is appropriate to offer assistance to a person with a disability, but one should wait until it is accepted before providing the assistance. Clarification should be sought from the individual with the disability if the group leader is unsure of how or what type of assistance is needed.

## Bill of Rights for People with Disabilities

We believe that all people should enjoy certain rights. Because people with disabilities have consistently been denied the right to fully participate in society as free and equal members, it is important to state and affirm these rights. All people should be able to enjoy these rights, regardless of race, creed, color, sex, religion, or disability.

1. The right to live independent, active, and full lives.
2. The right to the equipment, assistance, and support services necessary for full productivity, provided in a way that promotes dignity and independence.
3. The right to an adequate income or wage, substantial enough to provide food, clothing, shelter, and other necessities of life.
4. The right to accessible, integrated, convenient, and affordable housing.
5. The right to quality physical and mental health care.
6. The right to training and employment without prejudice or stereotype.
7. The right to accessible transportation and freedom of movement.
8. The right to bear or adopt and raise children and have a family.
9. The right to a free and appropriate public education.
10. The right to participate in and benefit from entertainment and recreation.
11. The right to equal access to and use all businesses, facilities, and activities in the community.
12. The right to communicate freely with all fellow citizens and those who provide services.
13. The right to a barrier-free environment.
14. The right to a legal representation and full protection of all legal rights.
15. The right to determine one's own future and make one's own life choices.
16. The right to full access to all voting processes.

Source: http://www.reachcils.org/home/disability_rights/index.php4
REACH –Resource Centers on Independent Living, Texas

## Effective Groups

Groups can be said to be effective if they accomplish three things: 1) goal achievement, 2) maintenance of good working relationship among members, and 3) adaptation to changing environmental conditions that allow effectiveness to be maintained. Johnson and Johnson offer a model of effective groups that includes nine dimensions:

1. Group goals must be clearly understood, be relevant to the needs of group members, highlight the positive interdependence of members, and evoke from every member a high level of commitment to their accomplishment.

2. Group members must communicate their ideas and feelings accurately and clearly.

3. Participation and leadership must be distributed among members.

4. Appropriate decision-making procedures must be used flexibly to match them with the needs of the situation.

5. Conflicts should be encouraged and managed constructively. . . . Controversies (conflicts among opposing ideas and conclusions) promote involvement in the group's work, quality, and creativity in decision-making, and commitment to implementing the group's decisions. Minority opinions should be accepted and used.

6. Power and influence need to be approximately equal throughout the group. Power should be based on expertise, ability, and access to information, not on authority.

7. Group cohesion needs to be high. . . . Cohesion is based on members liking each other, desiring to continue as part of the group, and being satisfied with their group membership.

8. Problem-solving adequacy should be high.

9. The interpersonal effectiveness of members needs to be high. Interpersonal effectiveness is a measure of how well the consequences of your behavior match your intentions. (1991:21–24)

## SUMMARY/TRANSITION

All of the perspectives, concepts, and dimensions we have considered in this chapter are important to help us understand groups. Currently as students and teachers and as social workers and future social work practitioners, we do and will continue to conduct much of our work in the context of small groups. We create groups, we facilitate groups, and we can expect on almost a daily basis to spend time as a member of some small-group effort.

In this chapter we have explored groups as contexts in which both process and product are inextricable concerns. We have examined a number of issues involved in the formation and achievement of group purposes and goals. The interrelated and interdependent nature of membership, leadership, followership, and decision-making was considered. A variety of roles and norms played by group members and their significance for the individuals playing them and for the group as a whole have been investigated. We have outlined a number of stage-based models of group development, recognizing that while stages are a part of group development they do not occur only in linear or fixed sequences. Social systems or ecological frameworks for explaining many aspects of groups have been sketched, along with recognition of some of the limitations of this common approach used by social workers to understand groups. We have stressed the absolute necessity of considering issues of oppression and of diversity in our work with and in groups. We noted that regardless of purpose or goal, serious attention must be given to issues concerning persons of color, persons with disabilities, and gender in all the groups with which we are associated.

Only by attending to the multiple, complex, interdependent, and interrelated dimensions of groups can we be effective in our group work. By doing so we can gain a much more complete and holistic picture of groups than we can from concentrating on any one perspective. This multiple-perspective approach is consistent also with our attempts in this book to develop a worldview that is inclusive and that incorporates a "both/and" rather than an "either/or" approach to understanding HBSE.

**Recall what you learned in this chapter by completing the Chapter Review.**

As throughout this book, the knowledge we explored here about groups is interdependent and interconnected with the things we have learned about individuals and familiness on our voyage toward understanding HBSE. The information we gathered during this part of our journey is related to and interconnected with our explorations in the chapters on organizations and communities that follow.

# Perspectives on Organizations

**9**

## INTRODUCTION

Organizations provide a significant context in which much of our daily lives are carried out. They form the environments in which a vast array of human behaviors takes place. For many of us, virtually all aspects of our lives are intertwined with and influenced by organizations. To give us some idea of how much of our own and others' lives are touched by organizations from the time we are born until the time we die, let us consider some examples of organizations. We very likely were born in or with the assistance of an organization—a hospital, public health agency, prepared childbirth program. We are likely to be socialized or educated in the context of organizations—day care, preschool/Head Start, grade and high schools, higher education institutions, vocational/technical schools. We very likely play in the context of organizations—organized sports, girls'/boys' clubs, Scouts, Jack and Jill, health/exercise clubs, fraternities/sororities. We may carry out much of our spiritual life in and mark major life events with rituals in the context of formal religious organizations—church, synagogue, temple, mosque. We probably do or will work in an organizational context—human service agencies, corporations, health and mental health organizations. We get many of our basic subsistence needs met through organizations—grocery, clothing, drug and department stores, food banks, housing authorities, banks, restaurants. We probably will grow old in the context of organizations—senior centers, home health or chore services, nursing homes, and assisted living organizations. We may very well die in an organizational context—hospital, hospice. While this sampling is not intended to be an exhaustive list of the organizations that influence us throughout life, it does give us a place to start in considering the far-reaching impact of organizations on our individual and collective lives (Etzioni, 1964).

If you reflect on the examples of organizational contexts earlier, it is not difficult to recognize that many of the organizations through which human needs are met are also contexts in which social workers work. Whether we are working to meet our own needs or those of other individuals, families, groups, communities, or nations we are very likely to be acting in or through an organizational environment. We are concerned here, of course, with what organizations do to help us meet human needs. We are also concerned with how organizations can and do present barriers to or may even prevent us from meeting our needs and reaching our full potential as humans. We are concerned, especially, with the role of organizations in helping or hindering diverse persons as they proceed through the life course. And we are concerned with the roles that diverse persons have in constructing the organizations that impact, so directly and comprehensively, their lives.

Organizations reflect and are reflected in the paradigms or worldviews of the persons who construct and operate them. Since organizations have such a high degree of influence on our day-to-day lives throughout our lives, it is imperative that we all share in creating and operating them. Only in this way will organizations be responsive to the needs of diverse persons.

As we begin to explore organizations, we need to recognize that much of the information on small groups from the previous chapter will apply to organizations as well. Much of the activity that organizations are engaged in happens through a variety of small groups. If you think about an organization in which you are involved, you can probably recognize that much of your involvement in relation to the organization is carried out through different small groups. You are likely, for example, to be a member of a committee or work group within the organization. You are also likely to have membership in informal groups within the organization—a group of organization members you eat lunch with on a regular basis, for instance. So much of an organization's activity is carried out in small groups that it begins to look as if the organization is really a collection of small groups. Because of this it is important that we use what we know about small groups to help us better understand organizations.

In this chapter we will explore a number of perspectives on formal organizations. We will explore the notion of organizational culture. We will look to history for some perspective on how we came to be a society and a world so reliant on the structures and processes of formal organizations. We will look to traditional notions of organizations for understanding the nature of the existing organizations we and the people with whom we work must deal every day. We will explore alternative notions of how organizations might/can be changed or structured to meet human needs and accomplish the core concerns of social work. We hope to use the understanding we gain about organizations in order to make them more responsive to our needs and to the needs of others. We seek avenues in this part of our journey to create and re-create organizations that are inclusive of the visions and voices of all the peoples with whom social workers are concerned.

# HISTORICAL PERSPECTIVE ON ORGANIZATIONS

We may think of a society characterized by so many different kinds and sizes of organizations directed toward a dizzying range of purposes and goals as a modern phenomenon. However, organizations have long been a basic context within which a wide range of human behavior and interaction takes place. It is true that the number and variety of organizations has increased greatly in the 20th century. However, organizations and the study of organizations have been with us for a long, long time. Etzioni reminds us that the pharaohs employed organizations in the creation of the pyramids. Chinese emperors over a thousand years ago made use of organizations to build irrigation systems. The first popes created the universal church as an organization to manage a world religion (Etzioni, 1964:1). Iannello (1992:3) notes that the philosophers of ancient Greece were interested in the study of organizations as a means of achieving specific goals and purposes.

Shafritz and Ott (1987:1) suggest it is safe to say that humankind has been creating organizations ever since we began hunting, making war, and creating families. Organizational study as a deliberate and focused field of exploration, especially in terms of managing large organizations, is largely a product of the 20th century, however. Much of the study of organizations during the 20th century has been done focusing on business or profit-making organizations. There is, though, a growing body of information that focuses on not-for-profit or public service organizations. Most students of organizations agree that the rise of industrial (and more recently the emergence of postindustrial) society in the 20th century has resulted in great increases in the quantity, size, and type of formal organizations in almost every area of life. This proliferation of formal organizations directed toward achieving a multitude of goals has greatly increased our interest in understanding formal organizations.

As we have learned about paradigms in general, our beliefs about what organizations are, what they do, and how they do it have not come about in a vacuum. They have been greatly influenced by the people, times, and cultures associated with their development. Shafritz and Ott (1987:2) suggest that "the advent of the factory system, World War II, the 'flowerchild'/anti-establishment/ self-development era of the 1960s, and the computer/information society of the late 20th and early 21st centuries all substantially influenced the evolution of organization theory." As we explore traditional and alternate perspectives on organizations, we will travel a route that parallels many of the historic influences of the early, middle, late 20th and early 21st centuries. To begin to understand organizations we need some basic concepts and definitions.

# BASIC CONCEPTS/DEFINITIONS

Whether exploring traditional or alternative notions about organizations, it is helpful to have at least a very general definition from which to explore differences in perspectives on organizations. Etzioni (1964:3) uses Talcott Parsons's basic definition of **organizations** as "social units (or human groupings) deliberately constructed and reconstructed to seek specific goals." Another common definition is that "an organization is a collection of people engaged in specialized and interdependent activity to accomplish a goal or mission" (Gortner, Mahler, & Nicholson, 1987:2). Iannello (1992:8) suggests that one might simply define organizations "as systems of continuous, purposive, goal-oriented activity involving two or more people." All three of these basic definitions differ slightly, but they share some essential common ground. All three recognize organizations as collectivities of people working together to accomplish a goal (or goals).

Within this common ground, however, there is a wide range of possibilities for differences in perspectives. The characteristics of the people involved in the organization, how those people are arranged in relation to one another, the nature of the goal (or goals), and the specific parts different organizational members play in accomplishing the goal (or goals) are just some of the sources of different perspectives on organizations.

An organizational *goal* can be defined simply as the desired or intended ends or results to be achieved by an organization (Neugeboren, 1985:27) or as a "desired state of affairs which the organization attempts to realize" (Etzioni, 1964:6). The nature of goals varies greatly from organization to organization and may even vary within the same organization over time. Different human service organizations may share a basic mission or purpose of improving the quality of life for people in the communities they serve. Human service organizations may vary greatly, however, in the specific goals they pursue in order to improve the quality of life.

Neugeboren (1985:5–17) suggests that there are three kinds of goals pursued by human service organizations. *Social care* goals are those directed toward changing the environment in order for people to improve the quality of their lives and reach their maximum potential.

*Social control* goals are those directed toward controlling the behavior of people who are deemed to be deviant and who interfere with the ability of others to maximize their potential and improve the quality of their lives. *Rehabilitation* goals are those directed toward changing individuals so they will have improved quality of life and better opportunity to reach their fullest potential. Organizations may have multiple goals. Human service agencies such as state departments of social or human services may encompass social care (day-care licensing to ensure high-quality environments for young children, provision of concrete services such as food stamps), social control (legal consequences for parents when child-abuse allegations are substantiated), and rehabilitation (parenting classes for abusive parents to assist in changing parenting behaviors that led to child abuse).

*Goal displacement* is characteristic of an organization that is pursuing goals contrary to the goals it originally and officially proclaimed. An example of organizational goal displacement is an adolescent group home originally begun to rehabilitate troubled teens that becomes a social control institution to incarcerate adolescents. Organizations may also be characterized by *goal succession*. This is the replacement of one goal by another goal when the original goal has been accomplished or it has declared itself unable to accomplish its original goal.

The March of Dimes was an organizational effort originally directed to obtaining resources necessary to find a cure for polio. Upon the virtual elimination of the threat of polio—in no small way a result of the efforts of the March of Dimes—the organization adopted a new goal that included combating birth defects. Goal succession is likely to be a functional change in goals; goal displacement is likely to be dysfunctional (Etzioni, 1964:10ff).

Organizations with multiple goals may experience conflict over the amount of organizational resources or energy to devote to their various goals. Such conflict may be especially pronounced if an organization is undergoing goal displacement in a situation in which the organization's stated goals are different from and may compete with

**Watch the video** "Providing Leadership to Promote Change to Improve Quality of Social Services" **to explore the need for advocacy by clients, social workers, and the larger community to change the environment to restore services to elders.**

Critical Thinking
Question: Should the social worker in the video have pressed the client harder to become part of the community efforts to restore program funding? Why? Why not?

227

its actual goals. Think about the potential for conflict within the adolescent group home in the example earlier. If some staff want the home to rehabilitate troubled teens so they can return to their families and the community, while other staff sees the goal as removal from the community and incarceration, the potential for significant conflict in the organization is great.

## Types of Organizations

There are three types of organizations or organizational sectors with which social workers are most likely to work and need to understand. One type, *private-for-profit* organizations, sometimes referred to as *market sector organizations*, include businesses and corporations organized with the primary goal of making an economic profit. A second type of organization is the *governmental* organization. Governmental organizations comprise the *public sector* and include local, state, national, and international (e.g., the U.N., the European Union) governmental organizations. Public health, education, and human service organizations are some of the most common public sector organizations. A third type of organization is the *private-not-for-profit* organization. These organizations are also referred to as *non-governmental organizations* or *NGOs*. (NGO is a term more often used to describe this type of organization outside the United States.) Non-governmental organizations comprise what is often referred to as the *voluntary* or *civil sector*. They include a wide range of organizations that provide civic and human services (e.g., Urban League, Lions Clubs, League of Women Voters), which are funded by private citizens (donations), fund-raising organizations (e.g., United Way), or privately funded foundations (e.g., Ford or Kellogg Foundations). Historically social workers have been more involved in public sector and voluntary or not-for-profit sector organizations. However, increasingly social workers are both working in or in partnership with market sector organizations in order to achieve human well-being and reduction of poverty and oppression (Rifkin, 1998).

Differing perspectives on organizational concepts and types result in very different notions about what organizations are like, what they should be like, and what they might be like. These differences have significant implications and consequences also for the organizations' ability to respond positively to the core concerns of social work we are addressing in this book. As in the chapters dealing with each level of human behavior we explore in this book, we will address notions about organizations from both traditional and alternative paradigmatic perspectives.

There are several traditional models of or approaches to organizations that have had major influences on the way the organizations we deal with every day are structured and operated. These perspectives did not emerge in a vacuum. They emerged from and along with the larger historical context of the 20th century. As we learned about paradigms generally, the different traditional paradigms often emerged as reactions to or extensions of prior notions of what organizations should be and do.

**Test your understanding of Basic Concepts/Definitions for understanding organizations by taking this short** Quiz.

## TRADITIONAL PARADIGMS

There are several broad categories of traditional perspectives on organizations. These broad areas are sometimes referred to as schools of thought. They include classical approaches (scientific management or machine theory and bureaucracy), human relations, systems, and contingency theory. Within these broad categories there are a number of basic concepts that can help us to understand the nature of the organizations with which we deal on a day-to-day basis. These theories and concepts also will help us, as social workers, to better understand the organizational context within which we work and through which the people with whom we work seek services to improve the quality of their lives. The organizational context, then, has important implications for both the quality of our own lives—for we spend so much of our time in this context—and the quality of life of the people with whom we work—for the organizational context is pivotal in determining whether or not people will receive the basic resources necessary to improve the quality of their lives. Once again we see that our interests and those of the people with whom we work are interconnected.

## Scientific Management or Classical Theory

*Scientific management* is a conceptual framework (or body of theory) for defining, structuring, and managing organizations that is consistent with the positivistic, scientific, objective, and quantitative dimension of the traditional paradigm. As its name implies, it is closely connected to and relies on the assumptions of science as the ideal approach to understanding organizations. Frederick Taylor put scientific management forward as a theory about organizations in the very early part of the 20th century. He presented a paper outlining his approach to the American Society of Mechanical Engineers as early as 1895. This school of thought has been tremendously influential in defining the structures and processes that make up much organizational life today. This is perhaps understandable, given the influence and power accorded scientific approaches to understanding human behavior generally during the 20th century (Pugh, Hickson, & Hinings, 1985).

Taylor's scientific management was directed toward maximizing efficiency in industry. Efficiency is an important basic concept related to organizations and is a major concern in virtually all organizational theories. *Efficiency* is defined as the production of the maximum amount of output for the least amount of input. It is, in other words, doing the most with the least possible amount of resources. Efficiency is often discussed in conjunction with another basic organizational concept, effectiveness. *Effectiveness* is defined simply as the degree to which the goals or purposes of an organization are accomplished. As we noted earlier, a primary concern of organizations is attainment or accomplishment of goals (Pugh et al., 1985).

According to Taylor, scientific management could achieve maximum effectiveness and efficiency in the attainment of organizational goals through four basic principles. Faithful adherence to these four principles would result in finding the "one best way" to perform a task, do a job, or manage an entire organization. The first principle involved creating a *science of work* for each worker's job or task. This included taking what was known about each task and objectively or scientifically studying what needed to be done to accomplish the task more efficiently. This new information was recorded, tabulated, and reduced to formal laws, rules, or even mathematical formulas that defined and standardized each task necessary to do a job. This process of studying, recording, and codifying work tasks is sometimes referred to as a "time and motion study." Time and motion studies sought to create a perfect match between the actions of workers and the activities carried out by machines. They sought to unite workers and machines into one smooth and efficient process for carrying out necessary tasks. While this principle applied in Taylor's model almost exclusively to production in factory settings, it was extended over the years to many other organizational settings as well. For example, studying human service office procedures to reduce unnecessary movement or effort in order to increase the number of clients seen is an example of this principle in a non-factory environment. Task analysis, workload analysis, and time studies are all examples of efforts to scientifically analyze tasks and processes in social work agencies to make operations efficient (Taylor in Grusky & Miller, 1981).

The second principle focused on the *scientific selection and training of workers*. The process of objectively studying each of the workers for their fitness for a particular task, then training them very deliberately to efficiently accomplish that task was quite different from traditional arrangements in which workers determined what they were suited for doing and then set about to train themselves as best as they could to do the work for which they were hired. This was yet another means of making work scientific. This concern for careful selection and training of workers was adapted far beyond the factory system. In social work education and practice, the education and selection processes used to ensure that individuals are suited and prepared for the professional jobs they will carry out is an example of this concern. The specific requirements for education of social workers as reflected in the Council on Social Work Education (CSWE), accreditation requirements, the continuing education requirements of many social work agencies, and the requirements for specific amounts and kinds of continuing education activities for renewal of social work licenses in many states are all examples of how this principle has influenced social work education and practice. If you have been through or will go through an application or screening process to be fully admitted to the social work program or school in which you are taking this course, your experience is consistent with this principle of scientific management (Taylor in Grusky & Miller, 1981).

Taylor's third principle focused on *bringing together management and workers to ensure that the scientific principles resulting from the study of the tasks to be completed and the careful selection and training of workers to carry out those tasks were successfully implemented in the work setting*. This principle involved management's taking responsibility for closely monitoring the workers to make sure they were performing their jobs in accordance with scientific principles. This principle also required that workers be rewarded appropriately for adhering to the standardized rules for carrying out specific tasks. Most often this reward took the form of economic benefits, specifically increases in pay. Taylor, though, suggested that there were other "plums" that could be offered, such as better or more kind treatment of workers and allowing workers greater say in what they preferred as rewards for adhering to scientific principles. There is some confusion about Taylorism—as scientific management is sometimes called—in respect to notions of reward. This theory is often described as seeing economic reward as the only motivator for workers. It is safe to say that economic rewards were considered the primary source of motivation, but as Taylor suggests, workers might also consider better treatment by management a kind of reward as well. Regardless of the kind of reward, the purpose of "plums" was to ensure that workers performed in accordance with the scientific standards for their jobs. The notion of supervision and evaluation of social workers and the relationship of salary increases to evaluation results as determined by managers or supervisors in agencies are examples of how this principle applies in social work settings (Taylor in Grusky & Miller, 1981).

The fourth principle of scientific management focused on *expanding the role played by managers in the overall production process*. Taylorism saw managers as having many responsibilities previously thought to be within the purview of the workers themselves. As can be seen from the preceding three principles, managers became responsible for studying, defining, standardizing, and monitoring the tasks carried out by workers.

Managers in effect took over from workers planning, decision-making, and judgments about what jobs were to be done and how those jobs were to be carried out. This change resulted in a re-division of labor in the work setting. In many ways a new class of managers was created within work organizations. These managers, while assuming new responsibilities previously held by workers themselves, simultaneously took away some of the freedoms workers had previously held. Examples of this new division of labor can readily be seen in social work settings today. Especially in large agency settings, the promulgation of regulations and procedures by managers about how tasks are to be carried out and the expectation that direct service workers will then implement those regulations and procedures is an example of this principle. The supervision, evaluation, and establishing of rewards in the form of salary increases by management are all examples of this new division of labor between workers and managers (Taylor in Grusky and Miller, 1981; Taylor in Shafritz and Ott, 1987; Pugh et al., 1985).

**Test your understanding of Scientific or Classical Theory of organizations by taking this short Quiz.**

---

## Scientific Management Themes

Organizations operating according to the principles of scientific management are characterized by several themes. These themes include:

- high degrees of specialization in jobs and the qualifications and training of personnel,

- clear division of labor,
- distinct hierarchy of authority, and
- assumptions that workers are motivated primarily by economic rewards.

---

### Bureaucracy

Another classic model of organizations was put forth by Max Weber in his formulation of bureaucracy. Weber (1864–1920) formulated the structure and characteristics of bureaucracy during approximately the same time period that Taylor's scientific management was emerging. Bureaucracy, in one form or another, defined in one way or another, and often symbolizing the shortcomings of organizational life, is almost a synonym for organizations today. Bureaucracy in a number of respects has similarities with the scientific management theory we explored earlier. Bureaucracy values highly two dimensions of the traditional or dominant paradigm. It puts a premium on many of the elements of the positivistic, scientific, objective, and quantitative dimension of the traditional paradigm and on rationality and impersonality (Pugh et al., 1985; Shafritz and Ott, 1987).

Weber outlined a number of *characteristics of bureaucracy*. First is the notion of a stable and officially stated structure of authority. Areas of authority within a bureaucracy are explicitly spelled out by rules or administrative regulations. Second, there is a clear "pecking order" or hierarchy of authority. This hierarchy clearly delineates who is responsible to whom within the bureaucratic organization. It provides a graded system of supervision in which lower offices are responsible to higher offices. Third, the organization's management is based on extensive written records of transactions, regulations, and policies that are kept over time. It is these written records that provide standardization and stability to the management of the organization. However, many people believe this emphasis on written records of activities and transactions is often taken to such extremes that workers' ability to do their jobs effectively is hindered. This over-emphasis on paperwork is disparagingly referred to as *red tape*. Fourth, the persons who fulfill management functions—those who run the organization—have specialized training and expertise that specifically prepares them for their jobs. Fifth, organizational responsibilities take precedence in the day-to-day life of personnel. In other words, one's official duties come first. Sixth, management of a bureaucracy follows a system of stable and comprehensive rules learned by managers through specialized education for their positions. Seventh, employment in a bureaucracy is seen as a "vocation" or career for which the person is specially trained and that the person sees as a duty to perform. Eighth, the persons who manage a bureaucratic organization should be separate from those who own the means of production. This prevents individual interests from interfering with decision-making for the good of the organization and helps ensure rational decision-making. To make sure this is the case, managers receive a fixed salary for their work rather than an hourly wage. Ninth, the resources of the organization must be free from outside control in order for managers to allocate and reallocate resources purely on the basis of the needs of the organization. This includes resources in the sense of personnel as well as financial resources. In other words, administrators must have the authority to hire, fire, and move personnel from one position to another within the organization (Pugh et al., 1985; Shafritz and Ott, 1987).

Weber's framework for bureaucracy was conceptualized as an *ideal type*. By this it is meant that this structure is one toward which organizations should strive. It is not assumed that this type necessarily exists in any complete or perfect way in any given organizational setting. However, it was assumed in this framework that the closer an organization can come to this ideal structure, the more efficient and effective it will be in accomplishing its goals. We know from systematic study of existing organizations, as well as from our individual personal experiences, that no single organization is likely to include all the characteristics of a bureaucracy. We also know from the many criticisms of bureaucratic organizational life that incorporating the ideal characteristics of bureaucracy does not necessarily guarantee that the organization will reach its goals, nor that it will do so with maximum efficiency (Grusky and Miller, 1981; Pugh et al., 1985; Shafritz and Ott, 1987).

There are a number of other considerations in addition to the characteristics of bureaucracies that are important to think about as we attempt to develop more comprehensive understanding of human behavior and the social environment (HBSE) in organizational contexts. Many of these other characteristics take us in the direction of alternative paradigm thinking. They include consideration of nonrational factors in organizational life, consideration of the impact of linkages to the external environment on the internal life of the organization, and consideration of personal as well as impersonal factors on our organizational experiences. Recognition of these other considerations leads to some approaches significantly different from those of scientific management and bureaucracy with their central concerns for rationality and efficiency.

Examples of these different approaches include human relations theory and Theories X and Y. While these approaches differ markedly from the classic approaches we have explored thus far, they are nevertheless considered here under traditional paradigms because they have more in common with traditional and dominant paradigmatic assumptions than with the dimensions of alternative paradigms we have outlined in this book. We might best think about these models as middle-range perspectives along a continuum leading us toward newer alternative or possible views of organizations.

## Characteristics of Bureaucracy

1. Stable and official structure of authority.
2. Clear hierarchy of authority ("pecking order").
3. Written records kept over time.
4. Specialized training and expertise.
5. Official duties come first.

6. Stable and comprehensive system of rules.
7. Career employment.
8. Managers separate from "owners" of organization.
9. Managers free to allocate and reallocate resources.

## Human Relations

What has come to be known as the human relations theory of organizational behavior emerged from and in many ways became a reaction to the focuses on rationality, machinelike precision, planning, and formality of classical scientific management and bureaucratic theory. Human relations thinking, however, did not discount entirely the traditional concerns of organizational life such as efficiency, effectiveness, and goal centeredness. Nor did it suggest that scientific management approaches be done away with entirely. It suggested instead that these concerns were insufficient to understand the complexities of modern organizational life (Etzioni, 1964).

### The Hawthorne studies

Human relations thinking emerged directly from classical scientific approaches. Elton Mayo (1880–1949) is considered by many to be the founder of the human relations school. It was in the process of seeking to extend understanding of the necessary factors for truly efficient and productive organizations that human relations emerged somewhat unexpectedly. In the process of carrying out a series of studies that have come to be referred to as the Hawthorne Studies, Elton Mayo and his colleagues happened upon the basic concepts of human relations approaches. Two of the studies within the Hawthorne series illustrate some of the fundamental "surprises" that became the human relations school. One study involved exploring the effect of lighting or illumination in the work area on worker productivity. In this study, illumination was manipulated according to the hypothesis that optimum illumination would result in improved worker output. Contrary to this hypothesis, the researchers found that whether illumination was increased, decreased, or left alone, worker output increased. This led to the finding that the attention given the workers in the experiment and their interpretation of this attention as symbolic of the organization's interest in and concern for their perspectives was a crucial factor in their productivity. This has come to be known as the *Hawthorne effect*. In other words, workers were motivated to produce by other than purely economic rewards. They were also motivated by informal factors such as individual attention and concern for their input in the operation of the organization (Etzioni, 1964; Pugh et al., 1985).

A second experiment in the Hawthorne series resulted in an equally "surprising" finding. This study is referred to as the Bank Wiring Room study because it involved observing and manipulating factors in a work setting in which telephone switchboards (called "banks") were being wired. This study resulted in the finding that not only informal factors such as individual attention affected worker productivity, but that groups of workers developed informal systems of managing output quite separate from the direction provided by management. The effect of this *informal group structure* was to set production norms or expectations about what were appropriate levels of production. On the one hand the group was concerned with not overproducing in the belief that overproduction would lead to layoffs of workers. On the other hand the group was concerned that production be "fair" in the sense that management and owners were not taken advantage of by unfairly low levels of production (Etzioni, 1964; Pugh et al., 1985).

A number of the basic concepts of *human relations thinking* emerged from these studies and many others carried out since the original Hawthorne studies. First, the importance of individual attention and positive social interaction as well as economic rewards in worker productivity and satisfaction uncovered a virtually unexplored level of organizational life that centered on informal, nonrational, emotional, and unplanned interactions. Second, the pivotal role of informal social groups in efficiency and productivity was discovered. These groups functioned according to informal and internal norms, leadership structures, communication patterns, and levels of participation that had not been considered at all important to the scientific management proponents (Etzioni, 1964; Gortner et al., 1987; Grusky and Miller, 1981; Pugh et al., 1985).

It is helpful to note here that these early studies of organizational life out of which the human relations school emerged significantly increased interest in understanding the role and behavior of small groups in our day-to-day lives. Many basic group concepts such as small-group norms, leadership, decision-making, roles, communication, and goals, which are explored in Chapter 8, have direct linkages to efforts to understand organizational life. This is consistent with our perspective in this book that sees HBSE as an interlocking and overlapping network of mutually interdependent processes and contexts.

The tendency here may be to see only the differences between scientific management and human relations perspectives. We need to keep in mind, though, that neither of these schools of thought questioned in any fundamental ways the traditional and dominant forms of organizational life. Both schools saw maximum efficiency and productivity as the consuming purpose of organizations. Both schools accepted hierarchies of power and control (whether they be formal or informal) as givens in organizational life. Neither of these schools saw significant conflict among the interests of the various groups within organizations. It was assumed in these traditional approaches that what was good for the organization's owners and managers at the top of the hierarchy was good for its line of lower-level workers at the bottom of the organizational hierarchy. In short, neither of these schools provided fundamentally new or alternative models within which to carry out our organizational lives.

**Test your understanding of Human Relations Theory by taking this short** Quiz.

## Theory X and Theory Y

As researchers continued to seek ways to maximize organizational efficiency, productivity, and goal achievement, the concerns of behavioral scientists began to influence organizational studies. Douglas McGregor (1906–1964), a social psychologist, became interested in the influence of managers' underlying assumptions about human behavior on their management practices. McGregor was specifically interested in managers' basic assumptions about what motivated people to behave as they do. His work led him to formulate two sets of assumptions about human motivation. One set he called *Theory X*.

Generally, Theory X reflects a belief on the part of managers that their role was to direct and control the activities of workers.

Theory X Assumptions about People:

1. They are lazy and will avoid work if at all possible.
2. They are antagonistic and cannot be trusted.
3. They must be coerced into putting for the effort for work.
4. They naturally prefer to avoid responsibility if at all possible.
5. They lack self-motivation.
6. They do not like to take risks.
7. They prefer to be told exactly what they are to do. (Smothers, 2011: 49–50)

The second set of assumptions he referred to as *Theory Y*. McGregor believed Theory Y assumptions reflected the beliefs of managers that their role was one of creating supportive relationships in which organizational members could exercise their inherent tendencies to grow, develop, and learn for their own benefit and that of the organization.

Theory Y Assumptions about People:

1. People are inherently good.
2. They do not inherently dislike and avoid work.
3. They are self-directed and exercise self-control in their work if they are committed to the organization's goals.
4. They seek responsibility and autonomy.
5. Creativity and resourcefulness are widely distributed among the population.
6. The intellectual capacity of workers is greatly underutilized. (Smothers, 2011: 49–50)

Clearly, McGregor believed Theory Y was a much-preferred alternative to the traditional Theory X. His position was summarized well by Gardner and Schermerhorn:

> Douglas McGregor's message endures like a timeless melody, well worth listening to over and over again . . . [He pursued] high performance not by manipulating people [with carrots and sticks] but by respecting them . . . His respect for innate human capacities – talent, willingness to accept responsibility, creativity, and capacity for personal growth, is well evidenced by many practices in our best-run organizations . . . self-directed work teams, employee involvement groups, job enrichment . . . and more [and reflect] the essence of Theory Y assumptions McGregor espoused almost a half-century ago. (2004: 270–71 in Kopelman, Prottas, & Falk, 2010: 121)

Theory X is more consistent with the assumptions of scientific management and traditional paradigm thinking. Theory Y assumptions about human motivation are more consistent with Human Relations Theory and are much more in line with the core concerns of social work. In addition, Theory Y assumptions are philosophically more consistent with the dimensions of alternative paradigms we have outlined in this book than are those of Theory X.

## Ethical Practice

**Practice Behavior Example:** Know about the value base of the profession, its ethical standards, and relevant law.

**Critical Thinking Question:** Assume you are working in a social work agency and the manager of your unit has many of the characteristics of a Theory X manager. What social work values and/or ethical standards might you expect to be sources of conflict in your relationship with the manager?

## Contingency Theory

Before we leave systems perspectives on organizations, we should visit briefly a close "relative" of organizational systems thinking. This is contingency theory. **Contingency theory** suggests that the effectiveness of any organizational action—a decision, for example—is determined in the context of all the other elements and conditions in the organization at the time the action is taken. Contingency theory posits that everything is situational and that there are no absolutes or universals. Contingency theorists assert that organizations always act in a context of relative uncertainty. In other words, they make decisions at any given point based on incomplete information. Given the incompleteness of the information, organizations must make the best decision they can with the information they do have.

Both systems and contingency theorists have as a major concern the processes of and variables influencing decision-making in organizations. A significant component of systems and contingency theories is decision-making. Shafritz and Ott (1987:234–238) suggest that use of complex quantitative tools and techniques to assist in gathering and processing the most information possible in order to make the best decision possible in an uncertain environment is a central theme of systems and contingency theorists. Such decision-making processes based on the assumption of incomplete information and uncertainty has been referred to as "satisficing" (March & Simon, 1958 in Gortner et al., 1987:258).

## Organizational Life Cycle Theories

Yet another traditional perspective on organizations, as is the case with individuals, families, and groups, is that of the life cycle. Researchers and theorists, primarily in the business disciplines, have posed a number of theories of organizations based on life cycles or stages. Howard and Hine (1997) suggest that, while there are differences in these theories, there are also similarities. They see these similarities as first a struggle for autonomy, followed by expansion, then stability.

More specifically, Hanks (1990 in Dodge & Robbins, 1992) outlines four organizational life cycle stages:

1. startup or entrepreneurial stage;
2. growth or expansion stage;
3. a domain protection stage and/or expansion stage;
4. a stability stage.

A third perspective on organizational life cycle theories (Miller & Friesen, 1980 in Jawahar & McLaughlin, 2001) suggests the following stages that tend to occur in sequence:

1. birth,
2. growth,
3. maturity, and
4. revival.

While these stage theories reflect a good deal of similarity, Miller and Friesen see organizations not only progressing to stability, but also having the potential to revitalize themselves after reaching maturity or stability. This approach is perhaps the least traditional of the three, given its less linear approach that allows for a rebirth or revitalization even at the later stages of the cycle.

## STRENGTHS, WEAKNESSES, CRITICISM

Before considering alternative paradigmatic perspectives on organizations, it is helpful first to consider some things that the traditional and dominant perspectives do and do not tell us about the realities of human behavior in organizational environments. The traditional perspectives on organizations we have explored so far tell us much about this level of human behavior that will be helpful in our social work practice and in our personal lives. These traditional notions, however, leave much untold or unclear about this important arena as well.

Classical traditional perspectives such as scientific management and bureaucratic theory (also referred to as rationalistic or mechanistic perspectives because of their concern with rational goal setting and decision-making aimed at achieving machinelike efficiency in organizations) told us much about the formal structure of organizations. Human relations thinking, with its concern for the nonrational and social elements of organizations, revealed much about the informal aspects of organizations. Systems and contingency theories presented us with perspectives that recognize both the formal and the informal aspects of organizations in addition to acknowledging the influences of the larger social environment on organizations.

However, Hasenfeld (in Patti, 2009:65) notes limitations of systems or ecological perspectives as they have been applied to organizational theory. He points out, for example, that research on organizations from an ecological perspective has not examined closely enough strategies to address macro-level system issues and changes such as changes "in the social, political, and economic environment in which [human service] agencies are embedded." In addition, he argues that too little ecologically based organizational theory has focused on "the role organizations play, individually and collectively, in constructing the environment in which they operate."

In other words, he suggests that ecological theory has not paid enough attention to "suprasystem" issues that form and continuously change the larger environment in which organizations exist and function. He has also posited that the theory has not been responsive enough to the ability of individual organizations to influence or change that larger environment in order for the organization to function better and more effectively meet its goals. Consistent with the perspective in this book, ecological or systems perspectives on organizations have not sufficiently accounted for the interdependence and interplay between the "focal" system (the individual organization) and elements in the larger macro-environment (the "suprasystem"). See Chapter 4 for a description of the more general systems perspective terms: focal and suprasystem.

These traditional perspectives, however, leave much unsaid about other important dimensions of organizational life. Classical perspectives (scientific management and bureaucracy) as well as human relations perspectives all assume, for example, that hierarchy is a necessary prerequisite for efficient and effective goal achievement in organizations. Systems approaches also assume some degree of hierarchy, although its specific characteristics may change in response to environmental conditions. Some alternative perspectives question the essential nature of hierarchy in organizations (Iannello, 1992).

Flowing from the assumption of hierarchy of traditional perspectives—classical, human relations, and systems—is the assumption that power must be divided unequally among the members of the organization. Power here is defined as the ability to influence movement toward accomplishment of goals. Whether this is according to formal and rational structures in bureaucracy, informal and non-rational networks in human relations approaches, or flexible and changeable arrangements based on environmental conditions in systems thinking, all of these traditional approaches include an inherent power differential among members.

In addition, these traditional perspectives see inequality or unequal distribution of power as basically functional for organizational members. In scientific management, lower-level workers benefit from power differences by having their basic economic needs met even though management and owners benefit materially to a greater extent in proportion to their greater power. In human relations thinking, not only are formal differences in power recognized, but the informal social networks reflect differences in power among network members as well. These formal and informal power inequities serve different, though overall functional, purposes. They support the realization of the organization's formal goals and they support the informal (social or personal) goals of members.

Another area in which alternative and traditional perspectives differ is that of conflict. Scientific-management approaches see truly rational and formal organizations as basically conflict-free. Human relations approaches when optimally implemented see informal structures as reducing the need for conflict to the point that these organizations have sometimes been referred to as "big happy families." Systems approaches go a bit further in recognizing that organizational conflict exists but they suggest that effective organizational systems will be "self-righting" in that they will make whatever adjustments are required to address and reduce conflict in order to return to a positive and mutually beneficial balanced state. Systems approaches, while recognizing the existence of conflict, see it as an exception, not a norm. (Buckley has addressed issues of conflict—he calls it "tension"—as a more "normal" part of systems behavior than most other systems thinkers.) Most systems approaches, nevertheless, operate from assumptions of cooperation and harmony (Barnard & Simon in Abrahamsson, 1977:151).

What is needed are alternative organizational perspectives that recognize the reality of differences or conflicts among members and that create mechanisms for using conflict resolution processes as an ongoing avenue for strengthening the organization (Abrahamsson, 1977; Iannello, 1992).

## ALTERNATIVE PARADIGMS

As we begin to explore alternative paradigms we emphasize that we do not want to exclude information provided by traditional perspectives. We want to extend that information in order to gain more comprehensive, inclusive perspectives on organizations. We are reminded here that alternative paradigms, while often critical of traditional perspectives, also often use traditional thinking as a departure point. In this respect it is helpful to recall the importance of historical perspective and the notion of continuum in our thinking about HBSE. Our goal, as we proceed on our journey to explore alternative perspectives on organizations, is to fill in some of the gaps in our knowledge and to clarify some of the areas left unclear by traditional organizational thinking. We are especially concerned with finding perspectives that are consistent with the core concerns of social work. Alternative perspectives are more "in process" than many traditional perspectives. Because many of the alternative perspectives are only now emerging, there are fewer examples of them around us. These alternative perspectives are also less "finished" in that their potential for improving the quality of our organizational lives has not been thoroughly studied or tested and can only be estimated in many respects. We begin our exploration of alternative perspectives with the notion of organizational culture as a way to think about organizations in more holistic ways.

## Organizational Culture/Climate

Regardless of whether an organization is in line with traditional paradigm or alternative paradigm thinking, it can be thought of as having an organizational culture that reflects and supports its prevailing view of the world. Earlier in this book we defined *culture* as the accumulation of customs, values, and artifacts that are shared by a group of people.

Schein (1992:7–15) suggests that organizations have many of the characteristics commonly associated with culture. He especially emphasizes that organizations are cultures by virtue of the shared experiences that organizational members hold in common. These shared experiences merge into a whole pattern of beliefs, values, and rituals that become the "essence" of the **organization's culture** and help provide stability. Organizational members adhere to these patterns, but they are not likely to be conscious of them in their day-to-day activities. This invisible or "taken for granted" aspect accounts for some of the difficulty outsiders have in fully understanding a given organization. It also accounts for some of the confusion and discomfort that new organizational members are likely to experience when they first enter the organization. This taken-for-granted aspect also helps explain why longtime members of an organization have difficulty explaining to new members or to outsiders exactly how the organization operates.

Schein (cited in Austin & Claassen, 2008:341) suggests there are three levels of culture, in this case organizational culture: 1) basic assumptions (fundamental nature of relationships among members to the larger environment and to each other), 2) values and beliefs (members' beliefs about what the organization should be and do), and 3) cultural artifacts (symbols that reflect the organization's values and beliefs—logos, promotional materials, etc.).

Schein (1992:11–12) stresses that all organizations do not develop smoothly integrated cultures shared equally by all organization members. When this integration is lacking the results are likely to be ambiguity and conflict. Lack of an integrated culture can come about because of turnover in organizational membership or because of the different experiences from outside the organization that its members bring with them. As a result, such organizations may be continuously trying to create an integrated whole from the shared and unshared experiences of members. Some organization members, leaders for example, are likely to play a larger role than others in the processes of creating or changing the culture.

This perspective on organizational culture can help us understand both stability and change in social work and human service organizations. This notion of culture combined with our perspective on traditional and alternative paradigms can help us to understand some of the problems within organizations and between organizations and the people they attempt to serve. For example, how can an organization with a culture characterized by patriarchal, white, quantitative, competitive, and privileged perspectives respond effectively to consumers and new organizational members whose worldviews are characterized by feminist, multicultural, qualitative, or cooperative perspectives? The concept of organizational culture can help us understand the difficulty faced by women, people of color, or persons with disabilities when they enter organizations (and they typically enter as lower-ranking members, rather than as members in formal leadership positions) that have historically been made up only of privileged able-bodied white males with a traditional paradigm perspective. It can also help us appreciate how important it is that the organizational culture of social work organizations reflect and respect the larger culture of the communities and people they serve.

In addition to the somewhat invisible but highly influential concept of organizational culture is the concept of organizational climate. These two concepts are highly interrelated. They both communicate the "feel" of an organization. *Organizational culture* includes such basic components as the fundamental beliefs and values of the organization. *Organizational climate*, on the other hand, reflects how organization members communicate organizational culture in more visible or observable ways both internally and externally. For example, how members interpret or communicate to others the organization's policies, practices, and procedures (Schneider, Brief, & Guzzo, 1996:7–9). It is important to assess the climate of an organization in order to determine the nature of the culture communicated to consumers, other organizations, and the larger community of which the organization is a part. One way to measure organizational climate is to ask a number of questions about key elements or aspects of the climate:

Measures of Climate According to Organizational Aspects

### Leadership

1. How much confidence is shown in workers?
2. How free do workers feel to talk to managers about their job?
3. To what extent are subordinates' ideas sought and used?

### Motivation

1. Is the use of fear, threats, punishment, rewards, or involvement used to motivate?
2. Is responsibility for achieving goal felt equally by workers and managers?
3. How much is cooperative teamwork used?

### Communication

1. Which way does communication flow in the organization (up, down, both directions)?
2. How is downward communication accepted by workers?
3. How accurate is information that flows upward?
4. How aware are managers of the problems faced by workers?

### Decision-Making

1. At what level in the organizations are decisions made?
2. To what extent are workers involved in decision-making?
3. Does the decision-making process result in positive or negative motivation?

### Goals

1. How are organizational goals established?
2. To what degree is there underlying resistance to goals?

**Controls**

1. How intense are evaluation and control mechanisms?
2. Is there an informal organizational structure resisting the formal one?
3. How are cost, productivity, and other data used in the organization? To motivate or to threaten?

Adapted from: (Kouzes & Posner, 1993)

## The "Iron Law of Oligarchy"

The concept of the "Iron Law of Oligarchy, an alternative to traditional approaches to organizational behavior, emerged at virtually the same time that Taylor's perspectives (discussed earlier) on scientific management and rationality in organizations were gaining prominence. This alternative appeared also at about the same time that Weber's notions about bureaucratic structure were being introduced. This alternative perspective preceded the more recent notions of organizational culture and climate. However, as you read this section, keep in mind the concepts of organizational climate and culture, which can help you understand the feel of the organization Michels described. Robert Michels published his work describing the "Iron Law of Oligarchy" in its original German in 1911. Scientific management and the theory of bureaucracy gained prominence roughly during the period from the turn of the century to 1930. Michels's work, however, took a decidedly contrary and pessimistic approach to the kinds of organizations Taylor and Weber were heralding as the answer to the organizational needs of the time.

Michels suggested that rather than organizations striving to meet the rationally specified needs of the organization as a whole, they instead serve the needs only of an elite few who gain control of the organization. He became convinced that formal organizations made democracy (participation and decision-making by a majority of organizational members) impossible and inevitably resulted in *oligarchy*—government or control by the few.

As organizations grew in scale their original goals would always end up being displaced by the goal of maintaining the organization in service to the interests of a small group of controlling elites. As an organization grew and became more bureaucratic it would employ a "ruling class" of managers or leaders. Their self-interests in maintaining the prestige and influence that accompanied their leadership positions resulted in a growing gap between the top and the bottom of the organizational hierarchy. Leaders no longer represented the interests of followers (Iannello, 1992; Michels in Grusky & Miller, 1981; Pugh et al., 1985).

Michels originally based his theory on his studies of revolutionary democratic political parties that grew into conservative political bureaucracies far removed from their original democratic goals. He came to believe that the development of oligarchy would happen to any organization regardless of its original purpose because oligarchy was a function of growing size or scale and the accompanying emergence of specialization and hierarchy. He was convinced that bureaucracy and democracy were inherently in opposition to one another (Michels in Grusky and Miller, 1981; Pugh et al., 1985).

As the self-interests of the organizational ruling class began to take precedence over original, more democratic goals of organizational members, Michels suggested the leaders of the organization would stress the need for internal unity. The harmony of ideas and views, along with the need to avoid or suppress tension and conflict, would become paramount. He also suggested that the ruling elite would put forth notions about dangers and hostility in the environment surrounding the organization, underscoring the need to hide internal differences from those outside the organization in order to maintain the status quo of the organization (Pugh et al., 1985:207–210).

Michels's view of the difficulty (the virtual impossibility, he came to believe) of large organizations' goals remaining consistent with democratic ideals was indeed a pessimistic one. Whether it was entirely justified is perhaps open to some argument. However, his alternative perspective does suggest that traditional models of organization are far from ideal and entail significant problems and risks in terms of ethics and values of which social workers need to be aware.

The tendency toward serving a select few powerful and prestigious leaders rather than the needs of all organizational members (and consumers of organizational services, as well, we might add) is certainly inconsistent with a number of core concerns of social workers. This tendency is contrary to concerns about maximum participation, self-determination, rights to resources, social and economic justice, and respect for diversity. As social workers and members of organizations (both as leaders and as followers), we need to recognize and act to prevent tendencies toward organizational oligarchy.

A concept similar to oligarchy, but applied to governments rather than organizations is **plutocracy**. Plutocracy is defined as a government ruled exclusively by and for the benefit of a wealthy elite. One might question, for example, if the U.S. government is trending toward plutocracy as powerful and super wealthy special interests, through their lobbyists and massive campaign contributions, dramatically increase their influence (control) over the federal government.

## A Critical Perspective

Kathleen Iannello (1992) presents a contemporary alternative perspective on organizations that follows in part from her belief that Michels's iron law of oligarchy, while criticized by a number of students of organizations, certainly has not been refuted. Indeed, she suggests that it is out of the hierarchical nature of traditional organizations that Michels's oligarchy grows (Iannello, 1992:3–25). If you recall, from our earlier exploration of traditional perspectives, hierarchy is considered a necessary component of modern organizational structures. This is especially so in a bureaucracy, perhaps the most common modern organization form (Iannello, 1992:3–7, 12).

Iannello's critical perspective suggests that alternatives to hierarchy are possible. However, to create alternatives we must first recognize that hierarchy is embedded throughout the values, norms, and ideologies of the larger society.

This critical perspective expands on traditional open-systems theory (explored earlier) in its emphasis on the interrelatedness of organizational structure and the values, norms, and ideologies of the surrounding environment. Iannello (1992:7–10) suggests that this critical perspective goes beyond traditional open-systems theory in recognizing the entire *society* as the environment having an "important and pervasive" influence on the nature of the organization. This perspective is in contrast to open-systems notions of an environment consisting only of those systems having a direct impact or influence on the organization, for example, other competing organizations in the immediate environment of the focal organization.

The critical perspective goes beyond open systems and much other traditional organizational thinking in another respect. It incorporates historical perspective as an additional pivotal consideration necessary for developing alternative models of organizations (Iannello, 1992:10). This perspective suggests, for example, that much is to be learned by asking "why," in a historical sense, an organization is structured as it is. How did it come to be the way it is? This questioning can engage us in paradigm analysis at the organizational level. For example, we might ask who founded the organization? What was their worldview? What were their values? Did they recognize the importance of difference? Did they see the organization's purpose as preserving or restoring human dignity and assisting members to reach their maximum potential? How was power distributed within the organization?

The critical perspective questions the necessity and inherent nature of hierarchy in organizations. It offers a different perspective on the meaning of hierarchy, and from this alternative perspective it calls attention to some of the problems created by hierarchy. Through its alternative analysis of hierarchy, the critical perspective raises a number of issues related to the dimensions of traditional and alternative paradigms with which we are concerned here. Specifically, it addresses such issues as power, domination, and privilege. It offers a definition of *hierarchy* as "any system in which the distribution of power, privilege and authority are both systematic and unequal" (Iannello, 1992:15).

This perspective's critique of hierarchy includes the concept of alienation of lower-level workers resulting from their lack of access to and participation in decision-making processes. The critique also questions the social control directed toward lower-level members of the hierarchy by those at the top in order to maintain their positions of power.

By looking beyond traditional narrow or closed-system organizational perspectives to include societal values and historical influences, the critical perspective reflects several dimensions of alternative paradigm thinking. This critical view allows the incorporation of a feminist perspective. It allows us to question the influence of patriarchal and masculinist societal values on organizational structures such as hierarchy.

Its historical perspective allows inclusion of broader interpretive, personal, experiential standpoints in addition to traditional "great person" accounts for thinking about the past and present structures of organizations. It allows serious consideration, for example, of power relations in organizations based on the experiences of all organization members rather than only the experiences of "key" administrators or decision makers (Iannello, 1992:3–13). In this respect it more readily allows for the inclusion of women's perspectives in thinking about organizations. For it is at lower levels in organizational hierarchies—clerical and administrative assistant positions, for example—that women have historically been concentrated.

## Consensus Organizations

Iannello develops a model of nonhierarchical organizations she refers to as consensus organizations. These organizations operate "primarily through a consensus decision-making process." The decision-making process followed in consensus organizations operates in a much more participative way in contrast to the centralized and alienating decision-making by managers and leaders at the top levels of the hierarchy in traditional organizations. *Consensus decision-making* occurs only after an issue has been widely discussed, with participation of a broad base (ideally all) of the organization members. After this discussion takes place, "one or more members of the assembly sum up prevailing sentiment, and if no objections are voiced, this becomes agreed-on policy" (Iannello, 1992; Mansbridge in Iannello, 1992:27).

Iannello notes that consensus organizations are also referred to by some as cooperative or collective organizations. She defines *consensus organization* as "any enterprise in which control rests ultimately and overwhelmingly with the members-employees-owners, regardless of the particular legal framework through which it is achieved" (Iannello, 1992; Rothschild & Whitt in Iannello, 1992:27). Consensus organizations attempt to "humanize the workplace, to put meaning and values back into jobs in order to reconnect the worker with society." To accomplish this goal these organizations focus on maximizing the level of commitment on the part of all workers to this primary goal. The means used to increase commitment and reduce alienation in consensus organizations is reducing hierarchy.

Examples of existing models of consensus organizations include the Israeli kibbutzim and a number of historical American Indian tribal organizations. However, we should be careful not to overgeneralize. We need to recognize that different kibbutzim and current American Indian tribal government organizations operationalize consensus principles to different degrees. Ideally, a kibbutz operates on consensus assumptions and principles. These include shared and egalitarian decision-making in all aspects of organizational life. This principle is implemented through weekly meetings of the entire organizational membership and a complex system of committees. This allows face-to-face decision-making. Leadership positions within the organization are elected and rotated among members to discourage hierarchy. Leadership positions offer no individual rewards for the individuals who hold them. Rewards within the organization are linked to achievement of collective rather than individual goals (Iannello, 1992:32).

As noted in the earlier discussion of consensus-based decision-making in small groups, Attneave stresses the central role played by consensus in many American Indian tribal government organizations. While the earlier discussion focuses on a preference for consensus in small-group decision-making, Attneave stressed that this form of decision-making operated whether the group was "the tribe, the band, the family or any other coherent cluster of people." Attneave noted, "tribal histories never suggested the impatient solution of majority vote so revered by 'democracies'" (Attneave, 1982:66–67).

### Comparison of consensus and bureaucratic organizations

How do consensus and bureaucratic organizations compare in terms of some of the basic issues and concerns of organizations generally? Rothschild and Whitt studied a number of consensus organizations, and Iannello used their findings to compare consensus and hierarchical bureaucratic organizations along several dimensions. A summary of this work follows:

1. *Authority:* In contrast to bureaucracy with its authority vested in individuals in the upper levels of the organizaiton, authority in the consensual organization rests with the collectivity.

2. *Rules:* In the consensual organization, rules are minimal and based on the "substantive ethics" of the situation. In the traditional organizations, rules are fixed, and emphasis is placed on conformity to the rules.

3. *Social control:* For the consensual organization, social control is based on something akin to peer pressure. Social control rarely becomes problematic, because of the homogeneity of the group. . . . Within a bureaucracy, social control is achieved through hierarchy and supervision of subordinates by their superiors, according to the formal and informal sanctions of the organizations.

4. *Social relations:* For the collective, social relations stem from the community ideal. "Relations are to be holistic, personal, of value in themselves." In the traditional model, the emphasis is placed on impersonality, which is linked to a sense of professionalism. "Relations are to be role based, segmental, and instrumental."

5. *Recruitment and advancement:* In the consensual organization, recruitment is based on friendship networks, "informally assessed knowledge and skills," and compatibility with organizations' values. The concept of advancement is generally not valued, since there is no hierarchy of positions and related rewards. Within the bureaucratic model recruitment is based on formal qualifications and specialized training. The concept of advancement is very meaningful for an individual's career and is based on formal assessment of performance according to prescribed rules and paths of promotion.

6. *Incentive structure:* For the consensual organization, "normative and solidarity incentives are primary; material incentives are secondary." For bureaucracy, "remunerative incentives are primary."

7. *Social stratification:* The consensual organization strives to be egalitarian. Any type of stratification is carefully created and monitored by the collectivity. In the bureaucracy, there are "differential rewards" of prestige, privilege, or inequality, each justified by hierarchy.

8. *Differentiation:* In the consensual structure, division of labor is minimized, particularly with regard to intellectual versus manual work. Jobs and functions are generalized, with the goal of "demystification of expertise." Bureaucracy maximizes division of labor to the extent that there is a "dichotomy between intellectual work and manual work and between administrative tasks and performance tasks." Technical expertise is highly valued and specialization of jobs is maximized. (Iannello, 1992:28–29)

### Limits of consensus organizations

There are a number of factors that limit the ability of organizations to successfully implement nonhierarchical structures. Some of these are summarized below:

1. *Time:* Consensus-style decision-making takes more time than bureaucratic decision-making, in which an administrator simply hands down a decision. . . . The idea of consensus, in which every member of an organization must agree to a decision, conjures up the picture of long, drawn-out sessions in which members may never agree. However, real-world experience has demonstrated that the endless rules and regulations of bureaucracies can also lead to protracted disputes. . . . It is important to recognize that both bureaucracies and consensual organizations are capable of making decisions quickly or slowly, depending on the nature of the issue.

2. *Emotional intensity:* There is more emotional intensity in the consensual setting. Consensual organizations provide face-to-face communication and consideration of the total needs of the individual. As a result, conflict within the organization may exact a much higher personal cost; individuals are held more accountable for their actions. In the bureaucratic organization, impersonality and formality make conflict less personal and therefore easier to handle.

But bureaucratic procedure also alienates people and is less satisfying personally. . . . [The] degree of emotional intensity has positive and negative aspects
for members of both organization types.

3. *Non-democratic habits and values:* As members of a hierarchical society, most
of us are not well prepared to participate in consensual styles of organization.
Our earliest contact with organizational life in educational and other settings is
bureaucratic.

4. *Environmental constraints:* Environmental constraints—economic, political, or
social pressures from the outside—are more intense in consensual organizations because such groups often form around issues that run counter to the
mainstream of society. . . . Consensual organizations can also at times benefit
because they provide a service or offer an avenue of participation that is not
available through other organizations. This has been true, for example, of organizations providing alternative health care or food co-ops providing natural
or organically grown foods.

5. *Individual differences:* While bureaucracies are able to capitalize on differences
in the attitudes, skills, and personalities of individual members, such differences may pose a problem for organizations based on consensual process. For
consensual organizations such diversity may lead to conflict. Yet while this
point has merit, it paints a somewhat false picture of both bureaucratic and
consensual organization. . . . Some argue that bureaucracy breeds sameness,
encourages lack of creativity, and provides little in the way of reward for anyone attempting to break out of set patterns. When such rewards exist they
are reserved primarily for those at the top of the organization. Yet others have
pointed out that bureaucracies, or at least public bureaucracies, have the most
diverse membership of any institutions. Thus, it is unsurprising that members
of consensual organizations, which are frequently homogeneous, are likely
to agree on issues that face the organization. (Rothschild & Whitt, Iannello in
Iannello, 1992:29–31)

An alternate perspective would suggest that it is possible for similarity and difference
to coexist. For example, it would seem that there can be homogeneity in terms of shared
philosophy and values simultaneous with diversity in ethnicity, gender, and sexual orientation. However, these limitations do leave the issue of conflict as a potential source of
growth and strength somewhat unaddressed.

## Modified Consensus Organizations

Based on the assumptions and principles of consensus organizations, their comparison
with hierarchical/bureaucratic organizations, and the limitations of both models, along
with her study of three different consensus organizations, Iannello develops an organizational type she refers to as "modified consensus." The elements of this model have a
good deal of consistency with core concerns of social work. Alternative structures and
processes from those of traditional models characterize modified consensus organizations. These differences include the areas of decision-making, nonhierarchical structures
and processes, empowerment, and clarity of goals.

Modified consensus organizations assure broad-based participation in decision-
making, but are also conscious of the need to make timely decisions for the sake of

operational efficiency. This is accomplished by differentiating between critical and routine decisions. Critical decisions are those that involve overall policy and have the potential for change in the fundamental direction of the organization. Critical decisions are made by the entire membership; in hierarchical organizations, only those at the top make critical policy decisions. In modified consensus organizations, routine decisions are those that are important in the day-to-day operation of the organization. Routine decisions are delegated horizontally within the organization according to the skills and interests of organizational members.

A second area of difference between modified consensus and traditional organizations is in concern for process. Process issues include concern for consensus, emerging leadership, and empowerment. Central to process is trust. Maintaining consensus through the participation and agreement of all organization members in the critical decisions faced by the organization fosters this trust. The trust built through consensus on critical decisions in turn engenders sufficient trust among members to allow routine decisions to be delegated. Without mutual trust among members, the domination of some by others in the organization, characteristic of traditional hierarchical organizations, would be difficult to avoid.

Leadership is essential in both traditional and alternative organizations. The nature of leaders and the processes for development of leadership varies significantly between traditional and modified consensus organizations, however. Modified consensus organizations look within their membership and recognize its variety of abilities and expertise as the source of leadership. Efforts are made to maximize the skills of members. Members with specific skills provide ongoing education and training of other members who want to learn these skills. Central to this process is rotation of members through various positions of leadership within the organization. The assumption is that all members have the potential for leadership in a wide range of areas. This perspective is very different from traditional notions of leadership that hold leadership to be characteristic only of the specialized experts at the top of the hierarchy. (See discussion of traditional and alternative notions of leadership in Chapter 8 for a detailed discussion of different perspectives on leadership.)

Modified consensus organizations also seek to minimize power and maximize empowerment. Iannello (1992:44–45) describes power as "the notion of controlling others, while empowerment is associated with the notion of controlling oneself." Therefore, within organizations based on empowerment, members monitor themselves. In organizations based on power, there must be an administrative oversight function. This perspective is consistent with our earlier discussions of empowerment as power to accomplish one's goals or reach one's potential rather than "power over" others.

Iannello argues that power "is a relational concept that has a win/lose element to it" (1992:120). The members of the women's organizations she studied and found most consistent with modified consensus structure and operation rejected the idea of voting on major decisions for this reason. To vote meant there would always be some members who perceived themselves to have "lost" (unless voting was unanimous). "With consensus decision making, based on the concept of empowerment, it is perceived that everyone 'wins' because all members agree to the final decision" (Iannello, 1992:120).

### Organizational leadership

In Chapter 8, we examined several leadership types and styles in the context of groups. While there are certainly similarities in the types and styles of leadership needed for effective group work practice and organizational practice, there are also differences. For example, the definition of leadership as "a process by which an individual influences a group of individuals to achieve common goals," clearly applies to both organizational and group contexts (Packard in Patti, 2009:144). However, leadership in the context of an organization, especially if it is a large, complex organization, is quite different from leadership in the context of a small group.

In Chapter 8, trait-based leadership theory was briefly described. However, even though this theory lost a good deal of its influence since its introduction in the first part of the 20th century, Packard notes that there has been renewed interest recently in efforts to understand traits associated with effective leadership. The more recent research in this area suggests the importance of a number of traits associated with effective organizational leadership. These include:

- A high energy level and tolerance for stress
- Self-confidence (including self-esteem and self-efficacy)
- An internal locus of control orientation (a sense that you, rather than external forces, control your destiny)
- Emotional stability and maturity
- Personal integrity (in Patti, 2009:156)

Packard cautions that "traits are important only to the extent that they are relevant to a particular leadership situation" (in Patti, 2009:146). In other words, as is so often the case—context matters.

Leadership skills and competencies have also received increased attention on the part of researchers and scholars. *Leadership competencies* are defined as "the combination of knowledge, skills, traits and attributes that collectively enable someone to perform a certain job." Competencies found to be associated with leadership effectiveness include:

- Character (displaying integrity and honesty)
- Technical and professional expertise
- Problem-solving and analytical ability
- Innovation
- Self-development
- A focus on results
- Setting "stretch" goals
- Taking personal responsibility for outcomes
- Effective communication
- Inspiring and motivating others
- Trust and interpersonal effectiveness
- Concern for others' development
- Collaboration and organizational change skills
- Ability to champion change
- Ability to relate well to outside stakeholders (Packard in Patti, 2009:146–147)

## Leadership styles

In Chapter 8 several traditional leadership styles applicable to small groups—autocratic/authoritarian, laissez faire, and democratic—were presented. Here we will address leadership styles within an organizational context with a focus on emerging or alternative styles. There has been considerable criticism of research in the area of leadership styles, especially in terms of its inconclusive nature. However, Yukl (cited in Patti, 2009:147) observes, "the overall pattern of results suggests that effective leaders use a pattern of behavior that is appropriate for the situation and reflects a high concern for task objectives and a high concern for relationships." Here again we see parallels between small-group concerns for task (or product) and relationship (or process/socioemotional) characteristics of leaders in larger organizations. In addition, Yukl adds the need for organizational leaders to attend to "change behaviors" as well. Change behaviors also reflect social work responsibilities related to change and advocacy on behalf of the systems we serve. A summary of examples of each type of leader behavior follows.

Task or product-focused behaviors

- Plan day-to-day activities to support task accomplishment.
- Help members understand task objectives and their roles in task achievement.
- "Big picture" oversight of processes and functions.

Relationship or process-focused behaviors

- "Cheer leader" offering support and inspiration.
- Recognition of successes and efforts.
- Support attainment of necessary skills and self-confidence of workers.
- Include members in decision-making.
- Encourage members to be self-directed in problem solving.

Change-focused behaviors

- Continuously scan larger environment to assess need for change
- Offer innovation and a "vision" when change is needed.
- Support member innovation in bringing about change.
- Encourage and demonstrate "Risk-taking" to bring about needed change.

Adapted from: Yukl, G., Gordon, A., & Taber, T. (2002). A Hierarchical Taxonomy of Leadership Behavior: Integrating a Half Century of Behavior Research. *Journal of Leadership and Organizational Studies, 9*(1), 18.

Emerging and more alternative leadership styles include Visionary Leadership, and Servant-Leadership.

*Visionary leadership* includes the ability to develop, articulate, and communicate a clear organizational vision. "A vision is 'a realistic, credible, attractive, and inspiring future for the organization" (Nanus & Dobbs cited by Parker in Patti, 2009:153). Parker notes, "while a mission statement describes why an organizations exists (its purpose) and what it does (its unique niche of programs and activities), a vision statement represents where the organization wants to be, its ideal future" (Patti, 2009:153).

*Servant leadership* is an alternative style with its roots in philosophical, ethical, and moral principles and it presents "the unorthodox idea that the leader should first serve followers" (Parker in Patti, 2009:153-154). This model seems particularly well suited to social work organizations.

Servant leaders achieve results for their organizations by giving priority attention to the needs of their colleagues and to those whom they serve. They are often seen as humble stewards of their organizations' resources (human, financial and physical).

Greenleaf identifies ways to tell if one is correctly practicing servant leadership, also known as the "best test":

- Do those [who are] served grow as persons?
- Do they, while being served, become healthier, wiser, freer, more autonomous, more likely themselves to become servants?
- And, what is the effect on the least privileged in society?
- Will they benefit or at least not be further deprived?
- Practicing servant leadership is to seek the best for other people and bring the maximum benefit to the organization.

The congruence of servant leadership with social work principles and values is evident in its ten characteristics:

1. Listening. Listens actively to his or her coworkers and supports them in decision identification.

2. Empathy. A servant leader attempts to understand and empathize with others.

3. Healing. The ability for healing one's self and others . . . . [Both the leader and worker share in the] search for wholeness.

4. Awareness. [Gains] general self-awareness to help understand issues involving ethics, power and values. He or she should have the ability to view situations from a more integrated, holistic perspective.

5. Persuasion. A servant leader does not take advantage of his or her power and status by coercing compliance; rather, he or she tries to persuade them in contrast to traditional authoritarian approaches to leadership

6. Conceptualization. A servant leader thinks beyond day-to-day realities [and can] focus on long-term operating goals.

7. Foresight. The ability to foresee the likely outcome of a situation. It enables the servant leader to learn about the past and to achieve a better understanding about the current reality.

8. Stewardship. Servant leadership is seen as an obligation to help and serve others . . . . Servant leadership, like stewardship, assumes first and foremost a commitment to serving the needs of others.

9. Commitment. A servant leader is convinced that people have an intrinsic value beyond their contributions as workers . . . . [And] nurture the personal, professional and spiritual growth of employees.

10. Building community. A servant leader identifies means to build a strong community within his or her organization and wants to develop a true community among businesses and institutions that reflect social responsibility on the part of the organizations.

(Adapted from Jones-Burbridge, 2012)

Interestingly, this style was developed by a retired executive, Robert Greenleaf of AT&T, an organization most would consider very traditional (Parker in Patti, 2009:15).

## Professional Identity

**Practice Behavior Example:** Commit themselves to the profession's enhancement and to their own professional conduct and growth.

**Critical Thinking Question:** Reflect on the leadership styles discussed in this section. Which style or styles reflect the style(s) of leadership you want to develop in continuing your development as a professional social worker?

## Feminist Approaches to Organizations

As indicated in the discussion of consensus-based organizations, feminist theory offers an important alternative perspective on organizational behavior. This theoretical perspective is increasingly being applied to thinking about organizational life. For example, Gilligan's theory that women's development (see Chapter 6) is based on an ethic of care and the centrality of relationships has been applied to organizational life and business enterprises. Liedtka notes, "Gilligan's metaphor of the web to represent feminine thinking, has been juxtaposed against the use of hierarchy to represent masculine thinking" (1996). Burton also suggests that "in one sense it might be said that traditional, economics-based approaches to management have concentrated on the legalistic, contractual, masculine side of human existence" (1996). These alternative organizations based on relationships and caring "are not bureaucracies. . . . The rules in a bureaucracy become, over time, the ends rather than the means. Thus, caring, even for the customer or client, is subordinated to perpetuation of the organization in its current state" (Liedtka, 1996).

Core concepts from Gilligan's theory are associated with other new management theories such as **stakeholder theory** and the notion of learning organizations (see discussion of learning organizations in this chapter). "Stakeholder theory, like the ethic of care, is built upon recognition of interdependence." Stakeholder theorists suggest that "the corporation is constituted by the network of relationships which it is involved in with employees, customers, suppliers, communities, businesses and other groups who interact with and give meaning and definition to the corporation" (Liedtka, 1996).

According to Burton, newer approaches such as "stakeholder theory might then be said to be the feminine counterpart to traditional management" theories (1996).

The concept of the learning organization, another alternative approach to organizational management, also reflects elements of feminist theory, especially the ethic of care. The

FELIPE TRUEBA/EPA/CORBIS

*How do the demonstrators in this photo, who are marching to commemorate International Women's Day in Santiago de Chile, Chile, March 8, 2012, portray an "ethic of care" and the "centrality of relationships" put forth in the theory of Carol Gilligan?*

learning organization also appreciates the importance of relationship and interconnectedness characteristic of much alternative paradigm thinking, including feminist perspectives. For example, the learning organization is closely linked with "communities that share a sense of purpose that connects each member to each other, and to the community at large. Learning organizations are characterized by an ability to maintain an open dialogue among members, that seeks first to understand, rather than evaluate, the perspectives of each. . . . Care-based organizations would seem ideally suited for such processes" (Burton & Dunn, 1996).

Caring organizations recognize the importance of employees and frontline workers as the primary providers of services to consumers: "It is the employees who deal directly with these customers who ultimately determine the firm's success or failure. The rest of the organization, including senior management, exists to support and respond to, rather than control and monitor, these frontline workers" (Liedtka, 1996). Such organizations will be characterized by listening to the needs of their consumers and by willingness to experiment to meet the changing needs of consumers. As Liedtka points out, "they will need to listen, to inquire, and to experiment. They will be collaborative enterprises . . . which value the diversity of their workforce, and who work in partnership with their suppliers and in the communities in which they reside" (Liedtka 1996). Certainly these perspectives are important approaches to consider in designing and operating social work organizations.

### Women's career paths

Research by O'Neil and Bilimoria (2005) resulted in uncovering recurring patterns and trajectories in the careers and life courses of women that differ from those of men. These differences emerge from three major factors:

1. The differential impact of family responsibilities on men's and women's careers.

2. Findings from women's developmental psychology . . . suggest a distinctive relational emphasis may pervade women's career development.

3. Women's relative under-representation and subsequent token status at higher organizational levels uniquely constrain their career progress. (O'Neil & Bilimoria, 2005:169)

With the earlier information as context, O'Neil and Bilimoria found, through their research, three general phases of career development among the women in their study.

The authors conclude that research on women in organizations "strongly suggests that organizations need to understand, recognize and support women's career and relationship priorities in order to retain talented professional women." However, in this particular study the researchers "found strong evidence that while organizations may agree on the importance of that support, they often fall short in practice, resulting in a lack of women who reach the higher rungs of management" (O'Neil & Bilimoria, 2005:185).

Next, we explore network organizations and social change theories of organizations (critical theory and empowerment theory). These theoretical approaches also share tenets of feminist theory consistent with the discussions in the previous section, "Feminist Theory and Organizations."

### Network organizations

Another emerging organizational theory is that of the network organization. This has been especially true for human service organizations. The increasing prominence of such organizational realities as privatization of services and managed care approaches have created the need, even the requirement, for human service organizations to devote more attention building and maintaining networks both internally and externally. *Network organizations* create network exchange relations, collaborations, and alliances with other organizations. In addition, "innovations in information technology, especially the Internet, have supported the transformation from traditional models of bureaucracy to network organizations" (Hasenfeld in Patti, 2009:61). Think, for example, about the organization of networks formed through such social networking sites such as Facebook, YouTube, and Instagram. Hasenfeld notes, "research suggests that in addition to external networks, internal networks, rather than hierarchical structures, may have greater advantages, especially in reducing costs and improving quality." However, he also notes that "despite the critical importance of networks to human services administration, they receive limited attention" (Patti, 2009:61).

### Social change theory and organizations

Critical theory is an alternative approach to social change in and through organizations. Alvesson and Deetz describe critical theory as an approach to understanding and changing organizations. They suggest, "the central goal of critical theory in organizational studies has been to create societies and workplaces which are free from domination, where all members have equal opportunity to contribute to the production of system which meet human needs and lead to the progressive development of all" (cited by Hasenfeld in Patti, 2009:71).

According to Alvesson and Deetz, critical theory as an approach to organizational analysis and change includes four major themes or premises:

1. Organizational forms need not be accepted as the natural order of things.

2. Management interests are not universal.

3. The emphasis on technical rationality represses understanding and mutual determination of the desired ends.

4. The organizational culture fosters the hegemony of dominant groups. (cited by Hasenfeld in Patti, 2009:71–72)

## Chaos/Complexity Theory and Organizations

In Chapter 4 we explored alternative theories that were extensions of social systems thinking. Included in these discussions were chaos and complexity theories. Students of organizations have begun to explore the application of these two theoretical perspectives to organizational behavior. These perspectives are increasingly presented as alternatives to traditional bureaucratic approaches to organizations. One of the most significant differences in the newer approaches of chaos and complexity is their focus on the importance of recognizing the positive aspects of change and flexibility, while traditional bureaucratic approaches seek stability and standardization. Evans points out, for example, that "traditional systems theorists have held that equilibrium or stability is the desirable state for an organization," but chaos theorists contend "that a condition of loosely bounded instability appears necessary to enable existing structures and patterns of interaction to respond to environmental demands." New paradigm managers focus more on developing "organizational processes and systems that support the agency's capacity, self-renewal, and self-organization" (1996). Wheatley suggests that consistent with newer extensions of systems thinking, organizations can be described as "living systems."

For social workers, a particularly helpful aspect of newer organizational thinking is its focus on the benefits and need for diversity in organizations. Evans stresses that "one excellent source of creative disorder is work force diversity. Organizational culture tradi-tionally works to smooth out, if not eliminate, difference, but public managers can en-deavor to counter this tendency by flexible job assignments, creating diverse work groups, and recognizing the unique contributions of individual women and men" (Evans, 1996).

Another element of new-paradigm organizational thinking is its emphasis on under-standing the multiple layers and complexity of organizational life. Zhu discusses the comple-mentary nature of Eastern philosophical recognition of complexity and interconnectedness within organizations. Zhu points out that complex "systems involve multiple dimensions which are at once differentiated and interconnected." From this "Oriental systems approach" the organizational environment is closely connected to the larger social environment in "a dynamic web of multiple relations: relations within the complexity of 'the world,' relations between the human mind and that world, and relations among human beings" (Zhu, 1999).

These newer approaches also incorporate a more spiritual approach to organiza-tional management. They shift the focus "from structural and functional aspects of or-ganization to the spiritual characteristics and qualities of organizational life." Overman suggests these managers focus "on energy, not matter; on becoming, not being; on coin-cidence, not causes; on constructivism, not determinism; and on new states of awareness and consciousness" (Overman, 1996). Alternative approaches to management stress the importance of relationships, social networks, and small groups.

## Organizations as Living Systems

As living systems, organizations possess all of the creative, self-organizing capacities of other forms of life. The people within all organizations are capable of change, growth, and adaptation—they do not require outside engineering or detailed design. People are capable of creating structures and responses that work, then moving into new ones when required. We possess natural capacities to work with change in a creative and effective way. (Wheatley and Kellner-Rogers, 1996)

## Theory Z

We included in traditional approaches to understanding organizations a discussion of Theory X and Theory Y. These were organizational theories based on sets of assump-tions about people held by managers. Douglas McGregor proposed Theory X as an ap-proach to management based on the assumption that people were basically lazy and irresponsible. Theory X held that because people would naturally seek to avoid work and responsibility, a major part of the manager's responsibility was to constantly watch workers to make sure they were working and fulfilling their responsibilities. Theory Y, on the other hand, held that people "are fundamentally hardworking, responsible, and need only to be supported and encouraged" (Ouchi, 1981:58–59).

William Ouchi (1981) developed an alternative theory of organizational management that he termed Theory Z. Like Theories X and Y, Theory Z was an approach to manage-ment premised on assumptions about humans. However, Theory Z had its basis not in traditional Western assumptions about humans, but in assumptions about humans based on Japanese culture and reflected in many Japanese organizations and approaches to man-agement. While not all Japanese firms displayed all Theory Z characteristics to the same degrees, Ouchi found a significant number of Japanese firms that reflected a Theory Z perspective. Ouchi compared U.S. corporations with these Japanese firms and found funda-mental differences in the assumptions underlying the business enterprises in the two coun-tries. He contrasted the elements of the two approaches as shown in Table 9.1, as follows:

---

**Table 9.1  Differences in the Assumptions Underlying the Business Enterprises in Japan and the United States**

| Japanese Organization | U.S. Organization |
|---|---|
| Lifetime employment | Short-term employment |
| Slow evaluation and promotion | Rapid evaluation and promotion |
| Non-specialized career paths | Specialized career paths |
| Implicit control mechanisms | Explicit control mechanisms |
| Collective decision-making | Individual decision-making |
| Collective responsibility | Individual responsibility |
| Holistic concern | Segmented concern |

*Theory Z: How American Business Can Meet the Japanese Challenge*, by William G. Ouchi. Copyright © 1981. Reprinted by permission of Perseus Books Publishers, a member of Perseus Books.

---

The Theory Z emphasis on job security, collective decision-making, and collective responsibility for decisions, along with a holistic perspective, has a good deal of similarity with the consensus and modified consensus models described earlier. Unlike consensus and modified consensus notions, Theory Z has been applied to very large profit-making organizations, including major U.S. and multinational business corporations.

Ouchi suggests that participative or consensus decision-making is perhaps the best-known feature of Japanese organizations. A consensus approach has also been widely researched and experimented within the United States and Europe.

A group or team approach is a central mechanism for implementing consensus-based decision-making in Theory Z organizations. A **team** approach, sometimes referred to as **quality circle** or **quality control circle**, is a cohesive work group with the ability to operate with a significant degree of autonomy in the areas for which it is responsible. While teams are often formal and official work groups, many times these teams are not officially created but simply form from among organization members to address a problem or issue that arises. Ouchi describes the function of quality control circles:

> What they do is share with management the responsibility for locating and solving problems of coordination and productivity. The circles, in other words, notice all the little things that go wrong in an organization—and then put up the flag. (1981:223)

A team approach is central to Theory Z–type organizations in both the United States and Japan. In the United States, the Theory Z organization's focus on consensus decision-making is usually implemented at the small-group level within the large organization. Ouchi describes the typical participative decision-making structure and process as it has been adapted in the West:

> Typically, a small group of not more than eight or ten people will gather around a table, discuss the problem and suggest alternative solutions.. The group can be said to have achieved a consensus when it finally agrees upon a single alternative and each member of the group can honestly say to each other member three things:
>
> 1. I believe that you understand my point of view.
> 2. I believe that I understand your point of view.
> 3. Whether or not I prefer this decision, I will support it, because it was arrived at in an open and fair manner. (Ouchi, 1981:36–37)

Our earlier discussion of organizational culture suggested that there is less ambiguity and conflict when there is an integrated and homogeneous organizational culture. In addition, it suggested that there is less organizational conflict when the external cultural experiences of organization members are similar to and compatible with the culture of the organization. The Japanese cultural value of collective decision-making and collective responsibility is reflected in and quite compatible with Japanese organizational culture based on long-term employment, trust, and close personal relationships.

A significant limitation of Theory Z organizations both in Japan and in the United States is their difficulty in dealing with cultural diversity. They tend to depend on a homogeneous internal organizational culture. This in turn makes it unlikely that people will be brought into the organization if they come from external cultures that are diverse. The consensus and modified consensus approaches discussed earlier also depended on or assumed a high degree of homogeneity among organizational members, at least in terms of organizational goals, philosophy, and values. While consensus, modified consensus, and Theory Z organizations reflect many values consistent with alternative paradigm perspectives and with the core concerns of social work, their reliance on similarity rather than diversity is a major limitation.

## Learning Organizations

The concept of a learning organization is an attempt to go beyond the notions of total quality management, especially the notion of adapting to changes as they occur. According to Hodgetts et al. **learning organizations** "not only *adapt* to change, but they *learn and stay ahead of* change" (1994:12). A learning organization is characterized by:

1.  *Systems thinking:* Certainly, systems thinking is central to much of social work theory and practice. See Chapter 4 for an extended discussion of social systems thinking.

2.  *Personal mastery:* The ability to continually clarify and deepen our personal vision, to focus our energies, to develop patience, and to see reality objectively.

3.  *Mental models:* Learning to "turn the mirror inward," to increase our awareness of how we view the world—our worldview or guiding paradigm, to bring our worldview to a surface or conscious level, and continually and critically examine our views.

4.  *Building shared vision:* The ability to uncover shared "pictures of the future" that can build genuine commitment and engagement. According to Senge, "people excel and learn, not because they are told [sic] to, but because they want to."

5.  *Team learning:* This begins with "dialogue" or the "capacity of members of a team to suspend assumptions and enter into a genuine 'thinking together.'"

(Senge, 1990: 6-10)

### Learning culture

Barrett (1995:40) provides a helpful list of competencies characteristic of organizational cultures that support and nurture a learning environment. These competencies include:

1.  *Affirmative Competence:* The organization draws on the human capacity to appreciate positive possibilities by selectively focusing on current and past strengths, successes, and potentials.

2. *Expansive Competence:* The organization challenges habits and conventional practices, provoking members to experiment on the margins, makes expansive promises that challenge them to stretch in new directions, and evokes a set of higher values and ideals that inspire them to passionate engagement.

3. *Generative Competence:* The organization constructs integrative systems that allow members to see the consequences of their actions, to recognize that they are making a meaningful contribution, and to experience a sense of progress.

4. *Collaborative Competence:* The organization creates forums in which members engage in ongoing dialogue and exchange diverse perspectives.

These levels of competence are quite compatible with alternative paradigm thinking generally and alternative thinking about organizational life more specifically. For example, they focus on strengths-based thinking and collaborative approaches. These competencies also reflect a postmodern tone in their call to focus on the margins of organizational discourse in order to be more inclusive of diverse perspectives and as a source of creative solutions beyond the status quo.

## Managing Diversity

R. Roosevelt Thomas, Jr., a scholar who addresses diversity in organizations, has done extensive research and consultation related to the realities of diversity in American corporations. Based on this research and experience he has developed an approach to organizations and management called "managing diversity" (MD). He defines this approach as a "'way of thinking' toward the objective of creating an environment that will enable all employees to reach their full potential in pursuit of organizational objectives" (Thomas, 1991:19). Other proponents of MD suggest that it means recognizing that individuals are different and that this diversity can be a strength rather than a weakness for organizations. Advocates of MD also stress that managing diversity is necessary to deal with current labor force and workplace realities.

Thomas (1991) suggests that MD goes beyond affirmative action approaches and recognizes the growing tendencies among employees to celebrate their differences. He suggests that while affirmative action was and continues to be necessary, it can only help get minorities and women into an organization. It cannot ensure that once in an organization they will be able to reach their full potential. The goal of MD is "to develop our capacity to accept, incorporate, and empower the diverse human talents of the most diverse nation on earth" (Thomas, 1990:17). MD is an approach that can pick up where affirmative action leaves off.

More recently Thomas (1996) has extended his work on MD to include what he refers to as "redefining diversity" from an organizational perspective. He suggests that a full definition of diversity must include not only differences, but similarities as well. "Diversity refers to any mixture of items characterized by differences and similarities," according to Thomas. He stresses the importance of understanding the "diversity mixture," which includes not only people but any other aspects of the organization as well. These other aspects can include product lines (or services), functions, marketing strategies, or operating philosophies.

Thomas also "has suggested that current notions of diversity need to be broadened to go beyond mere representation to a focus on diversity management: 'making quality decisions in the midst of difference, similarities, and related tensions.'" He suggests additionally that leaders of diverse organizations need to "become comfortable with tension and complexity" and "more strategic in their thinking, considering diversity issues in the context of mission, vision, and strategy" (2006, cited by Packard in Patti, 2009:160).

This expanded notion of diversity is helpful in thinking about human behavior in the context of organizational environments because it requires us to be more completely inclusive in our thinking and actions. It requires us to include similarities as well as differences in the diversity mixture. In addition, it requires us to think about differences not only in terms of people, but also in terms of all of the activities of the organization. These activities include the services we provide to consumers, the marketing of those services, and the philosophies used by the organization to plan, deliver, and evaluate its operations.

### The increasingly pluralistic workplace: Labor Force Projections

Clearly, the U.S. labor force is becoming more diverse. However, this increasing diversity is not yet reflected in the top leadership of the major organizations and corporations that control much of the overall labor force.

General Workforce

People of color make almost 1/3 of the total labor force (see Figure 9.1). Women make up almost half (47 percent) of the labor force (see Figure 9.2).

Gay and transgender workers make up an estimated 6.28 percent or 8,203,000 workers. However, these data are incomplete because the federal government does not yet collect data on sexual orientation and gender identity in many of its surveys. The chart reflects data collected by the Williams Institute, a national think-tank at the UCLA Law School.

People with disabilities contribute in significant ways to the U.S. economy. However, the talents of people with disabilities are dramatically underused in the labor force. The unemployment rate for people with disabilities is 15 percent compared to the U.S. unemployment rate overall, which is 8.7 percent.

As Figure 9.3 indicates, significant disparity remains in the representation of members of diverse groups who own businesses in the United States:

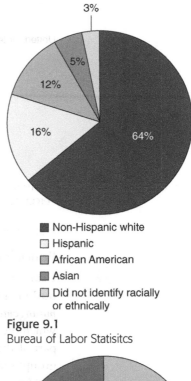

**Figure 9.1**
Bureau of Labor Statisitcs

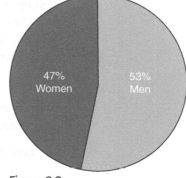

**Figure 9.2**
Bureau of Labor Statisitcs

**Figure 9.3**
Disparity in the Representation of Members of Diverse Groups Who Own Businesses in the United States

Source: http://quickfacts.census.gov/qfd/states/00000.html
Note: Most recent data available as of 11/6/2013

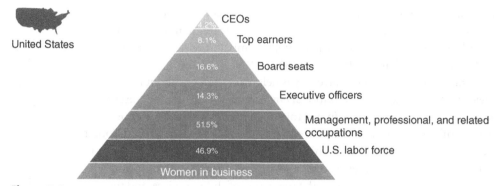

**Figure 9.4**
Percentage of Women Executives Compared to Women in the Workforce Overall

http://www.catalyst.org/knowledge/us-women-business

## Principles of pluralistic management

Using the work of Crable, Kunisawa, Copeland, and Thomas, Nixon and Spearmon outline a number of principles of pluralistic management. They define *pluralistic management* as "leadership that aggressively pursues the creation of a workplace in which the values, interests, and contributions of diverse cultural groups are an integral part of the organization's mission, culture, policies, and procedures and in which these groups share power at every level" (1991:156–157).

Nixon and Spearmon note that these principles "resonate with two central values of the social work profession: respect for the dignity and uniqueness of the individual and self-determination" (1991:157).

## A typology of organizational progression to pluralism

Nixon and Spearmon (1991:157–158) offer a helpful four-level typology to assess an organization's level of progress toward being a truly pluralistic workplace.

> *Level 1: Token EEO organization.* Hires people of color and women at the bottom of the hierarchy; has a few token (see definition of tokenism in Chapter 8) managers who hold their positions only as long as they do not question organization policies, practices, mission, and so on.
>
> *Level 2: Affirmative Action Organization.* Aggressively recruits and supports the professional development of women and people of color and encourages non-racist, non-sexist behaviors; to climb the corporate ladder, women and people of color must still reflect and fit in with policies, practices, and norms established by dominant white men.
>
> *Level 3: Self-renewing Organization.* Actively moving away from being sexist and racist toward being pluralistic; examines its mission, culture, values, operations, and managerial styles to assess their impact on the well-being of all employees; seeks to redefine the organization to incorporate multiple cultural perspectives.
>
> *Level 4: Pluralistic Organization.* Reflects the contributions and interests of diverse cultural and social groups in its mission, operations, and service delivery; seeks to eliminate all forms of oppression within the organization; workforce at all levels (top to bottom) reflects diversity; diversity in leadership is reflected in policymaking and governance structures; is sensitive to the larger community in which it exists and is socially responsible as a member of the community (Nixon & Spearmon, 1991:157–158).

### Diversity in Practice

**Practice Behavior Example:** Understand how diversity characterizes and shapes the human experience and is critical to the formation of identity.

**Critical Thinking Question:** Using Nixon and Spearmon's typology, assess the level of pluralism that you believe best describes your college or university. Provide examples to support your assessment.

# TECHNOLOGY, ORGANIZATIONS, AND SOCIAL POLICY

As in so many areas, technology is having a profound impact on the nature of organizations and organizational life. Technology may be seen as blurring the boundaries between organizational and community life in some ways. However, it might be more accurate to say that technology is providing organizations with alternative avenues for influencing community life and achieving organizational goals within communities. For example, the Internet can offer voluntary or civic sector organizations a very direct mechanism for communicating and achieving their purposes within communities.

However, as Westen notes, technology cannot determine the future and health of our democracy because "in the end, that outcome is determined by the spirit and skills of the people themselves. But technology can provide the electorate with the ability to make improved decisions" (Westen, 1998). Clearly, the 2008 and again in 2012 presidential campaigns President Barack Obama used Internet connectivity (e-mail, texting, Facebook, YouTube) to an unprecedented extent in organizing, funding, and promoting his campaign. For example, many have suggested that the greatly increased voter turnout among young people was in large part a result of his campaign's significant investment in communication and networking through the Internet.

# SUMMARY/TRANSITION

In this chapter we explored definitions and historical perspectives on organizations generally, in addition to discussing a number of specific traditional and alternative perspectives on organizations. In considering traditional perspectives, scientific management, bureaucracy, human relations, and Theory X and Theory Y were discussed. Theory Y, systems, and contingency theory perspectives were discussed as somewhat mid-range perspectives having some characteristics or qualities of both traditional and alternative paradigms.

We addressed alternative organizational approaches within the framework of organizational culture. Using organizational culture as a backdrop, Michel's "Iron Law of Oligarchy," Iannello's critical perspective, consensus, and modified consensus organizational approaches were addressed. Network organizations, social change theories of organizations, and organizational leadership theories were also addressed as alternative to traditional organizational thinking. Theory Z, teams or quality circles, and MD perspectives were also presented as alternative perspectives on organizations.

We concluded this chapter with the recognition that no single alternative perspective was entirely consistent with alternative paradigm principles or social work core concerns. The challenge we were left at the end of this chapter was to continue to search for newer alternatives that incorporate the separate strengths of alternative and traditional models while avoiding their shortcomings.

---

**Human Behavior**

**Practice Behavior Example:** Know about human behavior across the life course; the range of social systems in which people live; and the ways social systems promote or deter people in maintaining or achieving health and well-being.

---

**Critical Thinking Question:** Now that you have read this chapter, choose an organization, (work, faith-based, school, hospital, leisure, social work, etc.) and give one example of how the organization might promote and one example of how it might deter the achievement or maintenance of health and well-being.

---

**Recall what you learned in this chapter by completing the** Chapter Review.

# 10

RICHARD DEVERELL ILLUSTRATION/PHOTOEDIT

# Perspectives on Community(ies)

## INTRODUCTION

Each stop along our journey toward understanding human behavior
and the social environment (HBSE), thus far, has been important. In
some respects, though, this chapter on community may be the most
important. Such an assertion is not intended to lessen the importance of understanding human behavior at individual, family, group,
organizational, and global levels. Instead, the notions of community
we explore here highlight the importance of these other levels by
bringing them together into one arena.

In a sense we have been talking about community all through
this book. Who we are as individuals is influenced greatly by the
community contexts within which we live. Who we are as individuals significantly influences the nature of the communities in which
we live. Families, groups, and organizations also carry out their lives
and seek to fulfill their potential and goals in the context of community. Communities are an important element in complex global
issues. All of these levels of human behavior are intricately intertwined with community. The core concerns of social work are interconnected with and define qualities of community to which social
workers aspire. The dimensions of both traditional and alternate
paradigms reflect ways of viewing community—albeit very different views. The very concept of paradigm or worldview reflects the
elements that together form community (regardless of the nature of

the specific elements). When Kuhn (1970) discussed paradigm shifts in the natural sciences (see Chapter 1), he did so using the language of community. The assumptions we made at the beginning of our journey about the relationships among ourselves, social work, and the people with whom we work are also essential relationships to consider in defining and giving meaning to community.

It is not an exaggeration to say that we cannot talk about social work in the spirit in which we have done so here without also talking about community. It is always within the context of community that we practice social work. The individuals, families, groups, and organizations with which we work are fundamental building blocks of community. Communities are also fundamental building blocks of nations around the globe. It is in response to the needs and demands of humans at these levels that we construct and reconstruct community.

Community is an inclusive but somewhat elusive concept for many of us today. Much has been written about the "loss of community" and about the "search for community." These notions suggest the significant changes occurring in people's views of community. They are also consistent with our attempts in this book to embark on a journey in "search" of more holistic ways of understanding HBSE. In this chapter we embark on a journey in search of community.

Community is where the individual and the social environment come together. An inclusive perspective on community can help social workers answer the perennial question confronting our field: "Should the resources and interests of social workers best be directed toward individual or social change?" The answer, it seems, is a resounding yes! We must focus on both—and that focus must simultaneously be directed internally to us and externally to the world around us. We can do nothing else, for each is contained in the other. We must change ourselves in order to change the world. As the world changes, we change (Bricker-Jenkins & Hooyman, 1986). Community represents that level of human behavior at which we as individuals connect with the social or collective world around us.

As we explore notions of community both from traditional and alternative perspectives, we will see that as has been the case with paradigms generally, the kinds and quality of communities are influenced more by the worldviews of some of us than others. It will be our quest here to explore notions of community that will allow all members of communities to participate, learn from one another, and be represented in this important sphere of life. For community provides important opportunities and challenges to expressing individual and collective human differences as well as similarities.

## HISTORICAL PERSPECTIVES ON COMMUNITY

How people have thought about community in the past was influenced by the dominant worldviews in place at the time. The ways in which we think about community presently are greatly influenced by the dominant paradigms of the historical periods in which we live, as are the ways we think about HBSE generally.

The revolutionary changes in perspectives on the individual brought about by the Renaissance in Western Europe had a great impact also on perspectives on the individual's place in much of the larger collective world of community. Again, we are reminded that the individual and the social are indeed closely (even inseparably) interrelated. These revolutionary changes occurring in Western Europe had influence far beyond this relatively limited geographic region of the globe. The new paradigms of the Renaissance (you might recall from our discussion in Chapter 1) came to define and dominate the modern world. Central to this revolution was the belief in the centrality of the individual rather than of society or the collective. Anthropologist David Maybury-Lewis (1992:68ff) believes this shift from the centrality of the collective to the individual had significant implications, positive and negative, for both family and community.

In addition to the implications of the Renaissance view of the supremacy of the individual, the emergence of modern science in the 19th century also had significant influence on the global environment of which human communities are a part. The emergent philosophy of science was based in large part on the assumption that the natural world existed to be mastered by and to serve humans. A belief in humans' right to exploit nature had religious roots as well. "Medieval Christianity also taught that human beings . . . were created in God's image to have dominion over this earth." These beliefs in the supremacy of humans over nature were in stark contrast to the worldviews of many tribal peoples, who saw strong interconnections and mutuality between humans and the other elements of the natural world as well as the spiritual world (Maybury-Lewis, 1992:73).

A worldview focusing on mutual interdependence of individuals, families, communities, and the larger world rather than one based on individuality and exploitation of nature results in significantly different perspectives on the place of community in the scheme of things. A worldview based on interdependence has much to teach us about how to live together with each other; how to create "a sense of community through intricate and time-tested webs of inclusion" (Utne, 1992:2).

These alternative and historically older perspectives, from which we can learn much, have continued to exist, although they have been largely ignored in dominant worldviews. These alternatives represent, for the most part, roads not taken by the constructors of dominant paradigms as they defined what community is or should be. Examples of alternative perspectives continue to exist in the beliefs about and views of community held by many indigenous peoples in the United States and around the globe. Many of the alternate notions about community that we will explore here as "new" ways of thinking about community actually have their roots in ways of thinking about community that are much "older" than those views currently dominant. This is another way of recognizing that our journey to a more holistic understanding of community represents a completing of a circle through which we can begin anew to think about HBSE, rather than a linear notion of a journey that ends at a specific destination "at the end of the line" in the present.

## DEFINING COMMUNITY

Community is a complex and multifaceted level of human behavior. It is made even more complex, and hence somewhat more difficult to define, because it is such an inclusive (and, as noted earlier, a somewhat elusive) concept. Definitions of community need to incorporate human behavior at the individual, family, group, and organizational levels. To do this we take the position here that there are multiple ways of defining community. Different definitions focus on different facets of communityness. Different definitions may also reflect varying degrees of consistency with the dimensions of traditional or alternative paradigms.

As we explore traditional and alternative perspectives on community, we will encounter a number of basic elements used to think about community. These basic elements will include such notions as *community as a collective of people*. This *includes individuals, groups, organizations, and families; shared interests; regular interaction to fulfill shared interests through informal and formally organized means; and some degree of mutual identification among members as belonging to the collective.*

Anderson and Carter (1990:95–96) suggest that community is a perspectivistic notion. This notion of multiple "perspectives," rather than a "single definition of" community is perhaps appropriate here, because it implies that community is different things to different people. This broad notion allows inclusion of traditional as well as alternative perspectives as individuals, families, groups, and organizations come together or separate in distinct communities. It allows us to incorporate the multiple perspectives we have explored on all the other levels of human behavior throughout this book into our thinking about communities. For example, when we discuss the important roles of individuals in community, we can now think about the important roles played by all individual members, including women and men; people of color and white people; people with disabilities and temporarily able-bodied people; poor people and people who are financially well-off; old and young people; gay men, lesbians, bisexual, transgender, and heterosexual people. When we discuss the important roles played by families within the context of community, we can now think about alternative and diverse family forms, including gay and lesbian families and augmented or fictive families, as important elements of community in addition to traditional nuclear or simple extended family forms.

## TRADITIONAL PERSPECTIVES

### Community as Place

Perhaps the most traditional perspective on community is one that associates community first and foremost with a geographical location—a place, in which we carry out most of our day-to-day activities—our hometown or our neighborhood, for example. Reiss offers a typical example of place-focused perspectives on community. He suggests, "a community arises through sharing a limited territorial space for residence and for sustenance and functions to meet common needs generated in sharing this space by establishing characteristic forms of social action" (1959:118).

Traditional perspectives on community as territory or space were used as a basis to describe both small rural communities and large urban cities. Dwight Sanderson (in Warren & Lyon, 1988:258–260) described a rural community geographically as the rural area in which the people have a common center of interest (such as a village or town center) and a common sense of obligation and responsibility. Sanderson suggested a method developed by Galpin to locate the boundaries of rural communities. You locate the rural community by beginning at the village or town center and mark on a map the most distant farm home whose members do their business there (Sanderson in Warren & Lyon, 1988:259).

Weber defined *city* as an economic marketplace or market settlement that was a specific geographic space. He defined *city* as a place where local inhabitants could satisfy an economically substantial part of their daily wants on a regular basis in the local marketplace. He saw city as a place in which both urban (city dwellers) and nonurban (people from the surrounding rural area) could satisfy their wants for articles of trade and commerce. These articles of trade were produced primarily in the local area surrounding the city or were acquired in other ways and then were brought to the city for sale (Weber in Warren & Lyon, 1988:15–17). These notions of rural communities and cities as geographic locations (places) in which we carry out a variety of activities or functions to meet our needs are probably the most traditional ways we think of community.

## Community as Function

Warren extends the perspective on community as place by describing in more detail the nature of the functions that are carried out in the place or space that is community. He suggests that **community** is *"that combination of social units and systems that perform the major social functions having locality relevance. In other words, by community we mean the organization of social activities to afford people daily local access to those broad areas of activity that are necessary in day-to-day living"* (1978:9).

Warren describes these activities or functions as five types:

1.  Local participation in production-distribution-consumption of necessary goods and services by industry, business, professions, religious organizations, schools, or government agencies.

2.  Socialization or the transmission of knowledge, social values, and behavior patterns to members by families, schools, religious organizations, and other units.

3.  Social control to influence members' behaviors to conform to community norms through laws, the courts, police, family, schools, religious organizations, and social agencies.

4.  Social participation in activities with other members through religious organizations, family and kinship groups, friendship groups, business, government programs, and social agencies.

5.  Mutual support for community members in times of need through care for the sick, exchange of labor to help members in economic distress, and assistance for other needs by primary groups such as families and relatives, neighborhood groups, friendship groups, local religious groups, social service agencies, insurance companies, and other support units. (Warren, 1978:10–11)

## Community as Middle Ground, Mediator, or Link

Community has often been viewed as a kind of "middle ground" or context in which individuals' "primary relationships" such as those in family and close friendship groups come together with their "secondary relationships," which are more specialized associations such as those in formal organizations (work, school, religion). This notion of community suggests that community is that place where the individual and the society meet.

Warren (1978:9) stresses the linkages between the people and institutions of a local community and the institutions and organizations of the larger society. Another aspect of this approach, especially when combined with the notion of community as that location in which all our daily needs are met, is that community is a microcosm of society. It is an entity in which we can find, on a smaller or local basis, all the structures and institutions that make up the larger society (Rubin in Warren & Lyon, 1983:54–61). Later in this chapter we explore alternative perspectives on community; significant questions have been raised about whether this is a realistic or necessary way of perceiving community.

## Community as Ways of Relating

Another traditional approach to community shifts the central focus on community from the relatively concrete or instrumental notions of geographic place or a set of specific functions to a much more interactional or affective focus on community as ways people relate to each other. This is a much more affective-or "feeling"-focused way of defining community. As we will see, this perspective on community offers a number of avenues for expanding our notions of community to include alternative, more inclusive views of what community means.

This approach to community focusing on the ways members relate to one another emphasizes identification or feelings of membership by community members and feelings by others that a member is in fact a member. This notion also stresses sharedness. It emphasizes feelings of connectedness to one another on the part of community members. This perspective on community can be referred to as a sense of "we-ness" or a "sense of community" that is felt by members.

Ferdinand Tönnies (in Warren & Lyon, 1988:7–17) formulated what has become a classic way of describing two contrasting ways people relate to each other as members of collectivities. His formulations have often been used in relation to discussion of different ways people relate to each other in different community contexts. Tönnies's conceptualization is helpful here because while it focuses on ways of relating, it also lends itself to thinking about the nature of relationships that predominate in large urban communities compared to those in small rural communities. In other words, it allows us to incorporate place as well as relationships in our feelings about community. In addition, Tönnies's approach suggests a historical perspective on changes in the ways people have tended to relate to one another within community over time.

Tönnies's formulation is based on two basic concepts. One he referred to as gemeinschaft, the other he termed gesellschaft. *Gemeinschaft relationships* are ways of relating based on shared traditions, culture, or way of life and on a sense mutual responsibility arising out of that shared tradition. He associated gemeinschaft relationships with the ways people related to each other in small, stable rural communities where people knew each other well, shared many past experiences, and expected to continue long relationships with each other into the future. He suggested gemeinschaft relationships

## Human Behavior

**Practice Behavior Example:** Know about human behavior across the life course; the range of social systems in which people live; and the ways social systems promote or deter people in maintaining or achieving health and well-being.

**Critical Thinking Question:** As you read this chapter, can you find one example of how communities as social systems promote and one example of how community systems can deter people from maintaining and achieving health and well-being?

were based on what he called natural will. *Natural will* reflected a quality of relationship based on mutuality in which people did things for one another out of a sense of shared and personal responsibility for one another as members of a collective.

*Gesellschaft relationships,* on the other hand, were ways of relating to each other based on a contractlike exchange in which one member did something for another in order for that person to return the favor in the form of needed goods, money, or services. This way of relating was based in what Tönnies referred to as rational will. *Rational will* reflected impersonal ways of relating not based on shared culture, tradition, or personal relatedness over time. Gesellschaft relationships were founded on the rational reality that people needed things from each other to survive, and to get those things one had to exchange goods, services, or money for them. Gesellschaft relationships were more likely to characterize life in large urban cities where people were not likely to know one another well or share a past with the people with whom they had to interact to get their needs met (Tönnies in Warren & Lyon, 1988:7–17).

Tönnies believed that gesellschaft and gemeinschaft relationships could and often did exist simultaneously. Some needs were met contractually based on rational will and some were met out of a sense of mutual responsibility based on natural will. One form tended to predominate, however, depending on whether the community context was traditional and rural (gemeinschaft) or impersonal and urban (gesellschaft). Tönnies saw the emergence of capitalist industrial urbanized societies to replace traditional societies dominated by agrarian rural communities as a historical movement from gemeinschaft relationships predominating in collective life to their replacement by gesellschaft relationships (Tönnies:7–17 and Warren:2–3 in Warren & Lyon, 1988).

## Community as Social System

Notions of community as a social system offer a somewhat more comprehensive or holistic view of community than many of the other traditional notions. Like notions of community as relationship, approaches to community as a social system offer some helpful avenues to pursue as we search for more comprehensive and inclusive alternatives to traditional notions of community.

The advantages of a systems view of community are similar to the advantages of a systems view of some of the other levels of human behavior we have explored. A systems view allows us to see the various components or subsystems of communities—the individuals, families, groups, and organizations that make up communities. A social systems view allows us to recognize the influence on communities of other systems and subsystems in the larger environment—the influence of state and national governments on the local community, for example. A systems approach also acknowledges that influences among systems components and between communities and the environment is reciprocal. A systems view suggests that a community influences the larger environment at the same time that the community is influenced by the larger environment. In recognizing these reciprocal influences, a systems view can help us to appreciate the reality of ongoing change in community life.

**Test your understanding of Traditional Perspectives on community by taking this short** Quiz.

# ALTERNATIVE PERSPECTIVES ON COMMUNITY

Our efforts to explore alternative ways of knowing and viewing community will involve a number of the dimensions of alternative paradigms we outlined in Chapter 2. It will include interpretive, intuitive, qualitative, subjective approaches, feminist perspectives, diversity-focused visions, personal and integrative perspectives, and perspectives addressing oppression and discrimination in community. Our journey will use as points of departure a number of the elements of traditional perspectives on community as well. Some parts of our journey will involve looking in different ways at some of the traditional perspectives on community. In our search for alternatives, as was suggested earlier, we will return to some older visions of community held by indigenous peoples in various parts of the globe.

### Ethical Practice

**Practice Behavior Example:** Know about the value base of the profession, its ethical standards, and relevant law.

**Critical Thinking Question:** As you read and reflect on the alternative approaches to community that make up this section, give an example for each approach to illustrate how it reflects specific social work values. Did you find any approaches that you believe are inconsistent with social work values?

## Nonplace Community

A *nonplace community* is a community in which attachment to a specific place or geographic territory is absent and is not considered essential for community to exist. Nonplace communities are sometimes referred to as *communities of the mind, communities of interest,* or *identificational communities* (Anderson & Carter, 1990; Longres, 1990). It is perhaps difficult to perceive of community as not primarily associated with a place because we are socialized from early on to think of community primarily as a place (e.g., our "hometown"). Nonplace perspectives of community are also a bit more difficult to grasp because of our more general socialization to traditional paradigm thinking. If we cannot see, feel, hear, or observe objectively an entity through our senses (consistent with scientific thinking), we have difficulty accepting that that entity in fact exists.

On the other hand, this notion of community might be a bit easier to grasp if we recall that a number of aspects of traditional approaches to community have not been primarily place-based. When we talk about community in terms of relationships, or functions, or networks of linked subsystems, we are not talking primarily about place. However, we do usually assume that those relationships, functions, or networks exist in some more or less constant relationship to a place. Nonplace notions of community suggest that one need not associate these aspects of "communityness" with a specific or constant place. Community as social network is discussed as a special type of nonplace community later in this section.

The notion of nonplace communities as "identificational communities" can be a helpful one. It suggests that a central feature of a nonplace community is a feeling of commonalty or identification with the other members of the community. This perspective is a helpful way to conceptualize many diverse communities—the African-American community, the gay or lesbian community, the Catholic community, the community of cancer survivors. Nonplace notions of community can help us to recognize that it is possible, indeed likely, that we are members of several communities simultaneously.

*Identificational communities* include "groups such as ethnic/cultural/religious groups, patient groups, friendship groups, and workplace groups. While membership in these communities often overlaps with geographic communities, membership is not determined by place, but by interest or identification with the group" (Longres, 1990; Germain, 1991 in Fellin, 1993:60)

*Professions* can also be thought of as nonplace communities or "communities of interest"—the social work community, for example. As social workers, we share common interests with other members of the profession. We identify with and are identified by others as members of the social work professional community. If we think about the basic elements of community we began this chapter with, we can compare the social work profession with these elements and assess whether social work reflects these community elements. Certainly social workers form a collective of people (primarily comprised of individuals and groups rather than entire families and organizations) with shared interests. Our shared interests are even codified in the Code of Ethics of the profession. As social workers we interact regularly on an informal basis with other social workers—with our colleagues in our agency or with colleagues we went to school with and with whom we continue to maintain contact, for example. We also have formally organized mechanisms for fulfilling our shared interests—the National Association of Social Workers (NASW) sponsors state and national conferences and meetings for its members to share their common professional interests, for example. The Council on Social Work Education holds an Annual Program Meeting each year that brings together members of the social work education community from around the country to share their interests. Such meetings as these not only provide opportunities to share professional interests, but they also serve to allow members of the community to maintain their personal relationships with other members of the social work community. They help reinforce our feelings of membership in the larger social work community. The purpose of NASW itself is focused on furthering the professional interests of social workers. We mutually identify ourselves as members of the social work community and others identify us as members of the social work community (both other social workers and members of other communities). In all these ways we nurture our sense of community.

Nonplace perspectives on community can help us maintain a sense of community and can give us reassurance and security even when we are separated from other community members or when we move from one geographic location to another. A Cambodian refugee can "reunite" with his or her community by connecting with other Cambodian people in the new location. Even if there are no other Cambodian people in the new location, one's sense of identity as a member of the Cambodian community can remain with the person and help the person have a sense of belonging although separated from other community members.

In this respect our nonplace communities can have a historical dimension. Some of what provides us with a sense of belonging, a sense of community, does not exist in the present. Past experiences of community upon which we build our current beliefs about community exist primarily as memories. These memories of the past are important avenues for determining the nature of community for us today. Stories of ancestors and friends who have died also help provide a sense of community or communalness—connectedness to other humans—that is an essential part of community.

# INTENTIONAL COMMUNITIES

## Communes

Both McKnight's and Solomon's perspectives on community suggest that the boundary between community and family and small group often blurs. This is especially true when we consider intentionally formed communities, specifically communal perspectives on community. Communal living has often been studied as an alternative approach to traditional family forms. Communal living has also been studied as an intentional effort to construct new forms of community living. For our purposes this difference in perspective is not problematic. It helps us realize that the boundaries between different levels of human behavior are blurred and change according to the perspective of the observers and participants involved. It might be helpful to reconsider levels of human behavior as not mutually exclusive but existing on a continuum that is not linear but spiral. For example, as family forms change and expand from nuclear to extended or networks of fictive kin (see Chapter 7 on families) they spiral into forms that resemble community almost as much as (or perhaps more than) they resemble traditional family forms. So, while we consider communal living here as a form of alternative community, keep in mind that in many ways we might just as appropriately have included it in our chapter on families.

Whether viewed from the perspective of family or community, efforts in communal or communitarian living represent efforts to create alternatives to traditional arrangements for living together. The term "intentional community" is often and more recently used as a synonym for "commune." The use of the term "commune" was preferred in the early years (1970s–1990s) of the modern intentional community movement.

There are many different definitions of "intentional community." However, they all have a great deal in common. The definition below seems to capture the overall spirit of communes or intentional communities.

> a _community_ designed and planned around a social ideal or collective values and interests, often involving shared resources and responsibilities.

Communitarian movements tend to come about during times of social and cultural transition. Such movements have occurred periodically throughout history and have included religious, political, economic, and alternative family foundations. The most recent and most studied flurry of activity in communal-living experiments occurred in the United States during the 1960s and 1970s.

Aidala (1989:311–338) suggests that communes allow conditions of social and cultural change in which old patterns of living are questioned and new patterns have not yet emerged. She suggests that they are "intense ideological communities [which] allow limited experimentation with alternatives in work, family, politics, religion, and their intersections." She believes that "communal experiments functioned for their participants, and one might argue, for the larger society as well, as part of the process of changing norms for family life" (1989:312). She notes that commune members "were concerned with working out norms, justifications, and habitual practices to support cohabitation, delayed childbearing or childlessness, assertive women, emotionally expressive men, working mothers, child-tending fathers, and relationships based upon discussion and negotiation rather than predefined, obligatory roles" (1989:334). It is interesting to compare these goals with the core concerns and values of social work, such as self-determination, rights for each person to reach their fullest human potential, social and economic justice, and equality. Aidala suggests also that the very existence of communal experiments, whether they ultimately failed or succeeded in achieving their purposes, were important voices questioning the status quo of traditional family forms and human relationships (1989:335).

Aidala and Zablocki also find evidence that significant numbers of commune members were not explicitly seeking new family forms but joined communal groups in search of "consensual community" in which "to live in close relationship with others with whom one agreed about important values and goals. Communes were attempts to intentionally expand networks of emotional support beyond conventional bonds of blood and marriage" (1991:88). Nevertheless, the boundaries of family and community often merged in communal life. "Forming a communal household had to do not only with common location but with a particular type of relationship among members characterized by holistic, affectional bonds, and equally important dimensions of *shared belief and conviction*" (1991:113). Note the elements of family, groups, and community in these descriptions of communes. Aidala (1989) and Aidala and Zablocki (1991) refer to these communal arrangements as "wider families." This is perhaps a helpful way to appreciate the intersection of the several levels of human behavior reflected in these experiments.

Rosabeth Moss Kanter (in Warren, 1977:572–581) perhaps best summarized the core issues and concerns faced by communes or utopian communities. The central issue, she believed, was that of commitment. The basic concerns were how members arranged to do the work the community must have done to survive as a group, and how the group managed to involve and satisfy members over a long period of time.

The issue of commitment Kanter referred to reflects the important search for a fit between individual needs and interests and those of the community that is central to communal struggles. She suggested that "commitment . . . refers to the willingness of people to do what will help maintain the group because it provides what they need." When a person is committed, what that person wants to do is the same as what that person must do. The person gives to the group what it needs to maintain itself and receives in turn what the person needs to nourish her/his sense of self (1977:574).

Kanter listed several specific problems with which communes must deal in order to ensure both their survival and group and individual commitment:

1. How to get work done without coercion.
2. How to ensure decisions are made, but to everyone's satisfaction.
3. How to build close, fulfilling relationships, but without exclusiveness.
4. How to choose and socialize new members.
5. How to include a degree of autonomy, individual uniqueness, and even deviance.
6. How to ensure agreement and shared perception around community functioning and values. (Kanter in Warren, 1977:572)

These perspectives on communes may run counter to many of the stereotypes we might hold about communes as rather normless contexts for excessive and irresponsible behaviors such as drug abuse and irresponsible sexual activity. While these excesses may have been a part of some communal experiences (as they are a part of noncommunal life), those who have studied communal life have found that these intentional communities are much more likely to be serious attempts to find workable alternatives to the historic needs of individuals, families, groups, and communities.

### New towns

Communes are almost exclusively efforts on the part of private individuals and groups to find new visions of community by creating intentional communities. There have been government-assisted experiments in the creation of intentional communities as well. Government efforts to create new communities or "new towns" began as an effort to respond to the "urban crisis" that erupted during the 1960s. This crisis of community came about in large part because of the history of oppression and exclusion of many community members, especially persons of color and low-income persons, from meaningful participation in the life of the community. These individuals and groups had been denied access to participation in the locality-relevant functions of community necessary to meet individual and family needs (see Warren, in the previous page).

New towns were an effort to build new communities that would not be characterized by the oppression and discrimination that had been so harmful to so many people and had culminated in the explosions that were the urban crisis of the 1960s. New towns were sanctioned by the federal government in the form of loan guarantees to private developers who would literally build new communities. The federal government loan guarantees came with the requirement that new towns provide plans for including a wide representation of people as potential community members—people of color, low-income people, older persons, persons with disabilities. The fundamental concern was for new communities to ensure optimum "quality of life" or "the well-being of people—primarily in groups but also as individuals—as well as the 'well being' of the environment in which these people live" (statement from 1972 Environmental Protection Agency conference quoted in Campbell, 1976:10). Many people have pointed out that few if any new towns actually lived up to these high expectations.

The basic concept of new towns was not really new when it received renewed interest in the late 1960s. The "Garden City" concept had been in place in Britain since the turn of the century. In the United States new towns emerged after World War I, and government support for several so-called greenbelt towns began in 1929. The new towns of the 1960s were comprehensive efforts to build community with consideration for both physical and social environments. They were planned "to provide for a broad range of social, economic, and physical activities within a defined area of land and within a predetermined time period" (Campbell, 1976:17). Socially they were to include a full range of educational services and health, recreation, civic, and religious organizations. Economically they were to include businesses, industry, and professional endeavors. Physically they were to include "infrastructure" of roads and utilities as well as housing for a wide range of income levels. This comprehensive range of services was to be carried out in economically viable, environmentally sound, and socially interactive ways. Citizens of new towns were to have meaningful participation in governance and decision-making throughout the development process (Campbell, 1976:17).

Government support for new town development decreased to virtually nothing by the end of the 1970s. As a result, this experiment in government-supported intentional community development probably was not in place long enough even to effectively evaluate its success or failure. Certainly, as noted earlier, there is little doubt that new towns failed to reach the lofty potential declared for them by their proponents. New towns, like other experimental intentional communities, held great promise for the quality of life they hoped to provide and might serve as helpful models of what community life might be like under varying conditions. Campbell suggests that the greatest challenge of new towns was:

> to structure and maintain an environment . . . in which human potential is enhanced, and finally, one where people irrespective of age, sex, race, religion, or economic condition can positively interact with each other and nature. (1976:266)

### Community, technology, and social and economic justice

Another important consideration in nonplace notions of community is that of technology. Much of the ability to maintain a sense of community regardless of whether it is place-based or not is the ability to communicate with other members of the community. The communication technology available to many of us today enables us to maintain and access community relationships almost instantly. Modern transportation systems allowing us to physically travel from one place to another quickly and temporarily (air travel, freeway systems, high-speed rail, etc.) enable us to maintain some face-to-face contact with the members of our nonplace communities over time.

It is important to recognize that such avenues to expanded visions of community are unequally available to different members of the human community. Much of the technology necessary to maintain nonplace community is expensive. Think about the concerns most of us have about the amounts of our cell phone bills from month to month or of the cost of air travel or of owning and maintaining an automobile. Think about the reality that many of us do not have access to telephones at all and certainly cannot afford air travel or the cost of owning and maintaining a car. Consider that for some of us with disabling conditions the ability to create and maintain nonplace community may be essential to our survival, but unattainable without access to expensive technology or modes of transportation. If we are unable to move about freely in order to participate in place community to meet our daily needs, nonplace relationships and networks and the resources necessary to maintain them become extremely important means of establishing and maintaining a sense of belonging or any sense of community.

### Virtual community

One of the more recent notions of nonplace community is that of the virtual community created through the world wide web of the Internet.

Porter defines a *virtual community* as an aggregation of individuals or business partners who interact around a shared interest, where the interaction is at least partially supported and/or mediated by technology and guided by some protocols or norms (Porter, 2004). She provides a Typology of Types of Virtual Communities in Figure 10.1.

Parrish suggests that "virtual communitarians," advocates for and members of virtual communities, focus on a number of areas that are similar to more traditional ideas of community. These include:

- personal intimacy, moral commitment, and social cohesion
- goals, fears, and interests in common
- the recognition by individuals of other individuals who have goals, interests, and fears in common with themselves, and who manifest both recognition that these can best be dealt with interpersonally, and desire to do so. (2002:262–263)

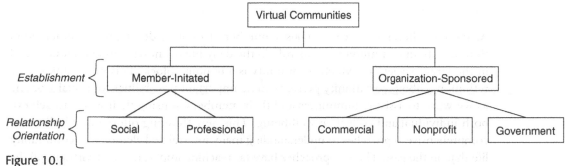

**Figure 10.1**
Types of Virtual Communities

In addition, Parrish suggests that advocates for virtual community also focus on elements that distinguish virtual from traditional notions of community:

1. transcendence of Cartesian [geographic] space;
2. emphasis on choice;
3. fluidity of identity;
4. evaluation by communication; and
5. equality (Parrish, 2002:273).

Parrish summarizes his assessment of virtual communities as presented by a number of scholars:

> Virtual communities are . . . exciting new forms of community which *liberate* the individual from the social constraints of embodied identity and from the restrictions of geographically embodied space; which *equalize* through the removal of embodied identity structures; and which promote a sense of connectedness (or *fraternity*) among interactive participants. (Parrish, 2002:279)

Virtual community is also often associated with and overlaps the increasing popularity of social networking sites such as Facebook, Instagram, and Twitter.

It is important that social workers understand that virtual communities exist and that for a growing number of people virtual communities can provide a significant opportunity for acquiring a meaningful "sense of community." It is equally important that we recognize both the advantages and disadvantages that virtual communities hold for individual and community life including those listed earlier. For social workers, it is especially important to recognize and continually evaluate the implications of technology and technological advances for the core social work concern of social and economic justice.

Notions of nonplace community highlight that community involves many important qualitative elements. Community is not necessarily a place and a place is not necessarily a community. Such a multidimensional and qualitative perspective on community does not rely on place, although it may be created from and associated with any number of places. A nonplace perspective on community allows us to create individualized communities that have meaning for us personally. Such perspectives are subjective and interpretive, but very valuable ways to think about community.

**Test your understanding of Alternative Perspectives on community by taking this short Quiz.**

## Alternative Approaches to Community Change

As the 1990s became the early 2000s, a number of exciting developments emerged in thinking about community and its role in the daily life of individuals and families and in the larger society of which community is a building block. This new thinking (or rethinking) about community presents some important possibilities for social workers as we work to assist communities and their members in using their assets to achieve both individual and collective well-being. This new thinking offers more holistic or comprehensive approaches to understanding many interrelated elements of community life than in the past. These approaches have far-reaching implications for virtually all the competencies and professional practice behaviors that make up social work education and practice: not just HBSE. These new developments integrate theoretical approaches to understanding community (the knowledge base) with policy and practice approaches to bring about positive community changes that are consistent with social work values and ethics. In addition, these alternative approaches reinforce the connections to well-being at the individual, family, group, organization, community, and global levels. Among the concepts and approaches that make up this exciting new direction for understanding and intervening in and with communities are:

- Community building
- Community renewal
- Community assets and strengths
- Social capital
- Civic ethic and civil society

## Poverty Reduction

One of the most promising themes that flows through these concepts and approaches is of fundamental concern to social workers: poverty reduction. As we have indicated in other chapters, the theme of poverty reduction is of critical importance to social work because it is at the core of so many of the other concerns that social workers attempt to address such as infant mortality, substance abuse, violence, racism and sexism, child abuse and neglect, hunger, homelessness, and teen pregnancy. Poverty reduction is also a theme that unites our efforts across all system levels—individual, family, group, organization, community, and society.

As is so often the case, many of these newer alternative approaches to community strengths and needs by addressing the overarching issue of poverty really take us back to social work history—a history that was first and foremost about addressing human needs resulting from lack of physical and social resources. However, these alternative approaches also integrate new developments in strengths-based and assets-based theory and practice that have emerged in the profession only recently. Next we will explore some of these alternative developments in thinking about community.

## Community Building/Community Renewal

A new response to poverty reduction at the community level is "known as *community building*; its goal is overhauling the nation's antipoverty approach and creating communities that work for the low-income families who live there" (Walsh, 1997). Community

*Trash and debris piled high in front of destroyed houses in Long Beach, NY after Hurricane Sandy.*

building is also referred to as **community renewal**. Walsh stresses that community building takes a more comprehensive approach to poverty in theory and practice because it goes beyond analyzing poverty only in terms of jobs or income "but [also] as a web of interwoven problems—poor schooling, bad health, family troubles, racism, crime, and unemployment—that can lock families out of opportunity, permanently." In addition, community-building initiatives work toward poverty reduction at multiple levels to address economic, social, and political marginalization that locks people and communities into poverty (1997).

Ewalt, a social worker, stresses, "it is clear that redeveloping impoverished communities requires a multifaceted approach that addresses the physical and economic conditions of neighborhoods as well as the social and cultural aspects" (1998b). Such strategies also acknowledge the "linkages and interconnectedness among the various strands of an individual's life and of the importance of family and neighborhood influences in determining individual level outcomes" (Connell, Kubisch, Schorr, & Weiss, 1995: 511). This recognition of the multilayered and ever-changing influences of the larger social environment on individual development is consistent with life course theory discussed in Chapter 4.

Central to community building or community renewal is the idea "that the path toward individual, neighborhood, and corporate renewal is indivisible from or, at the very least, dependent on efforts to rebuild a sense of community. Ultimately, the culture of renewal represents the individual American's revived search for meaning—but within the context of community" (Louv, 1997).

### Strengths/assets

The concept of community building also conveys an asset rather than a deficit approach to poverty reduction consistent with alternative paradigm thinking. For example, it uses a metaphor of "building"—a constructive concept—rather than earlier and traditional metaphors, such as that used in 1960s-era approaches to poverty reduction, which was often referred to as "the war on poverty." As Walsh points out, "war is about destruction, community building is about creation" (1997). Community building uses the existing assets of poor communities as the foundation for development. This approach focuses first "on the strong institutions, associations, and individuals that still exist in poor communities—from schools and churches to the corner grocer who employs teenagers and the stay-at-home mom who watches latchkey kids—rather than focusing solely on deficits like crime, unemployment, or school failure" (Walsh, 1997).

## People- and Place-Based Strategies

Another indication of the comprehensive or holistic approach taken by community builders is the attempt to reunite what Walsh refers to as the traditional split "between 'people' and 'place' strategies." Traditional antipoverty approaches tended to be divided into two parts: "human services—the 'people' people, [that] focused on the education, family support, and health care needs of the poor—and the 'place' strategists, the community development field that focuse[d] more on rebuilding neighborhoods—with housing, retail development, and attempts at job creation—than on human development" (Walsh, 1997).

Naparastek and Dooley point out the mutually reinforcing nature of an approach integrating both people- and place-based strategies: "A community-building approach looks at the whole picture, acknowledges the interconnectedness of people- and place-based strategies, and recommends a course of action in which solutions are tied together in such a way that they reinforce one another" (1998:11). Such approaches can help improve the effectiveness of community-based social work practice. "Linking place- and people-based strategies through community-building has significant implications for social work, because it means improving the delivery and quality of human services, strengthening community organization, stimulating economic development, and in every possible way improving the quality of life of residents while affecting physical improvements," according to Naparastek and Dooley (1998:11).

## Community Building and Physical Environment

A significant part of place-based community building involves the actual physical design of homes and neighborhoods. Community building strives for physical construction of homes and neighborhoods that support the creation of a "sense of community." This focus on physical design is referred to as an architecture of community renewal. Examples of these innovative design changes include:

- Placing the garage or carport around back, or hiding it on the side of the structure.
- Building houses with front porches to increase interactions with neighbors and a sense of community.
- Clustering housing and offices closer together so workers might be able to walk to their jobs.
- Using mass transit rather than cars. (Louv, 1996)

Louv suggests that the design of schools today should support a sense of community but often do not: "Schools in the late 19th and early 20th centuries strove for stateliness and grandeur. . . . Looking at the typical suburban school, one wants to

exhort it: 'Buck up! Show some pride! Remember that you're crucial to the community!'" Another innovative design approach is
to "allow each single-family house to have a garage apartment or
cottage at the rear of its lot. . . . [So grandparents] may be available for baby-sitting and other household assistance, but without
the frictions of sharing their children's living quarters 24 hours a
day. . . . These apartments also can be used by grown sons and
daughters, especially after a divorce or a job layoff" (1996).

### Three community development approaches

1.  Smart growth is a development approach that attempts
    to reduce urban sprawl. It is defined as "comprehensive,
    addressing such issues as natural resource protection,
    expanded housing diversity, regional collaboration, eco-
    nomic development that builds on local capacity and citizen involvement."

2.  New urbanism is . . . essentially an "'architecture of community' that is more
    humanized in scale and character." With a focus on physical appearance and
    neighborhood layout to improve quality of life, it calls for more compact,
    mixed-use development, housing diversity, architecture that is consistent
    and sensitive to place, common open space abundance (both functional and
    natural) and internal circulation that is pedestrian friendly and oriented. It
    seeks "the restoration of existing urban centers within 'coherent metropoli-
    tan regions' and 'the conservation of natural environments'." The process is
    dependent on citizen participation planning and design.

3.  The ecological cities approach takes a comprehensive and holistic systems
    approach. The "ecocity" promotes "land-use policies that maximize urban
    density, reduce non-renewable energy consumption, protect biodiversity,
    reduce travel distances, and maximize transportation options." Overall its goal
    is community sustainability. (Jepson Jr & Edwards, 2010:418–419)

All three of the community development approaches described earlier seek to create
and maintain sustainable communities. Below is a list of what community development
experts consider the basic principles of sustainability.

### 14 Principles of Sustainability

1.  *Jobs–housing balance:* Living closer to work can increase productivity and
    efficiency amd reduce use of natural resources and creation of waste.

2.  *Spatial integration of employment and transportation:* Improved access, usability, and
    connectivity of transportation to work can improve productivity and efficiency.

3.  *Mixed land use:* Can improve opportunity for community residents to interact
    with one another and result in less transportation energy consumption.

4.  *Use of locally produced, clean, and renewable energy sources:* Replacing imported
    energy with clean and renewable energy generated in the community itself
    will help maintain long-term sustainability.

5.  *Energy and resource efficient building and site design:* Using more energy efficient
    building guideline can reduce the depletion of natural resource and provide
    renewable energy alternatives.

**Policy Practice**

**Practice Behavior Example:** Analyze, formulate, and advocate for policies that advance social
well-being.

**Critical Thinking Question:** How do the
approaches to community building and revitalization in this section (Community Building and
Physical Environment) reflect policies or programs
that advance social well-being at the community
level? Give two specific examples.

6. *Pedestrian access (walking and biking) to work and leisure:* Reduces transportation energy use, pollution, and can have positive effects on residents' health.

7. *Housing affordability (for all income groups):* Affordable housing, especially for lower and working class residents can reduce social problems across multiple systems.

8. *Housing diversity (of style, type, and tenure):* A variety of housing styles and types can encourage more interaction among people with diversity backgrounds.

9. *Higher density residential development:* Development that is more compact can result in more open space for residents.

10. *Protection of natural and biological functions and processes:* Human systems rely on nature and biodiversity to function and they must be maintained and for community sustainability.

11. *Resident involvement and empowerment:* As social workers we know the importance of empowerment and the ability of residents to organize to address, identify, and solve problems effectively.

12. *Social spaces (public spaces to encourage social gathering):* Increased social contact among the residents of a community can improve the community's ability to organize and respond to changing conditions.

13. *Sense of place:* A sense of place increases attachment to place and in turn increases the likelihood of resident involvement and interaction to respond to issues as they arise.

14. *Inter-modal transportation connectivity:* Increased connectivity and variety in transportation options can increase resident interaction and reduce energy consumption and pollution. (Jepson Jr & Edwards, 2010: 421–422)

### Ideal neighborhood design

Perhaps a good way to get an overview of new urbanism is to consider the essential principles of an "ideal neighborhood." These elements include:

- The *neighborhood has a center and edge.* The center should be a public space, a square, a green or an important street intersection.
- The *"optimal size of a neighborhood* is a quarter mile from center to edge." What this 'optimal size' represents is . . . the equivalent of five-minute walk at an easy pace. Great emphasis is placed on restoring walking as the principal means of movement around a district. . . . The population of a neighborhood [is] within walking distance of many of their daily needs, such as a convenience store, post office, community police post, automatic bank teller, school, day-care center, and transit stop.
- The *neighborhood has a balanced mix of activities*—dwelling, shopping, working, schooling, worshipping, and recreating.
- The *neighborhood structures building sites and traffic* on a fine network of interconnecting streets.
- The *neighborhood gives priority to public space* and to the appropriate location of civic buildings. (Adapted from Hamer, 2000:116–117)

## Comprehensive Community Initiatives

Holistic and integrative approaches to community building and renewal are often referred to as *comprehensive community initiatives (CCIs)*. Ewalt cites the definition of comprehensive community initiatives (CCIs) by Kubisch, Weiss, Schoor, and Connell.

To make these new comprehensive community-building approaches work and for social workers to become effective in helping them work, Naparastek and Dooley suggest the need for linking community building "to social work practice in a form that requires competence in the processes of place-based and people-based strategies; . . . the need for social work practitioners who are familiar with community theory and community organizations, who understand the processes of physical and economic development, and who have core knowledge of social work values and commitment to grassroots participation" (Naparastek, Dooley, 1998:14).

### Community-building principles

The National Community Building Network, formed in 1993 by a number of private foundations (Ford, Casey, and Rockefeller) and other community-building initiatives, developed a set of eight principles to guide community-building efforts:

1.  *Integrate community development and human service strategies:* Traditional antipoverty efforts have separated "bricks and mortar" projects from those that help families and develop human capital; each approach needs the other to be successful.

2.  *Forge partnerships through collaboration:* Building community requires work by all sectors—local residents, community-based organizations, businesses, schools, religious institutions, health and social service agencies—in an atmosphere of trust, cooperation, and respect.

3.  *Build on community strengths:* Past efforts to improve urban life have too often addressed community deficits; our efforts build on local capacities and assets.

4.  *Start from local conditions:* There is no cookie-cutter approach to building community; the best efforts flow from and adapt to local realities.

5.  *Foster broad community participation:* Many urban programs have become professionalized and alienated from the people they serve; new programs and policies must be shaped by community residents.

6.  *Require racial equity:* Racism remains a barrier to a fair distribution of resources and opportunities in our society; our work promotes equity for all groups.

## Comprehensive Community Initiatives (CCI) Definition

CCIs contain several or all of the following elements and aim to achieve synergy among them: expansion and improvement of social services and supports, such as child care, youth development, and family support; health care, including mental health care; economic development; housing rehabilitation and/or construction; community planning and organizing; adult education; job training; school reform; and quality-of-life activities such as neighborhood security and recreation programs (Ewalt, 1998b:3).

**Test your understanding of Alternative Approaches to Community Change by taking this short Quiz.**

7. *Value cultural strengths*: Our efforts promote the values and history of our many cultural traditions and ethnic groups.

8. *Support families and children*: Strong families are the cornerstone of strong communities; our efforts help families help themselves. (Walsh, 1997)

These eight principles provide a framework for understanding newer approaches to community development and revitalization.

## Economic Perspectives on Community: Capital/Assets

Driving these new approaches to community renewal is a growing recognition on the part of social workers and others that poverty reduction at the individual, family, and community level is to a very great extent about assessing, using, and growing assets. "Asset building is a new way of thinking about antipoverty strategies; its emphasis on resources rather than problems has much in common with the strengths perspective in social work practice and policy development" (Page-Adams & Sherraden, 1997:432). Assets involve multiple types: human, physical, and fiscal. The concept of assets and asset development is closely related to the concepts of human, economic, and social capital discussed in sections that follow. A shift to an assets-based practice and policy framework would cause a paradigm shift in the profession that would result in social workers advocating for policies that "invest in people instead of programs" (Beverly & Sherraden, 1997:23ff).

A number of years ago, "Sherraden (1988, 1990, 1991) suggested that households and communities develop not by income alone (the dominant theme of the welfare state), but also by savings and asset building. In this usage, the term 'assets' is restricted to the concept of wealth, including both property and financial holdings" (Page-Adams & Sherraden, 1997:423). "Sherraden proposed a system of individual development accounts (IDAs)—matched savings for purposes such as education, home ownership, and small business development" (Page-Adams & Sherraden, 1997:423–424). Based on evaluation of asset development programs, Yadama and Sherraden concluded that "it appears that assets lead to more positive attitudes and behaviors, and the same attitudes and behaviors lead to more assets" (Ewalt, 1998b:68).

In addition to Individual Development Accounts (IDAs) to be used for home ownership, educational investments, or small business development, Sherraden also foresees other types of asset development accounts such as Individual Training Accounts (ITAs) to be used by individuals to invest in human capital development through education and training chosen by individuals to meet their education and training needs. Beverly and Sherraden note that the Council on Adult and Experiential Education and participating employers who set up ITAs for their employees "have found that workers make much better use of these training funds than of training that is offered *en masse* to all employees. Because the money is 'theirs' workers make careful choices about how to invest in themselves, and they are committed to the training" (1997:24).

## Types of Capital: Financial, Human, Social, and Cultural

Consistent with the community-building principle of combining or integrating both "people-" and "place-based" strategies is the increasing concern over the multiple types of capital necessary to comprehensively address poverty at the personal, family, and community levels. While there are numerous types of capital, perhaps the three most common and relevant for social workers are: financial (or economic), human, and social capital. Cultural capital is a more recent addition to the types of capital.

### Financial capital

Financial capital refers to money or property that is available for investment or "use in the production of more wealth" (*Webster's*, 1995). In other words, financial capital is resources available to use to create more resources. It is interesting that for a profession with a long history of concern for reducing poverty, we have been so hesitant to incorporate the concept of financial capital and capital or asset creation in the policies and programs we support. It would seem fundamental that many of the multitude of difficulties poor people face result from inadequate financial capital—they do not have access to the resources necessary to accumulate financial capital. A growing number of social workers are working to incorporate concepts such as capital and assets into social work programs and policies. For example, growing interest in social development in social work, both in the United States and internationally, reflects this increasing recognition of the importance of economic assets to individual and collective well-being. Midgley points out that "social development is characterized by the integration of social and economic processes and the promotion of the social welfare of all. At the same time, social development is 'particularly concerned with those who are neglected by economic growth or excluded from development'" (Midgley in Beverly & Sherraden, 1997:3).

### Human capital

Human capital refers "to an individual's skills, knowledge, experience, creativity, motivation, health, and so forth. . . . Like other forms of 'capital,' human capital is expected to have future payoffs, frequently in the form of individual employment opportunities, earnings, and productivity in market and non-market sectors" (Beverly & Sherraden, 1997:1–2). Beverly and Sherraden suggest that unlike financial capital, human capital can be used, but it cannot be used up because "individuals cannot be separated from their knowledge, skills, and other individual attributes" (Beverly & Sherraden, 1997:2).

The concept of human capital is of significance to social workers interested in alternative approaches and policies concerned with poverty reduction because it "represents a broad social development strategy" and because it is strengths- and assets-based (Beverly & Sherraden, 1997:3). Beverly and Sherraden argue that "because social workers have traditionally advocated for improvements in social welfare and have a particular concern for those who are marginalized, it is particularly appropriate to promote investments in human capital [and] . . . investments in human capital have the potential to integrate economic development with improvements in social welfare" (1997:25–26).

Human capital is also an important concept for social workers because there is a great deal of empirical evidence that building human capital has positive outcomes for people in areas such as improved employment opportunities, higher wages, and better fringe benefits (health insurance, retirement benefits, etc.). In addition, other assets accrue for individuals as a result of increases in human capital, including increased savings, improved health outcomes, and improved access to and use of social resources such as information and influence. Communities also benefit from increases in the human capital held by their members. For example, Beverly and Sherraden note that community members with higher levels of education are more likely to volunteer, make charitable donations, and participate in political activities in their communities. Communities with better-educated members also tend to be more economically viable. Finally, Beverly and

Sherraden also note intergenerational benefits to increases in human capital holdings. Increased levels of human capital on the part of mothers have a positive impact on the health of their children. Children of parents with higher levels of education generally obtain more education for themselves than their peers with less well-educated parents (Beverly & Sherraden, 1997:3–10).

All these positive outcomes suggest that social workers would do well to use human capital theory as a significant policy and practice framework. Beverly and Sherraden argue that the social work "profession should consider the formation of human capital as a central commitment and organizing theme. . . . Social work practice . . . should be viewed not merely as an endeavor to solve problems, but also as an opportunity to build human capital—in knowledge, skills, experience, credentials, position, health, physical ability, mental cap[a]city, and motivation—that can contribute to future well-being" (1997:16). These authors also suggest some quite specific and concrete areas in which social workers can help the people with whom we work build their human capital at both policy and practice levels. These areas include working to increase investments in early childhood development, including advocating for basic nutrition and health care for all preschool children because good nutrition in infancy and early childhood can offset some of the learning difficulties faced by many poor children. Advocating for increased financial support for college education, vocational education and training (including computer and information technology training), and lifelong learning is also important (Beverly & Sherraden, 1997:17–23).

### Social capital

One of the most engaging concepts and a cornerstone of the new or alternative community theory is that of social capital. Understanding the meaning, significance, and use of this core concept can help us link social work principles and values to the new work on community building and renewal. It can also help us appreciate the mutually reinforcing and interrelated nature of human behavior at the individual, family, group, organizational, community, and societal levels.

"The term *social capital* has been used for about forty years to describe resources that are neither traditional capital (money or the things money buys) nor human capital (skills or know-how). . . . *Social capital refers, then, to resources stored in human relationships, whether casual or close*" (emphasis added, Briggs, 1997). It "is the stuff we draw on all the time, through our connections to a system of human relationships, to accomplish things that matter to us and to solve everyday problems" (Briggs, 1997). "Defined simply, it consists of networks and norms of civic engagement" (Wallis, Crocker, & Schecter, 1998). Social capital means "the sum of our informal, associative networks, along with social trust—the degree to which we feel we can expect strangers to do right by us" (Lappé & DuBois, 1997).

Social capital is closely related to both financial and human forms of capital. For example, "businesses have never thrived, nor have economies flourished, without social capital. Not that social capital is an adequate substitute for the other kinds of capital. . . . Rather, social capital makes the other kinds work well. It greases the gears of commerce, along with other areas of life" (Briggs, 1997).

The concept of social capital is important in helping us understand both poverty and community development. It also has a significant role to play in empowerment approaches to reducing poverty and building strong families

**Watch the video** "Keeping Up With Shifting Contexts" **to explore the impact on a social work agency of larger forces in the social environment.**

Critical Thinking Question: Based on the situation described in the video, give an example of how the agency and social workers might use their social capital to help reverse the funding cuts.

and communities (Wallis et al., 1998). According to Wallis et al. "in both the public and nonprofit sectors, there is growing belief that programs that empower communities strengthen the resources they can provide to individuals. From this perspective, community development and individual development are intertwined, and social capital suggests the substance that is both binding and created between them" (1998). Robert Putnam, one of the early scholars to introduce the concept of social capital in the social sciences, stressed the connections between economic and social capital. Putnam concluded:

> after studying the role of informal relationships in economic success in Italy, that the "norms and networks of civic engagement contribute to economic prosperity and are in turn reinforced by that prosperity. . . . Chief among these norms is reciprocity, the willingness of people to help one another with the expectation that they in turn can call for help." (Wallis et al., 1998)

Warner suggests that the concept of social capital evolved from an initial individual and family emphasis to a community focus: "Early work on social capital focused at the individual or family level in an effort to understand how stocks of social capital contribute to individual education or economic achievement." However, Warner notes that Putnam later explored the nature of social capital at the community level or "public" capital that resides in groups or networks of groups within communities. This public- or community-based form of social capital comes about in the community through "organized spaces for interaction, networks for information exchange, and leadership development" (1999:375). According to Briggs, the concept of social capital is now used in connection with family, neighborhood, city, societal, and cultural system levels.

A number of scholars and practitioners who study and use the concept of social capital in their work stress that while the concept itself is value-neutral, the uses and impacts of social capital may be either negative or positive: "as a resource or means, social capital has no right or wrong to it until some judgment is made about the ends to which we put it. We covet social capital for the reasons that many people covet money: not for what it is but for what we can do with it" (Briggs, 1997).

## Social Capital Helps Us "Get By"

It is used by individuals . . . to "get by" (for social support), that is, to cope with the everyday challenges that life presents, from flat tires to divorces. When we confide distress to a friend or listen as a confidante, social capital is at work, directly serving the person in distress but also renewing the relationship in ways that will, over time, be used by the speaker and the listener. When poor moms share caregiving tasks and rides to church along networks of relatives, friends, and acquaintances, they each draw on social capital. . . . These kinds of support often, but not always, come from people who are alike in race, class, and other terms. What is more, we are born into many of these supportive ties (to kin, for example) (Briggs, 1997).

## Social Capital Helps Us "Get Ahead"

Social capital is used for social leverage, that is, to change or improve our life circumstances, or "opportunity set." When we ask a friend who is "connected" to put in a good word as part of a hiring or grantmaking decision, or when an inner-city kid, through a personal tie, gets a shot at a life-changing scholarship, this too is social capital (Briggs, 1997).

Wallis et al. for example, points out, "although social capital helps facilitate actions, those actions may be either beneficial or harmful. Social capital that benefits a narrowly defined social group may not benefit a larger social group or society in general" (1998). Briggs stresses that "social capital that benefits me may not benefit my neighbors. That is, individuals may further their own aims through social capital without doing much for the community at large" (1997). Briggs illustrates "that profitable youth gangs and mafia rings depend on social capital. Sweetheart corporate deals, including those that cheat taxpayers, depend as much on off-the-books social capital as they do on mountains of legal paperwork. The now impolitic 'old boy network' functioned, and still functions in many places, through trusting ties among the 'boys' involved, to the detriment of those excluded" (1997). Just as social capital can be used for negative or positive purposes, it is also not equally distributed among individuals and communities: "not all groups have equal access to social capital. Reserves of social capital are unevenly distributed and differentially accessible depending on the social location of the groups and individual who attempt to appropriate it" (Schulman & Anderson, 1999).

If social capital is to be a useful concept for social work policy and practice, two questions need to be asked. *First, can social capital be consciously created? Second, given the unequal distribution of social capital among individuals and communities, can the creation of social capital be facilitated by external entities such as governments?* Warner points out that government certainly has played a role in decreasing community opportunities and resources for social capital development, such as its "abandonment of inner city public institutions" and in rural areas through school consolidation, which results in loss of the personal, family, and local community networks necessary for social capital construction (1999:379–80). This being the case, she argues that governments can and should be active in supporting social capital development for poor rural and urban communities.

She suggests that "at the individual level [social capital is] formed within the bounds of family, work, and school. . . . In communities where forums for interaction no longer emerge as natural extensions of work, school, or play, they can be intentionally created and designed to encourage development of social capital to enhance community problem solving." Warner provides examples of intentionally creating or supporting "public spaces" that act as places for citizens to engage in conversations and activity to enhance community effectiveness and democracy. She suggests, "these spaces may be incidental (sidewalks), voluntary (clubs and associations), or quasi-official (planning board hearings), but they must be relatively participatory to enable the communication essential for public democratic discourse." Through these mechanisms "the citizen becomes a producer as well as a consumer of community" (Warner, 1999:376–379).

To facilitate the creation of social capital, governments must undergo a paradigm shift in the way they relate to communities: "Local government must shift from acting as controller, regulator, and provider to new roles as catalyst, convener, and facilitator. . . . Government programs are most effective in promoting community level social capital when they develop a facilitative, participatory structure and involve participant as partners, not clients, in program design." Warner illustrates the difference in traditional and alternative roles played by government entities by contrasting Head Start with its requirement that parents be involved in decision-making through its policy councils with traditional hierarchical school decision-making where most decisions are made by professionals rather than by parents (Warner, 1999:384–9).

## Spiritual Capital Religion and Social Capital

Houses of worship build and sustain more social capital—and social capital of more varied forms—than any other type of institution in America. Churches, synagogues, mosques, and other houses of worship provide a vibrant institutional base for civic good works and a training ground for civic entrepreneurs. Roughly speaking, nearly half of America's stock of social capital is religious or religiously affiliated, whether measured by association memberships, philanthropy, or volunteering. Houses of worship run a variety of programs for members, from self-help groups to job training courses to singles' clubs. Houses of worship also spend $15 to $20 billion each year on social services, such as food and housing for the poor and elderly. Regular religious services attenders meet many more people weekly than nonworshipers, making religious institutions a prime forum for informal social capital building (John F. Kennedy School of Government, 2000).

Warner also suggests the need for professionals, including social workers, to make fundamental changes in both their roles and their policies/programs. She suggests, for example, programs that narrowly focus on individual social capital development such as parenting skills or job training "are unlikely to connect participants to broader community or extra-community resources." These kinds of "social services and community development programs are designed to address deficits rather than assets in communities. Highly professionalized services assume that the professional has the expertise while the client has the problem." Shifting to participatory, partnership-based management on the part of traditional social service agencies and schools will involve a significant paradigm shift. Warner notes that "participatory management represents a major organizational innovation for hierarchical, professionalized government structures" (Warner, 1999:384–9).

The process of building social capital is similar to the concept of *synergy* in social systems thinking (see Chapter 4) in that "social capital is built up through repeated exchanges among people (or organizations) over time. It depends on regular borrowing and lending of advice, favors, information, and so on," and "depends on making regular deposits and withdrawals into a system of relationships, some of them quite casual, others very intimate" (Briggs, 1997).

The destruction or loss of social capital results from processes similar to those involved in entropic systems (see Chapter 4) in that "it breaks down through disuse as much as through the distrust that alienates" (Briggs, 1997).

**Test your understanding of Economic Perspectives on Community by taking this short Quiz.**

## Civil Society, Civic Culture, and Civic Ethic

The concept of social capital is often associated with the concept of *civil society*. Bradley suggests that "*civil society* . . . is the sphere of our most basic humanity—the personal, everyday realm that is governed by values such as responsibility, trust, fraternity, solidarity, and love" (emphasis added in Wallis et al., 1998). "The common element binding local and bridging capital is a norm of civic engagement (or civic ethic)" (Wallis et al., 1998).

The multiple layers that interact in the creation and use of social capital which result in and flow from civil society are sometimes referred to as a *nested structure*. This nested structure comes about in the following way: "The civic ethic begins with personal affinities and relationships that build trust, and it then brings small groups of citizens together in common purpose. These private networks in turn form the basic building blocks of civic culture, creating a climate that supports the growth of cooperative problem solving" (Wallis et al., 1998).

Using the nested structure concept, "family, neighborhood, and community represent basic levels of social organization. Social interaction, social capital, civic infrastructure, and a civic culture are the elements critical to building a healthy civil society. Each of these four elements is present in some form at each of the levels of social organizations and links different levels of social organizations together" (Wallis et al., 1998).

## Social Capital and Diversity

Social capital is a useful concept in understanding and addressing issues of diversity, discrimination, and oppression in communities. For example, people who work in community building suggest that social capital is "often created and expressed differently according to how it was influenced by race, class, and ethnicity" and stress that people who work in the area of community building in communities with diverse populations "need to have extensive familiarity with work in different cultural contexts to successfully identify and use social capital effectively" (Wallis et al., 1998).

In addition, to be effective in community building and renewal in poor and disenfranchised communities with populations of persons of color, efforts must include "addressing the impact of racism as part of their problem solving effort in community building" (Wallis et al., 1998). Racism and discrimination can "be tied in with the theme of social capital, especially in recognizing that some groups organize around racial prejudice and that this is a negative form of social capital" (Wallis et al., 1998). Individual and institutional racism are fundamental barriers to the creation of effective relationships among individuals, families, groups, organizations, and communities so essential to the creation and positive use of social capital.

## Cultural Capital

Cultural capital and the related concept of cultural wealth are used to help more completely understand social and racial inequalities. Yosso notes, "Franklin (2002) defines cultural capital as 'the sense of group consciousness and collective identity' that serves as a resource 'aimed at the advancement of an entire group'" (2005). Bourdieu (in Yosso, 2005:76), who originally developed the concept, defines *cultural capital* as "an accumulation of cultural knowledge, skills and abilities possessed and inherited by privileged groups in society." He also posited that cultural capital must either be inherited or gained through formal schooling. However, Yosso argues that cultural capital is not only inherited, possessed, and used by privileged groups, but also is widely available among members of communities of color. She suggests the traditional description of cultural capital as available only to privileged groups, who either inherit it or gain it through their access to formal education, reinforces a deficit view of communities of color. For example, she notes that Bourdieu's "theory of cultural capital has been used to assert that some communities are culturally wealthy while others are culturally poor. This interpretation of Bourdieu exposes White, middle class culture as the standard, and therefore all other forms and expressions of 'culture' are judged in comparison to this 'norm'" (Yosso, 2005:76). She argues that to the contrary communities of color possess large amount of cultural capital ("cultural wealth").

## Community as Social Network

Both computer-supported social networks (CSSNs) and the concept of social capital reflect an alternative approach to community as a social network. A social network approach is a nonplace perspective on community. The notion of social network represents somewhat of a middle ground between traditional and alternative paradigm thinking about community. Some suggest that it is not in itself a community, but that it is an important component of community for many people. Netting, Kettner, and McMurty (1993:103–104), in their discussion of the importance of social networks as community resources, use Balgopal's definition:

> Social networks such as kin, friends, neighbors, and coworkers are supportive environmental resources that function as important instruments of help. . . . Social networks provide emotional resources and strength for meeting the need of human relatedness, recognition, and affirmation. They also serve as mutual aid systems for the exchange of resources such as money, emotional support, housing, and child care.

Certainly this perspective suggests that social networks include many of the supports and resources commonly thought of as part of community whether it is a place or nonplace community.

Other researchers have attempted to trace or map social networks as a means of understanding community. This approach, referred to as network analysis, has included attempts to describe community by focusing on interpersonal relationships. This alternative was used by Wellman and Leighton (in Warren & Lyon, 1988:57–72) to try to discover if large urban *gesellschaft*-like communities had completely done away with personal *gemeinschaft*-like ways in which community members might relate to one another. They were especially concerned with if and how these personal and primary relationships could exist in the large and relatively impersonal urban context. Based on their analysis, they determined that personal relationships remained strong and important to urban dwellers but these relationships often extended well beyond the geographic boundaries of neighborhoods or communities and included relatives and friends in distant places. Although the primary personal relationships were not necessarily territorially or place-based, people were able to maintain them through modern communications technology and transportation systems. This approach to network analysis concluded that a more workable alternative perspective on community was one that included both place, in terms of neighborhood or geographically defined community, and nonplace community networks that functioned to meet primary mutual support and identification needs not met in the urbanized and mobile environment characteristic of much of modern society.

## Qualitative Aspects of Community

McKnight (1987:54–58) posits an ideal community vision that is inclusive of all community members and offers a qualitatively different experience in living from that possible in organizational or institutional life. McKnight suggests a number of other ways that communities can be defined by considering their differences from formally constructed and explicitly goal-directed organizations or institutions (see discussion of organizational goals, Chapter 9). McKnight sees community and formal organizations as oppositional in many ways. He suggests that institutions operate to *control* people while the means of association through community is based on *consent*.

McKnight's vision is inclusive in that he finds a place even for those who have been excluded from community and labeled as in need of institutionalization either in the traditional sense of a mental (or other social control) institution or in the more contemporary sense of human service systems that he sees as the equivalent of institutions without walls. The themes of community, he suggests, are shown in Figure 10.2.

### African-American community qualities

Barbara Solomon's (1976:57) discussion of ways of defining African-American community questions the appropriateness of traditional place-based and quantitative definitions. She suggests a way of defining African-American communities that is much more qualitative in focus:

> The physical proximity of peoples in some geographical location is not enough to define community. A degree of personal intimacy must also be present among the residents of the physical space. This aspect of community has generally been ignored by social scientists whose image of community has been colored by those characteristics amenable to quantitative analysis, e.g., income level, crime rate, or incidence of hospital admissions. Personal intimacy, however, is indicated through the existence of such relationships as friendship and marriage and such feelings as confidence, loyalty, and interpersonal trust (1976:57).

McKnight's and Solomon's community visions, with their recognition of the value of qualitative dimensions, including personal strengths and fallibilities; informality; collective efforts and responsibility; stories as avenues to knowing and understanding; accepting as real and legitimate both celebration and tragedy; and the importance of personal intimacy, relationships, confidence, loyalty, and trust have much in common with many of the dimensions of our alternative paradigm. Even though McKnight's vision is set in opposition to modern human service organizations, and Solomon's vision is offered in part as a critique of existing social science definitions of community (among which can be included those created and used by many social workers), they both include much that is consonant with the core concerns and purposes of social work.

## Community: Social and Economic Justice and Oppression

The challenges faced by new towns reflect the need to undo existing patterns of oppression and unequal distribution of power in traditional communities. Our alternative paradigm requires us to recognize and work toward the reduction of existing oppression at all levels of human behavior. Community, because of its inclusiveness of other levels of human behavior, is a critical context for recognizing—with the goal of reducing—oppression and unequal distribution of power.

An essential first step to reducing oppression and unequal distribution of power is the recognition of their existence. One way to begin to recognize the existence of oppression and inequality in communities is to think about the physical structure of the traditional communities within which we live. How are they arranged? How segregated are community members from each other in terms of color and income or class? How does this segregation come to be? How is it maintained?

### Community and discrimination

Where we live is a powerful influence on much of what we experience in other spheres of our lives. Where we live is a powerful influence on whom we have as friends; on whom we have as role models and associates; on where and with whom we go to school;

**Capacity**

- Recognition of the fullness of each member because it is the sum of their capacities that represents the power of the group.

- Communities are built upon recognizing the whole depth—weaknesses and capacities [strengths] of each member.

**Collective Effort**

- The essence of community is people working together.

- One of the characteristics of this community work is shared responsibility that requires many talents.

- Thus, a person who has been labeled deficient can find... support in the collective capacities of a community that can shape itself to the unique character of each person.

**Informality**

- Transactions of value take place without money, advertising, or hype.

- Authentic relationships are possible and care emerges in place of its packaged imitation: service.

**Stories**

- In universities, people know through studies.

- In businesses and bureaucracies, people know by reports.

- In communities, people know by stories.

- These community stories allow people to reach back into their common history and their individual experience for knowledge about truth and direction for the future.

**Celebration**

- Community groups constantly incorporate celebrations, parties, and social events in their activities.

- The line between work and play is blurred and the human nature of everyday life becomes part of the way of work.

- You will know you are in community if you often hear laughter and singing.

- You will know you are in an institution, corporation, or bureaucracy if you hear the silence of long halls and reasoned meetings.

**Tragedy**

- The surest indication of the experience of community is the explicit common knowledge of tragedy, death, and suffering.

**Figure 10.2**
The Themes of Community

Source: Based on McKnight, John L. (1987). Regenerating community. *Social Policy, 17*(3): 57–58.

on the kinds of jobs and resources to which we have access; and on the quality of our housing. Segregation in housing results in different people having fundamentally different experiences in relation to the influences we listed earlier. In the United States segregation is most often based on color and/or income. While segregation based on color in many areas of life (schools, public accommodations, jobs, housing) has been made illegal through such legislation as the 1964 Civil Rights Act and the 1954 Supreme Court ruling (*Brown versus Topeka Board of Education*) we need only to look around us to become aware of the continuing reality of segregation in our communities.

Logan (in Warren & Lyon, 1988:231ff) and Feagin and Feagin (1978:85ff) describe several types of institutionalized discrimination in communities that serve to create and maintain oppression and unequal distribution of power. These mechanisms of oppression include blockbusting, racial steering, and redlining.

*Blockbusting* is a practice followed by some real estate brokers in which the racial fears of whites about African-American families are used to manipulate housing markets. Blockbusting can happen when a previously all-white neighborhood begins to become integrated. After a few African Americans move into the neighborhood, white home owners are manipulated into selling their property, often at lower than market value, out of fear. These same homes may then be sold at significantly inflated prices to new incoming African-American persons. *Racial steering* is a process that perpetuates existing patterns of segregation. Racial steering involves realtors or rental-property management agents steering people to specific areas of communities in order to maintain racial or economic segregation. *Redlining* is a form of discrimination used by some banks and other lending institutions that declares certain areas or sections of communities as bad investment risks. These areas often coincide with poor neighborhoods or neighborhoods with larger populations of people of color. The term *redlining* came from the practice by some institutions of actually outlining in red on a map the areas in which they would not approve home loan or mortgage applications. This practice prevents low-income people or people of color from acquiring loans in order to become home owners rather than renters. It also negatively affects communities because it prevents community people from purchasing and rehabilitating deteriorating rental housing (Logan, 1988:231–241; Feagin & Feagin, 1978:85–115).

These practices provide examples of mechanisms for creating and maintaining segregation, discrimination, and oppression in communities. These processes are all directly related to housing. Housing is only one element of community life. However, because where we live influences so many of the other sectors of our lives, it seems fundamental that we recognize housing as a cornerstone of systems of oppression in communities. Housing segregation directly influences other patterns of segregation; perhaps most fundamental among these is school segregation. It can be argued that until we are willing to—indeed, until we insist on the opportunity and right to—live in truly integrated neighborhoods and communities we will most likely never be able to eliminate oppression and discrimination in this or the other sectors of life. All of us as humans must have the right to live in the communities and neighborhoods we choose.

By living close to others we come to know, respect, and understand the complexities of those persons different from ourselves. By living among people different from ourselves we can learn to compromise, to respect, and learn from difference, to celebrate and be

## Human Rights & Justice

**Practice Behavior Examples:**

Understand the forms and mechanisms of oppression and discrimination.

Advocate for human rights and social and economic justice.

**Critical Thinking Question:** How do the forms and mechanism of oppression and discrimination at the community level add to your understanding of oppression and discrimination? Can you think of an example of how you might advocate for human rights and social and economic justice in a community experiencing block busting?

strengthened by difference. The examples we have used here focus on low-income people and people of color. They can readily be applied also to people different from us in other ways—in sexual orientation, religious beliefs, disabling conditions, or age, for example.

## Diversity and Community

Recognizing and removing barriers to help create community environments in which the benefits of diversity can be realized are fundamental concerns for social work at the community level. The intentional communities we explored earlier, such as communes and new towns, reflect significant concerns for diversity in a number of respects. Certainly a central concern for us as social workers (or soon-to-be social workers) is the degree to which human diversity is respected and incorporated in community. Perspectives on communities consistent with the alternate paradigms we consider in this book will attempt to maximize and respect diversity among community members as a source of strength. At the same time, alternate perspectives must balance the importance of diversity in communities with the importance, especially for many members of oppressed groups, of living around and within communities of people with whom we have much in common and that can provide us with a sense of positive identity, security, and history.

### Religion and community

A significant element of community life for many people is that of religious institutions. Maton and Wells describe the potential for both positive and negative contributions of religion to community well-being. They define *religion* very broadly as "encompassing the spectrum of groups and activities whose focus extends beyond the material reality of everyday life (i.e., to a spiritual reality)" (1995:178). You might want to compare this definition of religion with our earlier definitions of religion and spirituality.

**Religious institutions and community development**  Maton and Wells (1995) point out the role that many religious organizations have played in community development efforts. They note:

> Religious organizations, especially those in urban areas, have a vested interest in revitalizing surrounding neighborhoods and communities. This form of environmental change may have a preventive effect by reducing stress related to urban infrastructure decay and enhancing supportive resources (Maton & Wells, 1995:182).

**Religious institutions and social action**  In addition to community development directed toward improving the physical structures and well-being of community members, religious organizations have often played significant roles in social action to bring about social and economic justice in communities. Church involvement in social action has an especially rich history and tradition in the African-American community. Maton and Wells point out:

> especially in the South, black churches functioned as the institutional centers and foundation of the [civil rights] movement. . . . Black churches provided the movement with the leadership of clergy independent financially from the white society and skilled at managing people and resources, an institutionalized financial base, and meeting place where strategies, tactics and civil rights organizations were developed. Furthermore, black churches supplied the movement with "a collective enthusiasm generated through a rich culture consisting of songs, testimonies, oratory and prayers that spoke directly to the needs of an oppressed group." (1995:187–188)

**Watch the video** "Case
Dover: Darwin's Judgement
(2/12)" **to explore the conflict
created in one community
by supporters of intelligent
design and supporters of
evolution.**

**Critical Thinking
Question:** Describe two
actions the religious leaders
and school board members
involved in this conflict might
take to de-escalate the situation for the good of the community and its children.

**Religious institutions as a negative force in community life** We must be aware that while churches and other religious institutions have played very positive roles in community life, they have also historically contributed to individual and community problems in a variety of areas. Maton and Wells point out:

> some religious principles and values can lead to inappropriate guilt and anxiety, or a limited view of the nature of emotional problems. . . . Organized religion's . . . considerable psychological and economic resources, can be used to subjugate and disempower rather than empower groups, such as women and racial minorities. . . . Religion's focus on helping the "less fortunate," while generating many volunteer and economic resources, can lead to a paternalistic, disempowering approach to those in need. Also, because mainstream religion is part of the current power structure in society, it often does not take part in empowerment activities that challenge the current structure (1995:189).

Social workers need to be aware of the significant potential for churches to assist communities and their members. At the same time we need to recognize their potential for exacerbating individual and community problems.

**Community and people with disabilities** Mackelprang and Salsgiver (1996:9ff) describe two alternative paradigms for achieving social and economic justice for people with disabilities: the Minority Model and the Independent Living Perspective. The minority model was the foundation for "the birth of disability consciousness" in the United States and arose out of the civil rights turbulence of the 1960s. Mackelprang and Salsgiver (1996) assert that this movement matured with the development of the independent living concept in the early 1970s.

*Independent living perspective* Mackelprang and Salsgiver stress, "Independent living encourages people with disabilities to begin to assert their capabilities personally and in the political arena" (1996:10).

Some principles and examples of the independent living model

1. Independent living proponents view people with disabilities not as patients or clients but as active and responsible consumers.

2. Independent living proponents reject traditional treatment approaches as offensive and disenfranchising and demand control over their own lives.

3. Independent living proponents retain their own personal responsibility to hire and fire people who provide attendant or personal care rather than allowing formal structures to provide and control the professional care givers.

4. Independent living proponents prefer attendants who are trained by the individuals with disabilities themselves instead of licensed providers like registered nurses.

5. Independent living proponents see empowerment as self-developed and not bestowed by someone else. For example, social workers are viewed only as consultants, not as prescribers of care or treatment plans.

6. Independent living proponents believe that the greatest constraints on people with disabilities are environmental and social.

7. Independent living proponents espouse a philosophy that advocates natural support systems under the direction of the consumer. (Mackelprang & Salsgiver, 1996:10–12)

*Independent living: strengths and limitations*  Mackelprang and Salsgiver suggest that social work has much to learn from the independent living perspective and "can benefit greatly from a shift in focus from case management in which clients are labeled 'cases' to a consumer-driven model of practice that acknowledges self-developed empowerment and not empowerment bestowed from others" (1996: 12–13). They also note, however, that "the independent living approach can be criticized as viewing problems too much from an external perspective. Independent living may be too quick to assume that consumers already have knowledge and abilities rather than recognizing that they may need assistance to develop their strengths" (1996:12). They recommend a partnership between social work and independent living proponents in which social work can contribute its multi-systems and ecological approach and the disability movement "can help social work enhance approaches to clients, better empower oppressed and devalued groups, and understand the needs of people with disabilities" (1996:13).

## Toward a strengths approach to community

Perhaps an ideal community is one in which individual identity and identity as a member of the community are integrated. Myers (1985:34–35) finds such a holistic-perspective in an Afrocentric worldview. The African concept of "extended self" actually includes community. Self and community are not separate or distinct systems. She notes that "self in this instance includes all of the ancestors, the yet unborn, all of nature, and the entire community" (Myers, 1985:35). Utne (1992:2) suggests the benefits and strengths of a non-Western, more inclusive perspective on community. He recommends that "perhaps we in the West will listen to what [indigenous] people have to teach us and start making different choices. Perhaps someday our children will know the experience of community conveyed by this common phrase of the Xhosa people of southern Africa: 'I am because we are.'"

Collins (1990) offers an important feminist perspective on community and diversity. Her perspective reflects the strength of African-American women in creating and maintaining communities in which they and their families have historically been able to survive in the struggle against oppression in the surrounding environment. Her perspective reflects an Afrocentric worldview in which holism and unity are central. Collins's (1990:53) perspective also recognizes the critical influence on African-American individuals, families, organizations, and communities of the slavery and oppression comprising so much of the history of African peoples in the United States. She suggests that these historical conditions resulted in significant differences between African American and white communities. She describes an alternative to traditional white communities in which family, extended family, and community merged and in which "Black communities as places of collective effort and will stood in contrast to the public, market-driven, exchange-based dominant political economy in which they were situated" (Bethel in Collins, 1990:53).

Black women played significant roles in the creation and maintenance of this alternative community. Women provided the stability necessary for these communities, whose primary concern was day-to-day survival (Collins, 1990:146). The empowering, but not overpowering, role played by African-American women in their communities and families is portrayed in the following excerpt:

> African American women worked to create Black female spheres of influence, authority, and power that produced a worldview markedly different from that advanced by the dominant group. Within African American communities Black

women's activities as cultural workers is empowering. . . . The power of Black
women was the power to make culture, to transmit folkways, norms, and customs,
as well as to build shared ways of seeing the world that insured our survival. . . .
This power . . . was neither economic nor political; nor did it translate into female
dominance (Radford-Hill in Collins, 1990:147).

Collins also summarizes the alternative meaning of community that emerges from
an Afrocentric worldview as one that stresses "connections, caring and personal accountability." This historical worldview, combined with the realities of oppression in the United
States, resulted in alternative communities that empowered their members. These communities were created not through theorizing, but instead they came about "through
daily actions" of African-American women. These alternative communities created:

> sanctuaries where individual Black women and men are nurtured in order to
> confront oppressive social institutions. Power from this perspective is a creative
> power used for the good of the community, whether that community is conceptual-
> ized as one's family, church community, or the next generation of the community's
> children (Collins, 1990:223).

## SUMMARY/TRANSITION

In this chapter, within the larger context of traditional and alternative approaches to
community, we explored a variety of different but often interrelated types of, and perspectives on, communities. Historical perspectives on community were reviewed. Issues
related to defining community were discussed.

Within the arena of traditional perspectives on community, a number of ways of
thinking about community were presented. Community as a specific place and community as a set of functions were explored. Community was discussed as a middle ground,
mediator, or link between small systems such as individuals, families or groups, and
larger societal systems. Community as ways of relating or as patterns of relationships
and community as a social system were described.

Alternative perspectives on community included the notion of nonplace community. Community as a social network or web of relationships and resources through
which members meet needs and face challenges in life was discussed as an alternative
to more traditional notions. Qualitative aspects of community were explored, including discussion of some qualitative aspects of African-American communities. Intentional
communities, including communes and new towns, were presented.

**Recall what you learned in
this chapter by completing
the Chapter Review.**

Issues of oppression and power at the community level were included among
alternative perspectives. The notion of heterogeneity or diversity and community life was presented. In this discussion a strengths approach to community was
included.

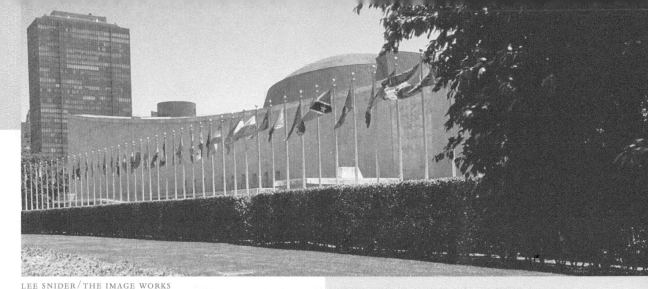

# 11

# Global Perspectives and Theories

## INTRODUCTION

This chapter addresses traditional and alternative as well as emerging approaches to theories and knowledge about international or global social work. It is important, as we begin to ground ourselves in knowledge about human behavior and the social environment in an international context, that we begin by looking at what exists currently at international and organizational levels. This chapter presents some of the fundamental thinking about international social work past, present, and future.

Specifically, it presents in full the fundamental document guiding much of the thinking about international social welfare, the U.N. Universal Declaration of Human Rights. While adopted in 1948, this essential document has received scant attention in U.S. social work education until recently.

This chapter will also introduce you to the missions and purposes of three of the major international organizations for social workers—the International Association of Schools of Social Work, the International Federation of Social Workers, and the International Council on Social Welfare. Becoming familiar with all these documents is critical to gaining a basic understanding of the current context of international social work. The reader is encouraged to visit the Web site citations for each of these organizations to learn about current plans and activities, as well as how to become a part of the international social work community. Clearly, human behavior and the social environment in a global context call for a life-long learning approach because the world is constantly and rapidly changing. The technological resources (Web sites) referenced in this chapter can provide access to the world of global social work as it responds to rapid change around the globe.

Certainly the events of September 11, 2001, and the resulting wars in Iraq and Afghanistan had an impact on individuals, families, groups, organizations, and communities throughout the United States and the world. These tragic events also presented an urgent reminder of the interrelationship of international concerns, needs, hatred, and actions with the well-being of people in the United States. It is safe to say that virtually every person in the United States was touched by these tragic events either directly or indirectly. It is also safe to say these events touched the lives of countless people and nations around the world. Social workers, because of our special concerns for the person *and* the environment, human dignity and worth of all people, and social and economic justice, have a special responsibility to understand and act to address such issues as those leading to and following September 11.

## SOCIAL WORK AND ISLAM

In the aftermath of 9/11, it has become increasingly clear how little the U.S. public in general, and social workers specifically, know about the Muslim or Arab world and Islamic religion and culture. In Chapter 7 we addressed Islam in the context of family. Here we will address some of the basic tenets of an Islamic worldview or culture that guide the lives of Muslims and that are important for improving social workers' understanding of Islam both from religious and societal vantage points. However, it is very important that the reader understand that Muslims and Muslim communities, like all humans and communities, differ in the degree to which the various tenets of Islam are perceived and practiced by different individuals and communities.

As Al-Krenawi and Graham note, "Ethnic Arab societies are highly diverse and consist of heterogeneous systems of social differentiation based on ethnic, linguistic, sectarian, familial, tribal, regional, socioeconomic, and national identities." They also note that at a societal level the greater emphasis is on "the collective over the individual, having a slower pace of societal change, and a greater sense of social stability" (2000a:10).

Rehman and Dziegielewski present seven basic beliefs that are included in an Islamic worldview:

1. the belief in one God, Allah . . . as the one and only Creator/Sustainer of the heavens and the earth;
2. the belief in Divine Will (Al-Qadr/ fatalism);
3. the belief in the angels of Allah;
4. the belief in the revealed books of Allah (the Torah, the Psalms, the Qur'an and the Gospel);
5. the belief in the messengers of Allah [prophets];
6. the belief in the day of judgment; and
7. the belief in life after death (2003:33).

Al Krenawi and Graham describe what are referred to as the "Five Pillars of Islam." These pillars are integrated in life of followers of Islam:

1. The *shahada*, or profession of faith, is the belief that there is no other god but Allah and that Muhammad is His last prophet.
2. The *salat* is the imperative to pray five times daily: at dawn, noon, mid-afternoon, sunset, and evening.
3. The *zakat* is the requirement to pay alms to the needy on behalf of one's family and business. It was customarily calculated as an annual payment of two and one half percent of all capital, assets, savings, and current income above a specified threshold.
4. The *siam* is the imperative to fast from food, drink, and sex during daylight hours during the month of Ramadan, which immediately precedes the

---

**Diversity in Practice**

**Practice Behavior Example:** Gain sufficient self-awareness to eliminate the influence of personal biases and values in working with diverse groups.

**Critical Thinking Question:** After reading about the basic tenets of Islam, give one example of how you can use this information to increase your self-awareness and help eliminate personal biases about Islam.

CELIA PETERSON/ARABIANEYE/CORBIS

*How does the family in this photo reflect the statement by Al-Krenawi and Graham that, "Ethnic Arab societies are highly diverse and consist of heterogeneous systems of social differentiation?"*

celebration of the date upon which Allah revealed the Koran to the Prophet Muhammad.

5.  The *Hajj* is a pilgrimage to Mecca, a holy city of Islam located where Allah revealed the Koran to the Prophet Muhammad. The pilgrimage should be undertaken at least once in a Muslim's lifetime, if financially, mentally, and physically capable (Al-Krenawi & Graham, 2000b:294–295).

**Test your understanding of Social Work and Islam by taking this short** Quiz.

In addition, "there are certain dietary rules in Islam. Muslims are not permitted to eat pork or consume alcohol or any other drugs that have the potential of impairing normal functioning" (Rehman & Dziegielewski, 2003:33).

## War, Refugees, and Immigrants

According to Nash, Wong, and Trlin, "social work is operating in an increasingly global environment. Nowhere is this more apparent than in work with immigrants, refugees and asylum seekers" (2006:345). They also note, "the movement of people (voluntary and forced) across borders is an international phenomenon, an expression of globalization with implications for national, economic and political stability and cultural identity" (Nash et al., 2006:345). For example, the context in which they discuss these issues is New Zealand.

In discussing the experiences of Bosnian refugees, Snyder et al., (2005) describe the impact on the development of children and families of war, becoming a refugee, and finding and settling in a new country. They note, for example, that during the Bosnian war "many women and children fled as refugees while men tended to stay behind to fight and protect property" (Snyder et al., 2005:614–615). The impact on these child refugees' development included numerous challenges. These included family separations, disruptions in socialization as a result of loss of familiar supports such as "schools and places of worship," and vulnerabilities to threats and actual experiences of violence. The results of having faced these challenges were many: difficulties developing trust and relating to peers, developmental delays, poor school performance, depression, post-traumatic stress disorder (especially for child victims of "rape, sexual abuse, and physical assaults"), nightmares and flashbacks, and survivor guilt (Snyder et al., 2005:615).

In addition to experiences related directly to having been in the midst of war, refugees also face a wide range of difficulties and vulnerabilities during resettlement and adaptation to new and unfamiliar environments during transit and after relocation. Snyder et al. delineate some of the stressors: "difficult transit experiences; culture shock; adjustment problems related to language and occupational change; and disruption in their sense of self, family, and community" (Lipson, 1993 and Worthington, 2001 in Snyder et al., 2005:616).

Refugees leaving their war-torn but home countries to settle in a new and unfamiliar place bring with them a history of multiple losses, including "severance from family and friends who have been left behind or killed, displacement from their homes and communities, social isolation, and the premature death of their children" (Snyder et al. 2005:616).

There are many other complex challenges and issues facing refugees and the social workers who attempt to provide them services. For example, social workers need to be informed about torture, both because it harms the lives of tens of thousands of people who might be or become social work clients and also because its effects are often missed. Torture is a corruption of the expected relationship between governmental authority and its citizenry; survivors know that they can neither trust the state nor rely on it to protect them. "Torture is toxic. It affects not only survivors, families, friends, and communities, but also those who would be healers (Engstrom & Okamura, 2004:296). Because torture has a lasting effect on the body, mind, and social system, social workers must play a key role in linking survivors to a broad array of medical, mental health, legal, and social services (Engstrom & Okamura, 2004). In other chapters in this book we will continue to address these challenges for individuals, families, communities, and the international community.

**Watch the video** "Refugees: Social Work Extreme" **to explore the experiences of a social worker working with refugees.**

**Critical Thinking Question:**
Give two examples from the video of stressors identified by Snyder et al., in the text. Defend your choices.

## DEFINING INTERNATIONAL AND GLOBAL CONTEXTS

Asamoah, Healy, and Mayadas (1997) note that the terms "international" and "global" are often used interchangeably. However, these scholars differentiate between the two. They consider the general term *international* to be "the narrower term, referring to anything involving two or more nations, whereas 'global' [generally] refers to a mode of thinking about the planet as a whole and the interactive effects of social phenomena, linking domestic and international concerns in a seamless web." Healy, on the other hand links the terms more specifically to issues of social welfare.

Healy (1995 in Midgely, 1997:9–10) differentiates between the terms *international* and *global*. She refers to *international* as "a broad umbrella term that refers to comparative accounts of social welfare activities in many countries." She defines *global* as "referring comprehensively to welfare activities that affect the planet as a whole" (1995 in Midgely, 1997:9–10). We will keep these differences in mind as we explore international and global perspectives on social work.

## HISTORICAL CONTEXT OF INTERNATIONAL SOCIAL WORK: TRADITIONAL AND ALTERNATIVE PERSPECTIVES

Mayadas and Elliot (1997) trace the history of international social work through four phases. Phase One they refer to as the Early Pioneers (1880s to 1940s). During this period there was a great deal of international exchange between Europe and the United States. This phase focused on the transfer of new social welfare approaches from Europe, primarily England to the United States. The two primary approaches were the Charity Organization Societies and Settlement Houses.

Proponents of scientific charity shared the poorhouse advocates' goals of cutting relief expenses and reducing the number of able-bodied who were receiving assistance, as well as the moral reformers' goal of uplifting people from poverty through discipline and religious education via private charity.

The basic approach of the Charity Organization Society (or scientific charity) was:

to have various groups already providing services to the poor coordinate their efforts. There would be a central office that served as a charity clearinghouse where "friendly visitors" (COS agents) involved in investigating the poor would meet to compare notes to determine who was worthy of relief and who was an imposter.

This collaboration would result in a complete registry of every person in the city who was receiving public or private assistance. The goal of this organized approach was to stop providing relief to the undeserving poor but continue to provide the deserving poor with the assistance to solve their own problems. (Myers-Lipton, 2006:68–69)

The settlement house, an approach to social reform with roots in the late 19th century and the Progressive Movement, was a method for serving the poor in urban areas by living among them and serving them directly. As the residents of settlement houses learned effective methods of helping, they then worked to transfer long-term responsibility for the programs to government agencies. Settlement house workers, in their work to find more effective solutions to poverty and injustice, also pioneered the profession of social work. (Johnson Lewis, 2013)

Mayadas and Elliott (1997:175–176) suggest that the professional values underlying these approaches "were paternalism, ethnocentrism, and protectionism, and were based on service models of charity, philanthropy, and social control of the poor."

Phase Two, according to Mayadas and Elliott, was Professional Imperialism (1940s–1970s). This phase focused on the development and export of social work education from the United States to other countries. Underlying values remained primarily paternalistic, ethnocentric, and colonialistic. Services were based on social control, remedial, medical, and crisis-oriented approaches. It was not sensitive to the cultural differences between the United States and the countries to which it exported a social work education model focused on practice with individuals, even though many of the cultures of the other countries were more collectively and group focused (Mayadas & Elliott, 1997:176).

Phase Three, the reconceptualization and indigenization of social work (1970s–1990s) was a response to the lack of fit between indigenous (native) people's needs and the model being exported in Phase Two. The extreme poverty and political repression in many countries of the developing world led to a rejection of Western models and the development of more radical, liberationist, and social development-oriented models. During this phase underlying values included regionalization, polarization, separation, and localization. This is consistent with a rejection by developing countries of Western-focused models (Mayadas & Elliott, 1997:177).

Phase Four, international social development in the 21st century is still in process, and represents a paradigm shift in international social work. Approaches to international social work are becoming more social development oriented, comprehensive, and sensitive to the needs of the cultural and social contexts of different countries and regions. Values underlying the emerging approach are mutual exchange of ideas, multicultural, and focused on democracy, diversity, social, cultural, and ethnic interchange (Mayadas & Elliott, 1997:177). We will look more closely at the social development approach later in this chapter.

## Social Work in a Global Context: Debates/Critiques

The issues surrounding social work in a global context are difficult, complex, and a source of disagreement and controversy in the profession. Midgley (2001 in Gray & Fook, 2004:625) notes several of the issues that face social workers in their efforts to understand social work in a global context:

- the nature of international social work;
- the profession's commitment to internationalising social work education and practice;
- the universality of social work values;

- internationalism as a desirable normative position; and
- on the nature of social work itself, that is, whether the profession should be committed to remedial, activist or developmental forms of practice.

Part of the overall debate surrounding social work in a global context is the issue of "professional imperialism." Gray and Fook (2004:626) note:

> Many social workers across the world are becoming ever more vocal about the forces of "professional imperialism," particularly in the developing world. Over the past 30 years social work writers have been trying to raise awareness of the dominance of Western influences on social work and have been stressing the need for social work in the developing world to free itself from the 'in-built assumptions and cultural biases of first world theories and models of practice' . . . and to develop indigenous education and practice.

Below is a discussion of indigenization flowing from and part of the position taken in the "professional imperialism" debate.

### Indigenization debate

The indigenization debate rests on two central premises:

1. Social work is a Western invention and a product of modernity. The notion of progressive change fits this paradigm. The question here is "whether or not, for example, Western perspectives on practice are really responsive to the personal and social needs of the population of other regions."

2. Indigenisation is postmodern to the extent that it questions the dominance of "social work as a Western invention" and seeks to relate it to local culture, history, and political, social and economic development. Implicit in the indigenisation side of the debate is the question of "whether it is incumbent on particular nations to develop their own orientations to social work practice." . . . This can also be extended into the question of whether national boundaries or commonalities make the most responsive basis for "localised" practice, or whether in fact there might be less structural or static boundaries, based on shared experiences, which provide a more appropriate framework for practice (Gray & Fook, 2004:634–635).

The two premises of the debate described earlier are addressed at more specific levels below:

1. *The globalisation–localisation debate:* The argument "that alongside the process of globalisation was a counter tendency towards the development of locally based solutions."

2. *The Westernisation–indigenisation debate:* Is western social work relevant "to third world or developing contexts, such as Africa and Asia. Is Western social work capable of addressing developing world issues "such as poverty, AIDS/HIV, hunger, drought, and war."

3. *The multicultural–universalisation debate:* What are the "implications of built-in cultural biases . . . within social work's multicultural or culturally sensitive

<hr>

## Human Rights & Justice

**Practice Behavior Example:** Recognize the global interconnections of oppression and are knowledgeable about theories of justice and strategies to promote human and civil rights.

**Critical Thinking Example:** After reading the "Indigenization Debate" section, do you believe Western social work is part of the solution or part of the problem in developing a truly global approach to social work? Do you believe a truly global approach to social work is possible and beneficial? Why or why not?

**Test your understanding of Social Work in a Global Context by taking this short** Quiz.

perspective, the notion that its values are universalisable and the potential conflict with non-Western and traditional cultures with collectivist values based [among other things] on kinship, community networks and the extended family system" (Gray & Fook, 2004:627).

## TECHNOLOGY AND INTERNATIONAL SOCIAL WORK

Increasingly, technology and access to technology are significant issues in the global environment and in international social work. New technologies can provide many opportunities for international social work and social development. However, their availability and access can also be serious barriers for people who lack the resources or countries that lack the infrastructures to acquire and use them. Midgely (1997:33) for example, notes that "many experts believe that the rapid expansion of information technology in recent decades has played a much more important role in fostering globalization than political or economic development." In other words, technology, particularly information and communication technology, can and does play a major role in the ability of people around the globe to communicate, in many cases instantly. The result of this is believed by many to be movement toward global integration and a world culture. The challenges, however, are significant in the area of technology and its potential for bringing people together. As is so often the case, lack of resources, education, and equal access create what has been referred to several times in this book as the digital divide—a world of "haves" and "have-nots" with great disparities among people and countries in their ability to acquire and use technology to communicate and improve the quality of their lives. Technology is certainly a central consideration in international social and economic development efforts. The influence of technology globally may play a large role in globalization, but neoliberalism has more direct and encompassing influences on global development.

## NEOLIBERALISM IN A GLOBAL CONTEXT

As Garrett notes, "within social work education, there may be a failure to adequately and critically examine neoliberalism and processes of neoliberalization" (Garrett, 2010:340). Neoliberalism both as national and global policy emerged during the 1970s with so-called "Thatcher/Reagan revolutions in Britain and the US." Since then the political and economic thinking and practices of neoliberalism have continued to spread globally including such diverse countries as the states of the former Soviet Union, post-Apartheid South Africa, and even China (Harvey, 2006:145).

Neoliberalism has been defined as "A 'conservative revolution' which 'ratifies and glorifies the reign of . . . the financial markets, . . . the return . . . of radical capitalism, with no other law than the return of maximum profit, an unfettered capitalism . . . .'" (Bourdieu, 2001:35 in Garrett, 2010:340). It is focused on maximizing the benefits of entrepreneurs and businesses through enforcement of "private property rights, individual liberty, free markets and free trade." Government's role is quite narrow and is primarily focused on removing as many barriers to entrepreneurs' and businesses' success (profit) as possible. In many cases the government also creates markets in areas that were formerly under the umbrella of government itself. This includes the privatization of such services as health care, education, social security, or even environmental protection (Harvey, 2006:145). The impact on social work and social work services is considerable given the profit motive central to capitalism or free markets.

Critics of neoliberalism refer to its tendency to extend privatization as far as possible as "Accumulation by Dispossession." The results include:

- *Privatization of public resources and services:* Transfer of assets from public and civic sectors to private and class-privileged domains.
- *Financializing economies globally:* Redistribution of wealth from workers and productive capital to finance capital—speculation, predation, and fraud.
- Management and manipulation of debt and disinvestment crises (the recent recessions in the United States and Europe) resulting in creating a sense of precariousness concerning the economy.
- *State Redistribution:* Large reductions in taxes on high incomes and capital wealth—agricultural and pharmaceutical subsidies leading to what critics call corporate socialism (Garrett, 2010; Harvey, 2006; Polivka & Estes, 2009).

For social work and other public service providers the process of privatization has direct implications in many areas previously thought to be services citizens had a right to regardless of their standing in society. Examples include:

- Public utilities of all kinds (water, telecommunications, transportation)
- Social welfare provision (social housing, education, health care, pensions)
- Public institutions (such as universities, research laboratories, prisons)
- Warfare (as illustrated by the 'army' of private contractors operating alongside the armed forces in Iraq) (Harvey, 2006)

Midgley identifies some of the consequences of neoliberalism for social work based on a book by Ian Ferguson. Social workers in public agencies as well as non-profit organizations are increasingly pressured to cut costs and increase efficiencies much the same as for-profit businesses. He also notes the increase in private-for-profit service delivery organizations (community mental health centers, inpatient psychiatric hospitals, etc.) that are driven primarily by the goal of making a profit. The increasing emphasis in social work on evidence based practice, strict or inflexible adherence to all agency rules, and close control by managers, Midgley believes have undermined historical role of social work "as a liberal and humane profession" (Midgley, 2009:185).

## INTERNATIONAL SOCIAL DEVELOPMENT

*Social development* has been defined in multiple and interrelated ways. It has been described as:

- "the process of planned change designed to bring about a better fit between human needs and social policies and programs." (Hollister)
- "directed towards the release of human potential in order to eliminate social inequities and problems" (Meinert, Kohn, & Strickler)
- "an intersystemic and integrated approach designed to facilitate development of the capacity of people to work continuously for their own welfare and the development of society's institutions so that human needs are met at all levels especially the lowest" (Billups & Julia)

- aiming "to foster the emergence and implementation of a social structure in which all citizens are entitled to equal social, economic, and political rights and equal access to status, roles, prerogative and responsibilities, regardless of gender, race, age, sexual orientation, or disability" (Chandler) (Sullivan, 1994:101).

All of these definitions share a concern for gaining access to basic resources to fulfill human needs. Sullivan argues, however, for an expanded notion of basic human needs from rather than the traditional notion of needs for housing, food, clothing, etc. He suggests the inclusion of "the provision of opportunities, the ability to maximize individual and collective potential, assurance of equal rights and protection of the natural environment" (Sullivan, 1994:107–108). This expanded notion of the goals of a social development approach is certainly consistent with social work values and ethics, respect for human diversity, and social and economic justice. Asamoah et al. provide a summary of social development specifically in the context of social work. They suggest:

> Social development emphasizes the values of human rights, social justice, equity in resources, and parity between human and economic development . . . values consistent with those of social work. Similarly, social development's focus on strengths, empowerment, self-sufficiency, and development support the change and growth orientation of social work. The broad applicability of social development provides a common worldwide identity for the profession. (Asamoah et al., 1997)

The definitions of social development earlier and the more inclusive notion of basic human needs are also consistent with such approaches as strengths, feminist, and empowerment perspectives on bringing about the necessary changes at the community and individual levels to accomplish the goals and fulfill the requirements of the definitions (see Chapters 1, 2, and 3).

Midgely suggests social development is "an approach for promoting human well-being that seeks to link social programs directly with economic development efforts. Its proponents argue that economic development should be harnessed for social purposes." Rather than the remedial and "band aid" approaches to social programs, advocates for social development suggest that "social programs should contribute positively to economic development" (Midgely, 1997:75–76). This approach has been used widely in the developing world and is increasingly being used in vulnerable areas of the developed world. In the global context social development has become of increasing interest to nations and organizations struggling to overcome dire poverty and great disparities in who benefits from economic development around the world.

As we have noted several times throughout this book, social work, especially social work in the United States, has historically struggled to balance its stated responsibilities in the areas of both individual and social change or micro and macro approaches. As we have also noted several times, this historic struggle is also present in the arena of human behavior and the social environment (HBSE). Within HBSE, this struggle often results in much more attention to human behavior at the individual or small system level than to the social environment or the larger systems, such as organizations, communities, and the global environment, that form the context of human behavior at the individual or small system levels. Some have suggested that a social development approach might offer a way to bring more balance to these competing responsibilities within the profession.

For example, Asamoah et al. note, "the United Nations Development Program links human development and sustainable development, both of which are elements of social development. This linkage of the micro and macro is reflected in Lowe's definition of social development as 'an encompassing concept that refers to a dual-focused holistic, systemic-ecologically oriented approach to seeking social advancement of individuals as well as broad-scale societal institutions'" (Lowe, 1995 quoted in Asamoah et al., 1997).

Next, we will explore the U.N. Universal Declaration of Human Rights.

# UNITED NATIONS UNIVERSAL DECLARATION OF HUMAN RIGHTS

This declaration of universal human rights is perhaps one of the most important documents guiding international social work organizations. It has been used widely to develop principles and missions of social work organizations around the world. Note that given the time periods in which it was created male pronouns are used predominantly. However, note also the inclusion of "sex" in Article 2. Adopted in 1948, its implementation in much of the world is far from complete, including in the United States.

**Test your understanding of the U.N. Universal Declaration of Human Rights by taking this short** Quiz.

## Articles of U.N. Declaration of Human Rights

*Article 1.* All human beings are born free and equal in dignity and rights. They are endowed with reason and conscience and should act towards one another in a spirit of brotherhood.

*Article 2.* Everyone is entitled to all the rights and freedoms set forth in this Declaration, without distinction of any kind, such as race, colour, sex, language, religion, political or other opinion, national or social origin, property, birth or other status. Furthermore, no distinction shall be made on the basis of the political, jurisdictional, or international status of the country or territory to which a person belongs, whether it be independent, trust, non-self-governing or under any other limitation of sovereignty.

*Article 3.* Everyone has the right to life, liberty and security of person.

*Article 4.* No one shall be held in slavery or servitude; slavery and the slave trade shall be prohibited in all their forms.

*Article 5.* No one shall be subjected to torture or to cruel, inhuman or degrading treatment or punishment.

*Article 6.* Everyone has the right to recognition everywhere as a person before the law.

*Article 7.* All are equal before the law and are entitled without any discrimination to equal protection of the law. All are entitled to equal protection against any discrimination in violation of this Declaration and against any incitement to such discrimination.

*Article 8.* Everyone has the right to an effective remedy by the competent national tribunals for acts violating the fundamental rights granted him by the constitution or by law.

*Article 9.* No one shall be subjected to arbitrary arrest, detention or exile.

*Article 10.* Everyone is entitled in full equality to a fair and public hearing by an independent and impartial tribunal, in the determination of his rights and obligations and of any criminal charge against him.

*Article 11.* (1) Everyone charged with a penal offence has the right to be presumed innocent until proved guilty according to law in a public trial at which he has had all the guarantees necessary for his defence. (2) No one shall be held guilty of any penal offence on account of any act or omission which did not constitute a penal offence, under national or international law, at the time when it was committed. Nor shall a heavier penalty be imposed than the one that was applicable at the time the penal offence was committed.

*(Continued)*

## Articles of U.N. Declaration of Human Rights *(Continued)*

*Article 12.* No one shall be subjected to arbitrary interference with his privacy, family, home or correspondence, nor to attacks upon his honour and reputation. Everyone has the right to the protection of the law against such interference or attacks.

*Article 13.* (1) Everyone has the right to freedom of movement and residence within the borders of each state. (2) Everyone has the right to leave any country, including his own, and to return to his country.

*Article 14.* (1) Everyone has the right to seek and to enjoy in other countries asylum from persecution. (2) This right may not be invoked in the case of prosecutions genuinely arising from non-political crimes or from acts contrary to the purposes and principles of the United Nations.

*Article 15.* (1) Everyone has the right to a nationality. (2) No one shall be arbitrarily deprived of his nationality nor denied the right to change his nationality.

*Article 16.* (1) Men and women of full age, without any limitation due to race, nationality or religion, have the right to marry and to found a family. They are entitled to equal rights as to marriage, during marriage and at its dissolution. (2) Marriage shall be entered into only with the free and full consent of the intending spouses. (3) The family is the natural and fundamental group unit of society and is entitled to protection by society and the State.

*Article 17.* (1) Everyone has the right to own property alone as well as in association with others. (2) No one shall be arbitrarily deprived of his property.

*Article 18.* Everyone has the right to freedom of thought, conscience and religion; this right includes freedom to change his religion or belief, and freedom, either alone or in community with others and in public or private, to manifest his religion or belief in teaching, practice, worship and observance.

*Article 19.* Everyone has the right to freedom of opinion and expression; this right includes freedom to hold opinions without interference and to seek, receive and impart information and ideas through any media and regardless of frontiers.

*Article 20.* (1) Everyone has the right to freedom of peaceful assembly and association. (2) No one may be compelled to belong to an association.

*Article 21.* (1) Everyone has the right to take part in the government of his country, directly or through freely chosen representatives. (2) Everyone has the right of equal access to public service in his country. (3) The will of the people shall be the basis of the authority of government; this will shall be expressed in periodic and genuine elections which shall be by universal and equal suffrage and shall be held by secret vote or by equivalent free voting procedures.

*Article 22.* Everyone, as a member of society, has the right to social security and is entitled to realization, through national effort and international cooperation and in accordance with the organization and resources of each State, of the economic, social and cultural rights indispensable for his dignity and the free development of his personality.

*Article 23.* (1) Everyone has the right to work, to free choice of employment, to just and favourable conditions of work and to protection against unemployment. (2) Everyone, without any discrimination, has the right to equal pay for equal work. (3) Everyone who works has the right to just and favourable remuneration ensuring for himself and his family an existence worthy of human dignity, and supplemented, if necessary, by other means of social protection. (4) Everyone has the right to form and to join trade unions for the protection of his interests.

*Article 24.* Everyone has the right to rest and leisure, including reasonable limitation of working hours and periodic holidays with pay.

*Article 25.* (1) Everyone has the right to a standard of living adequate for the health and well-being of himself and of his family, including food, clothing, housing and medical care and necessary social services, and the right to security in the event of unemployment, sickness, disability, widowhood, old age or other lack of livelihood in circumstances beyond his control. (2) Motherhood and childhood are entitled to special care and assistance. All children, whether born in or out of wedlock, shall enjoy the same social protection.

*Article 26.* (1) Everyone has the right to education. Education shall be free, at least in the elementary and fundamental stages. Elementary education shall be compulsory. Technical and professional education shall be made generally available and higher education shall be equally accessible to all on the basis of merit. (2) Education shall be directed to the full development of the human personality and to the strengthening of respect for human rights and fundamental freedoms. It shall promote understanding, tolerance and friendship among all nations, racial or religious groups, and shall further the activities of the United Nations for the maintenance of peace. (3) Parents have a prior right to choose the kind of education that shall be given to their children.

*Article 27.* (1) Everyone has the right freely to participate in the cultural life of the community, to enjoy the arts and to share in scientific advancement and its benefits. (2) Everyone has the right to the protection of the moral and material interests resulting from any scientific, literary or artistic production of which he is the author.

*Article 28.* Everyone is entitled to a social and international order in which the rights and freedoms set forth in this Declaration can be fully realized.

*Article 29.* (1) Everyone has duties to the community in which alone the free and full development of his

personality is possible. (2) In the exercise of his rights and freedoms, everyone shall be subject only to such limitations as are determined by law solely for the purpose of securing due recognition and respect for the rights and freedoms of others and of meeting the just requirements of morality, public order and the general welfare in a democratic society. (3) These rights and freedoms may in no case be exercised contrary to the purposes and principles of the United Nations.

*Article 30.* Nothing in this Declaration may be interpreted as implying for any State, group or person any right to engage in any activity or to perform any act aimed at the destruction of any of the rights and freedoms set forth herein. http://www.un.org/Overview/rights.html

## Millennium Goals

Consistent with principles outlined in the U.N. Declaration of Human Rights, in 2000 the United Nations Development Program, in collaboration with numerous countries, private-for-profit, nonprofit, nongovernmental (NGOs), and public governmental organizations, set an agenda for ending world poverty by the year 2015. In his foreword to the United Nations Millennium Development Goals Report 2008, Secretary-General Ban Ki-moon noted the lofty purpose of the goals: "in adopting the Millennium Declaration in the year 2000, the international community pledged to 'spare no effort to free our fellow men, women and children from the abject and dehumanizing conditions of extreme poverty.'"

The Secretary-General also notes that the grand intentions of the Millennium Development Goals (MDGs) "encapsulate the development aspirations of the world as a whole. But they are not only development objectives; they encompass universally accepted human values and rights such as freedom from hunger, the right to basic education, the right to health and a responsibility to future generations" (U.N., 2008:3). The eight goals are as follows:

1. Goal: Eradicate extreme poverty and hunger
2. Goal: Achieve universal primary education
3. Goal: Promote gender equality and empower women
4. Goal: Reduce child mortality
5. Goal: Improve maternal health
6. Goal: Combat HIV/AIDS, malaria and other diseases
7. Goal: Ensure environmental sustainability
8. Goal: Develop a Global Partnership for Development (U.N., 2008)

### Human Behavior

**Practice Behavior Example:** Know about human behavior across the life course; the range of social systems in which people live; and the ways social systems promote or deter people in maintaining or achieving health and well-being.

**Critical Thinking Question:** Based on the information about the Millennial Goals and the progress and challenges involved in achieving the goals, estimate which of the goals you believe can be realistically fully achieved by 2015 and provide evidence to support your estimates.

**Progress and challenges**

The most recent Millennium Goals Report (2012) notes the early achievement or some of the goals and recounts where achievement of goals is lagging. In the report, U.N. Secretary-General, Ban Ki-moon notes several milestones reached prior to the 2015 deadline set originally for the achievement of all eight goals. Specifically, he notes, the target of reducing world poverty by half has been reached well ahead of the 2015 deadline as has the goal of cutting in half the proportion of people without access to dependable drinking water. In addition, improving the conditions of people living in slum conditions has been achieved for 200 million people—this is double the original goal. Primary school enrollment for girls now equals that for boys. Finally, he points out increasing progress in reducing child and maternal mortality.

The Secretary-General cautions, however, that the work of achieving the goals is far from over. For example, projections suggest that in 2015 over 600 million people will still not have access to a dependable source of drinking water and almost one billion people will still be living on less than $1.25 a day. Hunger continues to be a daunting challenge, as does completion of primary school education for all. The goal of gender equality is unfulfilled. The unevenness of progress within countries and regions and the severe inequalities that exist among populations, especially between rural and urban areas, continue as grave concerns.

Perhaps the environment-related goals are the most elusive, specifically, the continuing loss of biodiversity, the lack of safe sanitation, and greenhouse gas emissions remain threats to a sustainable future for all who live on the planet (United Nations, 2012:3–5).

Both the U.N. Universal Declaration of Human Rights and the Millennium Goals are founded on the fundamental belief in human rights. In the following section, we explore the notion of social work as a human rights profession.

## Social Work as a Human Rights Profession

There are different definitions of human rights, but they all have much in common, as the definitions and discussion provided below reflect. In 1988, the International Federation of Social Workers (IFSW; see information on IFSW in a following section) declared, "social work was and always has been a human rights profession." Healy presents the basic tenet associated with the IFSW declaration as "the intrinsic values of every human being and as one of its main aims the promotion of equitable social structures, which can offer people security and development while upholding their dignity." Healy provides a basic definition of *human rights* as "those rights that belong to all just because we are human." She finds Articles 22 and 25 of the U.N. Universal Declaration of Human Rights particularly applicable to social work as a human rights profession (see these articles in the preceding section, "United Nations Universal Declaration of Human Rights") (Healy, 2008:735–737). In addition, Lundy and van Wormer provide the *Social Work Dictionary*'s definition of social justice: "an ideal condition in which all members of a society have the same basic rights, protection, opportunities, obligations, and social benefits" (Barker quoted in Lundy & Van Wormer, 2007:727).

The concepts of social and economic justice are also fundamental elements of social work's purpose and are closely related to the concept of human rights, but are not the same thing. Lundy and van Wormer, for example, argue, "economic justice is a narrower concept, referring to the standard of living that ideally should be equitable. All persons ought to have opportunities for meaningful work and an income that provides them with adequate food, shelter, a level of living that contributes to good health." They further explain, "whereas social and economic justice is a general term that relates to society in general, human rights is a term that, from the point of view of the people, refers to specific universal standards relevant to freedom and well-being, personal and collective rights" (Lundy & Van Wormer, 2007:727–728).

In their discussion of the "potential for human rights to serve as a unifying framework" for the profession, Asamoah et al. note that the UNDHR (see preceding section) actually defines four categories of human rights:

1. Recognition of human dignity.

2. Recognition of civil and political rights.

3. Economic and social rights—including government responsibility to guarantee that human needs for shelter, health care, education, and old age security will be met.

4. Solidarity rights "stress the need for individual and international cooperation to realize such rights as a clean environment, peace, and international distributive justice" (Asamoah et al., 1997).

These scholars argue that in the United States the first two categories of rights have been considered "as the totality of human rights." However, they also argue, "for social work as a global profession . . . the other two categories are equally or more important" (Asamoah et al., 1997).

One of the greatest violations of human rights is torture. In Illustrative Reading 10.1: A Plague of Our Time: Torture, Human Rights, and Social Work, the authors address this egregious violation of human rights. They present information on the prevalence of torture and they note that social workers in the United States are often ill prepared to deal with survivors of torture, though many immigrants and refugees who come to the United States have been victims of torture. In addition, they provide information on intervention approaches and outline resources that may be helpful to social workers who work with victims of torture.

Next, we explore the major international social work organizations that are actively engaged in the struggle to bring human rights and social and economic justice to the forefront of social work in a global context.

## INTERNATIONAL SOCIAL WORK ORGANIZATIONS

There are a number of international social work organizations concerned with the implementation of the U.N. Universal Declaration of Human Rights. In addition, these organizations share many concerns about the mechanisms for and responsibilities of social workers in effectively creating a global environment consistent with social work ethics and values, especially those concerned with social and economic justice and well-being for all people. Three of the major international organizations of social workers are the International Federation of Social Workers (IFSW), the International Council on Social Welfare (ICSW), and the International Association of Schools of Social Work (IASSW). These organizations often work collaboratively to provide leadership and direction for the development of effective international approaches to social work education and practice. For example, IFSW and IASSW worked jointly to put forth an International Definition of Social Work in 2001. It is included below after the missions and principles of these organizations.

## International Association of Schools of Social Work (IASSW)

The *International Association of Schools of Social Work (IASSW)* is an international association of institutions of social work education, organizations supporting social work education, and social work educators. Its mission is:

a. To develop and promote excellence in social work education, research, and scholarship globally in order to enhance human well-being.

b. To create and maintain a dynamic community of social work educators and their programs.

c. To support and facilitate participation in mutual exchanges of information and expertise.

d. To represent social work education at the international level.

In fulfilling its mission, IASSW adheres to all United Nations Declarations and Conventions on human rights, recognizing that respect for the inalienable rights of the individual is the foundation of freedom, justice, and peace.

Members of IASSW are united in their obligation to the continued pursuit of social justice and social development. In carrying out its mission, IASSW fosters cooperation, collegiality, and interdependence among its members and with others.[1]

## International Council on Social Welfare (ICSW)

The *International Council on Social Welfare (ICSW)*, founded in Paris in 1928, is a nongovernmental organization which now represents national and local organizations in more than 80 countries throughout the world. Our membership also includes a number of major international organizations.

### Mission

The ICSW is a global nongovernmental organization which represents a wide range of national and international member organizations that seek to advance social welfare, social development, and social justice.

ICSW's basic mission is to promote forms of social and economic development which aim to reduce poverty, hardship, and vulnerability throughout the world, especially amongst disadvantaged people. It strives for recognition and protection of fundamental rights to food, shelter, education, health care, and security. It believes that these rights are an essential foundation for freedom, justice, and peace. It seeks also to advance equality of opportunity, freedom of self-expression and access to human services.

In working to achieve its mission, ICSW advocates policies and programs which strike an appropriate balance between social and economic goals and which respect cultural diversity. It seeks implementation of these proposals by governments, international organizations, nongovernmental agencies, and others. It does so in cooperation with its network of members and with a wide range of other organizations at local, national,

---

[1]http://www.iassw.soton.ac.uk/Generic/Mission.asp?lang=en

and international levels. ICSW's main ways of pursuing its aims include gathering and disseminating information, undertaking research and analysis, convening seminars and conferences, drawing on grass-roots experiences, strengthening nongovernmental organizations, developing policy proposals, engaging in public advocacy, and working with policy-makers and administrators in government and elsewhere.[2]

## International Federation of Social Workers

The *International Federation of Social Workers (IFSW)* recognizes that social work originates variously from humanitarian, religious, and democratic ideals and philosophies; and that it has universal application to meet human needs arising from personal-societal interactions, and to develop human potential.

Professional social workers are dedicated to service for the welfare and self-fulfillment of human beings; to the development and disciplined use of scientific knowledge regarding human behavior and society; to the development of resources to meet individual, group, national and international needs and aspirations; to the enhancement and improvement of the quality of life of people; and to the achievement of social justice.

### History

The IFSW is a successor to the International Permanent Secretariat of Social Workers, which was founded in Paris in 1928 and was active until the outbreak of World War II. It was not until 1950, at the time of the International Conference of Social Work in Paris, that the decision was made to create the IFSW, an international organization of professional social workers.

The original agreement was that the IFSW would come into being when seven national organizations agreed to become members. After much preliminary work, the Federation was finally founded in 1956 at the time of the meeting of the International Conference on Social Welfare in Munich, Germany.[3]

## INTERNATIONAL DEFINITION OF SOCIAL WORK

The social work profession promotes social change, problem solving in human relationships and the empowerment and liberation of people to enhance well-being. Utilizing theories of human behavior and social systems, social work intervenes at the points where people interact with their environments. Principles of human rights and social justice are fundamental to social work.

## Commentary

Social work in its various forms addresses the multiple, complex transactions between people and their environments. Its mission is to enable all people to develop their full potential, enrich their lives, and prevent dysfunction. Professional social work is focused on problem solving and change. As such, social workers are change agents in society and in the lives of the individuals,

### Professional Identity

**Practice Behavior Example:** Serve as representatives of the profession, its mission, and its core values.

**Critical Thinking Question:** Compare the international definition of social work and the related components outlined in this section with the U.S. definition (see Chapter 1 for a refresher on the CSWE definition of social work in terms of its mission, goals, and purposes). What are the differences? Similarities?

[2]http://www.icsw.org/
[3]http://www.ifsw.org

families, and communities they serve. Social work is an interrelated system of values, theory, and practice.

## Values

Social work grew out of humanitarian and democratic ideals, and its values are based on respect for the equality, worth, and dignity of all people. Since its beginnings over a century ago, social work practice has focused on meeting human needs and developing human potential. Human rights and social justice serve as the motivation and justification for social work action. In solidarity with those who are disadvantaged, the profession strives to alleviate poverty and to liberate vulnerable and oppressed people in order to promote social inclusion. Social work values are embodied in the profession's national and international codes of ethics.

## Theory

Social work bases its methodology on a systematic body of evidence-based knowledge derived from research and practice evaluation, including local and indigenous knowledge specific to its context. It recognizes the complexity of interactions between human beings and their environment, and the capacity of people both to be affected by and to alter the multiple influences upon them including bio-psychosocial factors. The social work profession draws on theories of human development and behavior and social systems to analyze complex situations and to facilitate individual, organizational, social, and cultural changes.

## Practice

Social work addresses the barriers, inequities, and injustices that exist in society. It responds to crises and emergencies as well as to everyday personal and social problems. Social work utilizes a variety of skills, techniques, and activities consistent with its holistic focus on persons and their environments. Social work interventions range from primarily person-focused psychosocial processes to involvement in social policy, planning, and development. These include counseling, clinical social work, group work, social pedagogical work, and family treatment and therapy as well as efforts to help people obtain services and resources in the community. Interventions also include agency administration, community organization, and engaging in social and political action to impact social policy and economic development. The holistic focus of social work is universal, but the priorities of social work practice will vary from country to country and from time to time depending on cultural, historical, and socioeconomic conditions.[4]

## SUMMARY

A number of aspects of international or global social work have been addressed in this chapter. Social workers, especially social workers in the United States and other affluent nations, have both unique opportunities and serious responsibilities in the global arena.

---

[4]International Association of Schools of Social Work/ International Federation of Social Workers. Definition of Social Work Jointly Agreed on 27 June 2001 in Copenhagen.

For social work to fulfill its purposes as a profession, it must increasingly move into the international arena. In order to more fully understand human behavior and the social environment, it is essential that we become knowledgeable about international issues and people. If we are members of affluent groups and societies, we must recognize that our privilege is not shared by many others on the planet. In addition, we have the responsibility of using the benefits of our privileged status to advocate both locally and globally for social and economic justice in its fullest sense. As social workers we need to develop a true worldview that transcends national borders, belief systems, and ways of life.

**Recall what you learned in this chapter by completing the Chapter Review.**

# References

## References for Chapter 1

Berman, M. (Winter 1996). "The shadow side of systems theory." *Journal of Humanistic Psychology, 36*(1).

Boulding, Kenneth E. (1964). *The meaning of the 20th century: The great transition.* New York: Harper-Colophon.

Capra, Fritjof. (1983). *The turning point: Science, society, and the rising culture.* Toronto: Bantam Books.

Cormode, G., & Krishnamurthy, B. (2008). "Key Differences between Web 1.0 and Web 2.0." *First Monday, 13*(6). Retrieved from http://www.uic.edu/htbin/cgiwrap/bin/ojs/index.php/fm/article/view/2125/1972

CSWE. (2008). *Educational policy and accreditation standards.* Retrieved July 1, 2008, from http://www.cswe.org/CSWE/accreditation/

Goldstein, Howard. (1990). "The knowledge base of social work practice: Theory, wisdom, analogue or art?" *Families in Society, 71*(1), 32–43.

Kirby, A. (2010). "Successor States to an Empire in Free Fall, Feature." *The Times Higher Education Supplement,* p. 42.

Kuhn, Thomas S. ([1962] 1970). *The structure of scientific revolutions* (2nd ed.). Chicago: The University of Chicago.

Lather, P. (1991). *Getting smart: Feminist research and pedagogy with/in the postmodern.* New York: Routledge.

Lincoln, Y. S., & Guba, E. G. (1985). *Naturalistic inquiry.* Beverly Hills: Sage.

Logan, Sadye. (1990). "Black families: Race, ethnicity, culture, social class, and gender issues." In Logan, S., Freeman, E., & McRoy, R. *Social Work Practice With Black Families.* New York: Longman.

Lonner, W. J. (1994). "Culture and human diversity." In E. J. Trickett, R. J. Watts, & D. Birman (Eds.), *Human diversity: Perspectives on people in context.* San Francisco: Jossey-Bass.

Manchester, William. (1992). *A world lit only by fire: The medieval mind and the renaissance: Portrait of an age.* Boston: Little, Brown and Company.

Myers, Linda J. (1985). "Transpersonal psychology: The role of the afrocentric paradigm." *Journal of Black Psychology, 12*(1), 31–42.

National Center for Cultural Competence, G. U. (2004). *Achieving cultural competence: a guidebook for providers of services to older Americans and their families.* Retrieved February 22, 2009 from http://www.aoa.gov/PROF/adddiv/cultural/CC-guidebook.pdf

Persell, Caroline Hodges. (1987). *Understanding society: An introduction to sociology.* New York: Harper and Row.

Sahakian, William S. (1968). *History of philosophy.* New York: Barnes and Noble Books.

Schutz, Alfred. (1944). "The stranger: An essay in social psychology." *American Journal of Sociology, 49,* 499–507.

## References for Chapter 2

AmeriStat. (2000). *Race and ethnicity in the census: 1860–2000,* [Web site]. AmeriStat Population Reference Bureau and Social Science Analysis Network. Available: http://www.ameristat.org/racethnic/census.htm [2000, 4/4/00].

Armas, G. (2000, March 13, 2000). "Administration puts out new guidelines for multiracial categories." *Northwest Arkansas Times.*

Beaver, Marion. (1990). "The older person in the black family." In *Social work practice with black families.* Logan, Sadye, Freeman, Edith, & McRoy, Ruth (Eds.). New York: Longman.

Belenky, Mary F., Clinchy, Blythe M., Goldberger, Nancy R., & Tarule, Jill M. (1986). *Women's ways of knowing: The development of self, voice, and mind.* New York: Basic Books, Inc.

Bent-Goodley, T. B. (2005). "An African-centered approach to domestic violence." *Families in Society,* 86(2), 197.

Berlin, Sharon B. (1990). "Dichotomous and complex thinking." *Social Service Review,* 64(1): 46–59.

Bottomore, Tom. (1984). *The Frankfurt school and critical theory.* London: Tavistock Publications.

Capra, Fritjof. (1983). *The turning point: Science, society, and the rising culture.* Toronto: Bantam Books.

Cobb, A., & Forbes, S. (2002). "Qualitative research: What does it have to offer to the gerontologist?" *Journals of Gerontology,* 57A(4), 6.

Collins, P. H. (1986). "Learning from the outsider within: The sociological significance of black feminist thought." *Social Problems,* 33(6): 14–32.

Collins, P. H. (1989). "The social construction of black feminist thought." *Signs,* 14(4): 745–773.

Collins, P. H. (1990). Black feminist thought: Knowledge, consciousness, and the politics of empowerment. Boston: Unwin Hyman, Inc.

Collins, P. H. (1996). "What's in a name? Womanism, black feminism, and beyond." *Black Scholar,* 26(1), 9–17.

Dawson, Betty G., Klass, Morris D., Guy, Rebecca F., & Edgley, Charles K., (1991). *Understanding Social Work Research.* Boston: Allyn & Bacon.

Evans-Campbell, T., Fredriksen-Goldsen, K., Walters, K., & Stately, A. (2007). "Caregiving exeriences among American Indian two-spirit men and women: Contemporary and historical roles." *Journal of Gay & Lesbian Social Services,* 18(3/4), 75–92.

Everett, J. E., Chipungu, S. S., & Leashore, B. R. (Eds.). (1991). *Child Welfare: An Africentric Perspective.* New Brunswick, NJ: Rutgers University Press.

Freire, P. (1993). *Pedagogy of the Oppressed: 30th Anniversity Edition.* (M. B. Ramos, Trans.). New York & London: Continuum.

Graham, M. (1999). "The African-centred worldview: Developing a paradigm for social work." *British Journal of Social Work,* 29, 251–267

Heineman Pieper, M. (1995). "Preface." In Tyson, K. (Ed.). *New foundations for scientific social and behavioral research: The heuristic paradigm.* Boston: Allyn & Bacon.

Helms, J. E. (1994). "The conceptualization of racial identity and other 'racial' constructs." In Trickett, E. J., Watts, R. J., & Birman D. (Eds.). (1994). *Human diversity: Perspectives on people in context.* San Francisco: Jossey-Bass.

hooks, bell. (1989). *Talking Back: Thinking Feminist, Thinking Black.* Boston, MA: South End Press.

Imre, Roberta Wells. (1984). "The nature of knowledge in social work." *Social Work,* 29(1): 41–45.

Kerlinger, Fred N. (1973). *Foundations of behavioral research.* New York: Holt, Rinehart and Winston, Inc.

Lorenz, W. (2012). "Response: Hermeneutics and Accountable Practice: Lessons from the History of Social Work." *Research on Social Work Practice,* 22(5), 492–498. doi:10.1177/1049731512444167

Lyubansky, M. (2011). *The Meaning of Whiteness. In Between the Lines: Perspectives on Race, Culture, and Community.* Web Blog. Retrieved from http://www.psychologytoday.com/blog/between-the-lines/201112/the-meaning-whiteness

Manheim, Henry L. (1977). *Sociological research: Philosophy and methods.* Homewood, IL.: The Dorsey Press.

McIntosh, Peggy. (1992). "White privilege and male privilege. A personal account of coming to see correspondences through work in Women's Studies." In Margaret Anderson & Patricia Hill Collins (Eds.). *Race class and gender: An anthology.* Belmont, CA: Wadsworth Publishing Co.

Myers, L. J., & Speight, S. L. (1994). "Optimal theory and the psychology of human diversity." In Trickett, E. J., Watts, R. J. & Birman D. (Eds.). (1994). *Human diversity: Perspectives on people in context.* San Francisco: Jossey-Bass.

Pharr, Suzanne. (1988). *Homophobia: A Weapon of Sexism.* Inverness, CA: Chardon, Press.

Population Reference Bureau. (2010). *PRB Discuss Online: What Is Your "Race"? A Question Increasingly Difficult to Answer.* Retrieved February 23, 2013, from http://www.prb.org/Articles/2010/discussionjan12010.aspx

Population Reference Bureau. (2013). *Changing the way U.S. Hispanics are counted.* Retrieved from Population Reference Bureau website: http://www.prb.org/Articles/2012/us-census-and-hispanics.aspx

Rampton, M. (2008). "The Three Waves of Feminism." *PACIFIC: The Magazine of Pacific University, 41*(2). Retrieved from PACIFIC: The Magazine of Pacific University website: http://www.pacificu.edu/magazine_archives/2008/fall/echoes/feminism.cfm

Reason, Peter. (1981). "Methodological approaches to social science by Ian Mitroff and Ralph Kilmann: An appreciation." In Peter Reason and John Rowan. (Eds.). *Human inquiry: A sourcebook of new paradigm research.* New York: John Wiley and Sons.

Reason, Peter, (Ed.) (1988). Human inquiry in action: Developments in new paradigm research. London: SAGE Publications.

Ruth, Sheila. (1990). *Issues in feminism.* Mountain View, CA: Mayfield Publishing Co.

Ryan, J. (2011). *Quotes from Tim Wise's Lecture the Pathology of Privilege: Racism, White Denial and the Costs of Inequality. Web Blog: Gender, Power and Privilege Blog.* Retrieved from http://ws405.blogspot.com/2011/01/quotes-from-tim-wises-lecture-pathology.html

Scott, Joan W. (1988). *Gender and the politics of history.* New York: Columbia University Press.

Sherman, Edmund. (1991). "Interpretive methods for social work practice and research." *Journal of Sociology and Social Welfare, 18*(4): 69–81.

Tyson, K. (1995). "Editor's Introduction" Heuristic research. New foundations for scientific social and behavioral research: The heuristic paradigm. Boston: Allyn & Bacon.

U.S. Census Bureau. (March 14, 2001). *Questions and Answers for Census 2000 Data on Race.* Retrieved February 19, 2014, from https://www.census.gov/census2000/raceqandas.html

Van Den Bergh, N. (Ed.). (1995). *Feminist practice in the 21st century.* Washington, DC: NASW Press.

*Webster's New Universal Unabridged Dictionary* (2nd ed.) (1983). In Edmund Sherman, "Interpretive methods for social work practice and research." *Journal of Sociology and Social Welfare, 18*(4): 69–81.

Weick, Ann. (1991). "The place of science in social work." *Journal of Sociology and Social Welfare, 18*(4): 13–34.

## References for Chapter 3

Alix, E. K. (1995). *Sociology: An everyday life approach.* Minneapolis: West Publishing.

Asamoah, Yvonne, Garcia, Alejandro, Hendricks, Carmen Ortiz, and Walker, Joel. (1991). "What we call ourselves: Implications for resources, policy, and practice." *Journal of Multicultural Social Work,* 1(1): 7–22.

Brault, Matthew W., "Americans With Disabilities: 2010," *Current Population Reports,* P70-131, U.S. Census Bureau, Washington, DC, 2012.

Brown, Edwin G. (1981). "Selection and formulation of a research problem." In Richard M. Grinnell, Jr., *Social work research and evaluation.* Itasca, IL.: F. E. Peacock Publishers, Inc.

Dawson, Betty G.,Klass, Morris D., Guy, Rebecca F., and Edgley,Charles K., (1991). *Understanding Social Work Research.* Boston: Allyn& Bacon.

Diller, J. (1999). *Cultural diversity: A primer for the human services.* Belmont: Brooks/Cole Wadsworth.

Gambrill, E. (2007). Special section: Promoting and sustaining evidence-based practice views of evidence-based practice: Social workers of ethics and accreditation standards as guides for choice. *Journal of Social Work Education, 43*(3), 447–482.

Germain, Carel. (1986). "The life model approach to social work practice revisited." In Francis Turner (Ed.). (3rd ed.). *Social work treatment.* New York: Free Press.

Gingerich, W. J. (2000). Solution-Focused Brief Therapy: A Review of the Outcome Research. *Family Process, 39*(4), 477.

Green, J. (1999). *Cultural awareness in the human services: A multi-ethnic approach.* (3rd ed.). Boston: Allyn and Bacon.

Grinnell, R. (1981). *Social Work Research and Evanluation.* Itasca, IL: F. E. Peacock.

Henslin, J. M. (1996). *Essentials of sociology: A down-to-earth approach.* Boston: Allyn and Bacon.

Jung, C. G. (1964). *Man and his symbols.* New York: Doubleday.

Kuhn, Thomas S. ([1962] 1970). *The structure of scientific revolutions.* (2nd ed.). Chicago: The University of Chicago. p. 175

Lee, M. Y. (2003). A solution-focused approach to cross-cultural clinical social work practice: Utilizing cultural strengths. *Families in Society, 84*(3), 385–395.

Leigh, L. (1998). *Communicating for cultural competence.* Boston: Allyn and Bacon.

Lum, D. (1999). *Culturally competent practice: A framework for growth and action.* Pacific Grove: Brooks/Cole.

Martin, Patricia Yancey, and O'Connor, Gerald G. (1989). *The social environment: Open systems applications.* White Plains, NY: Longman, Inc.

Mullen, E. (1981). Chapter 31: Development of Personal Intervention Models. In Ginnell, R. (Ed.), *Social Work Research and Evaluation* (pp. 606–634). Itasca, IL: F. E. Peacock.

Newsome, W. S., and Kelly, M. (2004). Grandparents raising grandchildren: A solution-focused brief therapy approach in school settings. *Social Work with Groups, 27*(4), 65–84.

Norman, J., and Wheeler, B. (1996). "Gender-sensitive social work practice: A model for education." *Journal of Social Work Education, 32*(2): 203–213.

Patterson, J. B., McKenzie, B., and Jenkins, J. (1995). "Creating accessible groups for individuals with disabilities." *The Journal of Specialists in Group Work, 20*(2): 76–82.

Persell, Carolyn. (1987). *Understanding society* (2nd ed.). New York: Harper and Row.

Pool, C. (1997). "A new digital literacy: A conversation with Paul Gilster." *Educational Leadership, 55:* 6–11.

Queralt, M., and Witte, A. (1998). "A map for you? Geographic information systems in the social services." *Social Work, 43*(5): 455–469.

Rudd, R. D. (2007). Defining Critical Thinking. Techniques, 82(7), 46–49.

Sackett, D. L., Straus, S. E., Richardson, W. S., Rosenberg, W., and Haynes, R. B. (2000). *Evidence-based medicine: How to practice andteach EBM* (2nd ed.). New York: Churchill Livingstone.

Scheyett, A. (2006). *Danger and Opportunity: Challenges in Teaching Evidence-Based Practice in the Social Work Curriculum.* Journal of Teaching in Social Work, 26(1/2), 19–29.

Scott, Joan W. (1988). "Deconstructing equality-versus-difference: Or, the uses of poststructuralist theory for feminism." *Feminist Studies, 14*(1): 33–50.

Shafritz, Jay M., and Ott, J. Steven. (1987). *Classics of organization theory.* Chicago: The Dorsey Press.

Szasz, Thomas Stephen. (1987). *Insanity: The idea and its consequences.* New York: John Wiley and Sons, Inc.

Thyer, B. (2001). "What is the role of theory in research on social work practice?" *Journal of Social Work Education, 37*(1):9–25.

Tilbury, C., Osmond, J., & Scott, T.(2009). Teaching critical thinking in social work education: A literature review. *Advances in Social Work & Welfare Educatiion*, 11(1), 31–50.

Tyson, K. (1995). *New foundations for scientific and behavioral research: The heuristic paradigm.* Boston: Allyn and Bacon.

Van Den Bergh, N. (Ed.). (1995). *Feminist practice in the 21st century.* Washington, DC: NASW Press.

Weaver, H. (1998). "Indigenous people in a multicultural society: Unique issues for human services." *Social Work, 43*(3): 203–211.

Weaver, H. N. (1999). "Indigenous people and the social work profession: Defining culturally competent services." *Social Work, 44*(3): 217.

Weick, Ann. (1991)."The place of science in social work." *Journal of Sociology and Social Welfare, 18*(4): 13–34.

Williams, C. (2006). "The epistemology of cultural competence." *Families in Society, 87*(2): 111–143.

## References for Chapter 4

Abrams, L., & Moio, J. (2009). Critical race theory and the cultural competence dilemma in social work education. *Journal of Social Work Education, 45*(2), 245–261.

Anderson, R., & Carter, I. (1990). *Human behavior in the social environment: A social systems approach* (4th ed.). New York: Aldine de Gruyter.

Anderson, R., Carter, I., & Lowe, G. (1999). *Human Behavior in the social environment: A social systems approach* (5th ed.). New York: Aldine de Gruyter.

Bengston, V., & Allen, K. (1993). The life course perspective applied to families over time. In P. Boss, W. Dogherty, R. LaRossa, W. Schumm, & S. Steinmetz (Eds.), *Sourcebook of family theories and methods: A contextual approach*. New York: Plenum.

Bergen, D. (1994). *Assessment methods for infants and toddlers: Transdisciplinary team approaches*. New York: Teachers College Press, Columbia University.

Berman, M. (1996, Winter). The shadow side of systems theory. *Journal of Humanistic Psychology, 36*(1), 28–54.

Besthorn, F., & McMillen, D. (2002). The oppression of women and nature: Ecofeminism as a framework for an expanded ecological social work. *Families in Society, 83*(3), 221–232.

Bränström, R., Kvillemo, P., & Moskowitz, J. (2012). A randomized study of the effects of mindfulness training on psychological well-being and symptoms of stress in patients treated for cancer at 6-month follow-up. *International Journal of Behavioral Medicine, 19*(4), 535–542. doi: 10.1007/s12529-011-9192-3

Canda, E. R. (1989). Religious content in social work education: A comparative approach. *Journal of Social Work Education, 25*(1), 36–45.

Cole, E., & Omari, S. (2003). Race, class and the dilemmas of upward mobility for African Americans. *Journal of Social Issues, 59*(4), 785–802.

Collins, P. H. (1990). *Black feminist thought: Knowledge, consciousness, and the politics of empowerment*. Cambridge: Unwin Hyman, Inc.

Cowger, C. D. (1994). "Assessing client strengths: Clinical assessment for client empowerment." *Social Work, 39*(3): 262–268.

Cowley, A.-D. S., & Derezotes, D. (1994). *Transpersonal psychology and social work education*. Available from EBSCOhost a9h (10437797). Retrieved on February 24, 2014, from Routledge: http://0-search.ebscohost. com.library.uark.edu/login.aspx?direct=true&db=a9h&AN=9502011998&site=ehost-live&scope=site

CSWE. (2008). *Educational policy and accreditation standards*. Alexandria, VA: Author.

DeJong, P., & Miller, S. D. (1995, November). How to interview for client strengths. *Social Work, 40*(6) 729–736.

Gaia Hypothesis: Section 3: Dr. Lynn Margulis: Microbiological Collaboration of the Gaia Hypothesis. (1996). Retrieved April 12, 2014, from http://www.mountainman.com.au/gaia.html

George, L. (1996). Missing links: The case for a social psychology of the life. *Gerontologist, 36*(2), 248–255.

Germain, C. (1979). *Social work practice: People and environments, an ecological perspective*. New York: Columbia University.

Germain, C. (1991). *Human behavior in the social environment: An ecological view*. New York: Columbia University Press.

Gleick, J. (1987). *Chaos: The making of a new science*. New York: Penguin Books.

Gray, M. (2011). Back to Basics: A Critique of the Strengths Perspective in Social Work. *Families in Society, 92*(1), 5–11. doi: 10.1606/1044-3894.4054.

Gray, M., Coates, J., & Hetherington, T. (Eds.). (2012). *Environmental social work*. London: Routledge.

Hwang, Y.-S., & Kearney, P. (2013). A systematic review of mindfulness intervention for individuals with developmental disabilities: Long-term practice and long lasting effects. *Research in Developmental Disabilities, 34*(1), 314–326. doi: 10.1016/j.ridd.2012.08.008

Hyland, T. (2012). Mindfulness and the myth of mental illness: Implications for theory and practice. *Contemporary Buddhism, 13*(2), 177–192. doi: 10.1080/14639947.2012.716705

Krippner, S. (1994, Summer). Humanistic psychology and chaos theory: The third revolution and the third force. *Journal of Humanistic Psychology, 34*(3), 48–61.

Lang, A. J., Strauss, J. L., Bomyea, J., Bormann, J. E., Hickman, S. D., Good, R. C., et al. (2012). The theoretical and empirical basis for meditation as an intervention for PTSD. *Behavior Modification, 36*(6), 759–786. doi: 10.1177/0145445512441200

Lovelock, J. (2000). *Gaia: A new look at life on earth* [E-reader version]. Retrieved from http://www.amazon.com/gp/product/B005EXD2T4/ref=wms_ohs_product?ie=UTF8&psc=1

Lynn, M. (2004). Inserting the 'race' into critical pedagogy: An analysis of 'race-based epistemologies. *Educational Philosophy & Theory, 36*(2), 153–165.

Martin, P. Y., & O'Connor, G. G. (1989). *The social environment: Open systems applications.* White Plains, NY: Longman, Inc.

McGarrigle, T., & Walsh, C. (2011). Mindfulness, self-care, and wellness in social work: Effects of contemplative training. *Journal of Religion & Spirituality in Social Work: Social Thought, 30*(3), 212–233.

Miovic, M. (2004). An introduction to spiritual psychology: Overview of the literature, East and West. *Harvard Review of Psychiatry, 12*(2), 105–115.

Murphy, Y., Christy-McMullin, K., Stauss, K., & Schriver, J. (2010). Multi-systems life course: A new practice perspective and its application in advanced practice with racial and ethnic populations. *Journal of Human Behavior in the Social Environment, 20*(5), 672–687.

Murphy, Y., Hunt, V., Zajicek, A., Norris, A., & Hamilton, L. (2009). *Incorporating intersectionality in social work practice, research, policy, and education.* Washington, DC: NASW Press.

Newman, B., & Newman, P. (1991). *Development through life: A psychosocial approach* (5th ed.). Pacific Grove, CA: Brooks/Cole Publishing Company.

Pastrana, A. (2004). Black Identity Constructions: Inserting Intersectionality, Bisexuality, and (Afro-) Latinidad into Black Studies. *Journal of African American Studies, 8*(1/2), 74–89.

Pharr, Suzanne. (1988). Homophobia: *A Weapon of Sexism.* Inverness, CA: Chardon, Press.

Saleebey, D. (1996, May). The strengths perspective in social work practice: Extensions and cautions. *Social Work, 41*(3), 296–305.

Saleebey, D. (1997). Introduction: Power in the people. In D. Saleebey (Ed.). *The strengths perspective in social work practice* (2nd ed., pp. 3–19). New York: Longman.

Scannapieco, M., and Jackson, S. (1996). Kinship care: The African American response to family preservation. *Social Work, 41*(2): 190–196.

Schiele, J. H. (2007). Implications of the equality-of-oppressions paradigm for curriculum content on people of color. *Journal of Social Work Education, 43*(1), 83–100.

Dr. Lynn Margulis. (1996). Microbiological Collaboration of the Gaia Hypothesis. *In The Gaia Hypothesis* (Section 3). Retrieved on April 12, 2014, from http://www.mountainman.com.au/gaia.html

Sermabeikian, P. (1994). Our clients, ourselves: The spiritual perspective and social work practice. *Social Work, 39*(2), 178–183.

Stewart, A., & McDermott, C. (2004). Gender in psychology. *Annual Review of Psychology, 55*(1), 519–544.

Swigonski, M. E. (1993, Summer). Feminist standpoint theory and the questions of social work research. *Affilia, 8*(2), 171–183.

Walsh, R., & Vaughan, F. (1994). The worldview of Ken Wilber. *Journal of Humanistic Psychology, 34*(2), 6–21.

Whitechurch, G. G., & Constantine, L. L. (1993). Systems Theory. In P. G. Boss et al. (Eds.), *Sourcebook of family theories and methods: A contextual approach.* New York: Plenum Press.

Yosso, T. (2005). Whose culture has capital? A critical race theory discussion of community cultural wealth. *Race, Ethnicity and Education, 8*(1), 69–91.

## References for Chapter 5

Achenbaum, W. A., & Bengtson, V. L. (1994). Re-engaging the disengagement theory of aging: On the history and assessment of theory development in gerontology. *The Gerontologist, 34*(6), 756–763.

Bergen, D. (1994). *Assessment methods for infants and toddlers: Transdisciplinary team approaches.* New York: Teachers College Press, Columbia University.

Berzoff, J. (1989). From separation to connection: Shifts in understanding. *Affilia, 4*(1), 45–58.

Bloom, M. (Eds.). (1985). *Life span development* (2nd ed.). New York: MacMillan.

Bronfenbrenner, U. (1977). Toward an experimental ecology of human development. *American Psychologist, 32*(7), 513–531. doi: 10.1037/0003-066X.32.7.513.

CSWE. (2008). *Educational Policy and Accreditation Standards.* Alexandria, VA: Author.

Cumming E. and Henry W., *Growing Old: The Process of Disengagement.* Basic Books, New York, 1961. (Reprint: Arno, New York, 1979, ISBN 0405 118147.).

D'Augelli, A. R. (1994). Identity development and sexual orientation: Toward a model of lesbian, gay, and bisexual development. In E. J. Trickett, R. J. Watts, & D. Birman (Eds.), *Human diversity: Perspectives on people in context* (pp. 312–333). San Francisco: Jossey-Bass.

Erikson, E. H. (1950). *Childhood and society.* New York: W. W. Norton and Company, Inc.

Erikson, E. H. (1963). *Childhood and society* (2nd ed.). New York: W. W. Norton and Company, Inc.

Erikson, E. H. (1968). *Identity: Youth and crisis.* New York: W. W. Norton and Company, Inc.

Gardner, H. (1993). *Multiple intelligences: The theory in practice.* New York: Basic Books.

Gemmill, G., & Oakley, J. (1992). Leadership an alienating social myth? *Human Relations, 45*(2), 113–139.

Gilligan, C. (1982). *In a different voice: Psychological theory and women's development.* Cambridge: Harvard University Press.

Green, M. (1989). *Theories of human development: A comparative approach.* Englewood Cliffs, NJ: Prentice Hall.

Healy, W., Bronner, A., & Bowers, A. M. (1930). *The structure and meaning of psychoanalysis as related to personality and behavior.* New York: Alfred A. Knopf.

Helms, J. E. (1994). The conceptualization of racial identity and other racial constructs. In E. J. Trickett, R. J. Watts, & D. Birman (Eds.), *Human diversity: Perspectives on people in context* (pp. 285–311). San Francisco: Jossey-Bass.

Herrnstein, R. J., & Murray, C. (1994). *The bell curve: Intelligence and class structure in American life.* New York: Free Press.

Jendrek, M. P. (1994). Grandparents who parent their grandchildren: Circumstances and decisions. *The Gerontologist, 34*(2), 206–216.

Levinson, D. J. (1986). A conception of adult development. *American Psychologist, 41*(1), 3–13.

Levinson, D. J. (1996). *The seasons of a woman's life.* New York: Knopf.

Levinson, D. J., Darrow, C. N., Klein, E. B., Levinson, M. H., & McKee, B. (1978). *The seasons of a man's life.* New York: Alfred A. Knopf.

Loevinger, J. (1987). *Paradigms of personality.* New York: W. H. Freeman and Company.

Miller, J. B. (1986). *Toward a new psychology of women.* Boston: Beacon.

Miller, J. B. (1991). The development of women's sense of self. In J. Jordan, A. Kaplan, J. B. Miller, I. Stiver, & J. Surrey (Eds.), *Women's growth in connection: Writings from the stone center* (pp. 51–66). New York: Guilford Press.

Miller, R. L. (1992). The human ecology of multiracial identity. In M. P. P. Root (Ed.), *Racially mixed people in America* (pp. 24–36). Newbury Park, CA: Sage.

Parks, E., Carter, R., & Gushue, G. (1996, July/August). At the crossroads: Racial and womanist identity development in black and white women. *Journal of Counseling and Development, 74,* 624–631.

Pharr, S. (1988). *Homophobia: A weapon of sexism.* Inverness, CA: Chardon Press.

Richards, R. (1996, Spring). Does the lone genius ride again? Chaos, creativity, and community. *Journal of Humanistic Psychology, 36*(2), 44–60.

Spencer, M. B. (1990). Development of minority children: An introduction. *Child Development, 61,* 267–269.

Spencer, M. B., & Markstrom-Adams, C. (1990). Identity processes among racial and ethnic minority children in America. *Child Development, 61,* 290–310.

Steenbarger, B. (1991). All the world is not a stage: Emerging contextualist themes in counseling and development. *Journal of Counseling and Development, 70,* 288.

Szasz, T. S. (1961). *The myth of mental illness: Foundations of a theory of personal conduct.* New York: Harper and Row Publishers, Inc.

Tornstam, L. (1999/2000, Winter). Transcendence in later life. *Generations, 23*(4), 10–14.

Trickett, E. J., Watts, R. J. and Birman, D. (Eds.). (1994). *Human diversity: Perspectives on people in context.* San Francisco: Jossey-Bass.

University of Arkansas Nursery School. (1996, September). *Play: Typescript.* Fayetteville, AR: Author.

Weick, A. (1981). Reframing the person-in-environment perspective. *Social Work, 26*(2), 140.

Weick, A. (1991). The place of science in social work. *Journal of Sociology and Social Welfare, 18,* 13–33.

Wheeler-Scruggs, K. S. (2008). Do lesbians differ from heterosexual men and women in Levinsonian phases of adult development? *Journal of Counseling & Development, 86*(1), 39–46.

## References for Chapter 6

Abrams, L., & Gibson, P. (2007). Reframing multicultural education: Teaching white privilege in the social work curriculum. *Journal of Social Work Education, 43*(1), 147–160.

Americans with Disabilities Act of 1990, Title I, Pub. L. No. 101-336, § 101 (1990).

ADA AMENDMENTS ACT OF 2008, http://www.eeoc.gov/laws/statutes/adaaa.cfm, Pub. L. No. p. 110-325 (S 3406) § SEC. 3. CODIFIED FINDINGS (U. S. Equal Employment Opportunity Commission 2008 September 25, 2008).

Aldarondo, F. (2001). Racial and ethnic identity model, and their application: Counseling U.S. biracial individuals. *Journal of Mental Health Counseling, 23*(3), 238–255.

Andrews, A., & Ben-Arieh, A. (1999). Measuring and monitoring children's well-being across the world. *Social Work, 44*(2), 105–115.

Belenky, M. F., Clinchy, B. M., Goldberger, N. R., & Tarule, J. M. (1986). *Women's ways of knowing: The development of self, voice, and mind*. New York. Basic Books, Inc.

Bent-Goodley, T. B. (2005). An African-Centered approach to domestic violence. *Families in Society, 86*(2), 197.

Bower, B. (1992). Gene influence tied to sexual orientation. *Science News, 141*(1), 6.

Burgess, C. (2000). Internal and external stress factors associated with the identity development of transgendered youth. *Journal of Gay and Lesbian Social Services, 10*(3/4), 35–47.

Burdge, B. J. (2007). Bending gender, ending gender: Theoretical foundations for social work practice with the transgender community. *Social Work, 52*(3), 243.

Cass, V. C. (1984). Homosexual identity formation: Testing a theoretical model. *Journal of Sex Research, 20*(2), 143–167.

Chodorow, N. (1978). *The reproduction of mothering: Psychoanalysis and the sociology of gender*. Berkeley: University of California Press.

Coleman-Jensen, A., Nord, M., & Singh, A. (2013, September). *Household food security in the United States in 2012*. (Economic Research Report (ERR 155). Washington, DC U.S. Department of Agriculture.

Collins, P. H. (1990). *Black feminist thought: Knowledge, consciousness, and the politics of empowerment*. Cambridge: Unwin Hyman, Inc.

Cross, W. E. (1971). The Negro to Black experience: Towards a psychology of Black liberation. *Black World, 20*(9), 13–27.

Department of Justice. (2010). *Americans with Disabilities Act Title III regulations: Nondiscrimination on the basis of disability by public accommodations and in commercial facilities*. Retrieved April 24, 2014, from http://www.ada.gov/regs2010/titleIII_2010/titleIII_2010_regulations.htm

D'Augelli, A. R. (1994). Identity development and sexual orientation: Toward a model of lesbian, gay, and bisexual development. In Trickett, E. J., Watts, R. J., and Birman, D. (Eds.). *Human diversity: Perspectives on people in context*. San Francisco: Jossey-Bass.

Eliason, M. J. (1996). Working with lesbian, gay, and bisexual people: Reducing negative stereotypes via inservice education. *Journal of Nursing Staff Development, 12*(3): 127–132.

Evans-Campbell, T., Fredriksen-Goldsen, K., Walters, K., & Stately, A. (2007). Caregiving exeriences among American Indian two-spirit men and women: Contemporary and historical roles. *Journal of Gay and Lesbian Social Services, 18*(3/4), 75–92.

Fong, R., Spickard, P. R., & Ewalt, P. L. (1995). A Multiracial Reality: Issues for Social Work, Editorial. *Social Work*, pp. 725–728.

Franklin, A. (1999). Invisibility syndrome and racial identity development in psychotherapy and counseling African American men. *Counseling Psychologist, 27*(6), 761–793.

Gardner, H. (1983). *Frames of mind: The theory of multiple intelligences*. New York: Basic Books.

Gardner, H. (1993). *Multiple intelligences: The theory in practice*. New York: Basic Books.

Gates, G. (2006). *Same-sex couples and the gay, lesbian, bisexual population: New estimates from the American Community Survey*. Los Angeles: Williams Institute on Sexual Orientation Law and Public Policy, UCLA School of Law.

Gates, G. (2011). *How many people are lesbian, gay, bisexual, and transgender?* Los Angeles: The Williams Institue, UCLA School of Law, 8.

Gilligan, C. (1982). *In a different voice: Psychological theory and women's development*. Cambridge: Harvard University Press.

Goswami, A. (1996). Creativity and the quantum: A unified theory of creativity. *Creativity Research Journal, 9*(1), 47–61. doi: 10.1207/s15326934crj0901_5

Graham, M. (1999). The African-centred worldview: Developing a paradigm for social work. *British Journal of Social Work, 29,* 251–267.

Greene, D. C., & Britton, P. J. (2012). Stage of sexual minority identity formation: The impact of shame, internalized homophobia, ambivalence over emotional expression, and personal mastery [Article]. *Journal of Gay & Lesbian Mental Health, 16*(3), 188–214. doi: 10.1080/19359705.2012.671126

Hammack, P. L. (2005). An integrative paradigm. *Human Development, 48*(5), 267.

Harding, S. (1986). *The science question in feminism*. Ithaca, NY: Cornell University Press.

Harvey, A. R. (2001). Individual and family intervention skills with African Americans: An Africentric approach. In R. Fkong & S. Furuto (Eds.), *Culturally competent practice: Skills, interventions, and evaluations (pp. 225-240)*. New York: Haworth.

Harvey, A. R., & Hill, R. B. (2004). Africentric youth and family rites of passage program: Promoting resilience among at-risk African American youths. *Social Work, 49,* 65–74.

Helms, J. E. (1994). The conceptualization of racial identity and other 'racial' constructs. In E. J. Trickett, R. J. Watts, & D. Birman (Eds.), *Human diversity: Perspectives on people in context*. San Francisco: Jossey-Bass, 285–312.

Hoefer, R., & Curry, C. (2012). Food security and social protection in the United States. *Journal of Policy Practice, 11*(1–2), 59–76.

Jackson, K. F., & Samuels, G. M. (2011). Multiracial competence in social work: Recommendations for culturally attuned work with multiracial people. *Social Work, 56*(3), 235–245. doi: 10.1093/sw/56.3.235

Jacobs, J. (1992). Identity development in biracial children. In M. P. P. Root (Ed.), *Racially mixed people in America*. Newbury Park, CA: Sage, 190–206.

Jordan, J., Kaplan, A., Miller, J. B., Stiver, I., & Surrey, J. (1991). *Women's growth in connection: Writings of the Stone Center*. New York: Guilford Press.

Keller, E. F. (1985). *Reflections on gender and science*. New Haven: Yale University Press.

Kerwin, C., & Ponterotto, J. G. (1995). Biracial identity development: Theory and research. In J. G. Ponterotto, J. M. Casas, L. A. Suzuki & C. M. Alexander (Eds.), *Handbook of multicultural counseling* (pp. 199–217). Thousand Oaks, CA: SAGE Publications, Ltd.

Kich, G. K. (1992). The developmental process of asserting a biracial, bicultural identity. In M. P. P. Root (Ed.). *Racially mixed people in America*. Newbury Park, CA: Sage, 304–320.

Kimmel, M. S., & Messner, M. A. (Eds.). (1995). *Men's lives* (3rd ed.). Boston: Allyn and Bacon.

Kinsey, A. C. (1948/1998) *Sexual behavior in the human male*. Philadelphia: W. B. Saunders; Bloomington: Indiana University Press.

Kopels, S. (1995, Fall). The Americans with Disabilities Act: A tool to combat poverty. *Journal of Social Work Education, 31*(3), 337–346.

Levy, B. (1995). Violence against women. In Van Den Bergh, N. (Ed.), *Feminist practice for the 21st century*. Washington, DC: NASW, 312–329.

Malone, M., McKinsey, P., Thyer, B., & Starks, E. (2000). Social work early intervention for young children with developmental disabilities. *Health and Social Work, 25*(3), 169–180.

Martin, E. P., & Martin, J. M. (2002). *Spirituality and the Black helping tradition in social work.* Washington, DC: NASW Press.

McQuaide, S. (1998). Women at midlife. *Social Work, 43*(1), 21–31.

Miller, J. B. (1976). *Toward a new psychology of women.* Boston: Beacon Press.

Miller, J. B. (1986). *Toward a new psychology of women* (2nd ed.). Boston: Beacon Press.

Myers, L. J., Speight, S., Highlen, P., Cox, C., Reynolds, A., Adams, E., et al. (1991). Identity development and worldview: Toward an optimal conceptualization. *Journal of Counseling and Development, 70,* 54–63.

NOMAS (Producer). (n.d.).NOMAS Brochure. Retrieved from http://site.nomas.org/wp-content/uploads/2012/05/BrochureBordered.pdf

Orlin, M. (1995). The Americans with Disabilities Act: Implications for social services. *Social Work, 40*(2), 233–234. Reprinted with permission.

Parham, T. (1999). Invisibility syndrome in African descent people: Understanding the cultural manifestations of the struggle for self-affirmation. *Counseling Psychologist, 27*(6), 794–801.

Parks, E. E., Carter, R. T., & Gushue, G. V. (1996, July/August). At the crossroads: Racial and womanist identity development in Black and White women. *Journal of Counseling and Development, 74,* 624–631.

Pierce, C. M. (1988). Stress in the workplace. In A. F. Coner-Edwards & J. Spurlock (Eds.), *Black families in crisis: The middle class* (pp. 27–34) New York: Brunner/Mazel.

Pierce, C. M. (1992, August). *Racism.* Paper presented at the conference on the Black Family in America, New Haven, CT.

Rank, M., & Hirschl, T. (1999). The likelihood of poverty across the American adult life span. *Social Work, 44*(3), 201–216.

Rothblum, E. D. (1994). Transforming lesbian sexuality. *Psychology of Women Quarterly,* 18.

Sanders Thompson, V. (2001). The complexity of African American racial identification. *Journal of Black Studies, 32*(2), 155–165.

Schiele, J. H. (1997). The contour and meaning of Afrocentric social work. *Journal of Black Psychology, 27,* 800–819.

Schroots, J. (1996). Theoretical developments in the psychology of aging. *The Gerontologist, 36*(6), 742–748.

Seipel, M. (1999). Social consequences of malnutrition. *Social Work, 44*(5), 416–425.

Sellers, R., Smith, M., Shelton, J., Rowley, S., & Chavous, T. (1998). Multidimensional model of racial identity: A reconceptualization of African American racial identity. *Personality and Social Psychology Review (Lawrence Erlbaum Associates), 2*(1), 18.

Spencer, M. B., & Markstrom-Adams, C. (1990). Identity processes among racial and ethnic minority children in America. *Child Development, 61,* 290–310.

Stack, C. B. (1986). The culture of gender: Women and men of color. *Signs, 11*(2), 321–324.

Vrangalova, Z., & Savin-Williams, R. (2012). Mostly heterosexual and mostly gay/lesbian: Evidence for new sexual orientation identities [Article].*Archives of Sexual Behavior, 41*(1), 85–101. doi: 10.1007/s10508-012-9921-y

Yeh, C. (1999). Invisibility and self-construct in African American men: Implications for training and practice. *Counseling Psychologist, 27*(6), 810–819.

Wastell, C. A. (1996). Feminist developmental theory: Implications for counseling. *Journal of Counseling and Development, 74,* 575–581.

## References for Chapter 7

Al-Krenawi, A., & Graham, J. (2000). "Islamic theology and prayer." *International Social Work, 43*(3), 289.

American Association of Retired Persons. (2012). *Putting the Parent in Grandparents*. Retrieved March 31, 2013, from http://www.aarp.org/home-family/friends-family/info-08-2012/putting-parent-in-grandparent-fl1845.html

American Immigration Lawyers Association. (1999). *American is immigration*. [Web site]. American Immigration Lawyers Association. Available: http://www.aila.org/aboutimmigration.html [2000, 3/20/00].

Annie E. Casey Foundation, 2012 Annie E. Casey Foundation. (2012). *Stepping up for kids: what government and communities should do to support kinship families. Policy report: Kids count* (pp. 1–20). Baltimore, MD: Author.

Atkin, K. (1991). "Health, Illness, Disability and Black Minorities: A Speculative Critique of Present Day Discourse." *Disability, Handicap & Society, 6*(1), 37–47. doi:10.1080/02674649166780031

Ayala-Quillen, B. A. (1998). "The Adoption and Safe Families Act of 1997 kinship care report: An analysis of key areas." *Protecting Children, 14*(3), 12–14.

Bailey, D., Skinner, D., Rodriquez, P., Gut, D., & Correa, V. (1999). "Awareness, use, and satisfaction with services for Latino parents of young children with disabilities." *Exceptional Children, 65*(3), 367–381.

Bengston, V. L., & Allen, K. R. (1993). "The life course perspective applied to families over time." In P. G. Boss, Doherty, W. J., LaRossa, R., Schuman, W. R., and Steinmetz, S.K. (Eds.). *Sourcebook of family theories and methods: A contextual approach.*
New York: Plenum Press.

Billingsley, Andrew. (1968). *Black families in white America*. Englewood Cliffs, NJ: Prentice Hall.

Blocklin, M., Davis, K., Kelly, E., King, R., & Fox, K. (2012). *Work Characteristics and Barriers to Family Formation*. Paper presented at the Work and Family Researchers Network Conference, Philadelphia, PA.

Boyd-Franklin, Nancy. (1993). "Race, class and poverty." In *Normal family processes*, Walsh, Froma. (Ed.). New York: Guilford.

Carter, B., & McGoldrick, M. (1999). Eds. *The Expanded Family Life Cycle*. (3rd ed.). Boston: Allyn and Bacon.

Chesters, J. (2013). "Gender convergence in core housework hours: Assessing the relevance of earlier approaches for explaining current trends." *Journal of Sociology (Melbourne, Vic.), 49*(1), 78–96. doi: 10.1177/1440783311427482

CNN (Producer). (2009, May 27, 2009) "Lawmakers approve same-sex marriage in N.H., Maine." Podcast retrieved from http://www.cnn.com/2009/POLITICS/05/06/maine.same.sex.marriage/.

Crawford, J.M. (1999). "Co-parent adoptions by same-sex couples: From loophole to law. Families in Society." The *Journal of Contemporary Human Services, 80*, 271–278.

Demo, D. H., & Allen, K. R. (1996). "Diversity within lesbian and gay families: Challenges and implications for family theory and research." *Journal of Social and Personal Relationships, 13*(3), 415–434.

Devore, Wynetta, & Schlesinger, Elfriede G. (1991). *Ethnicsensitive social work practice* (3rd ed.). New York: Macmillan Publishing Company.

Dubowitz, H. (1994). "Kinship care: Suggestions for future research." *Child Welfare, 73*, 553–564.

Duvall, Evelyn M. (1971). *Family development* (4th ed.). Philadelphia: J. B. Lippincott Company.

Duvall, Evelyn M. (1988). "Family development's first forty years." *Family Relations, 37*, 127–134.

English, Richard. (1991). "Diversity of worldviews among African American families." In Everett, Joyce, Chipungu, Sandra, and Leashore, Bogart, eds. *Child welfare: An Africentric perspective*. New Brunswick, NJ: Rutgers University Press.

Elder, G. H. (1998). "The life course as developmental theory." *Child Development, 69*(1), 1–12.

Espinoza, C. (2012). Millennial Values and Boundaries in the Classroom. *New Directions for Teaching & Learning, 2012*(131), 29–41. doi: 10.1002/tl.20025

Evans, R. R., & Forbes, L. (2012). "Mentoring the "Net Generation": Faculty Perspectives in Health Education." *College Student Journal, 46*(2), 397–404.

Ferree, Myra M. (1990). "Beyond separate spheres: Feminism and family research." *Journal of Marriage and the Family, 52,* 866–884.

First Focus. (2012). *America's Report Card 2012: Children in the U.S.* Retrieved March 6, 2014, from http://sparkaction.org/resources/124188

Fong, R., Spickard, P. R., & Ewalt, P. L. (1996). "A multiracial reality: Issues for social work." In Ewalt, P. L., Freeman, E. M., Kirk, S. A., & Poole, D. L. *Multicultural issues in social work.* Washington, DC: NASW.

Fujiura, G. T., & Yamaki, K. (1997). "Analysis of ethnic variations in developmental disability prevalence and household economic status." *Mental Retardation, 35*(4), 286–294.

Fujiura, G. T., & Yamaki, K. (2000). "Trends in demography of childhood poverty and disability." *Exceptional Children, 66,* 187–199.

Geen, R. (2000). "In the interest of children: Rethinking federal and state policies affecting kinship care." *Policy & Practice of Public Human Services, 58*(1), 19–27.

Goyer, A. (2010). *More Grandparents Raising Grandkids.* Retrieved March 31, 2013, from http://www.aarp.org/relationships/grandparenting/info-12-2010/more_grandparents_raising_grandchildren.html

Hall, R., & Livingston, J. (2006). "Mental health practice with Arab families: The implications of spirituality vis-à-vis Islam." *American Journal of Family Therapy, 34*(2), 139–150.

Harrison, Algea, Wilson, Melvin, Pine, Charles, Chan, Samuel, and Buriel, Raymond. (1990). "Family ecologies of ethnic minority children." *Child Development, 61,* 347–362.

Harry, B. (2002). "Trends and issues in serving culturally diverse families of children with disabilities." *The Journal of Special Education, 36*(3), 131–138.

Hartman, Ann, and Laird, Joan. (1983). *Family-centered social work practice.* New York: Free Press.

Healthychildren.org. (2005). *Gay and Lesbian Parents.* Retrieved March 30, 2013, from http://www.healthychildren.org/English/family-life/family-dynamics/types-of-families/pages/Gay-and-Lesbian-Parents.aspx

Hernandez, M., & McGoldrick, M. (1999). "Migration and the life cycle." In B. Carter and M. McGoldrick. (Eds.). *The expanded family life cycle: Individual, family, and social perspectives* (3rd ed., p. 541). Boston: Allyn and Bacon.

Hetherington, E. Mavis, Law, Tracy, & O'Connor, Thomas. (1993) "Divorce, changes, and new chances." In *Normal family processes.* Walsh, Froma. (Ed.). New York: Guilford.

Hill, Reuben. (1986). "Life cycle stages for types of single parent families: Of family development theory." *Family Relations, 35,* 19–29.

Ho, Man Kueng. (Ed.). (1987). *Family therapy with ethnic minorities.* Newbury Park, CA: Sage Publications.

Hodge, D. (2005). "Social work and the house of Islam: Orienting practitioners to the beliefs and values of Muslims in the United States." *Social Work, 50*(2), 162–173.

Hollingsworth, L. (1998). "Promoting same-race adoption for children of color." *Social Work, 43*(2), 104–116.

Jendrek, M. P. (1994). "Grandparents who parent their grandchildren: Circumstances and decisions." *The Gerontologist, 34*(2), 206–216.

Kaye, H. S., LaPlante, M. P., Carlson, D., & Wenger, B. L. (1996) Trends in disability rates in the United States, 1970-1994. *Disability Statistics Abstract*, Number 17. Washington, DC: National Institute on Disability and Rehabilitation Research. (ERIC Document Reproduction Service No. ED 410 696)

Kennedy, Carroll E. (1978): *Human development: The adult years and aging.* New York: Macmillan Publishing Co., Inc.

Laird, Joan. (1993). "Lesbian and gay families." In *Normal family processes.* Walsh, Froma. (Ed.). New York: Guilford.

Lichy, J. (2012). "Towards an international culture: Gen Y students and SNS?." *Active Learning in Higher Education, 13*(2), 101–116. doi: 10.1177/1469787412441289

Lofquist, D., Lugaila, T., O'Connell, M., & Feliz, S. (2012). *Households and Families: 2010* (C2010BR-14). Washington, MD: U.S. Census Bureau.

Logan, Sadye, Freeman, Edith, and McRoy, Ruth. (Eds.). (1990). *Social work practice with Black families: A culturally specific perspective*. New York: Longman.

Malone, M., McKinsey, P., Thyer, B., & Straka, E. (2000). "Social work early intervention for young children with developmental disabilities." *Health and Social Work, 25*(3), 169–180.

Martin, Joanne, & Martin, Elmer P. (1985). *The helping tradition in the black family and community*. Silver Spring, MD: NASW.

Mather, M. (2009). *Children in Immigrant Families Chart NewPath*. Washington, DC.

McDaniel, S.H., Cambell, T.L., Hepworth, J., & Lorenz, A. (2005). *Family-oriented primary care (2nd ed.)*. New York, NY: Springer.

McGoldrick, Monica, Pearce, John, & Giordano, Joseph. (Eds.). (1982). *Ethnicity and family therapy*. New York: Guilford Press.

Meesan, W., & Rauch, J. (2005). Gay marriage, same-sex parenting, and Americas children. *Marriage and Child Wellbeing, 15*(2). Retrieved from The Future of Children: Princeton-Brookings website: http://futureofchildren.org/publications/journals/article/index.xml?ournalid=37&articleid=108&sectionid=699

Mosby's Medical Dictionary. (2009). *Family of Procreation* (8th ed.). Retrieved March 31, 2013, from http://medical-dictionary.thefreedictionary.com/family+of+procreation

Myers, Linda. (1985). "Transpersonal psychology: The role of the Afrocentric paradigm." *The Journal of Black Psychology*. 12(1), 31–42.

Parker, K., & Wang, W. (2013). Modern parenthood: Roles of moms and dads converge as they balance work and family. *Pew Research: Social and Demographic Trends*. 68(2): 151–170.

Park, J., Turnbull, A., & Turnbull III, H. (2002). "Impacts of poverty on quality of life in families of children with disabilities." *Exceptional Children, 68*(2): 151–170. http://www.pewsocialtrends.org/2013/03/14/modern-parenthood-roles-of-moms-and-dads-converge-as-they-balance-work-and-family/

Pequegnat, W., & Bray, J.H. (1997). Families and HIV/AIDS: Introduction to the special section. *Journal of Family Psychology, 11*(1), 3–10.

Perren, E., & Siegel, B. (2013). "Promoting the Well-Being of Children Whose Parents are Gay or Lesbian." *Pediatrics, 131*(4). Retrieved March 6, 2014, from Pediatrics website: http://pediatrics.aappublications.org/content/early/2013/03/18/peds.2013-0377

Pew Research Center (Producer). (2010). *Generations 2010* [Research Report]. Retrieved February 8, 2013, from http://pewinternet.org/Reports/2010/Generations-2010/Introduction/Defining-Generations.aspx

Pew Research Center. (2013). "Growing support for gay marriage: Changed minds and changing demographics." *PewResearch: Center for the People and the Press*. Retrieved March 30, 2013, from http://www.people-press.org/2013/03/20/growing-support-for-gay-marriage-changed-minds-and-changing-demographics/

Piotrkowski, Chaya, & Hughes, Diane. (1993). "Dual-earner families in context." In *Normal family processes*. Walsh, Froma, ed. New York: Guilford.

Rehman, T., & Dziegielewski, S. (2003). "Women who choose Islam." *International Journal of Mental Health, 32*(3), 31–49.

Rothausen, T.J. (1999). "'Family' in organizational research: A review and comparison of definitions and measures." *Journal of Organizational Behavior, 20*, 817–836.

Rounds, K. A., Weil, M., & Bishop, K. K. (January 1994). "Practice with culturally diverse families of young children with disabilities." *Families in Society: The Journal of Contemporary Human Services*. 75(1), 3–14.

Scannapieco, M., & Jackson, S. (1996). "Kinship care: The African American response to family preservation." *Social Work, 41*(2), 190–196.

Scanzoni, John, and Marsiglio, William. (1991). "Wider families as primary relationships." *Wider families*. Binghamton, NY: The Haworth Press.

Seelman, K., & Sweeney, S. (1995). The changing universe of disability. *American Rehabilitation, 21*, 2–13

Slater, Suzanne, & Mencher, Julie. (1991). "The lesbian family life cycle: A contextual approach." *American Journal of Orthopsychiatry, 61*(3), 372–382.

Stack, C.B. (1996). *All our kin.* New York, NY: Basic Books.

Staveteig, S., & Wigton, A. (2000). *Racial and ethnic disparities: Key findings from the national survey of America's families.* [Web site]. Urban Institute. Available: http://newfederalism.urban.org/html/series_b/b5/b5.html [2000, 4/8/00].

Time Inc. (2012). *Time Inc. Study Reveals That "Digital Natives" Switch between Devices and Platforms Every Two Minutes, Use Media to Regulate Their Mood.* Retrieved from Time, Inc. website: http://www.timeinc.com/pressroom/detail.php?id=releases/time_inc_study_digital_natives.php

UC Berkeley Gender Equality Resource Center. (n.d.). *Family of Choice.* Retrieved March 13, 2013, from http://geneq.berkeley.edu/lgbt_resources_definiton_of_terms - family_of_choice

Universal Declaration of Human Rights, Resolution 217 A (III), Article 16 § 3 (United Nations December 10, 1948).

U.S. Department of Health & Human Services Administration for Children & Families. (n.d.). Key Elements of Family-Centered Practice. *Child Welfare Information Gateway: Protecting children, strengthening families.* Retrieved March 31, 2013, from https://http://www.childwelfare.gov/famcentered/overview/elements.cfm

Walsh, F. (2003). *Normal Family Processes.* (3rd ed.) New York: Guilford.

Wight, V. R., Bianchi, S. M., & Hunt, B. R. (2013). "Explaining Racial/Ethnic Variation in Partnered Women and Men Housework: Does One Size Fit All?" *Journal of Family Issues, 34*(3), 394–427. doi:10.1177/0192513x12437705

Wilhelmus, M. (1998). "Mediation in kinship care: Another step in the provision of culturally relevant child welfare services." *Social Work, 43*(2), 117–126.

Winokur, M. A., Crawford, G. A., Longobardi, R. C., & Valentine, D. P. (2008). "Matched Comparison of Children in Kinship Care and Foster Care on Child Welfare Outcomes." *Families in Society: The Journal of Contemporary Social Services, 89*(3), 338–346.

Young, N. (2012). "To teach millennials, understand them." *Quill, 100*(2), 12–12.

## References for Chapter 8

Anderson, R., & Carter, I. (1990). *Human behavior in the social environment: A social systems approach* (4th ed.). New York: Aldine de Gruyter.

Attneave, C. (1982). American Indians and Alaska Native families: Emigrants in their own homeland. In M. McGoldrick, J. Pearce, & J. Giordano (Eds.), *Ethnicity and family therapy*. New York: Guilford.

Brown, L. N. (1991). *Groups for growth and change*. New York: Longman.

Bruce, W. T., & Mary Ann, C. J. (1977, December). Stages of small-group development revisited. *Group & Organization Studies, 2, 4*.

Bunch, C., & Fisher, B. (1996, Spring). What future for leadership. *Quest, 2*, 2–13.

Curran, D. J., & Renzetti, C. (1996). *Social problems: Society in crisis* (4th ed.). Boston: Allyn and Bacon

Davis, L. E., Galinsky, M. J., & Schopler, J. H. (1995). RAP: A framework for leadership of multiracial groups. *Social Work, 40*(2), 155–165.

Davis, L. E. (1985). Group work practice with ethnic minorities of color. In M. Sundal et al. (Eds.), *Individual change through small groups* (2nd ed., pp. 324–344). New York: The Free Press.

Estrada, M., Brown, J., & Lee, F. (1995). Who gets the credit? Perceptions of idiosyncrasy credit in work groups. *Small Group Research, 26*(1), 56–76.

Garland, J. A., Jones, H. E., & Kolodny, R. L. (1973). A model for stages of development in social work groups. In S. Bernstein (Ed.), *Explorations in group work: Essays in theory and practice*. Boston: Milford House.

Gastil, J. (1992). A definition of small group democracy. *Small Group Research, 23*(3), 278–301.

Gastil, J. (1994). A definition and illustration of democratic leadership. *Human Relations, 47*(8), 953–975.

Gemmill, G., & Oakley, J. (1992). Leadership: An alienating social myth? *Human Relations, 45*(2), 113–139.

Hare, A. P. (1994). Types of roles in small groups: A bit of history and a current perspective. *Small Group Research, 25*(3), 433–448.

Harris, B. (2010). *7 ways to avoid groupthink*. Retrieved April 17, 2013, from http://critical-thinkers.com/2010/12/7-ways-to-avoid-groupthink/

Harrison, D. A., Price, K. H., & Bell, M. P. (1998). Beyond relational demography: Time and the effects of surface-and deep-level diversity on work group cohesion. *Academy of Management Journal, 41*(1), 96–107.

Hartford, M. E. (1971). *Groups in social work* (pp. 94–137). New York: Columbia University Press.

Janis, I. L. (1982). *Groupthink* (2nd ed.). Boston: Houghton Mifflin.

Johnson, D., & Johnson, F. (1991). *Joining together: Group theory and group skills* (4th ed.). Englewood Cliffs, NJ: Prentice Hall.

Kanter, R. M. (1977). Women in organizations: Sex roles, group dynamics and change strategies. *Beyond sex roles*, 371–386.

Knouse, S., & Dansby, M. (1999). Percentages of workgroup diversity and work-group effectiveness. *The Journal of Psychology, 133*(5), 486–494.

Kolb, J. A., Jin, S., & Song, J. H. (2008). A model of small group facilitator competencies. *Performance Improvement Quarterly, 21*(2), 119–133.

Krech, D., Crutchfield, R. S., & Ballanchey, E. L. Individual in society (2nd ed.). New York: McGraw-Hill, 1962.

Lewis, E. (1992). Regaining promise: Feminist perspectives for social group work practice. *Social Work with Groups, 13*(4), 271–284.

Manz, C. C., & Sims, H. P., Jr. (1982). The potential for "groupthink" in autonomous work groups. *Human Relations, 35*, 773–784

McGoldrick, M., Pearce, J., & Giordano, J. (Eds.). (1982). *Ethnicity and Family Therapy*. New York: Guilford Press.

McLeod, P. L., Lobel, S. A., & Cox, T. H. (1996). Ethnic diversity and creativity in small groups. *Small Group Research, 27*(2), 248–264.

Miranda, S. M. (1994). Avoidance of groupthink: Meeting management using group support systems. *Small Group Research, 25*(1), 105–136.

Mitchell, D. H., & Eckstein, D. (2009). Jury dynamics and decision-making: A prescription for groupthink [Article]. *International Journal of Academic Research, 1*(1), 163-169.

Moorhead, G., Ference, R., & Neck, C. (1991, June). Group Decision Fiascoes Continue: Space Shuttle Challenger and a Revised Groupthink Framework. *Human Relations, 44*(6), 539–550.

Napier, R., & Gershenfeld, M. K. (1985). *Groups, Theory and Experience* (3rd ed.). Boston: Houghton Mifflin Company.

Neck, C. P., & Manz, C. C. (1994). From groupthink to teamthink: Toward the creation of constructive thought patterns in self-managing work teams. *Human Relations, 47*(8), 929–952.

Neck, C. P., & Moorhead, G. (1995). Groupthink remodeled: The importance of leadership, time pressure, and methodical decision-making procedures. *Human Relations, 48*(5), 537–557.

Oetzel, J. (2001). Self-construals, communication processes, and group outcomes in homogeneous and heterogeneous groups. *Small Group Research, 32*(1), 19–54.

Patterson, J. B., McKenzie, B., & Jenkins, J. (1995). Creating accessible groups for individuals with disabilities. *The Journal for Specialists in Group Work, 20*(2), 76–82.

Sabini, J. (1995). *Social psychology* (2nd ed.). New York: W. W. Norton.

Sarri, R. C., & Galinsky, M. J. (1985). A conceptual framework for group development. *Individual Change Through Small Groups, 2*, 71–88.

Scott, M., Hollingshead, A. B., McGrath, J. E., Moreland, R. L., & Rohrliaugh, J. (2004). Interdisciplinary perspectives on small groups. [Article]. *Small Group Research, 35*(1), 3–16. doi: 10.1177/1046496403259753

Sundell, M., Glasser, P., Sarri, R., & Vinter, R. (Eds.). (1985). *Individual change through small groups* (2nd ed.). New York: The Free Press.

Thomas, D. (1999). Cultural diversity and work group effectiveness: An experimental study. *Journal of Cross-Cultural Psychology, 30*(2), 242.

Worchel, S., Wood, W., & Simpson, J. A. (Eds.). (1992). *Group process and productivity.* Newbury Park, CA: SAGE Publications.

## References for Chapter 9

Abrahamsson, B. (1977). *Bureaucracy or participation: The logic of organization.* Beverly Hills: SAGE Publications.

Attneave, C. (1982). American Indians and Alaska Native families: Emigrants in their own homeland. In M. McGoldrick, J. Pearce, & J. Giordano. (Eds.), *Ethnicity and family therapy.* New York: Guilford Press.

Austin, M. J., & Claasen, J. (2008). Impact of organizational change on organizational culture: Implications for introducing evidence-based practice. *Journal of Evidence-Based Social Work, 5*(1/2), 321–359.

Barrett, F. (1995). Creating appreciative learning cultures. *Organizational Dynamics, 24*(2), 36–49.

Burns, C., Barton, K., & Kerby, S. (Producer). (2012, July). *The state of diversity in today's workforce: As our nation becomes more diversity so too does our workforce* [Online Brief]. Retrieved March 15, 2014, from http://www.americanprogress.org/issues/labor/report/2012/07/12/11938/the-state-of-diversity-in-todays-workforce/

Burton, B., & Dunn, C. (1996). Feminist ethics as moral grounding for stakeholder theory. *Business Ethics Quarterly, 6,* 133–147.

Dodge, R., & Robbins, J. (1992). An empirical investigation of the organizational life cycle. *Journal of Small Business Management, 30*(1), 27–37.

Etzioni, A. (1964). *Modern organizations.* Englewood Cliffs, NJ: Prentice Hall.

Gortner, H. F., Mahler, J., & Nicholson, J. (1987). *Organization theory: A public perspective.* Chicago: The Dorsey Press.

Grusky, O., & Miller, G. (Eds.). (1981). *The sociology of organizations: Basic studies* (2nd ed.). New York: The Free Press.

Hanks, S. H. (1990). The organization life cycle: Integrating content and process. *Journal of Small Business Strategy, 1*(1), 1–13.

Hodgetts, R. M., Luthans, F., & Lee, S. M. (1994). New paradigm organizations: From total quality to learning to world class. *Organizational Dynamics, 22*(3), 5–19.

Howard, D., & Hine, D. (1997). The population of organisations life cycle (POLC): Implications for small business assistance programs. *International Small Business Journal, 15*(3), 30–41.

Iannello, K. P. (1992). *Decisions without hierarchy: Feminist interventions in organization theory and practice.* New York: Routledge.

Jawahar, I., & McLaughlin, G. (2001). Toward a descriptive stakeholder theory: An organizational life cycle approach. *The Academy of Management Review, 26*(3), 397–414.

Jones-Burbridge, J. A. (2012). Servant leadership. *Corrections Today, 73*(6), 45–47.

Kopelman, R. E., Prottas, D. J., & Falk, D. W. (2010). Construct validation of a theory X/Y behavior scale. *Leadership & Organization Development Journal, 31*(2), 120–135.

Kouzes, J. M., & Posner, B. Z. (1993). *Credibility: How leaders gain and lose it, why people demand it* [E-reader version]. San Francisco: Jossey-Bass Publibactions.

Liedtka, J. (1996). Feminist morality and competitive reality: a role for an ethic of care? *Business Ethics Quarterly, 6,* 179–200.

March, J. G., & Simon, H.A. (1958). *Organizations.* Oxford, England: Wiley.

Miller, D., & Friesen, P. H. (1980). Momentum and revolution in organizational adaptation. *Academy of Management Journal, 23*(4), 591–614.

Neugeboren, B. (1985). *Organizational policy and practice in the human services.* New York: Longman.

Nixon, R., & Spearmon, M. (1991) *Building a pluralistic workplace.* In Edwards, R. & Yankey, J. (Eds.), Skills for Effective Human Services Management. Silver Spring, MD: National Association of Social Workers, 142–154.

O'Neil, D. A., & Bilimoria, D. (2005). Women's career development phases: Idealism, endurance, and reinvention. *Career Development International, 10*(3), 168.

Ouchi, William G. (1981). *Theory Z*. New York: Avon Books.

Overman, E. S. (1996). The new science of administration: chaos and quantum theory. *Public Administration Review, 56*: 487–491.

Patti, R. (Ed.). (2009). *The handbook of human services management* (2nd ed.). Los Angeles: Sage.

Pugh, D. S., Hickson, D. J., & Hinings, C. R. (Eds.). (1985) *Writers on organizations*. Beverly Hills: SAGE Publications.

Rifkin, J. (1998). A civil education for the twenty-first century: preparing students for a three-sector society. *National Civic Review, 87*, 177–181.

Schein, E. (1992). *Organizational culture and leadership* (2nd ed.). San Francisco: Jossey-Bass.

Schneider, B., Brief, A. P., & Guzzo, R. A. (1996). Creating a climate and culture for sustainable organizational change. *Organizational Dynamics, 24*(4), 7–19.

Senge, P. (1990). *The fifth discipline: The art and practice of the learning organization*. New York: Currency Doubleday.

Shafritz, J. M., & Ott, J. S. (1987). *Classics of organization theory* (2nd ed.). Chicago: The Dorsey Press.

Smothers, J. (2011). Assumption-based leadership: A historical post-hoc conceptualization of the assumptions underlying leadership styles. *Journal of Applied Management and Entrepreneurship, 16*(3), 44–59. doi:10.1108/00251740510634930

Thomas, R. R., Jr. (1990 March–April). From affirmative action to affirming diversity. *Harvard Business Review*, 107–117.

Thomas, R. R., Jr. (1991 Winter) The concept of managing diversity. *The Bureaucrat: The Journal for Public Managers*, 19–22.

Thomas, R. R. (1996). Redefining diversity. *HR Focus, 73*(4), 6–7.

Westen, T. (1998). Can technology save democracy? *National Civic Review, 87*, 47–56.

Wheatley, M., & Kellner-Rogers, M. (1996). Breathing life into organizations. *Public Management, 78*, 10–14.

Zhu, Z. (1999). The practice of multimodal approaches, the challenge of cross-cultural communication, and the search for responses. *Human Relations, 52*(5), 579–607.

## References for Chapter 10

Anderson, R., & Carter, I. (1990). *Human behavior in the social environment* (4th ed.). New York: Aldine De Gruyter.

Aidala, A. A. (1989). Communes and changing family norms: Marriage and lifestyle choice among former members of communal groups. *Journal of Family Issues, 10*(3), 311–338.

Aidala, A. A., & Zablocki, B. D. (1991). The communes of the 1970s: Who joined and why? *Marriage and Family Review, 17*(1–2), 87–116.

John F. Kennedy School of Governmen. (2000). *Better Together: Report of the Saguaro Seminar on Civic Engagement in America*. Harvard University: Cambrige, MA. Retrieved from bettertogether.org

Beverly, S., & Sherraden, M. (1997). *Human capital and social work* (97–2). St. Louis: Washington University George Warren Brown School of Social Work, Center for Social Development.

Bricker-Jenkins, M., & Hooyman, N. R. (Eds.). (1986). *Not for women only: Social work practice for a feminist future*. Silver Spring, MD: National Association of Social Workers, Inc.

Briggs, X. de Soyza. (1997). Social capital and the cities: Advice to change agents. *National Civic Review, 86*, 111–117.

Campbell, C. (1976). *New towns: Another way to live*. Reston, VA: Reston Publishing, Inc.

Collins, P. H. (1990). *Black feminist thought: Knowledge, consciousness, and the politics of empowerment*. Cambridge: Unwin Hyman, Inc.

Connell, J., Kubisch, A., Schorr, A., & Weiss, C. (1995). *New approaches to evaluating community initiatives: Concepts, methods, and contexts*. Washington, DC: Aspen Institute.

Ewalt, P. (1998). The revitalization of impoverished communities. In P. Ewalt, E. Freeman, & D. Poole (Eds.), *Community building: Renewal, well-being, and shared responsibility* (pp. 3–5). Washington, DC: NASW Press.

Feagin, J. R., & Feagin, C. B. (1978). *Discrimination American style: Institutional racism and sexism*. Englewood Cliffs, NJ: Prentice Hall.

Fellin, P. (1993). Reformulation of the context of community based care. *Journal of Sociology and Social Welfare, 20*(2), 57–67.

Germain, C. (1991). *Human behavior in the social environment: An ecological view*. New York: Columbia University Press.

Hamer, D. (2000). Learning from the past: Historic districts and the New Urbanism in the United States. *Planning Perspectives, 15*(2), 107–122. doi: 10.1080/026654300364047

Jepson, E. J., Jr., & Edwards, M. M. (2010). How possible is sustainable urban development? An analysis of planners' perceptions about New Urbanism, smart growth and the ecological city. *Planning Practice & Research, 25*(4), 417–437. doi: 10.1080/02697459.2010.511016

Kanter, R. M. (1977). Communes and commitment. In R. L. Warren (Ed.), *New perspectives on the American community: A book of readings*. Chicago: Rand McNally College Publishing Company, 577–581.

Kuhn, T. S. (1970). *The structure of scientific revolutions* (2nd ed.). Chicago: The University of Chicago Press.

Lappé, F. M., & DuBois, P. M. (1997). Building social capital without looking backward. *National Civic Review, 86*, 119–128.

Logan, J. R. (1988). Realities of black suburbanization. In R. L. Warren & L. Lyon (Eds.), *New perspectives on the American community* (5th ed.). Chicago: The Dorsey Press, 231ff.

Longres, J. (1990). *Human behavior in the social environment*. Itasca, IL: F. E. Peacock.

Louv, R. (1996). The culture of renewal, part I: Characteristics of the community renewal movement. *National Civic Review, 85*, 52–61.

Louv, R. (1997). The culture of renewal, Part 2: Characteristics of the community renewal movement. *National Civic Review, 86*, 97–105.

Mackelprang, R. W., & Salsgiver, R. O. (1996). People with disabilities and social work: historical and contemporary issues. *Social Work, 41*(1), 7–14.

Maybury-Lewis, D. (1992). Tribal wisdom. *Utne Reader, 52*, 68–79.

Maton, K. I., & Wells, E. A. (1995). Religion as a community resource for well-being: Prevention, healing and empowerment pathways. *Journal of Social Issues, 51*(2), 177–193.

McKnight, J. L. (1987). Regenerating community. *Social Policy, 17*(3), 54–58.

Myers, L. J. (1985). Transpersonal psychology: The role of the Afrocentric paradigm. *The Journal of Black Psychology, 12*(1), 31–42.

Naparastek, A., & Dooley, D. (1998). Countering urban disinvestment through community-building initiatives. In P. Ewalt, E. Freeman, & D. Poole (Eds.), *Community building: Renewal, well-being, and shared responsibility* (pp. 6–16). Washington, DC: NASW Press.

Netting, E., Kettner, P., & McMurty, S. (1993). *Social work macro practice.* New York: Longman.

Page-Adams, D., & Sherraden, M. (1997). Asset building as a community revitalization strategy. *Social work, 42*(5), 423–434.

Parrish, R. (2002). The changing nature of community. *Strategies, 15*(2), 259–284.

Porter, E. (2004). A Typology of Virtual Communities: A Multi-Disciplinary Foundation for Future Research. *Journal of Computer-Mediated Communication, 10*(1). Retrieved from Wiley Online Library website: http://onlinelibrary.wiley.com/doi/10.1111/jcmc.2004.10.issue-1/issuetoc doi:DOI: 10.1111/j.1083-6101.2004.tb00228.x

Putnam, R., & Feldstein, L. (2003). *Better together: Restoring the American community.* New York, NY: Simon and Schuster.

Reiss, A. J., Jr. (1959). The sociological study of communities. *Rural Sociology, 24*, 118–130.

Schulman, M. D., & Anderson, C. (1999). The dark side of the force: A case study of restructuring and social capital. *Rural Sociology, 64*(3), 351–372.

Solomon, B. (1976). *Black empowerment: Social work in oppressed communities.* New York: Columbia University Press.

Utne, E. (1992). I am because we are. *Utne Reader, 52*, 2.

Wallis, A. D., Crocker, J. P., & Schecter, B. (1998). Social capital and community building: Part one. *National Civic Review, 87*, 253–271.

Walsh, J. (1997). Community building in theory and practice: Three case studies. *National Civic Review, 86*, 291–314.

Warner, M. (1999). Social capital construction and the role of the local state. *Rural Sociology, 64*(3), 373–393.

Warren, R. (1977). *New perspectives on the American community: A book of readings* (3rd ed.). Chicago: Rand McNally College Publishing Company.

Warren, R. L. (1978). *The community in America* (3rd ed.). Chicago: Rand McNally College Publishing Company.

Warren, R., & Lyon, L. (1983). *New perspectives on the American community.* Homewood, IL: The Dorsey Press.

Warren, R., & Lyon, L. (1988). *New perspectives on the American community* (5th ed.). Chicago: The Dorsey Press.

*Webster's II new college dictionary.* (1995). Boston: Houghton Mifflin Co.

Yosso, T. (2005). Whose culture has capital? A critical race theory discussion of community cultural wealth. *Race, Ethnicity and Education, 8*(1), 69–91.

## References for Chapter 11

Al-Krenawi, A., & Graham, J. (2000a). Culturally sensitive social work practice with Arab clients in mental health settings. *Health and Social Work, 25*(1), 9–22.

Al-Krenawi, A., & Graham, J. (2000b). Islamic theology and prayer. *International Social Work, 43*(3), 289.

Asamoah, Y., Healy, L. M., & Mayadas, N. (1997). Ending the international-domestic dichotomy: New approaches to a global curriculum for the millennium. *Journal of Social Work Education, 33*(2), 389–402.

Bourdieu, P. (2001). *Acts of resistance: Against the new myths of our time* (2nd ed.). Cambridge: Polity Press.

Engstrom, D. W., & Okamura, A. (2004). A plague of our time: Torture, human rights, and social work. *Families in Society, 85*(3), 291–300.

Garrett, P. M. (2010). Examining the revolution: Neoliberalism and social work education. *Social Work Education, 29*(4), 340–355. doi: 10.1080/02615470903009015

Gray, M., & Fook, J. (2004). The quest for a universal social work: Some issues and implications. *Social Work Education, 23*(5), 625–644.

Harvey, D. (2006). Neoliberalism as creative destruction. *Geografiska Annaler Series B: Human Geography, 88*(2), 145–158. doi: 10.1111/j.0435-3684.2006.00211.x

Healy, L. (1995). Comparative and international overview. In T. D. Watts, D. Elliott, N. S. Mayadas (Eds.), *International handbook on social work education* (pp. 421–439). Westport, CT: Greenwood Press.

Healy, L. (2008). Exploring the history of social work as a human rights profession. *International Social Work, 51*(6), 735.

Johnson Lewis, J. (2013). *Settlement houses: Basics about the settlement house movement.* Retrieved April 15, 2013, from http://womenshistory.about.com/od/settlementhouses/a/settlements.htm

Lipson, J. G. (1993). Afghan refugees in California: Mental health issues. *Mental Health Nursing, 14*, 411–423.

Lowe, G. (1995). Social development. In R. Edwards (Ed.-in-Chief), *Encyclopedia of social work* (19th ed., pp. 2168–2173). Washington, DC: National Association of Social Workers.

Lundy, C., & Van Wormer, K. (2007). Social and economic justice, human rights and peace: The challenge for social work in Canada and the USA. *International Social Work, 50*(6), 727.

Mayadas, N., & Elliot, D. (1997). Lessons from international social work. In M. Reisch & E. Gambrill (Eds.), *Social work in the 21st century.* Thousand Oaks, CA: Pine Forge Press.

Midgely, J. (1997). *Social welfare in global context.* Thousand Oaks, CA: Sage Publications.

Midgley, J. (2009). Reclaiming social work: Challenging neoliberalism and promoting social justice. *Journal of Sociology & Social Welfare, 36*(2), 185–186.

Myers-Lipton, S. (2006). *Social solutions to poverty: America struggle to build a just society.* Retrieved April 15, 2013, from http://www.solvingpoverty.com/ScientificCharity.htm

Nash, M., Wong, J., & Trlin, A. (2006). Civic and social integration. *International Social Work, 49*(3), 345–363.

Polivka, L., & Estes, C. L. (2009). The economic meltdown and old age politics. *Generations, 33*(3), 56–62.

Rehman, T., & Dziegielewski, S. (2003). Women who choose Islam. *International Journal of Mental Health, 32*(3), 31–49.

Snyder, C., May, J. D., Zulcic, N., & Gabbard, W. (2005). Social work with Bosnian Muslim refugee children and families: A review of the literature. *Child Welfare, 84*(5), 607–630.

Sullivan, W. P. (1994). The tie that binds: A strengths/empowerment model for social development. *Social Development Issues, 16*(3), 100–111.

United Nations. (2008). *The millennium development goals report 2008.* New York: United Nations.

United Nations. (2012). *The millennium development goals report 2012* (p. 72). New York: United Nations.

Worthington, G. J. (2001). *Threads of hope: A qualitative analysis of applied coping strategies utilized by Bosnian refugees.* Unpublished dissertation, Chicago School of Professional Psychology, Chicago, IL.

# Index